My Sister, My Daughter, and Me

(Tres Señoritas Locas)

A Memoir

Shirley Rose Webb

PORTLAND • OREGON
INKWATERPRESS.COM

Scan this QR Code for more information on this title.

Copyright © 2017 by SHANNON34, LLC
Copyright No. TXu 1-989-819

Cover and interior design by Paige Asay
Floral illustrations © lokko studio. CreativeMarket.com
Editor and Publishing Consultant: Cliff Carle
Photographs on page 335 and back cover by Richard Bornstein. All other photographs are from author's own collection. Subjects in images have all consented to the publication of their likeness.

All rights reserved. No part of this book may be reproduced or transmitted in any form or by any means whatsoever, including photocopying, recording or by any information storage and retrieval system, without written permission from the publisher and/or author. The views and opinions expressed in this book are those of the author(s) and do not necessarily reflect those of the publisher, and the publisher hereby disclaims any responsibility for them. Neither is the publisher responsible for the content or accuracy of the information provided in this document. Contact Inkwater Press at inkwater.com. 503.968.6777

LCCN 2017902118

Publisher: Inkwater Press | www.inkwaterpress.com

Paperback
ISBN-13 978-1-62901-417-3 | ISBN-10 1-62901-417-6

Kindle
ISBN-13 978-1-62901-418-0 | ISBN-10 1-62901-418-4

ePub
ISBN-13 978-1-62901-419-7 | ISBN-10 1-62901-419-2

Printed in the U.S.A.

3 5 7 9 10 8 6 4

Reviews

"**My Sister, My Daughter, and Me** is fantastic! Every chapter, including the Female Fire-fighter Try-outs to The Disappearing Husband, are **#1!**"
—Rick Dees

"**Vibrant, engaging, and heartfelt.** Webb is an inspiration to us all."
—Urban Lit Magazine

"There are many **pearls of truth and beauty** throughout this book."
—Portland Book Review

"**Entertaining** and **heartwarming** book."
—Readers' Favorite 5-Star Seal Award

Northern California Book Festival Runner-Up.

Distinguished Favorite of New York City Big Book Seal Award.

Honorable Mention at the 2017 New England Book Festival.

Honorable Mention at the 2017 San Francisco Book Festival.

Honorable Mention at the 2017 Southern California Book Festival.

Honorable Mention at the 2017 New York Book Festival.

Honorable Mention at the 2017 Hollywood Book Festival.

Dedication

To my loving daughter, and my dear sister.
Two beautiful and unique souls.
I will love you both forever!

Author's Note

This book is a memoir of my life experiences. However, I have used fictional names and other identifying details for all friends and all members of my extended family, (including in-laws), with the sole exception of my husband. I have also fictionalized my places of employment. Any similarity between these fictional names and real people or businesses is strictly coincidental.

Table of Contents

Introduction — i
Chapter 1 **Don't Mess With Mamma Pig – 1962-1966** — 1
Chapter 2 **A Serious Injury – 1963** — 5
Chapter 3 **Welcome to the USA – 1966** — 9
Chapter 4 **My Loco Dad – 1972** — 11
Chapter 5 **An Unexpected Pregnancy – 1972-1977** — 15
Chapter 6 **The Fun & Wacky Job – 1978** — 18
Chapter 7 **My First (and Only) True Love – October 1978** — 25
Chapter 8 **Meeting Michael Jackson – 1980s** — 32
Chapter 9 **Playboy Audition – 1980s** — 34
Chapter 10 **Chosen by Elizabeth Taylor – 1980s** — 35
Chapter 11 **The Ghetto House – 1980s** — 37
Chapter 12 **Wild Night at Chippendale's – 1980s** — 48
Chapter 13 **Sexy Lingere Contest – 1980s** — 50
Chapter 14 **Girl's Night Out – 1980s** — 52
Chapter 15 **Female Firefighter Tryouts – 1980s** — 54
Chapter 16 **L.A. Raiders Cheerleader Tryouts – 1980s** — 58
Chapter 17 **Freeway Antics – 1980s** — 61
Chapter 18 **Julio Iglesias Fiasco – 1980s** — 64
Chapter 19 **A Brief Moment With John Travolta– 1980s** — 67
Chapter 20 **A Day With Jose Luis Rodriguez (El Puma) – 1980s** — 68
Chapter 21 **The Crazy Cop – 1980s-2008** — 71
Chapter 22 **Kim West / Steve Garvey & Steve Sax – 1980s-2006** — 73
Chapter 23 **Date With El Debarge – 1985** — 75
Chapter 24 **Famous Motown Lover – 1980s** — 76
Chapter 25 **In Love With A Mobster – 1980s** — 78
Chapter 26 **Playboy Magazine Shoot – 1986-1987** — 81
Chapter 27 **A Night at the Playboy Mansion – 1989** — 87
Chapter 28 **The Chapel of Love – 1990** — 91
Chapter 29 **Southern Lover – 1980s** — 95
Chapter 30 **Bike vs. Car – 1990s** — 99
Chapter 31 **My Daughter the Fashion Model – 1992** — 104
Chapter 32 **A Visitor From Italy – 1993** — 106
Chapter 33 **The Engagement is On – 1994** — 109
Chapter 34 **Goodbye Dave – 1996** — 110
Chapter 35 **The Disappearing Husband – 1996** — 112

Chapter 36 **Fun Times in Mississippi – 1996**	115
Chapter 37 **Parasailing in Ensenada – 1997**	118
Chapter 38 **Off-Key Wedding Bells – 2000**	123
Chapter 39 **Misery in Mississippi – 1998**	127
Chapter 40 **Cancer Scare – 2003**	130
Chapter 41 **Sad Sunny – 2003**	139
Chapter 42 **Victoria's Secret – October 2004**	143
Chapter 43 **Disneyland Disaster – 2005**	150
Chapter 44 **Tempestuous Divorce – 2006**	157
Chapter 45 **She's Gone – 2003-2008**	160
Chapter 46 **New Love – March 2008**	177
Chapter 47 **Dirty Tricks – 2009**	179
Chapter 48 **Skiing at Bear Mountain – 2009**	183
Chapter 49 **Water Damage – 2010**	187
Chapter 50 **Cinco de Mayo – 2010**	189
Chapter 51 **A Dragon in My Dreams – 2010**	213
Chapter 52 **The Vanishing Wheelbarrow – June 2010**	215
Chapter 53 **Rescued Pets – 2010**	222
Chapter 54 **A Bird Brings a Message – 2010**	226
Chapter 55 **Mental Healing – 2010**	228
Chapter 56 **Vehicular Homicide – 2010-2012**	230
Chapter 57 **Aerobics Fanatic – 1980s-2015**	233
Chapter 58 **Competitive Tennis – 2002-2015**	241
Chapter 59 **Community Property Dispute – 2010-2012**	247
Chapter 60 **The One-Year Coincidence – May 5, 2011**	252
Chapter 61 **Fighting For My Grandson – 2010, 2011 & 2012**	254
Chapter 62 **Memorial Counseling Center – June 2011**	266
Chapter 63 **Honorary Tennis Tournament 2011-2012**	267
Chapter 64 **Derby Daze – 2013-2014**	273
Chapter 65 **Awesome Friends in Mississippi – 2010-2015**	283
Chapter 66 **Pinata Vengeance – 1994-2014**	286
Chapter 67 **My Loco Elvis-Loving Brother – 2011-2012**	292
Chapter 68 **In a Search of a Father – 2010-2012**	301
Chapter 69 **Rebel Niece – 2008-2012**	305
Chapter 70 **Graciella's Surprise – December 2012**	313
Chapter 71 **BFF Blondie – 2010-2015**	319
Chapter 72 **The Invincibles – 1978-2015**	322
Acknowledgements	343

Introduction

This is a true story about my favorite younger sister, (Lina Emi Collins) my only daughter, (Natalie Emi Collins) and me (Shirley). It details my beautiful, crazy, fun and sometimes sad life. It's about love, laughter, struggles, happiness, tears and death.

If there's one thing I want you to gain from reading this book, it's the understanding that you can change your life if you want to. We all make mistakes, nobody's perfect. Learn from your mistakes and follow your dreams. Be positive and fight for what you want. Dreams do come true. It may not happen overnight, it might take years. I know it will though, because it happened to me through sheer force of will.

My story follows three crazy, fun, Hispanic women (Tres Senoritas Locas) who had big dreams of a better life for themselves. The first, with her irrepressible sense of humor, struggled mightily with some very wise and very foolish choices along the way. The second, with her beauty and charm, showed great promise, but kept falling over and over for the wrong men. The third, loving and kind, painstakingly reinvented herself after a cheating husband threw her out. And one of the three, through freakish circumstances, met with a heartrending death.

"Life can be equally beautiful, painful and unexpected."

Chapter 1

Don't Mess With Mamma Pig - 1962-1966

I was born in San Jose, Costa Rica. It is the second smallest country in Central America, about the size of West Virginia. Costa Rica has hundreds of beaches; most are uncrowded with white, black, yellow or red sand. It has ten volcanoes, three of them active. There are jungle waterfalls and areas that have monkeys, birds, iguanas and sloths when you walk to the beach for a swim. The butterfly farm is the best place to see many varieties up close in a big walk-in enclosure full of tropical plants. It's amazing!

I was six years old when my parents moved to the United States leaving six of my siblings and me with our grandmother, plus Aunt Pachi and her five children, until they could afford to send for all of us. Even though we were very poor, I was a happy little girl. I don't remember missing my parents much. I had plenty of brothers and sisters and cousins to play with everyday. I was very energetic and always thinking about what to do next. Something fun or crazy was always on my mind.

My favorite place to visit was Aunt Pachi's farm. Twice a year, Aunt Pachi, my two cousins Mina, Dalia and me, took the train trip that lasted almost all day to get there. From the train station, my aunt's brother, Chui, would be waiting for us with his two sons, some horses and a couple of mules for us to ride the forty minutes to the farm. I, of course, enjoyed every minute of it. I've had a tremendous love for animals for as long as I can remember.

On the farm, we picked mangos, hocotes, vegetables and many other exotic and delicious fruits. We also gathered fresh eggs from the chickens, and of course milked the cows. It was so much fun.

One day at the farm, while one of the cows was giving birth, there was an emergency. The calf was coming out backwards. The mother cow was going to die without help.

"Chiquillas vengan aqui. Ayudenme con la vaca." ("Girls, I need you to assist me with the cow.") The cow was in labor and making loud scary noises. Aunt Pachi was the funniest person I had ever met. She always made us laugh. She said, "Rub the cow's head and talk to her."

I gently caressed the cow, sang, and whispered, "Te amo, vaquita." ("I love you, my little cow.") My cousins joined in. Aunt Pachi was crying and cursing at the same time in Spanish: "Hueputa vaca, ayudeme!" ("Son-of-a-bitch cow, help me out!")

The cow was lying on the ground on her side when suddenly my aunt stuck her whole arm inside the cow's vagina and turned the baby around. The calf was born and the cow survived. Aunt Pachi had saved both the cow and the calf's lives; however, the cow rejected her calf, so we had to bottle-feed it.

In the mornings after milking the cow, we poured ourselves a cup of warm foamy milk. We laughed so hard at each other's foamy white mustaches. After our little laughing attack it was time to pour some milk into a baby bottle. Then we walked a few feet from where the cow was to feed the baby calf that was resting on some hay.

"I go first!" I yelled out. My two cousins gently touched the baby's head while I placed the bottle inside its mouth. Oh my God, this is the most beautiful thing I've ever done! I thought. Watching the calf eat and kissing her on the forehead was unreal. It was like a dream come true, living life on the farm.

Another time, a mama pig gave birth to a litter of piglets. Aunt Pachi told us, "Whatever you do, DO NOT TOUCH THE BABY PIGS!"

Of course I didn't listen to her and went inside the fenced enclosure to see the babies up close while the mother pig was preoccupied, out of sight, inside the barn. My two cousins were against it, but I convinced them to tag along. The little piglets were beautiful. We were staring at them and I couldn't help myself. I wanted to hold them.

Mina saw me reach for this one piglet and cried out, "Don't Shirley!"

But I did it anyway. "It's okay, no one's gonna know," I exclaimed.

A second after I grabbed the piglet, he let out the loudest scream I'd ever heard. My two cousins ran for the fence. I was scared to death and thought I had hurt the baby pig. Mina and Dalia looked back and one of them yelled, "Put him down! Run! The mother pig is on her way!

I quickly placed the piglet alongside his brothers and sisters, and looked up to see the mother pig barreling out the barn door and directly toward me. I let out a scream and ran for the fence. By then Aunt Pachi was already out the door of her house, and could see mama pig gaining ground on me.

My aunt threw open the gate and yelled, "Run faster!"

I never looked back; all I wanted was to get through that gate. I could hear the mother pig squealing loud and angrily; she really wanted a piece of me for disturbing her babies. I flew through the gate and Aunt Pachi closed it in the nick of time. I was safe and my cousins were jumping up and down and laughing at the same time.

Fortunately for me, my aunt was also laughing. She wagged a finger at me and said, "I told you not to touch the baby pigs, chiquilla necia." ("Foolish girl.")

Another time, some baby chicks and ducks were born. The farm was full of animals with babies. It was such a beautiful experience that I have treasured my entire life. To experience the birth of animals and to be around them was pure love and like a beautiful dream to me. Except that it was real.

The farmhouse had no bathrooms or running water. When we needed to relieve ourselves we had to exit the house and walk about forty feet to an old wood potty with four little walls around it and a door latch. In the middle of it was the hueco, ("the big hole") where you would sit to pee or poop. The hole was about five to six feet deep. Every night before it got dark, our aunt made sure that we all had used the hueco before going to bed. She didn't want us to go out in the dark because of the snakes and other varmints. There were no exterior lights. Except for full moons, the nights were pitch black.

Once in a while somebody desperately needed to use the hueco in the middle of the night. None of us wanted to stay in bed by ourselves because we were afraid of La Llorona, ("The Weeping Woman"). La Llorona is a legend about a woman who killed her baby, and her spirit comes out at night looking for a child to replace her dead baby. Most Latin people know the story, especially if you live in a Latin American country. We Latinos are very, very superstitious, so anytime any of us had to go to the bathroom in the middle of the night, Aunt Pachi woke up all of us kids, grabbed the lantern and walked in front of us to the hueco. I was six years old, cousin Dalia was five and Mina was six. If we heard a weird noise, we'd cling to Aunt Pachi's nightgown. It was scary but exciting.

Aunt Pachi's brother Chui came to San Jose to visit every year. On one of his visits he brought along a rooster, a couple of baby chicks and a turkey. We fed them every day and watched them grow. My cousins and I named the turkey Pepe. I loved chasing Pepe around the yard, but I could never catch him because he was too fast. When the hens were old enough we had fresh eggs for breakfast. Our rooster woke up singing every morning at 5:00 a.m. And Aunt Pachi's talking amazon parrot was hilarious. She was a beautiful green with bright red and yellow feathers, and had a big vocabulary. Her name was Lorita, meaning little parrot. Every morning the first thing she'd say was, "Buenos dias, Lorita." Once my aunt got her out of the cage and placed her outside of the door to the backyard where she had a standing perch, Lorita couldn't stop talking, singing and laughing. She imitated Aunt Pachi's voice. She'd been at the house ever since I was a baby.

I loved all the animals but my favorite was Pepe. He was ugly as hell! And I felt sorry for him. Then one Christmas, Aunt Pachi said, "Girls go back inside the house and don't come out." She sounded upset.

But of course I was already thinking "Why?" Aunt Pachi must be up to something, and I decided to sneak up and watch her. I saw Aunt Pachi crying, cursing, and chasing Pepe. When she finally caught him, very quickly, she snapped his neck and broke it. And that was the end of Pepe.

She stuck Pepe into a huge metal pot with boiling water that she had on top of some burning wood. OMG, I couldn't believe it. My teardrops were falling and my heart was broken. Aunt Pachi had warned us about Pepe when we first got him, saying, "Do not fall in love with the turkey! I have to kill it for our Christmas tamales."

Chapter 2

A Serious Injury - 1963

When I was seven years old, I was playing with my brothers and some of the kids in the neighborhood. We were throwing rocks at each other; but not in a mean way; it was all in fun. However, one of the bigger rocks glanced off my shin and my leg started bleeding. I ran inside the house and my Aunt Pachi cleaned the wound with alcohol. Over the next few days, I banged my open wound repeatedly. Nothing could stop me from playing on the street with the rough boys. Soon I was limping. My wound was now bigger, beet red, and had a big blister on top of it.

Over the weekend, my other cousins invited me to spend the night at their home. My cousin's mom, Soti, looked at the wound and said, "I'm going to pop the blister on your shin." Aunt Soti grabbed a sewing needle and placed it on the stove burner to disinfect it. The needle turned black and my aunt said, "Shirley, stay very still while I puncture the wound to let the pus drain."

I closed my eyes and held on tight to my cousin's hand. When I felt the needle I screamed, and tears rained down my face. The pain was like nothing I'd ever felt before.

She then placed a bandage around the wound.

Days later after my aunt's "surgery", my leg began to throb. I didn't complain to anyone and kept playing on the street with my brothers and the rest of the boys.

Two weeks later, I couldn't walk and was limping badly. I'd had also developed a high fever. My grandmother took a good look at me and said, "Shirlita, ("Little Shirley") you're going to the hospital."

The doctor looked at my wound and explained to my grandma, "Her leg is infected and the infection is on the bone going all the way up to her hip. The condition is called osteomyelitis. She needs an IV with antibiotics right away and will need to stay in the hospital for observation." His face became grave when he said to my grandma, "Let's step outside of the room so we can talk." In the hallway he said, "If the infection doesn't stop spreading, we'll have to amputate her left leg."

I wasn't told this until later in life.

My grandma came into my hospital room, hugged and kissed me, and whispered, "I love you, Shirlita! You have to stay here for a while. I'll come everyday to see you. Okay?"

'Si, abuelita," ("Yes, grandma,") I responded sadly.

Grandma was my favorite person in the world; she was the sweetest woman you'd ever meet; and I loved her as if she was my own mother.

Seven days later my fever was still not going down. I couldn't get up and walk. The nurses had to place a basin under my butt for me to pee and poop.

Two weeks later, I was still not feeling better. I was always a very energetic little girl but this time I was content to stay in the hospital bed. There were two other little girls about my age in the room with me. In a bed to the left side of me was Nadia. She loved to sing and was very sweet. Nadia had leukemia, but I didn't know it at the time. Across from Nadia and I was another little girl. I don't remember her name but I will call her Lily. Lily was burned over 90% of her body. Her bed had a canopy of white mesh fabric. I never saw Lily's face, but the three of us talked, sang, laughed and sometimes cried together when something was hurting us.

Except for the pain, I really enjoyed my time at the hospital. The food was excellent compared to what we ate at home, which was mostly rice and beans topped with a few drops of lemon juice. In the hospital, I actually got a glass of orange juice with every meal and real ice cream for dessert! "Hmm."

A month went by and I was still not feeling well. Grandma visited every day like she told me she would.

Six weeks later, one morning, I was in bed when all of a sudden my nose started bleeding heavily. I began crying and screaming, "Nadia, please help me!"

Nadia looked at me and saw the blood dripping on my hospital gown. She cried and yelled out, "Shirley, I'm pressing the button like crazy for the nurses to come!"

After that I vaguely remember a couple of nurses around my bed. My grandmother had just come in to visit when the nurses told her to step away from me. I looked at my grandma scared and crying and said, "Please hold me, Grandma." I then went into a deep sleep.

The next day when my grandma came to see me, I was awake and had oxygen to help me breathe. I was half asleep and wanted to stay awake for my grandma. She was rubbing my arm like she always did.

"Grandma," I said with a weak voice, "last night I had a dream with Chica in it."

Chica was my grandmother's aunt. She lived with all of us, but had died the year before. Chica was in her eighties and lived in the basement of the house.

Chica loved me as if I was her own child. She always took me to church with her. She'd put a hat on me and she'd rub beets on my cheeks to make them rosy. I always felt like a little princess with Chica. We had a special bond. I was her favorite of all twelve kids who lived in the house. She taught me how to play cards and she loved for me to read to her. I loved and missed her so much.

"Grandma," I said, "in my dream Chica came to the hospital to see me. She sat at the foot of the bed and reached her arm out to me. She had a beckoning smile on her face, and that was the end of my dream."

My grandma smiled and said, "Chica was taking care of you. She wants you to get better soon."

When I was older, my grandma informed me that I had died for a few seconds during the episode of the nosebleed, and that my dream with Chica was real. Chica came to take me, but it was not my time yet.

One morning after breakfast, Nadia and I were talking and laughing when all of a sudden, Nadia made a grim face and said, "Shirley, I don't feel good, I'm cold. I need another blanket. Please jump on my bed and hug me!"

"Nadia," I cried, "I can't. I'm all hooked up to this oxygen tank. I can't move."

"Please press the button to call the nurses for help!" Nadia said with shivering voice.

I immediately pressed the button repeatedly, but the nurses never came. It was even more frustrating because I could hear them laughing down the hall from us. In the meantime, Nadia was trying to reach for me so that we could at least hold hands.

"Shirley, I'm cold and I'm scared," Nadia cried.

To this day, I have never forgotten how her voice trembled when she told me this. I tried to reach for Nadia's hand, but our beds were too far apart from each other. All we could do was to stare at each other. In the next instant, blood was coming out Nadia's nose, mouth, and ears; her eyes were rolling backwards. I was terrified and screamed for help as loud as I could and madly pressed the button.

Finally the nurses came in and immediately closed the curtain around Nadia's bed to prevent me from seeing her anymore, but the curtain didn't close all the way; there was a crack big enough for me to see Nadia. I was crying, while silently watching the nurses stick cotton in her ears, nose and mouth. I didn't understand what was going on; I was only seven and had no idea that Nadia was in what here in America would be called a "Code Blue".

Nadia died that day in front of me; but I didn't realize this until I was older.

Later that afternoon when the nurse came in to check on me, I asked, "What happened to my friend, Nadia?"

The nurse didn't look me in the eyes when she said, "Nadia was transferred to another room because she needs special care."

Two months later, I was recovering and had to learn to walk again. I had no control of my left leg; it was as if I didn't have a leg at all.

The doctor said, "You'll be going home soon." He had saved my leg from amputation, but it was extremely weak. The nurses forced me to walk and walk around the hospital with a cane that I took home after they released me.

Before going home I said, "Bye, Lily. I'm going to miss you!" She would be staying in the hospital for a long while.

Chapter 3

Welcome to the USA - 1966

As I mentioned earlier, I was born in Costa Rica, as were my parents. My mom's grandmother was somehow part Chinese. According to some family members, in the1800s the Atlantic Railroad contracted six hundred plus Chinese laborers hoping to duplicate the success of rail projects. That's where our Chinese background comes from and why some of my siblings and I look more Asian than Latino.

In 1964 my parents left Costa Rica and moved to the United States for a better life. They left their seven children with our grandmother, Aunt Pachi and her five kids until they could save enough money for us to fly to Los Angeles, California.

A year later we got the news that our mother had another baby girl named Ceci. We were now a total of eight children, seven in Costa Rica, and one in the USA.

Two years later, in the summer of 1966, at the age of eight, my parents obtained green cards for all of us, including our grandma, to fly to the USA legally. We were all excited to get on a plane and fly to America. Our grandmother stayed with us for a year before returning back home to Costa Rica. Once grandma was gone I only had limited contact with her. I missed her dearly, but phone calls were extremely expensive. I spoke to her once a year and wrote as often as I could.

Seven years later, at the age of fifteen, my sister Gia and I flew to Costa Rica and spent some time with our grandmother, aunt and cousins. Mom thought is was a great idea since we were hanging out with some friends she didn't approve of. After returning from Costa Rica, Gia and I had no interest in hanging out with our old acquaintances and we both decided to concentrate on school instead. Several years later, our grandmother died of a massive heart attack. I was sad and heartbroken that I never got to say goodbye to my dear grandma. As for Aunt Pachi, I missed her too but I wasn't as close to her as I was with my grandmother. Grandma gave me the love of a mother I didn't have.

A year later, Mom gave birth for the last time to another girl, Graciella. We were now nine kids living in Los Angeles in a 2 1/2-bedroom apartment. The girls' room had three single beds; two of us shared a bed. I slept in one bed with my five-year-old sister, Lina. The boys' bedroom had bunk beds and one single bed to the side.

Lina and I never played together as children; I was a tomboy who liked playing marbles on the dirt and trading baseball and Topo Gigo cards with the boys. I loved competing with the boys and dancing with the girls.

Lina liked playing with the girls. She was an emotional little girl who cried about everything. Her nickname was "La Mona Gritona". ("The Screaming Monkey".) We didn't become best sisters and friends until the seventies.

Chapter 4

My Loco Dad - 1972

Every morning, Mom rode the bus to a Downtown Los Angeles factory where she worked as a seamstress. She also had a second job sewing at home. She rented a factory sewing machine and worked in the evenings and weekends to make more money to survive.

I was nine years old when Mom taught me how to sew. I couldn't wait to get home from school and sew pieces of the garments. At the end of the week, Mom handed me a $20 bill. Oh boy, I thought, this is a lot of money! So for sure I wanted to learn more and more. Months later, I was sewing more intricate pieces of each garment. Sometimes when she came home I'd already had most of the dress, blouse or skirt done, except for some of the more difficult pieces. I knew that only Mom could finish the entire garment herself.

By the time I was ten I had become a good seamstress. The factory had a gentleman who brought the pieces of clothing to our apartment; then he'd pick up the finished garments the following week. We had a week to finish one hundred dresses or blouses. We were paid for each piece 25, 50, 75 cents and sometimes $1.00.

I wanted to help Mom on the weekends but we only had one sewing machine. Since I was so dedicated and good at it, Mom decided to rent a second machine for me.

One year, Mom said, "Shirley, here are your earnings," and handed me five twenty dollar bills. She patted my head and said, "Good job! I'm so proud of you."

I couldn't believe my eyes. I had never made so much money. Our dad, as usual, had gone to Costa Rica to party. This was Easter week and mom had used all of her earnings to pay bills. I knew my sisters and I didn't have dresses for Easter Sunday, so I asked, "Mom, can you take me to buy dresses for my five sisters?"

"Of course I will," she said, caressing my hair. Is that what you really want to do with your money?"

"Yes!" I said, smiling.

Mom and I left and came back with six dresses and baskets too. My sisters were thrilled and we all couldn't wait for Sunday to wear our beautiful gowns.

Out of respect to my mom and because she's still here with us, I will not mention the many horrible things my dad did to her. Our dad was a very selfish man. He hated to work and when he did, he'd save his money and go to Costa Rica to party with his friends and spend it on loose women.

When he returned home from Costa Rica, he'd have his friends over to get drunk while mom was sewing.

By the time I was 11, I was still a very skinny little girl. My oldest sister always teased me about it, so I grew up somewhat insecure. She was three years older than I was, and quite voluptuous for a fourteen year old girl.

One day I was in the bedroom by myself playing picture cards while mom was in the sewing machine room working. My dad and his drunken friends were in the living room partying and making a lot of noise. Unexpectedly, one of my dad's friends, a very tall man, came into the bedroom, grabbed me by the shoulders, stuck his tongue inside my mouth, and began touching my private parts. I screamed for help but no one could hear me. I kicked him and I don't remember exactly how I got away, but I did. I ran out of the house as fast as I could and never wanted to come back home. After the incident, every time Dad's friends came over, I either left the house or hid in the closet. I was traumatized and afraid to tell anyone about it until I became an adult.

When dad got angry with mom he'd do horrible things to all of us kids. One evening he got crazy and said, "Kids come in the living room right now! Sit on the floor and listen."

We all sat there very quietly, waiting to hear what he had to say. Our mom was next door visiting her friend.

Our dad's eyes were like the devil. Loudly, he said, "This is your last evening. When you go to bed I'm going to turn the gas on so all of you and your mom can die."

We all started screaming and running from the living room to the front door or back door trying to escape from him. Our mom heard the screams and came running to rescue us.

My little sister, Graciella, took off outside crying hysterically and screaming, "We're all going to die tonight!"

Mom, with the help of some of the neighbors, got us back into the apartment. At this point, Mom was now yelling, crying and telling Dad, "Leave my children alone! Go back to Costa Rica and stay there for good."

"You're going to die with them too!" he said, laughing in her face.

Another time, he came into the living room again yelling out loud, "I need all of you in here now!" This time we already knew he was up to something crazy again.

Graciella was sitting on my lap already shaking, crying and saying, "No! No, more!" I held her tight, crying along with her.

Our crazy dad grabbed the telephone. In the sixties the telephones had a long cord that you could carry all over the house if you needed to go into a different room. He took the long cord of the telephone and wrapped it tight against his neck and said, "I'm going to kill myself in front of you because your mom doesn't want to be with me anymore."

With the cord around his neck he turned red and was making crazy ugly faces as if he was dying. He was shouting like a maniac while we all screamed and ran away from him.

He left so many scars on his children's hearts that some of my siblings are, even now, not capable of coping with their lives. Some of us are strong and can deal with it, some of us cannot. Some of us forgave him, but we can never forget what he did, he destroyed our hearts forever!

Our mom was afraid of him and stayed in the relationship out of fear for her children. As we got older, we did our best to protect our mother against our dad. Mother got stronger and later filed for divorce in 1972. I was sixteen at the time. Her children were getting older and the boys could stand up to their father, so she found the strength she needed to send our father away for good.

To this day, my dad is not a part of my life.

We all grew up on our own. We didn't have hugs, kisses, or help with our homework. We never heard the words "I love you." Mom wasn't an affectionate mother; her way of showing us love was by working hard. I don't blame her; that's just the way she was. Not only was she our mom but our dad too. She was not only an amazing woman but indeed our hero too!!

Many Thanksgivings we didn't have the money to buy a turkey, and often we had no toys for Christmas. Our mom cried because she couldn't give us toys or food. We ate rice and beans, but it was okay with me, I never craved anything special. The neighbors knew very well about our situation. My mom was like the lady who lived in a shoe. She had so many children she didn't know what to do.

To our surprise, one Thanksgiving, we heard a knock on the front door. There on our front porch was the Fire and Police Department with boxes of food. They brought us a turkey and all kinds of canned food. We were thrilled. Our mom was crying with happiness. We didn't speak much English but we gave them hugs to thank them. It turned out that one of our neighbors had placed the call and told them we needed help.

When Christmas came, again the Fire Department arrived at our house with food and toys. I got my first Barbie doll. I was the happiest girl and couldn't wait to make clothes for her. For as long as we lived in Los Angeles the firemen and the policemen came to our door every Thanksgiving and Christmas.

And every Christmas for the last 30 years of my life, I have been repaying those firemen by delivering toys to the fire station for needy children. It makes me feel good to know that many children will have toys and a big smile on their faces just like we did.

Chapter 5

An Unexpected Pregnancy - 1972-1977

In the fall of 1972, I was seventeen when I met Roger and fell in love. I brought him home to meet Mom and she liked him right away. Mom wasn't shocked that he was six years my senior. She was born and raised in Costa Rica, and back in her days, many girls my age were already married, to older men. This was part of the Latin American culture. Roger was German-American. He was 6'4, with long hair, soft spoken, polite, kind, and very likeable. I was swept off my feet and crazy in love. I guess I can call it my teenage puppy love.

Roger wasn't perfect, by any means. He didn't like to work, loved smoking marijuana, and he lived in a fantasy world every day of his life. He was all about peace, love, pot with no ambition at all. At times, I'd smoke pot with him but I wasn't crazy about it like he was. I just did it because Roger liked it and I was still too young to know what I wanted out of life. I thought smoking pot was the cool thing to do.

In March of 1974 I got pregnant and four months later in July we tied the knot. We moved into the garage at the house my mom rented in Hollywood, across from Hollywood High School. On December 10, 1974 we had our first baby, a boy we named Dean Luke Parker. Luke, as we came to call him, was a beautiful well-behaved boy. We were on welfare because as usual Roger didn't have a job. The following year I was pregnant again, and on December 17, 1975 gave birth to a girl and we named her Natalie Emi Parker.

We now needed a bigger place to live and moved into a two-bedroom apartment in front of where my mom lived.

I had dropped out of school because of my first pregnancy. I wanted a better life for my kids and myself. I was seeing life in a very different way. I had matured a lot and was growing tired of doing nothing except taking care of the kids, cleaning, cooking – while Roger smoked pot and daydreamed about making easy money. He always had some kind of crazy idea on his mind.

In 1977, at twenty years old, I was falling out of love with Roger. I was seeing things I didn't like about him that I never paid attention to before. I realized I'd had been too young and naïve when I thought I was going to love him for the rest of my life.

Roger got worse as he got older; he became lazier and hated to get out of bed in the morning. He was a slob and stayed up until two or three every night watching television. He slept during the day. He was like a fucking vampire. He didn't care since welfare was paying our rent, food, medical, etc.

One day, Roger came up with an idea that scared the shit out of me. He said, "Hey Cutz (his nickname for me), we could sell the kids for $50,000 each, have more kids and continue doing this for a while. We could go away and live very well somewhere in South or Central America." He was dead serious about this.

I looked him straight in the eyes, and with an evil stare I said, "You're fucking crazy! Are you out of your mind? I'd never do anything like that! Get the fuck out of my face."

Roger was smoking way too much pot and for sure doing hard drugs behind my back. I was terrified and didn't know what to do; I didn't have any friends and wasn't close to my sisters. Mom was always working, and I never really felt close to her until much later in life.

Roger never brought up the subject again. But I never forgot about it, and decided I needed an exit strategy. A month later I enrolled myself into an evening adult school to finish high school. Seven months later I received my diploma. I was so proud of myself and thought, "Now I can change my life and leave this lazy ass of a husband." At twenty-one, I'd had enough and said, "Roger we need to talk. I'm moving out with my two kids into my mom's house next month. And I want a divorce, too."

Roger was shocked. He wasn't expecting this at all. His face turned ghost white and he began to cry, begging, "Please, Cutz, don't leave me. I promise I'll change."

Of course by then I knew better than to believe him. "It's too late, I have already made up my mind," I replied in a firm voice.

Since he wasn't working, Roger had no other choice but to move to Richmond, Virginia where his parents lived. He never bothered to call the kids or send money, birthday or Christmas cards. It was as if he never had any children.

I moved into Mom's rental house and paid my share of the rent, utilities and food. I registered the kids in a nursery school that the government helped me pay for. And I enrolled myself in a Medical Assistant Training school for nine months. I woke up every morning at 5:00 a.m. By 6:00 a.m, rain or shine, the kids and I were at the corner of Sunset Blvd. and Highland waiting for the bus. It was California winter and many days we were rain soaked by the time we got to the school.

After dropping them off, I'd take two more buses to get to the medical school. I was definitely struggling but I never once complained. I had no car, no money, but I was content. I was young, ambitious, had a lot of energy, and wanted more out of life. After leaving Roger I felt like I'd taken something heavy off my shoulders and the feeling was good.

My life totally changed. Sometimes on the weekends, I'd go dancing at nightclubs with my older sister, Gia, my younger brother Evan, and Ray, a friend of the family who owned a car. This was during the seventies and disco clubs where everywhere in L.A. I loved dancing and felt so lucky that I lived with my mom and siblings who'd watch over my children so I could go out and play!

Latin people love to dance. As a kid you learn to dance at a very young age; it's all you have for recreation. Music is a big part of life for most Latin people. When I was out dancing I completely forgot about my problems. I enjoyed myself like there was no tomorrow. I felt like I was in another world. That's how I dealt with life back then, and to this day I still do. Music and dancing is still my passion. Cannot live without them!

November 1977, Luke (age 3), Natalie (age 2) in their Chinese PJs at our apartment in Hollywood.

Chapter 6

The Fun & Wacky Job - 1978

My sister Lina was three years younger than I. She was beautiful with brown hair and eyes, exotic looking, olive skin, a gorgeous body, sweet, and a cute personality – although she could be very moody at times. She also had a bad temper.

Lina was going to high school and had a part-time job in Hawaii at McDonald's. She was living with our older brother Edgar and his wife Marisa. A year later in 1978, she decided to come back home to Hollywood, California and moved in with mom, me, my kids, our two brothers and three other sisters.

One Saturday morning while having breakfast, Lina came into the kitchen and announced, "I don't know what to do with myself."

"I have an idea!" I yelled out, swallowing a mouthful of food.

Her eyes got bigger and with an arched brow said, "What? What? Please tell me."

"Why don't you enroll at the medical school I'm going to?"

Lina smiled at me, then enthusiastically said, "Sounds like a plan."

Since we didn't own a car we rode the big bus. Every morning we were up at 5:00 a.m., taking my kids to the nursery, then us to school.

We always had a blast riding the bus; we laughed at ourselves all of the time. Many times while on the bus, we'd look out the window and I'd whisper, "Hey look at that pretty girl driving a Jaguar… (Mercedes Benz, or other sports car)" Lina and I would look at each other and say, "Bitch! Someday we'll be driving one of those fucking cars too!"

During class, I noticed that Lina and our instructor, Roy, had eyes for each other. That afternoon after school, Roy invited Lina out on a date. But no one at school was supposed to know, except me of course. School rules stated no hanky-panky between teacher and student.

Come the weekend, I said, "Lina, you wanna go disco dancing with me?"

"You know I do, but I don't know how to dance disco," she frowned.

"Oh, don't worry about it, you'll learn fast," I guaranteed her.

A short week later, Lina was in love with disco dancing just like me. We couldn't stop from dancing; we were crazy about disco clubs. We'd go to Circus, Circus in Hollywood, Moody's in Santa Monica, Chippendale's in West Los

Angeles, etc. But Osco's in West Hollywood was our number one go-to club. We became friends with the bouncers and one of the bartenders. We never had to wait in line like the rest of the patrons and on top of that, we got unlimited free drinks from the bartender.

Our only problem was that we didn't have a car. Sometimes we'd ask our neighbors for a ride; other times we'd take a bus or two to get to the nightclubs. We'd be all dressed up like dolls, sitting, giggling and cursing in Spanish at the back of the bus. I'd say, "Hueputa mierda," ("Shit son-of-a-bitch,") and Lina always busted out laughing.

One evening we decided to go to a nightclub on La Brea Blvd., just five blocks from where we lived in Hollywood. Next to the club was the Laundromat where we sometimes washed our clothes. So I came up with a brilliant idea: "Lina, let's take our clothes to the laundry to wash while we dance at the club."

"Yeah, let's do it!" Lina agreed.

We didn't waste any time getting ready with our sexy outfits and six-inch high heel shoes. We went to the side of the house where we kept a supermarket cart, and loaded it with two plastic bags of dirty clothes. We pushed the cart on Sunset Blvd. to La Brea laughing hysterically and saying, "I bet you people think we're fucking prostitutes." During the 70s Disco era, Sunset Boulevard was lined with prostitutes, day and night. We couldn't even go to the supermarket without being accosted by a pervert asking, "How much?" We just flipped them off.

When we got to the Laundromat, we hurried and placed the clothes in the washers, stuck the quarters into the machines and off we were to the club next door.

We danced for a couple of hours, then, returned to the Laundromat to load our clothes into a dryer, then it was back for more dancing. Oh my God, we were so happy we could do this and thought we'd do it every week. An hour later we returned to fold our clothes and go home. But to our surprise, when we opened the dryers our clothes were gone. Someone had stolen all of our clothing.

Lina went absolutely insane, screaming and kicking the washing machines, "Shit! You fucking assholes!"

I just stood there frozen with my hand over my mouth. I didn't know what to do or say. I knew it was my fault. It was my fucking crazy idea to do this. All I could think about was, "How am I going to replace the clothes when I don't have enough money? Hay que mirda!" ("Shit!")

Well there was nothing we could do except to grab the cart and walk our sorry asses back home while I cursed and cried too. A week later I replaced some of the kids' clothes by going to the Salvation Army. Lina and I decided not to try this again.

Lina and I were so crazy about dancing that we were out on Fridays, Saturdays, Sundays – and sometimes Mondays or Wednesday. Disco dancing was the hottest thing on earth; we were young and full of energy. All we wanted to do was to dance, dance, and dance! We didn't have time to study and weren't passing the exams on Fridays. Lina was more dyslexic than I was; she couldn't pass any of the exams at school.

We needed to get our Medical Assistant Certificates. So I, of course, came up with a plan. "Lina," I said, "after school, go into Roy's office and seduce him while I go in the room were the test sheets are kept. I need at least fifteen minutes, okay?"

Lina did her thing and I did mine. I got more test sheets than we needed. On test days we were more than ready. We'd write the answers a, b, c, d on our left hand and on Fridays we always had a passing score. I don't know if Roy ever knew what we were up to, but we sure had to do this to pass and get our certificates. *OMG, what a sweat!*

One thing we both had was lots' of laughter; and we were young with our whole lives ahead of us. I was 21 years old and Lina was 18.

Nine months later, I graduated before Lina and went to work in a personal injury doctor's office for my internship. From there I quickly moved up from intern to full-time employee, taking only a month to start earning a regular paycheck. That's when I called the welfare department and told them I didn't need their help any longer. I was extremely proud of myself and thought; *All right girl, keep going. You're doing just fine.*

A month later, Lina completed her training and began searching for a place to do her internship.

We needed extra help in the doctor's office, so I asked the office receptionist-manager Laila, "Can my sister Lina do her internship for a month with us?"

Laila agreed and we got Lina for a month.

Lina and I were thrilled to be working together. Carmen, the other medical assistant, was helping me train Lina. Carmen was from El Salvador (we called her Carmela). She was tall and slender with a sweet smile and fortunately a lot of patience.

Laila was from Mexico. She was small, thin, and always dressed professionally.

Lina, Carmen and I wore white nurses' uniforms. We all spoke Spanish and got along well with each other. We worked hard and laughed a lot too. About 90% of the patients were Hispanic; most of them didn't speak English so it was the perfect place for us to work. Most of our patients were involved in auto accidents; their insurance companies referred them to our office for treatment.

Our duties included treating the patients with hot packs, ultrasound, a ten-minute massage, traction to the spine, and drawing blood.

Lina was learning, but she didn't feel comfortable drawing blood.

We all hated doing massages, especially to the men. We suspected that some of the guys were faking it just so they could get a massage from one of us. Some of the patients had real bad body odor. Lina would occasionally come out of the massaging room and go straight to the bathroom to throw up. Carmen and I would run to the back of the office to laugh at Lina. Other times Carmela or I got the stinky patient. We were always laughing at each other, and made it crazy fun while we were working.

One day at the office I started thinking on what to do about the stinky patients, and I came up with an idea. "Girls, listen and watch me." I tore two small pieces of a napkin, poured a tincture of rubbing alcohol on each piece, rolled the pieces into a miniature cigarette and stuck one piece in each of my nostrils.

Lina and Carmela looked at me and were about to have a laughing fit; they couldn't believe what I was doing. They both took off running to the back of the office to laugh out aloud. "Hay que mujer mas loca!" ("Crazy girl!") Carmela said, trying to catch her breath.

The girls came back to the front of the office and watched me go inside the massage room with the sticks protruding from my nose like premature walrus tusks. "I'll be back out in fifteen minutes," I said with a wink.

A stinky male patient was already on his stomach waiting for me. I approached him, oiled my hands and began massaging his back. The guy of course had no idea what I had done. But all I knew was that my idea worked. No more stinky smell for me.

Before I finished with the massage, Lina and Carmela opened the door slightly and peeked in so they could have another good laugh on me. The look in their eyes and funny expressions were over the top. I just couldn't finish the massage and had no other choice but to run out of the room as fast as I could, and ended up at the back of the office holding my stomach and laughing with the girls.

"You're so fucking crazy!" Lina said, almost choking from her laughter.

"It worked! It worked!" I said, whispering and giggling at the same time.

And of course, Lina and Carmela tried my invention and they were happy not to have to smell the stink any longer. Lina most of all hated to give the men massages. She'd say, "Jueputas viejos ni tienen dolor solo quieren que los toquemos." ("These sons-of-a-bitch men don't have any pain, they just want us to rub them.")

Our boss, Howard, the owner of the clinic, was in his forties. Howard was a cocaine addict and a heavy pot smoker. He came in the office only once a week; sometimes we walked in his office and found him snorting cocaine. He was cool about it, though. He even asked us a few times if we wanted some coke, but we always told him, "We don't do drugs, Howard." After a while he never bothered to ask again.

Dr. Marvis worked for Howard; he was in his fifties and we all thought he'd had some hair implants; pieces of his hair were always on his face. He was funny looking and most of the time he was asleep in his recliner chair in his office. We each took turns knocking on his door and announcing loudly, "Dr. Marvis you have a patient waiting." He'd jump up out of his chair disoriented. It was hilarious to watch. We laughed our asses off. The poor doctor looked more like a homeless person than a physician.

One day we needed to use the traction machine on one patient who had whiplash. I had already trained Lina and it was now her turn to treat him. There was a brace that we placed around the patient's neck. We'd then set the machine on one of the four available levels. Level one was a very slow pull, level two a little faster, level three medium pull, and level four was the strongest pull. You always needed to start the patient on level 1 and add on every two or three weeks to the next level until you reached level four.

Lina was very excited about using the traction machine for the very first time.

Carmela and I were busy in other rooms with patients, so Lina decided to do it all by herself. She got the patient, a short Hispanic man, all set up and pressed the button for the level. Lina wasn't paying attention and had pressed LEVEL four, the strongest pull to the neck. She walked away from the patient and closed the door for the fifteen-minute neck traction.

Carmela and I rushed out of the rooms we were in when we heard a man screaming, "AUXILIO, AUXILIO!" ("HELP, HELP!") We ran and opened the door with Lina right behind us. The poor man was pleading, "Senorita, senorita, esque me esta horcando," ("Miss, miss, the machine is choking me.")

Carmela ran over and pressed the Off button. I quickly removed the neck brace and said to him, "Esta maquina no sirve." ("There must be something wrong with the machine.") I didn't want to blame Lina.

Lina was already nervous and asked him, "Esta bien? Hay perdon." ("Are you okay? I'm so sorry.")

The little guy responded, "La maquina me iva a matar!" ("The machine was going to kill me!")

We all looked at each other and busted out laughing – as did the little man. Lina learned her lesson. But after that, every time she was about to use the traction machine, Carmela and I whispered, "Hay caramba otra victima." ("Another victim.")

One day this three hundred pound Caucasian man showed up at the clinic. He was a friend of Howard's. "I'm having problems with my back and Howard suggested I come in for treatments," he announced.

Carmela looked at me and said in Spanish, "You take him."

"Cabrona!" ("Asshole!") Oh, I wanted to kill her.

She turned to the big man and said, "Please, come right in one of the rooms. Remove your shirt and lay on your stomach. Shirley will be with you in a minute."

Lina turned to me with broad smile and said, "Carnitas is waiting for you!"

I glared at both of them. "You bitches are going to get it!"

I walked in the room and politely asked "carnitas" (pork skin) about his back problem. I began his treatment with a fifteen-minute hot pack on his back. Then I oiled my hands and began massaging his back. Carnitas had the hairiest fucking back I'd ever seen. OMG, I wanted to throw up and couldn't wait to get out of there. When I was finally done and left the room I found Lina and Carmela laughing it up.

"Was it fun massaging carnitas?" Lina smirked.

"You bitches are pissing me off." I said, pretending to be angry. "Hay, carnitas tiene la espalda llena de pelos" ("He has a hairy back.") I told them, making a nauseated face.

Carmela and Lina covered their mouths while laughing and making funny faces at me.

"Next time he comes he's yours!" I declared.

Since my hands were covered with oil I decided this was the perfect time. I moved in real close to both of them and rubbed my oily hands on both of their arms.

Lina and Carmela took off running and screaming to the back of the office. "No, get away from us, it's gross!"

We had so much fun working together; we were all hoping that our boss would hire Lina. A month went by and Lina finished her internship. But Howard didn't hire Lina because he was too cheap to pay an extra girl. We were sad to see Lina go. Her school found her a job with a doctor across the street from our office and we got to see each other every day for lunch.

A year and a half later, the receptionist-manager (Laila) got her ass kicked by an African-American intern, Brenda, following an argument.

I yelled at the intern, "Leave her alone!" But Brenda just kept banging Laila's head on the tile floor.

I made a mad dash to the back of the office were the X-ray technician was usually sleeping on the X-ray table. His name was Fred; he was a sweet kind of guy, super skinny, and he smoked way too much pot every day. He'd light up a joint in the X-ray room and we could smell it all the way to the front of the office. I flung the door open and yelled, "Fred, get your ass up and help me with Laila!"

Fred and I ran to the front, but by then Brenda was already gone. I helped the disoriented Laila up, while Fred called our boss and told him what had happened.

"Don't call the police. We don't know if Brenda is coming back to do something even worse," was Howard's advice. For reasons we couldn't understand he refused to call the police and report the incident. My guess is Howard had something to hide, and he was more afraid of the police than Brenda.

Laila and I both left the office extremely frightened. We were scared to go back to work. We were actually afraid for our lives. The next day I called Howard and told him I wasn't coming back. Laila and Carmela did likewise.

Chapter 7

My First (and Only) True Love - October 1978

In October 1978, I met Torreey while disco dancing at Moody's nightclub in Santa Monica. He was 6 feet tall, light hair, brown eyes and an incredible physique. Lina didn't go with me that evening, but my brother Evan, my oldest sister Gia and our friend Ray came along. I was dancing nonstop with several different guys and never wanted to sit down. On one of my rare breaks, Torreey walked up and asked, "Would you like to dance?"

"Sure." I said and got up while he held my hand and lead me to the floor.

I had already noticed him earlier and thought he was a pretty good disco dancer – for a white guy. "Where did you learn to dance?" I asked.

"I've been taking private disco dancing lessons every week for a while now," he responded, twirling me.

Disco dancing was so much fun; I think it was by far the best thing that ever happened to just about every person who loved dancing.

"What's your name?" Torreey asked.

"Shirley," I said.

"You don't look like a Shirley," he said, smiling.

We danced and danced until it was time for the club to close down for the night. "Can I get your phone number?" Torreey asked.

"Okay?" I said and wrote it on a bar napkin.

The following day I said, "Lina, guess what? I met this guy named ... T something? Shit, I don't remember. Maybe Terry or Tony. Fuck, I don't know. For now, I'll just call him Tweety, like Tweety Bird. I couldn't understand him over the loud music. But anyway, he asked me for my phone number and wants to take me out dancing."

"What?" Lina shook her head in disbelief, laughing, and said, "Okay, Tweety Bird it is?"

Tweety was a CPA working for Price Waterhouse at the time. But he certainly didn't look like your typical CPA – more like a pro football linebacker.

Tweety indeed called me the next day and invited me out dancing. "Meet me at Osco's nightclub," I told him over the phone. I didn't want him picking me up because I had just met him; besides my kids had never seen me with another man and I didn't want to confuse them. Also I didn't feel comfortable riding home by myself with him at 1:00 or 2:00 in the morning, so I came up with a plan. I said, "Lina, were going to Osco's around 10:00 p.m. ... that way if he offers us a ride home we'll be together."

According to plan, we'd showed up at Osco's shortly after 10:00. I immediately introduced Lina to Tweety and the three of us danced until 2:00 in the morning. I loved how he'd hold my hand on one side and with his other hand he'd hold Lina's hand twirling us at the same time; while Lina and I smiled, giggled and never wanted to sit down. It was so much fun, and the best time of our lives!

At the end of the night, Tweety offered us a ride home. Lina and I already had a plan in case he tried anything weird with us. I reminded Lina while we were in the ladies room, "You grab him from behind and I'll punch him in the face. Okay?"

He was super fit and honestly we really didn't have a chance with him, but fortunately nothing happened. He was a real gentleman and invited me out again the next evening.

Tweety and I continued seeing each other for about two months and finally I had the nerve to say, "I have a secret to tell you."

Tweety looked surprised and said, "Are you married?"

"Yes, but I'm separated and have been living with my mom for the last seven months – on top of that, I have two kids – and by the way, do you have a problem if I sometimes hang out with my sister and girlfriends, you know, girls' night out?" I said it all in one breath.

"That's okay with me. I've dated women with children before, and I don't have a problem with 'girls' night out,' " he said with a slight smile. "Oh, and how old are your kids?"

"Three and four," I replied, biting my nail.

"When do I get to meet them?"

Tweety Bird's stock just went up. "Next weekend if you like," I said with a smile.

After all that, Lina and I finally got his name right, and he went from Tweety to Torreey, when I had him write it down on a piece of paper.

The following weekend he came by the house and met my kids. The minute Torreey entered the door and Luke saw him, I could tell right away that Luke was already jealous. Luke was very close to me, a lot more than Natalie was.

"Hi. I'm Torreey," he said, bright eyed.

Luke looked at Torreey, said, "Hi," and then glued his eyes on his toy.

Natalie came running from the bedroom and into the living room with a big smile on her face. The minute *she* saw Torreey, she asked with a lisp, "Are you gonna be my new daddy?" At the time she'd had lost her baby front teeth and had a slight speech impediment.

And from then on, Torreey called me "Momsie."

Torreey sometimes stopped by the medical office where I worked and took me out to lunch; other times he came by and gave me a ride home. He knew I rode the bus every day to work and back home again to my kids. He was that kind of a guy, very caring, and a gentleman who opens the door to the car or any door for me or anyone else.

Torreey was a UCLA graduate with a degree in business. In high school, his water polo team was perhaps the strongest in their history (Fullerton High School 1963).

Torreey was Fullerton High School's top scoring player. A national panel of swimming coaches to the All-American high school water polo team named him that. The All-American selections were made from 4500 players in schools throughout the nation.

Torreey began his UCLA career in 1966. A shoulder injury he suffered in the summer of 1967 forced him to sit out that season; and contributed to his withdrawal from the 1968 Olympic Trials.

Both Torreey and his brother Craig, UCLA All-Americans, were selected as participants in the Olympic trials.

Torreey's older brother brought home the bronze medal for water polo in the 1972 Olympics in Munich, Germany.

One day Torreey asked me out to dinner with some of his friends. I was very nervous; I wasn't used to going out to fancy restaurants and sitting with strange people asking me all kinds of questions.

At the restaurant we had a few cocktails, then we all ordered our meal. The table had the formal silverware setting and I had no idea which fork to use for the salad, so when the food arrived I decided to watch Torreey pick the salad fork. I slowly grabbed my matching fork and started eating my salad. I thought to myself, *Okay, I'm safe for now, but what next? Hueputa mierda!*

When I got home, Lina asked, "How was dinner?"

"OMG, I was nervous and confused about the fucking utensils." Then I told her what I did and we ended laughing like always.

Torreey loved to snow ski. One day he said, "You want to go skiing with me to Mammoth Mountain?"

"I don't know how to ski," I lamented.

"Don't worry, you can take a few lessons when we get up there," he assured me.

"Really?" I shouted, super excited! I'd never been to the snow before.

A few days later he took me shopping for a ski jacket, gloves, etc., for our trip. On our way back home he said, "The trip to Mammoth is about six hours. I need you to help me with the drive for three or four hours, then I'll drive the rest of the way, okay?"

I didn't reply; I just pretended I didn't hear anything.

He dropped me off at my mom's house in Hollywood, gave me a kiss and said. "I'll see you on Friday evening around 6:00 p.m. for our trip."

"Oh, okay," I said, but was thinking, *Oh shit!*

The minute I got inside the house, Lina looked at me and said, "What's wrong? You look worried."

"Fuck," I cried, "I don't know how I'm going to get out of this one! Torreey wants me to drive his car for a couple of hours so he can sleep. He's going to be too tired after working all day to drive all the way to Mammoth."

Lina laughed hysterically. "Didn't you tell him you don't know how to drive? Oh shit, you're in fucking trouble."

"Of course not! I'm too fucking embarrassed! What's he going to think of me? I'm just this fucking girl who doesn't know how to drive, has two kids, no money, and no car."

Lina couldn't stop laughing; tears were rolling down her cheeks, so I ended up busting a gut too. After our laugh attack, Lina seriously said, "You better tell him on the phone before he picks you up on Friday."

"Fuck, I don't even want to think about it anymore." I wanted to tell him but I just didn't know how. It was too embarrassing. He assumed I knew how to drive, I guess he'd never dated anyone like me. I knew there was no way I could get out of this mess, not this time.

Friday came and I was a nervous fucking mess. Lina couldn't believe I still hadn't said anything to Torreey. He arrived at our door to pick me up; said hello to my mom, the kids, and Lina.

Lina said hello, then came over to me, and whispered in my ear in Spanish, "Hueputa que miedo." ("Son-of-a-bitch, how scary.")

I looked at Lina, wide-eyed, and said, "Bye Mom, Lina, thanks for watching the kids." I grabbed Natalie and Luke, hugged and kissed them and said, "I love you. I'll be back on Sunday." As I walked away I could see Lina from the corner of my eye, making funny faces at me.

Lina never complained about watching my kids while I was out with Torreey. She was always very sweet and caring toward them. She saw me struggling and trying hard to make a better life for us.

"How do you do it?" she asked several times. "No way I could do what you're doing if I had kids. I'm not strong enough like you are."

Torreey and I left the house and walked to the front were he'd parked the car, a yellow Camaro. He placed my little suitcase in the trunk, then turned around and said, "Okay, you can drive first, so get in the car and adjust the seat and mirrors."

By now, I was fucking shaking, I wanted to start running but stupid me went ahead and sat in the driver's seat. He opened the passenger door, sat down, gave me the key to the car and said, "Go ahead and start the engine."

I was holding the key. My hand began to shake and I broke down crying.

Torreey looked at me, confused. "What's wrong?"

Finally the words poured out of my mouth. "I can't drive, I can't drive!"

He didn't know what I meant. "Calm down and tell me what's wrong! Do you have a bunch of tickets or something?"

"No, no, it's nothing like that," I sobbed. "I never learned how to drive because I've never had any money to buy a car."

He shook his head in disbelief. "Why didn't you just tell me that the other day?"

"I was too embarrassed," I mumbled.

He got out of his seat, came around to where I was, and wrapped his arms around me.

"It's okay! It's no big deal," he soothed.

I knew he felt bad for me and didn't want to embarrass me any further. *For sure*, I thought, *he's never going to call me again*. To date, that was the most humiliating moment of my life.

Torreey drove all the way to Mammoth, fighting off the urge to fall asleep. The next few days we skied from 8:00 a.m. to 4:00 p.m. At first, Torreey skied by himself while I took lessons. After skiing all day, we went back to the lodge, put on our swimsuits and sat outside in the Jacuzzi while the snowflakes cascaded down.

"This is magical!" I told Torreey.

An hour later we headed to the restaurant for a romantic dinner by the fireplace. Our evening ended back at the lodge, making love and falling asleep in each other's arms. We had an amazing trip and couldn't wait to do it again. What a blast!

Shortly after we returned home, Torreey said, "Call the driving school and I'll pay for your lessons."

Two weeks after that I could drive an automatic. I was so excited; it was like a dream come true!

He then said, "Go to the DMV and get your license."

After I passed my driving test, he took me to a used car lot and bought me my first little car, a white Honda Civic. Here I was twenty-three with my own car! I'd drive to work, to pick up the kids, to the market, etc. Life was so much easier with wheels. I was the happiest girl in the world!

Torreey rented a bedroom from his roommate, Tim. The house was up in the hills of Redondo Beach with an ocean view. Tim owned the house and had his girlfriend, Gwen, living with him too. Torreey wanted me to come by and spend the weekends with him. I did it for a while until I felt that Tim didn't want me there. Torreey's friend was very moody and I could feel his animosity. Besides, I couldn't bring the kids with me because it wasn't Torreey's house.

One day I finally said, "Torreey, I don't want to come and stay at Tim's house anymore. He's rude to me most of the time. I don't feel comfortable being there."

Torreey nodded. "I know how Tim can be, and I don't want you to feel uncomfortable." He was very understanding. "Don't worry, I'll figure something out."

When Torreey was in college at UCLA, he was an officer in the Navy (ROTC) for eighteen months, stationed in Long Beach while he was training for the Olympic and Pan American teams. He decided to buy a house with a Veteran loan.

He found a small one-bedroom in Redondo Beach two blocks from the beach, which was all he could afford at the time. He never expressed a desire to get married or have children, and that was okay with me. I also didn't want any more children and marriage wasn't on my mind, either. I wasn't even divorced at the time. I was having fun with him; I'd learned to snow ski, play beach volleyball, work out in the gym, participate in aerobics classes; went disco dancing a lot, out to dinners with friends, parties, etc. I was having the time of my life. I never had anyone care for me that much. I kept crossing my fingers that it would last.

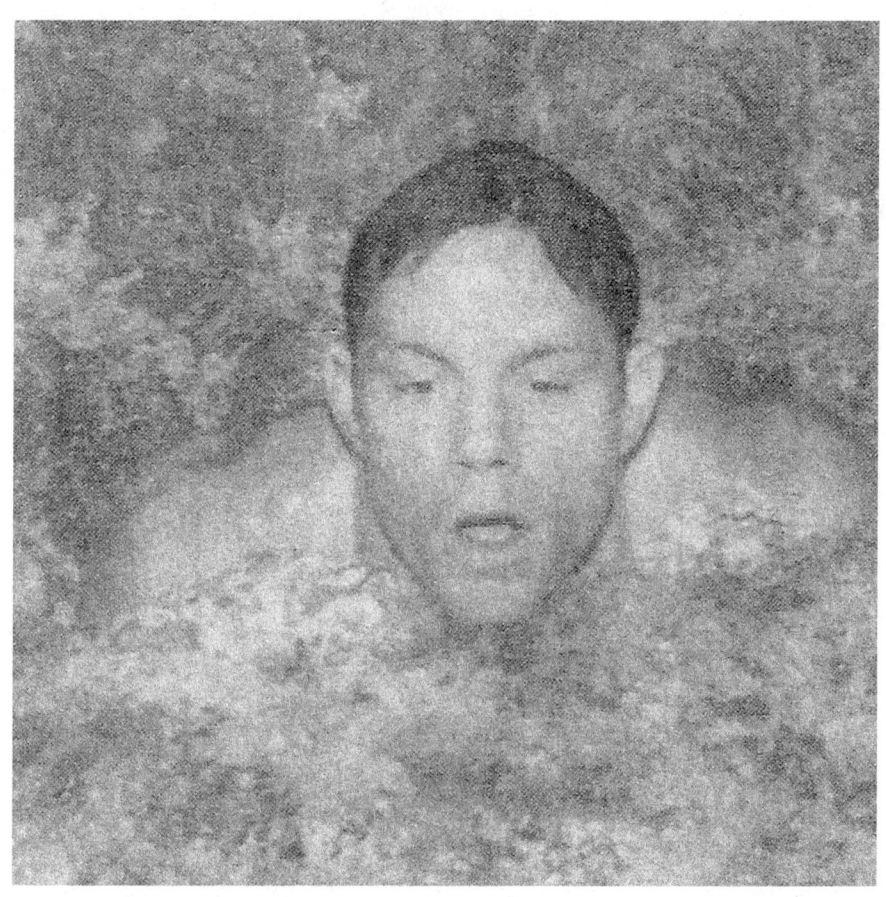

Torreey in 1969 NACAA championship UCLA water polo. Daily Bruins Newspaper.

Chapter 8

Meeting Michael Jackson - 1980s

I was unemployed and looking for a new job. One of Torreey's accounting clients had an employment agency in West Los Angeles. The agency sent me to an interview at an advertising agency, John's & John's, located on Sunset Blvd., near Vine in Hollywood on the 9th and 11th floors. The agency needed a mail clerk. I interviewed and got hired. I was super excited! My job was to deliver the mail all day long to the two floors of the agency.

Since I was a mail clerk, I didn't have to dress up like most of the other women did. It was perfect for me since I didn't own a lot of designer dresses. Instead, I wore my tight jeans most of the time. And of course the men began to notice and complimented me quite often. "Nice jeans, Shirley!" Or, "Looking good!" Or, "Um, Um!" Even some of the women who liked me would say something nice as well.

I not only enjoyed my new job, but relished all the attention I was getting, as well. I was the twenty-three-year-old new kid in town with the tightest jeans and the sexiest walk. But I still had to watch out for the female women haters. And believe me there were plenty of them. As long as I was a good worker I knew they couldn't complain and get rid of me. I was always very polite even to those who didn't like me for any reason at all.

Joe Jackson Productions was on the sixth floor (Michael Jackson's father). Fourteenth floor: Motown. Fifteenth: KISS/FM radio – with Rick Dees. Sixteenth: Joseph Isgro Productions. A lot of cool action was going on in this building.

One day, I met Michael Jackson in the lobby cafeteria. My best friend, Lorraine, the main receptionist, and I took the mandatory ten-minute break twice a day. We went to the cafeteria in the lobby to play Pacman every morning and afternoon. We were addicted to the video game. I moved my butt a lot while playing because I had to push my body toward the machine while trying to score points. And I screamed and laughed whenever I won or lost.

Lorraine always had a great time watching me, especially when I cursed, "Shit, fuck, hueputa!" Whatever came out of my mouth, Lorraine thought it sounded funny because of my accent.

We hung out together a lot and for a long time until she became very ill with leukemia. When I visited Lorraine at the hospital while she was on chemo, it brought back childhood memories of the Costa Rica hospital and my little friend Nadia. I closed my eyes and held Lorraine's hand while she slept, and I could see Nadia dying in front of me. My heart ached and was broken into little pieces as my sweet dear friend Lorraine wasted away.

I couldn't believe this was happening to me again. Only this time I was an adult watching my best friend die.

But long before that, one day Michael Jackson came in with his bodyguards while Lorraine and I were playing Pacman and making a lot of noise laughing and screaming. Next thing I knew, Michael was standing behind me looking over my shoulder. He whispered, "You're very good!" Then ended up laughing with us. I'll always remember his sweet soft voice behind me. Michael Jackson, his sister Latoya and their mother Katherine came in the building many times. Sometimes we saw them in the elevator or walking to their limo or the Rolls Royce that his mother drove. Latoya and Mrs. Jackson were also very sweet.

One year later, the receptionist, Linda, in the media department on the 9th floor got promoted. Linda and I had become pretty good friends. She was from Nicaragua.

"Shirley, would you be interested in working full-time in the position I'm vacating? I can train you next week," she offered.

I couldn't believe it. "Yes! Yes!" I immediately responded.

The media department was a fun place to work, especially for a young woman like me. Good-looking men came to our department to meet with the media buyers to sell them radio or television commercial spots. I was always very polite, pleasant, and dressed sexy but classy. I knew the men loved it! Every time I got up from my desk to go deliver a message to one of the account managers, I could feel their eyes staring at me from behind. I flirted playfully and didn't think there was anything wrong with it. I did it simply for amusement, with no intention of developing any further relationship. I was both loyal, and honest with Torreey, besides I've never liked dating more than one man at a time. It was just a game that some of the women and I enjoyed playing.

Chapter 9

Playboy Audition - 1980s

Lina was having a hard time keeping a job; her dyslexia made her so insecure and upset at times. One day, a talent scout gave her a card to try out for Playboy, and I told her to go for it! She auditioned the following week. This was not a written test, but a nude photo test. She PASSED with an A!

Hurray! Lina started working for Playboy. In addition to modeling, she also performed in videos, and traveled to Mexico, Spain, etc. as a spokesmodel for Playboy. She did music videos; one by the Smithereens, *Only a Memory*. Another by Tony! Toni! Tone! *Baby Doll*. But they had her working only part-time and she wasn't making enough money to pay the bills; she needed a full-time job.

To pick up some extra cash, she took a part-time job at Jack In The Box working the drive-thru window. One day she came home crying and said, "I got fired!"

"Why? What did you do?" I asked with a frown.

"A woman was placing an order and I couldn't understand her, so she started calling me names over the intercom. I got so mad at her I called her names too: fucking bitch, motherfucker... step out of your car so I can kick your ass."

"OMG, Lina!" I said, holding my hand over my mouth, and laughing out loud. "Lina, you don't need that fucking job. FUCK JACK IN THE BOX, HIS HAMBURGERS AND CUSTOMERS TOO!" We ended up laughing on the couch until our tears were running down our faces and our bellies were aching.

Chapter 10

Chosen by Elizabeth Taylor - 1980s

A year later I was promoted to a word processor and we now needed a new receptionist as soon as possible. I thought for a second, and then raced into my boss's office asking, "Tom, can my sister interview for the job?"

Tom looked me in the eye and said, "Is she cute?"

"You kidding? She's a Playboy model," I said raising my eyebrows. My boss was openly gay, so I knew he wouldn't be hitting on Lina.

"Okay, have her come in for the interview tomorrow," he said with a wink.

"Thank you! Thank you!" I said and left Tom's office jumping with joy. I immediately called Lina and gave her the news.

The next day, Lina came for the interview; Tom loved her and offered her the job.

Lina and I were thrilled that we'd be working together in the same department.

One day we met Rick Dees, the wildly popular DJ from KISS-FM Radio, in the elevator of the lobby. He looked kind of boyish with big blue eyes, a cute smile and a friendly personality. "*Rick Dees in the morning!*" Lina sang his signature promo line with a smile while Rick and I laughed.

After running into him over and over, we both decided it was time to sing "*Disco, Disco Duck. Quack, quack.*" It was a goofy song he'd written and occasionally played on his show. Rick opened his eyes wide, laughed, and before stepping out of the elevator he said, "Very funny girls!"

Every time after that when we ran into Rick, he'd look at us with a big smile on his face and say, "Hi girls."

Besides Michael Jackson and Latoya, we met celebrities like Smokey Robinson, Elizabeth Taylor, Rod Steward, Rick James, Julio Iglesias, John Travolta, Steve Garvey and Steve Sax (L.A. Dodgers).

When Lina and I met Smokey Robinson in the elevator of our building, we immediately said, "Hi Smokey!"

"Hi ladies!" he responded with that beautiful smile of his, and cute dimples, too.

"Wow, you have beautiful green eyes!" Lina told him, smiling. That was our sweet few minutes with him.

I met Elizabeth Taylor one afternoon after hearing Rick Dees on the radio announcing that she was going to be his guest. Lina was not at work that day. When the interview was over some of my co-workers and I rushed our asses to the elevator and up to the KISS-FM Radio floor to get a glimpse of Liz Taylor. Ten of us waited outside the door; four bodyguards were already standing by to protect Ms. Taylor. They didn't allow us to get too close to the door. All of a sudden, the door flew open and the bodyguards took their positions in front of and behind Liz Taylor.

I couldn't believe my eyes, looking at this beautiful lady. Some of my co-workers yelled out her name: "Miss Taylor can we get your autograph?" The bodyguards kept saying, "No, no."

As Liz Taylor was walking away from us, I yelled, "Miss Burton, may I please have your autograph?"

Immediately, Liz Taylor turned around and asked, "Who said that?"

I raised my hand and responded nervously, "I did!"

Liz Taylor walked back to where I was standing with a pen and a piece of paper. She was now directly in front of me, looking me over, and with a soft and polite voice said, "What is your name?"

"Shirley," I replied, gripping my pen and the blank paper that I handed to her with hands that were shaking from the excitement.

I looked at her straight in the eyes and saw the most beautiful orbs I'd ever seen. I stared at her hands while she was autographing my paper and saw the gargantuan rock on her finger. I believe she was wearing the famous ring that Richard Burton had given her many years ago. It was the biggest, most gorgeous diamond I had ever seen.

When she returned my pen and paper, I said, "Thank you so very much!" and bounced on my toes with joy. I was the only one who got an autograph from Liz Taylor ... I mean, Miss Burton that day.

Chapter 11

The Ghetto House - 1980s

From Hollywood, our family moved to North Hollywood, in the San Fernando Valley, into a three-bedroom in a horrible neighborhood. There were now eleven people living in a rundown house. One bedroom was for my brother Evan, his wife Jen, and their little boy, Bobby. The second: three of my sisters Tanya, Ceci, and Graciella. The third: Mom, Lina, my kids and I.

Lina and I were still working for the advertising agency in Hollywood. I stayed home with my kids Monday through Thursday nights. Most Fridays, after work, I'd spend the weekend at Torreey's tiny house. And on Mondays I was back at the ghetto house in North Hollywood. Lina, Mom or other family members were watching my kids on those weekends.

The North Hollywood house was a total nightmare; there were fights all of the time. My brother and his wife drank a lot. Two of my sisters were always out partying, and whenever they were home they fought with everyone. Another sister was pregnant, always in a bad mood and argued about everything until she moved out and went to live with her boyfriend. Lina was dating a baseball player, Larry, who played for the minor league California Angels and later for the Milwaukee Brewers. He was moody with a horrible attitude and hardly ever smiled.

My kids were now five and six. Luke was a very hyperactive child, had a lot of energy, and he loved to watch cartoons. We only had one old TV in the living room. One Monday I came home early from work, opened the front door of the house, and to my shock, one of my sisters was on top of Luke, beating him up. Luke was screaming and crying hysterically, so I ran over, grabbed my sister by the hair and pulled her away from my son. My sister called me names and screamed, "Get the fuck out of my house, and take the fucking brats with you!"

Another time, after arriving home from work, I noticed that Natalie wasn't in the living room with Luke. I went looking for her in the bedrooms but she wasn't there either. I knocked on the bathroom door when I faintly heard Natalie talking to someone. "Natalie? Natalie, are you in there?"

An adult female voice said, "Natalie and I are taking a bath."

"Get Natalie out of the tub, RIGHT NOW!" I angrily yelled.

A few seconds later, Natalie came out of the bathroom with a towel wrapped around her body.

"Why were you taking a bath with...?" I demanded to know.

Natalie innocently said, "We were playing games in the bathtub."

"Natalie, never to do that again." I wanted to scream, but restrained myself.

Later in life, Natalie and I were having a conversation when she suddenly said, "Mom, remember the day when you came home and I was in the bathtub with...

"Yes, I was fucking pissed!"

"Well, she had me play a game." Natalie said, matter-of-factly. "Touch my boobs and then I'll touch yours back."

"Oh that fucking BITCH!" I will not mention her name, but she knows whom I'm talking about.

"Mom, please promise me you'll keep this story away from grandma," Natalie begged.

"Okay, I will," I said. I kept my promise to Natalie, I never told my mom, but I did tell two of my siblings.

By the time my kids were six and seven, I'd had enough of all the shit that was going on in our crazy house. I had to think and think repeatedly on what to do and how to handle this or that situation. Finally, I decided I had no other choice but to call my in-laws, whom I'd never met, and ask them for help. The grandparents sent Luke and Natalie's birthday and Christmas cards with a check for $25 every year, so I knew they cared about my kids.

"Hi Jereldine, this is Shirley. I need to talk with you. I need help!" I said in desperation, and told her what was going on at the house.

"I know some things about your family through Roger. I know you come from a dysfunctional family, but I had no idea what the poor kids were going through," Jereldine said, sounding a bit sour.

"I want to move to an apartment with the kids, but I can't afford it with my salary. Is there anything you could do to help me and your grandkids?" I pleaded, feeling like I wanted to pull my hair out.

"I'll talk it over with my husband and Roger." Jereldine hesitated, then went on to say, "Roger is not mentally well...he's trying to get his life together again."

I knew Roger was full of shit. Mental illness was just an excuse; he was probably smoking more pot than ever.

Jereldine concluded with, "I'll call you back in a few days."

When Jereldine called, she made an offer: "We can't help you with money, but we'll take the kids for a while until you get back on your feet. Perhaps by having the kids around, Roger might come out of his depression."

"I'll think about it and call you back in a week," I said with a shaky voice. After hanging up the phone I started crying. I felt deep down inside of me I was going to make the biggest mistake of my life, but I had no other choice. My kids were already hanging out with bad kids in the neighborhood. One day I came back from work and found out that both Luke and Natalie had gone to Sears with some of the kids in the neighborhood. Natalie and Luke both came home with brand new toys. Lina was home when the kids showed up. Natalie was carrying a big radio. Lina and my brother Evan knew right away that it was all stolen; they quickly got confessions out of both kids. Lina and Evan decided to take the pilfered merchandise to the backyard of the house and have Luke and Natalie destroy the toys one at a time while saying, "I will never steal again." My kids had been mentally and physically abused, and now they were stealing!

I couldn't take it anymore; I called Jereldine and said, "Okay, take the kids for a while. After all, Roger is their father and I need help from him right now!" Roger had not seen or talked to the kids since he first left.

I didn't mention anything to anyone at the house that I'd talked to Jereldine Parker about taking the kids. In the meantime, Jereldine arranged for the kids to fly to Richmond, Virginia.

A few days later, I said to the kids, "I'm sending you both to Virginia to live with your dad and grandparents for a while."

Luke immediately started crying and hugging me. "No, I don't wanna go!"

Natalie was never a crier; she was always a strong little girl. She asked, "Why? Why?" That was one of her favorite words. I sat down with both of them and made them understand that for now it was the right decision. I couldn't protect them, I had no money, and their grandparents and their dad would take care of them for a period of time. "I love you very much and I'll come see you for your birthdays and Christmas. Okay?"

Natalie asked, "Are we going on a plane?" Her eyes became bigger and bigger with excitement.

Luke, on the other hand, continued crying and said, "I already miss you, Momma."

"I miss you too. You'll both be okay," I said through tears, but also assuring them.

Natalie was already running around the house, yelling, "Luke and I are moving to Virginia with our dad and grandparents! And Christmas is going to be full of snow!" That was my Natalie, always excited about traveling.

Mom and my sister Gia came and asked, "Is this true?"

"Yes," I confessed.

Gia frowned and said, "Don't do it. Let me have Luke and I'll take care of him with my boyfriend, Manuel,"

I shook my head firmly. "I'm not going to separate them. Besides, this is their grandparents and father."

"Shirley, please don't send them away," Mom pleaded. But there was no turning back for me.

"Mom, Gia," I said, "I can't go on the way the kids and I are living anymore."

Mom was very unhappy about my decision. And as much as I didn't want to bring this up, I had no other choice but to remind her: "You and Dad left seven children in Costa Rica with our grandmother and aunt for a better life in America. If you did it, I can do it too. It isn't that I want to get rid of my kids – it's that I want a better life for them and myself."

Believe me, it was the hardest decision I have ever made in my life. No one understands the sacrifices another person has to make until they themselves are put in that position.

On Friday after work I picked up the kids and drove to Torreey's house for the weekend. I'd made my decision not to tell him what had been going on at my mom's house with the kids. I was too embarrassed to say anything to him; besides he never wanted children so I kept it to myself for as long as I could.

A week later, I finally said, "Torreey, I'm sending the kids to live with their dad and grandparents for a while. Roger and I talked, and he wants to help out with the kids." I didn't tell him about talking to Jereldine. While I was always honest with Torreey, this time I was determined to take care of my personal problems without involving him in any way.

Torreey shrugged and said, "It's about time Roger acts like a father."

In July of 1980, Roger's sister Pattie flew from Virginia to LAX to pick up my kids. I drove them to the airport and waited for Pattie's airplane to arrive. Pattie met the kids and me for the very first time. We sat and waited for an hour for the kids and Pattie to board their plane. Natalie was excited, but Luke was holding on to me with all his might. When it was time to board the plane, Luke screamed, "No, I don't want to go." He didn't want to let loose of my hand. Natalie didn't cry at all, she was already holding on to Pattie's hand. I held Luke very tight with tears streaming down my face and said, "Luke, I love you and I will see you soon. Okay, baby?"

I gave Natalie a kiss and a hug and told her, "I love you too, Natalie."

Pattie grabbed Luke's hand and said, "We're going to have fun in Virginia."

Luke finally let go of me but cried all the way to the gate saying, "I miss you! I miss you!"

I can still see the two little bodies walking away from me to what I prayed would be a better life for a while. I felt horrible afterward, ashamed of what I'd done. I cried and cried all the way back home.

Luke and Natalie began their new life, for now, with their dad and grandparents. They enrolled the kids in school. I called them every week, but Luke just wanted to come back home. Luke missed me more than Natalie; he was very close to me. Winter came and their birthdays were right around the corner, so I decided to surprise them by flying to Virginia for their birthdays and Christmas. Pattie came by the airport to pick me up and we got home in the evening after 10:00 P.M.. My kids had no idea I was coming; I went into their bedroom and saw Luke and Natalie both asleep in their own beds.

I gave Luke a kiss on the cheek. He opened his eyes and screamed, "MOMMA, MOMMA, you're here!"

I held him tight with teardrops of happiness falling down my face. "Yes, I am here, baby!"

Natalie woke up and rushed over to Luke's bed. I hugged her tight, gave her a kiss, and told them both, "I love and miss you so much."

"Momma, are you moving to Virginia?" Luke asked, smiling wide.

As much as I hated to say no I had to. I didn't want to lie to them. "I'm here for your birthdays and Christmas, and then I have to go back home. But I'll be back again, soon."

Their little faces got sad but I immediately grabbed them again and pulled them close to me. A few minutes later we all went to sleep happy to see each other. We woke up the next morning to a beautiful snowfall; and the kids couldn't wait to go outside and play in the snow with me.

During my three weeks with the kids I never saw Roger. He had decided to stay at a friend's house and not face me. To this day, I still don't understand why he never called or sent birthday or Christmas cards to the kids. It was like he was too embarrassed to face us, or he was too fucking high on drugs. I believe he didn't want me to ask him why he chose to do what he did – go away and ignore his kids. It wasn't fair to the three of us that he left all the responsibility to me, knowing how dysfunctional and crazy my family was. Roger knew about the ongoing fights at my mom's house. That's why his parents agreed to take the kids until I could straighten out my life. Roger's parents really believed the kids would be good to have around the house, because maybe it would help Roger come out of his depression. Thankfully, he was in therapy; he never knew what he wanted out of life.

The three weeks went by too fast for me. I was already crying, thinking about having to leave them again. But I could see they were well taken care of by their grandparents. The Parker's were retired, and Roger was living with them, and of course not working. The kids brought a lot of joy to them, but I never knew anything about Roger. The only information his mom offered was that his depression was mental not physical.

The day came when I had to return to California. Luke once again didn't want to let go of me; this time Natalie was crying too. Natalie rarely showed her emotions; she just stood there looking at me with her teary eyes. I grabbed her and Luke and said, "I love you both and will miss you – and I'll call you every week." I left the Parker's house in tears, got to the airport, and returned to my turbulent life in L.A.

Torreey was waiting for me at the airport. The minute he saw me his face lit up. He threw his arms around me tight. I could tell from his expression that he missed me. "How was the trip?" he asked.

"It was happy and sad too. I need to go see them again soon."

Weeks later Torreey asked, "Why don't you move in with me?"

"Really?" I replied, surprised. "I guess I can do that?" I said, at the same time thinking about the kids. I also wanted to move forward in our relationship. So it was the perfect opportunity for me to test the waters and really find out if the two of us were going to work out.

Torreey had just bought a little one-bedroom, one-bath house two blocks from the beach. He was remodeling the house himself on the weekends and I helped with certain things. I knew for a fact that there was no room for my two kids in this very tiny house. In the meantime, I was trying not to show how much I missed Luke and Natalie. I kept my pain of missing my kids where no one ever saw it.

By now, the kids had been gone for about nine months. One evening while I was visiting my mom at her madhouse, Jereldine Parker called me and said, "I need to have an important conversation with you." She continued saying, "The kids are great, but my husband and I can't take care of them anymore. The children require a lot of attention and we feel we're too old to continue with their care."

"What about Roger? Isn't he helping you with them?" I said, incredulously.

Jereldine said flatly, "Roger can't do it either." She then surprised me with: "Are you going to marry Torreey and take the kids with you?"

"I don't think that's going to happen any time soon!" I explained my situation with Torreey's tiny house, and added that he and I never discuss marriage.

To my shock, Jereldine then said, "My husband and I and Roger have decided that the best thing for the kids is to give them up for adoption to a young couple that lives in the area."

I didn't think this was Jereldine's idea, I believed it was all Roger's brainchild; I had heard this scheme before from her crazy son when we were married. And now I was hearing it from his mother. I was speechless. Jereldine kept talking, telling me to think about it, and she'd start getting the adoption documents prepared for me to sign.

All of a sudden, I opened my mouth and yelled at her: "What are you telling me? I am shocked and disgusted at what you're saying! This can't be true. Where is that piece-of-shit son of yours? I need to talk to him. Put him on the phone!"

Jereldine stammered, "R-Roger isn't home." She tried to get me to calm down, saying, "This is going to be the best thing for the kids. We cannot take care of them and you can't either."

I practically shouted, "Now you listen to me lady! I know very well that I come from a dysfunctional family, but you and you're family are out of your fucking mind. I can take care of my kids if that asshole son of yours will help me out!"

Jereldine calmly said, "That is not going to happen. He can't even take care of himself."

Jereldine reiterated that she was going to take care of the paperwork, and that the best thing for me was to sign the documents.

I yelled at her, "You are not going to arrange for any paperwork! You are going to put my two kids on a plane back home where they belong!"

Jereldine held it together and replied, "I'm not going to do that, because the kids don't deserve to come back to that awful home with your crazy family."

I yelled even louder, "IF YOU DON'T PUT THEM ON A PLANE THIS WEEK, I AM COMING TO GET THEM MYSELF – AND IT WON'T BE PRETTY!" The words came out of my mouth before I realized what I'd said, but I was glad I did.

This was my final conversation with the woman. The next day I got a call from her husband, Roger Sr., giving me the day and time of the kids' arrival. That was the last time my kids saw their father, Roger.

Torreey, my mom, Gia, her boyfriend Manuel and I took off to the airport to pick up the kids. I of course was nervous as can be. When I saw the two little bodies coming out of the gate my tears were falling down. The kids immediately yelled out, "Momma! Momma!" and threw themselves into my arms. "I miss you so much," I said, holding on to them tight.

I had no choice but to bring them back to the crazy house. I began taking the kids with me every weekend to Torreey's little house. I'd put blankets and pillows on the small living room floor for them to sleep. They were both so happy to be with me. Torreey and I played beach volleyball every weekend, and the kids were enjoying their limited time with the two of us. We'd barbeque in the evenings, or have a babysitter come by and take care of them so we could go out to dinner with friends. I'd drive them back home on Sunday evening so they could go to school the next morning.

By then the kids where hating going back to the crazy house. "Mom, why can't we live with you and Torreey?" Luke asked every week.

I had to explain as best as I could. "Well, I wish that was possible, but Torreey's house is too small.

Natalie would automatically say, "Why?" That was always the first word out of her mouth. "We like sleeping in the living room, it's a lot of fun!" she added. Natalie always had an answer for everything.

Luke just made a sad face and pretended to cry.

Eight months later, I started seriously thinking about my relationship with Torreey. I knew that he never wanted to get married, or have children either. Marriage or having any more kids was not on my mind either, but I did want to have my children with me. I couldn't go on like this for the rest of my life. I stayed at mom's house from Monday through Friday. Then picked up the kids late Friday afternoon and kept them with me at Torreey's house until Sunday. I'd drive them back Sunday evening for school on Monday. I was really getting tired of this; I wanted my own place with my kids.

So one weekend I decided to have a serious conversation with Torreey. I didn't bring the kids that weekend in case I had to leave right away.

"Torreey," I said, "I appreciate the car you bought for me, and all the fun things I've learned to do with you, but I'm getting older and my kids need their mother with them. I can't do this anymore." I had to be honest with him and didn't mean to hurt him in any way. He had been so kind and patient with me, I just wanted to let him know how I felt. "I love you and I've enjoyed all of the things we've done together, but I don't think you want the same things I do. You need to find a girl who never wants to settle down, and I need someone who either has kids or wants to help me raise my kids and have a home together.

"At work I have many men asking me out, and I seriously need to find the right man for myself. I'm not asking for a rich man, all I want is to have a home big enough for my two kids to be with me."

I thought I was losing the opportunity to go out with other men and find someone who wanted what I did before I got too old. I just wanted to give my kids a better life. They didn't have a dad because he was a coward who decided to run away from them. My kids deserved a better life.

I think Torreey was shocked by what I told him. I don't think he expected any of this at all. I'd surprised myself that I'd let everything out at once. I thought I could never say this to him but I did and I was proud of it; I did it for my kids. They were innocent victims and I was the only person who could fight for them. No matter what, I knew something good was going to happen for us because of the stance I'd taken.

Torreey didn't say too much. He looked at me with sad eyes and said, "I always thought you would do this." He was such a kind and incredible man, he didn't even ask me to give him back the car he'd bought for me.

That evening I drove back to the crazy house where my kids were. I took them to school in the mornings and drove to work and stayed with them on the weekends. As sad as I felt, and as much as I missed him, I felt relief and proud of myself. I did it for my kids.

Three weeks later, Torreey called. "Hi, how are you and the kids doing?"

"We're good," I replied casually.

"Would you like to come over for the weekend?" Torreey entreated.

"Well, I'm not sure I should? Remember our last conversation?"

"Yes, but I want to show you something," he insisted.

"Okay, but I have to be back by Sunday," I told him.

On Friday after work I drove to Torreey's house. From there we took off to the health club to exercise, and after we sat in the club's outside Jacuzzi. Ten minutes later, Torreey turned to me and said, "My dad helped me buy a bigger house for you and the kids to come and live with me. The house is in escrow and it will probably be ready for us to move in a couple of weeks."

My eyes became bigger. My mouth dropped. I was in shock! I couldn't believe what I had just heard come out of his mouth. I was speechless, frozen, whatever.

He said it again but I noticed that now he was nervous and waiting for my answer. "I bought a three bedroom house in Redondo Beach. Is that what you want? Do you want to come back?"

Somehow I came out of my paralyzed body and immediately jumped over to where he was sitting, hugged and kissed him with tears running down my face and a big "YES!" came out of my mouth. I was the happiest girl on the planet! I couldn't wait to get back to the crazy house and give my kids the wonderful news; they were going to be thrilled! They'd be going to a better school, have their own bedrooms, and best of all we were going to be together forever.

A month later we moved into the Victorian yellow wood house. It was built back in 1915, and it was slightly tilted to the left. So we named it the "crooked" house. The kids and I were very happy.

I registered them at the new school, took them with me to the health club in the evenings where I taught aerobics while they swam in the club's pool. I also enrolled them in karate classes were Torreey was a black belt and sometimes a judge.

One day while I was on my way home from the advertising agency in Hollywood, I started getting stomach cramps, goose bumps on my arms, and chills all over my body. I needed to use a bathroom immediately. I was trembling while driving, hoping to see a gas station nearby so I could pull over and use the restroom. A block away, I happened to see a Chevron gas station on the right side of the street. I continued driving, hoping I'd make it there on time. I was still trembling and the cramps were getting worse. I was almost there when all of a sudden, the signal turned yellow and the car in front of me screeched to a halt. I rammed my foot on the brake and my body went forward causing me to crap all over the car seat and myself.

"Fuck!" I screamed. I sat in my car waiting for the light to turn green but it was already too late. The shit was all over my dress and the car seat. When the light finally turned green I pressed my foot on the accelerator and hurried to the station. I parked my car and ran to the restroom with my dress full of shit. At this point I didn't care if anyone saw me full of caca. I sat on the toilet for a while until I felt it was okay for me to head home; I had another half-hour drive ahead of me.

When I finally got to the house, my kids were sitting outside on the stairs waiting for me to take them to their karate class. Of course, I was late and on top of that, my kids were upset and saying, "Mom, you're late, and Master Johnson is gonna yell at us!"

The instructor didn't allow any of his students to be tardy; it was considered disrespectful.

I hollered back at them, "I'm late because I crapped all over my dress in the car. You got it?"

They immediately climbed inside the car covering their noses, screaming, laughing, and begging, "No, I can't stand this. Please let me out of the car."

I was laughing my ass off just watching them through my rear view mirror.

After dropping them off I drove back home to shower, take Pepto Bismol, and clean the seat of my car before picking them up. I was now driving a brand-new light blue Honda Civic Sedan with blue velvet seat covers that were now coated with a nasty caca stain. Torreey had traded the used white

Honda Civic and surprised me with a new one. And that year we had our first Halloween party for the kids.

Luke (age 7), Natalie (age 6) celebrating their birthdays at Torreey's 650 sq. ft. house in Redondo Beach.

Chapter 12

Wild Night at Chippendale's - 1980s

One evening, Lina and some of her friends got together and went out to Chippendale's nightclub. Chippendale's was the hottest nightclub in town for women. Gorgeous men were everywhere, dancing and removing their clothes down to their teeny-tiny underwear.

The men came out dressed in cowboy, fireman, and policeman outfits. The music started playing and the women screamed as loud as they could. A gorgeous male would prance out and dance on stage for about fifteen minutes. The men started by removing a piece of clothing at a time while the women went crazy. They'd walk toward the women who were sitting in the first row, get very close to them and shake their thing in front of them.

The women fought to tip the dancers. They placed a $1, $5 or more in the dancer's crotch.

That particular evening, Lina met Ronny, a good-looking Italian Chippendale's waiter. The waiters and bartenders were also totally gorgeous. They wore skintight black trousers, no shirt, a black bow tie around their necks, and cuffs on their wrists. Their bodies were amazing!

Lina and Ronny started dating and she was hanging out at Chippendale's a lot. She'd go on weekends with a few of her girlfriends and didn't have to wait in line or pay for anything.

One weekend I decided to go along with Lina and her friends. When I walked in, I said, "Holly shit, I'm in men heaven. Hueputa que viejos mas lindos." ("Son-of-a bitch all these gorgeous men.")

Lina looked at me, nodded her head, grabbed my hand and giggling said, "Let's go to the dance floor before the show starts while Ronny brings us some drinks."

The place was so packed you couldn't even move from one side of the room to the other. The show started at 10:00 p.m. We sat in the first row and had a blast. We screamed as loud as we could and got up and danced with the male strippers and grabbed their butts while the rest of the women yelled louder! They also wanted their turn.

I noticed one of the male dancers; he was dressed in a police officer costume. He was blond with beautiful hair, blue eyes, tan, and an amazing body.

After the show was over, Lina jumped on the dance floor with the girls and I decided to go to the bar to get a glass of water. While I was waiting for the bartender, the good-looking male dancer who'd been dressed as a cop, and was now wearing a nice pair of slacks and a tight knit shirt, walked up beside me and said, "Hi."

I got very nervous; this man was too good looking, and I didn't even think he was speaking to me, so I first looked around to see who he was talking to. Then I said, "Hello, I've enjoyed the show very much."

The ensuing conversation we had was not very long before he said, "Would you like to go to my place, sit by the fireplace, and have a glass of champagne?"

Wow. This gorgeous man doesn't waste any time with women. I immediately said, "No thank you," and walked away thinking, *Yeah right, dude! "A glass of champagne"– and a piece of ass, too. You've got the wrong girl, Mr. Gorgeous Hair.*

He looked completely surprised; I don't think any of the women ever rejected him.

I jumped on the floor where Lina and the girls were dancing, grabbed Lina and her friends and said, "The male dancer with the cop costume asked me to go to his place."

Lina smiled and said, "That's John Gibson! He's a soap opera actor. He has a girlfriend that comes here all the time... I don't see her here tonight."

Lina's friend Elsa turned to me and said, "OMG, I can't believe you turned him down. No woman would do that to him, are you fucking crazy?"

At the time, John Gibson's girlfriend was the not-yet-famous Vanna White.

Lina, Ronny and most of the Chippendale's dancers and waiters including John Gibson roller-skated in Venice Beach on the weekends. Gibson later died in a plane crash.

Chapter 13

Sexy Lingere Contest - 1980s

At the time of this particular story, I was living with Torreey part-time, Friday, Saturday and Sundays only. The rest of the week I lived at the ghetto house with my kids, mom, sisters and brother.

In the five years before moving in with Torreey permanently, my sister Lina and I kind of lived a wild life. I call it a wild life because we did a lot of crazy shit, BUT we only behaved in this manner when we were out with each other or with a bunch of girlfriends. We had girls' night out at least twice a month. We didn't give a shit on these nights; all we wanted was to have fun and laugh.

When Lina went out on dates and I came along, we always conducted ourselves in a lady-like manner. We never in any way acted cheap or slutty. We knew when to behave and when to let it all out.

One day after work, Lina and I went home wondering how we were going to make it through the end of the week. We were almost out of money for food to feed the kids and ourselves. We didn't get paid until the end of the week, we were broke, and it was only Tuesday. I turned to Lina and said, "Hey, I have an idea. Let's enter the Lingerie Contest at Zash's nightclub in the Valley."

"Yeah, let's do it!" Lina happily agreed.

The first prize was $100, second prize $50, and third prize $25. We hurried home, fed the kids and helped them get ready for bed. Mom was going to watch them while we were out.

We put on some lingerie and miniskirts, and then took off to the nightclub. Marisa, our sister-in-law, also entered the contest. She's from Argentina, good-looking with long black hair down to her waist and a stunning figure.

We got to the nightclub and danced until the competition started at 10:00 p.m. Men squeezed into the club like sardines in a tin can, salivating to see some skin. There were ten of us girls who were brave enough to do this. We all went into the back of the nightclub and removed our skirts or dresses.

The DJ then announced the start of the contest. He called the first girl to the center of the dance floor. Each young woman had to dance to the music by herself. I don't remember who went first. All I know is that he called my name and I was feeling good and ready to shake my booty. "Hay hueputa que miedo." ("Son-of-a-bitch, I'm scared.") I said to Lina and Marisa while walking to the dance floor by myself.

The DJ played the music and I started dancing. I had low-cut lingerie exposing my boobs; I began moving and grabbing my boobs, and shaking my booty. The men went crazy, screaming, yelling and applauding. I was having a ball dancing. I couldn't see the crowd because of the bright spotlight in my eyes, which made me even more uninhibited. I ended my dance with a wink, a wave, and a squeal – and they all applauded like crazy.

Lina came out next. She danced and did her little sexy thing that she always did: a sexy pose, a wink, then blew kisses at the crowd – and the men clapped loudly.

Marisa came after, did her dance but not provocative like Lina and I. She was more of a conservative and timid person. She finished her dance and only got a few mild cheers from the audience.

When all of the contestants had finished dancing, it was time to select the three winners. We were all standing in line on the dance floor of the night-club. The DJ asked the crowd of people, mostly men, to shout as loud as they could to select the three finalists. The DJ started calling the numbers and the crowd began to scream for each girl. Lina, I, and another girl were selected as the top three. Again the DJ called #1 (the other girl) and the crowd screamed, but you could tell she wasn't their favorite. When he called my number, I stepped forward, grabbed my boobs, and shook my booty. The viewers went crazy for me.

Lina stepped up next and the men did the same for her.

It was now between Lina and me to win first and second prize. We hugged each other and I whispered in her ear, "We fucking got it girl! The money is ours." I really didn't care since we were going to end up with $150 altogether. We'd agreed beforehand to pool our winnings, so I knew it was fine with Lina too. Lina and I were never jealous of each other.

The DJ called my number and then Lina's and at the end, I ended up with the loudest screams. The announcer gave me $100 and Lina $50 in cash.

After the show was over and we had the money, we drove home laughing, cursing and talking about me grabbing my boobs and ass too. OMG, it was so much fun! I never really cared about what people thought of me; all I wanted was to have fun and laugh. Laughter is the best therapy in life.

Chapter 14

Girl's Night Out - 1980s

Another weekend, Lina and I decided to go dancing, so we called some of our fun and good friends. We ended up with five girls. I was now driving a black Jaguar (a gift from Torrey) so we all fit into one car. We first drove to downtown L.A. to a restaurant for dinner, where we met some other girlfriends, then went to a huge nightclub in Santa Monica.

We were all dressed to kill and danced till 2:00 a.m. The place was just starting to close when here comes our friend "Blondie" – 5'7, beautiful, with plush blonde hair, great figure, and the sweetest and kindest of all of my friends – with a tall blond guy in tow. He had a cast on one of his legs and was using crutches.

"Hey girls, this is Patrick!" Blondie yelled out and we started a conversation with him. Seconds later, Patrick convinced us to go to his place for more partying.

"Okay," I said. "Lets go!"

We all got in the Jag again, but this time we had to fit the big guy and his cast and crutches in the car with us. Blondie sat on his lap, and we were off. We were having a ball in the car, laughing and screaming, when all of a sudden it occurred to me to ask, "Hey, cast man! Where the hell do you live anyway?"

"Just keep driving. Were almost there," he kept saying.

I needed to use the bathroom and couldn't hold it any longer. I yelled, "Girls, I've got to pee right this fucking minute! And I'm not gonna do it in my car." Everyone cracked up again. As I pulled the car off the freeway onto Mulholland Drive and to the side of the road, everyone was silent.

"What are you doing?" Lina asked. She was sitting in front on the passenger's side.

I jumped out of the car and yelled, "Got to pee. You know?"

"Oh, I've got to see this, no way is she going to do it," Cast guy said, maneuvering for a better view.

Lina, who knew me better than anyone said, "Oh, yes she will!"

Before I pulled my panties down in front of the car and squatted down to pee, I yelled, "Girls… cover his eyes!" The sound of everyone laughing was making me laugh. Lina stuck her head out the window and shouted, "Hey, hurry up before a snake bites your ass." I was laughing and squatting, and peeing at the same time. It was probably the longest pee I had ever done. Totally insane!

Girls night out in the 80s. Rocky, me, Blondie, Lina & Sally

Chapter 15

Female Firefighter Tryouts - 1980s

One morning, Lina and I were in the car driving to work when we heard Rick Dees on the radio announcing "women's firefighter tryouts." We both opened our eyes big, looked at each other, and I yelled out, "Let's sign up for that!"

Lina squealed, "Yeah, let's do it!"

She always went along with anything I suggested. When I got to the office I called the telephone number for registration and got the information about the date, time, and venue.

That night, I casually said to Torreey, "Tomorrow, Lina and I are going to the firefighter tryouts."

He looked at me, laughed, then shook his head and said, "You guys are crazy. Do you have any idea how hard the training is? You never stop, do you?"

"It's okay, were still doing it," I said with a shrug.

On a Saturday, Lina and I drove to downtown LA, and were surprised to see about three hundred other women had shown up. We both looked at each other while making crazy funny faces and laughing.

"Damn, them bitches are huge!" I said, scared shitless. Most of the other women were bigger than the two of us put together. They were obviously body builders and looked more like men than women.

Lina and I are 5'1 and about hundred pounds. There were many good-looking firemen watching all of the women compete for the few openings. A couple of veteran firefighters came over to talk to Lina and me and one said, "Are you girls sure you want to become firefighters?"

"Yes we are!" we both said at the same time.

The firemen looked at each other with big smiles on their faces. Clearly, they thought we were cute, crazy, and funny too.

We didn't know what we'd gotten ourselves into but we decided, what the hell, let's try it. Someone blew a whistle and all of the women were instructed to form a line. The head fireman called each girl one at a time to perform the same task.

The first task was to run on top of a ladder without missing a step. The ladder lay on the ground. They had a stopwatch and we had to finish before the clock ran out. Lina and I watched a couple of the women perform the first task. We both looked at each other with a smile and said, "Si nosotros podemos hacer esa mirda!" ("Yeah, we can do that shit!")

I was in front of Lina, and went first. The fireman announced, "Are you ready?"

I snapped off a "Yes!"

He pushed the button on the stopwatch. I ran as fast as I could and busted my ass trying to finish the fucking ladder. Well, let's just say it was NOT as easy as it looked.

Lina's turn came and the fireman asked her if she was ready.

"Yeah," she said, slightly less confident after watching my mediocre performance.

The fireman yelled, "Go!"

Lina started running in between the steps of the ladder, screaming and laughing at the same time.

I yelled at her as loud as I could, "Go! Go! Go! You can do it!"

Midway, she suddenly decided to stop, looked at me, and sat her ass down on top of the ladder, gasping for air.

By now I was practically doubled over with laughter. I ran over to her and said, "Here, let me help you get up." We were holding on to each other, laughing like maniacs, while I cursed in Spanish, "Hueputa en que mierda nos metimos?" ("Son-of-a-bitch what kind of shit did we get into?")

Between laughs, Lina managed to say, "Why in the fuck did you tell me I could do it, when you didn't even make it?"

"Damn it, I didn't want you to give up, silly girl!" I grinned proudly.

The firemen were all looking at each other and laughing. The women were also amused, but probably thinking we were fools.

The second task: We had to climb up the ladder that was on the fire truck. The first couple of women tried it and passed. Then came my turn. I ran to where the fire truck was, jumped to get a hold of the first step so I could climb up the ladder while the timer was on. I don't remember how many fucking times I jumped but I couldn't get a hold of the first step of the ladder. The firemen and women were all laughing.

My sister quickly came to my rescue and said, "Here, I'll help you," and clasped her hands together.

I placed my foot in the stirrup of her hands and pushed myself up. At this point Lina was cursing in Spanish, "Apurese Hueputa me va a quebrar mis dedos." ("Hurray up you son-of-a-bitch, you're going to break my fingers.") Finally I grabbed the first step of the ladder and I could hear Lina screaming with joy. I was hanging by the ladder like a monkey off a tree and could not go any further. A fireman came and helped me down while his buddies were having a great laugh on us, pointing and slapping each other on their backs. The firemen couldn't believe we wouldn't give up.

"Shit, I'm not trying this one!" Lina shouted.

The third task: We had to run as fast as we could, grab the hose and extend it as far as were able. Again, the firemen had a timer going. The firemen decided to let Lina and I do this together. When our turn came, we ran, grabbed the hose, but no matter how we tried we couldn't extend it at all. Lina was cursing in Spanish, "Hueputa mangera." ("Fucking hose.") We both were stuck like glue; the hose was very heavy. Again, we failed! We both looked at each other and I exclaimed, "This shit is hard!"

The fourth task: This one I think was the funniest of them all. The women in front of us went first. When my turn came, the firemen thought it would be a good idea again if Lina and I try this one together. I think they had a plan, they already knew that we weren't going to pass at all. They just wanted a really good laugh at the last one.

First, they asked how much we weighed.

"Hundred pounds!" we yelled out together.

The two firemen looked at each other and smiled. Both firemen were holding a firefighter jacket, a hat, hammer and an ax. They put the hats on us and one said, "You girls look cute." Then he told us to spread our arms out and they started placing the jackets on us.

Lina and I looked at each other and smiled. After they finished placing the jackets on our bodies, the fireman gave Lina and I each a hammer and an ax. By this time I couldn't stand up anymore, the jackets were already very heavy for our weight, and my legs were trembling. I was trying desperately not to fall to the ground. I looked at Lina and she was halfway to the ground. By now, Lina was cursing in Spanish, "Hueputa mierda, ya no puedo mas." ("Shit son-of-a-bitch I can't take it anymore.") Lina dropped to the ground making funny faces at me. I couldn't take it either so I ended on the ground with Lina hugging each other laughing and cursing, "Hueputa que mierda!" By then everyone was laughing with us and at us. The firemen took the axes and hammers from our hands and helped us remove the jackets. Lina and I got up from the ground still laughing hysterically. There was no way we could manage all that equipment on our bodies when it practically outweighted us.

At the end of the day, Lina and I were pooped but we didn't regret trying out. It was a blast!

Before leaving, a couple of the firemen came over and one said, "We're sorry you girls didn't make it, but we want to let you know that if you apply for a secretarial job we'll make sure you get hired."

"Thank you so much for putting up with us," I told them hugging and kissing them on their cheeks. And before walking away I turned to them with a wide smile and said, "We'll be back next year."

Chapter 16

L.A. Raiders Cheerleader Tryouts - 1980s

While driving to work, Lina and I heard Rick Dees on KISS-FM radio announce the L.A. Raiders Cheerleader tryouts. So of course we decided to give it a shot and showed up that weekend ... along with approximately one thousand other hopefuls. Lina and I were in our twenties and anytime there was something new to try, we were up for it. It was fun and exciting, plus we were doing it together, and that made it more enjoyable for both of us. We went out to the Raiders' field for the tryouts. Out of the thousand girls, apparently on looks alone, they selected about two hundred – and we were two of those girls. We were so excited, jumping, giggling, screaming and hugging each other. We met a real nice girl, Sandy, who had dancing experience and was also selected.

While the 200 girls who'd made the first cut looked on, the choreographer stepped in and showed all of us a dancing routine that we had to practice and learn in the next two weeks. Lina and I learned some of the moves, but needed more work; we didn't have enough time to go over all of the steps. So we befriended the knowledgeable dancer and the three of us agreed we'd get together over the next two weeks and learn the routine to prepare for the finals.

This was more like a beauty pageant. Besides having to learn the steps to the music and perform it in front of the judges, we also had to buy an evening dress for the finals and intelligently answer questions for them. Being in a beauty pageant wasn't something I liked doing, except for the dancing part.

I knew Lina was good at the beauty pageant part. She'd been in a few contests in the past; the only problem with Lina, as previously ponied out, she was a lot more dyslexic than I. When we were practicing the dance, Lina would go left instead of right. We ended up laughing a lot while learning the routine. Lina sometimes would lose it and sob, "I can't do this shit, fuck it!"

But I always encouraged her, saying, "Cut the bullshit, Lina. You can do it!"

The day of the finals we headed to a hotel near LAX. The event started in the morning and it went on until midnight; by then we were exhausted.

We met some of the football players. I especially remember shaking hands with Marcus Allen. We took pictures with them and afterwards they all repeated, "Good luck ladies!"

Each girl had a number pinned on her waist. We all started with the dancing routine in groups of eight girls at a time. Lina, Sandy, and I were in the same group. We each wore a leotard; mine was yellow and Lina's was blue; and tennis shoes. Some of us had on headbands and leg warmers.

When the judges called our group we were a little nervous, especially Lina. She kept saying, "I'm probably gonna fuck it up." We did our routine and Lina went to the left instead of the right on a couple of the moves. She looked at me and rolled her eyes. I wanted to fucking laugh but decided to ignore her. We finished our routine, ran back stage and changed into our evening gowns.

I wore a white evening dress with a silver glitter feather boa on the side of it. We didn't have money to buy a new dress so we made them with our mom's help.

Lina's dress was black and she looked gorgeous!

We looked and felt beautiful. Our hairdos grabbed the eye; in the 80s most girls' hairstyles were immense.

The judges began calling the girls to walk to the front of the stage. We all wore a number on the front of our chests. We waited and waited patiently for our number to be called. Then I heard mine announced. "OMG, I'm scared!" I gasped and walked onstage all by myself, my heart pounding out of my chest and my legs trembling. I thought I was going to faint. *God, I hate beauty contests.* I loved dancing and would dance in a contest all night long if I had too. That was my passion. While standing in front of the judges, one of them, Raiders owner Al Davis, asked me a question. I don't remember what it was or how I answered it.

Another judge asked, "Shirley, your dress is beautiful! Where did you buy it?"

Smiling with my bottom lip shivering, I replied, "I made it with my mom's help." I stood there thinking to myself, *What da hell am I doing here? I'm no fucking beauty queen.*

I don't remember when they called Lina or what her questions were; by then I was wiped out. We waited until nearly midnight for the judges to make their final selection of twenty girls. We were on the floor holding hands when we found out we wouldn't be Raiderettes, but we'd tried as hard as we could. We looked at each other and I said, "Oh shit! Who the fuck wants to be a cheerleader anyway? FUCK 'EM!"

Me in white, Lina in black at the Raiderrette cheerleader tryouts in the 1980s.

Chapter 17

Freeway Antics - 1980s

One evening in the middle of spring, my sister Lina, a friend Selma, and I took off dancing (downtown LA) until 1:00 a.m. We got on the freeway with the radio playing loud and singing along to, Girls Just Wanna Have Fun. The highway at that time of night was very quiet.

I was driving like always. Lina was in the front passenger seat, and Selma sat in the back. Suddenly I opened my mouth and shouted, "Lina! You see the couple driving next to us on the right side of the freeway?"

"Yeah! What's your crazy idea?"

"A-ha! Flash your boobs right after I honk the horn. Okay?" I turned the music down and said, "Go!"

By now, Lina had her boobs pressed against the window. The guy driving turned his head once, then twice. The woman sitting next to him began hitting him on the head. She then turned and flipped her finger at us.

"Ha! Ha! Ha!" Lina, Selma and I were laughing like crazy.

"Hueputa mierda le esta patiando el culo." ("Oh shit, she's kicking his ass.") I said almost chocking from laughing so hard. I honked the horn one more time and we all waved goodbye with big smiles.

Minutes later, I was bored again when I saw this nerd driving very slowly, all by himself. He looked sad and lonely. "Girls," I said, "let's get this one real good. Lina, do the same thing, but this time squeeze your boobs against the window. Selma, press your butt on the window." She was wearing a G-string underwear. We were laughing and screaming while I tried keeping the car from swerving.

"We need to wake up the nerd," I yelled.

I began to slow down, got closer to the geek, waved and threw kisses at him. He was wide-awake by now, smiling at us and kept driving parallel to our car.

"Okay, girls ... time to flash him," I gave the command.

Lina immediately pressed her boobs against her window; Selma pushed her butt on the back window, and I layed on the horn.

The nerd turned his head, his eyes went wide, he opened his mouth very big, and his car began swerving all over the freeway.

"OMG, fucking crazy dude!" I screamed, but couldn't stop laughing! Luckily there was no sign of cops. The nerd decided to follow us, so I started speeding while Lina and Selma were blowing kisses at him until we lost him.

The following day, on Sunday evening, I came up with an idea while Lina and I were at home having some margaritas. "Lina, I think we need to become U.S. citizens. We've been in this country since the sixties. "I'm tired of carrying this damn green card around with me. So, let's do it! Okay?"

"Yeah, why not?" Lina replied, sounding brave, but I could tell she wasn't all-in like me.

On Monday morning I spoke with a representative from the Immigration offices. She told me she'd mail me a package with all the details.

Days later I received the info. Read everything, and that evening when Torreey came home I said, "Guess what?"

"Oh! Oh! It sounds like trouble," he said staring at me.

"Damn, dude! I'm up to something real good. Do you wanna hear it?" I said dead serious.

"Yeah, go ahead," he said skeptically.

"Lina and I are going to become U.S. Citizens." I beamed with pride.

"Wow! It's about time! You go, Momsie! That's the best idea you ever had! You're finally going to be able to vote," he said, tickling me.

"Yep! You bet I will!" I responded, giggling.

In the meantime, Lina and I were studying the booklet with questions and answers for our upcoming test. Months later we drove to the immigration offices near downtown L.A. for our verbal exam.

When an older Hispanic gentleman called my name I immediately stood up, looked at Lina in panic and followed the little guy to a room. Once inside he told me not be nervous. He was extremely nice. He began asking me questions while I answered each one correctly; questions like: "Who's the president of the United States?" "How many stars does our flag have?" And so on. Ten minutes later I was done; came out with a big smile and told Lina, "Its easy. You can do it."

Lina followed the little man and ten minutes later she came out with a frown on her face.

"What the fuck happened? You knew all the answers. We went over and over them." I said, surprised.

"I don't know what happened?" Lina frowned. "I was nervous and got stuck with a couple of the answers. But he wants me to go over the ones I missed and he'll give me one more chance."

"Okay! Go over there and study and concentrate," I insisted, pointing to a row of tables and chairs.

Fifteen minutes later, he called Lina, and this time when she came out she had a smile on her face.

"Alright, you did it!" I said, hugging her.

A month later, we both took off to a field in downtown L.A. for the ceremony. The place was huge. There were approximately a thousand people becoming US Citizens that day. We were each given a small flag of the United States and when the ceremony ended we all raised our flags in the air. It was an amazing day for Lina, me and every one else who was there. We were now two super proud American citizens.

Chapter 18

Julio Iglesias Fiasco - 1980s

One morning while Lina and I were at work we heard Rick Dees on KISS-FM announce that Julio Iglesias was his guest that day. Lina and I already knew the trick to seeing the celebrities who appeared on Rick Dees' show. We listened to the interview and shortly before it was over we'd rush our asses to the elevator and park ourselves outside of the KISS-FM door with pen and paper ready for an autograph. Moments later Julio exited with two other men.

Lina and I couldn't believe our eyes; we were directly in front of the famous Latin lover, Julio Iglesias. We approached him and said in Spanish, "Hola, Julio. Podemos darte un beso y un abrazo?" ("Hi, Julio. Can we give you a kiss and a hug?")

"Claro que si," ("Yes, of course you can.") Julio responded with a wide smile, showing us his piano teeth.

We both approached and kissed him on his cheek. We continued a conversation with him in Spanish.

"De donde son vosotras?" ("What country are you both from?") He asked.

"Costa Rica," I replied.

After another minute of chitchat, he said, "Adios, chicas," (Bye, girls,") and got into the elevator.

We waved good-bye and I thought, *Wow that was exciting! Can't wait to tell Mom.*

That same day around 4:00 p.m., Julio's manager called Lina at the office and said, "Julio is inviting you both to the studio on Melrose Boulevard, in Hollywood, to watch him record at around 6:00 p.m." The manager gave Lina the address and Lina told him we'd be there.

Lina appeared at my desk shaking with excitement. "Hueputa, no lo puedo creer? ("Son-of-a-bitch, I can't believe it?) We're going to the studio. Shit, I didn't think he'd call me!"

"What?" I was totally confused. "How did he get our number?"

"Well, when I kissed him on the cheek I slipped a piece of paper with my name and number on it on his hand." Lina said, fluttering her eyes.

"You clever little shit!" I said, but I was excited too.

We arrived at the recording studio a little after 6:00 p.m., both shaking with laughter. "OMG, this is crazy. Never in my wildest dreams did I ever think we'd be watching the most famous Latin lover sing. It brought back memories of my childhood in Costa Rica when I use to sit in the living room of the house with my grandma, aunt and cousins listening to Julio Iglesias's romantic songs on the radio. My grandma and aunt were madly in love with Julio. They always thought of him as a classy singer.

My Julio reverie was interrupted when a man opened the door.

"Hi!" Lina said. "Julio invited us to watch him record."

"Come in," he said, and took us into the taping room where Julio was already recording.

We walked inside and could see him through a glass window singing. We sat down next to the producer who kept talking to Julio through the microphone. We were wildly excited to be inside a recording studio. It was unbelievable!

After a while, Julio took a break and came over to see us. We left the recording room and went into a hallway and sat down with him. On our way to the studio, we had stopped at a liquor store and purchased a disposable camera to take pictures. We snapped a few shots with Julio, but to our surprise, when we later got to our car there was no trace of the camera. And more surprising, Julio was not the kind of person we thought he was.

First of all, while sitting in the hallway on a couch, without any warning, Julio made an inappropriate move toward my sister.

Lina pushed him away and snapped, "Don't do that again!"

Apparently, he then decided I might be more "compliant" and moved toward me. I quickly backed out of his reach and said, "De ningun modo!" ("No way!")

He made a disgusted face and said, "Vosotras estan loquitas. Ustedes no tienen ninguna idea cuantas mujeres quisieran estar en vuestros zapatos, ahorita mismo!" ("You gals are a little crazy. Do you have any idea how many women would love to be in your shoes, right now!") I guess he was used to women throwing themselves at him.

At this point, his manager stepped outside and called Julio to come back to the recording, then gestured to us as well.

Lina and I probably should've of gotten the hell out of there. But we decided to go back inside. It was a once in a lifetime experience to watch a superstar recording his beautiful new songs. Plus we'd have a great story to share with family and friends.

While sitting inside the studio I turned to Lina and said, "No puedo creer lo que nos hizo ese hombre? Abuelita amaba a Julio. Si todavia estuviera aqui estaria tan decepcionada" ("Do you believe what just happened?

Our grandmother loved Julio. How disappointed she would be if she were still here.")

The gentleman sitting next to us was Julio's producer; a Hispanic and very well-known person in the music industry. But at the time, Lina and I didn't have a clue who he was. He turned to us and said, "Julio no vale la pena, ustedes son chicas buenas." ("Julio is not worth it, you're both nice girls.")

"Gracias, senor!" I exclaimed.

"De nada," replied Emilio Estefan, who was producing Julio's album that year. Mr. Estefan was a true gentleman. Thank you once again, Emilio.

A little later, Julio came over to where Lina and I were sitting. With a friendly grin on his face, applauding softly and sounding more like he was making fun of us, he said, "Ballanse para sus casitas," ("Go home to your little houses.")

We didn't understand why Julio behaved in this manner. We hadn't acted cheap in front of him to deserve being treated like we were prostitutes.

After our experience with Julio we could never again look at him the same, but what didn't change was we still loved his music.

Chapter 19

A Brief Moment With John Travolta- 1980s

Lina and I were at the office when we heard Rick Dees announcing on the radio that he was interviewing John Travolta tomorrow. The following day, Lina and I listened to the interview on the radio and before it was over, we did our thing and took the elevator to the KISS-FM floor. We waited by the back door near the elevator. To our surprise, Travolta came out all by himself, no bodyguards.

We approached him with a smile and said, "Hi John! Can we hug you?"

"Sure," he said with a broad smile.

We hugged and kissed him on his cheeks while he embraced us both at the same time. He was sweet, very thin and had the most beautiful blue eyes I have ever seen. We didn't ask for his autograph nor did we have a camera to take a photograph with him. That was our brief time and beautiful experience with John Travolta.

Chapter 20

A Day With Jose Luis Rodriguez (El Puma) - 1980s

One Thursday afternoon my sisters, Lina and Gia, took off to a record store in the Valley near Gia's home.

Jose Luis Rodriguez (El Puma) was promoting his new album and signing autographs.

Lina and Gia were in line with the rest of his fans. Twenty minutes later, they where in front of him, nervous as can be.

"Hola nenas, como se llaman?" ("Hi girls, what are your names?") He asked with his sexy smile.

"Me llamo, Lina." ("My name is Lina.") Lina replied with a wink and handed him the record she was holding for him to sign.

Lina and Gia of course hugged and planted a kiss on his cheek, which is very common in Latin America.

El Puma is a famous sexy Latin singer and actor from Venezuela. Women all over Latin America would die to meet this man. He has a beautiful voice and sings romantic songs that have many Latin women falling in love with him.

Before my sisters left, El Puma's manager approached them and gave them two tickets and backstage passes for his concert on Saturday evening at the Greek Theater.

On Saturday, Lina and Gia got all made up and took off to the concert, super excited.

Following the concert, Lina and Gia went backstage to chat with El Puma. Lina was not only beautiful, but also funny and had a natural sexy way of talking to men.

Before going home, El Puma gave Lina his telephone number at the place he was staying, the Montage Hotel in Beverly Hills. "Come by and see me," he said.

When Lina got home, she called me excited. "Shirley, guess what?" And related everything that happened that evening. "You have to come with me to see him. Please!" she begged.

"Well… I already have plans," I said like I wasn't going to change my mind. And then I screamed, "Estas loca mujer? Claro que si voy. Esto no me lo pierdo!" ("Are you crazy girl? Of course I will go.")

On Sunday, Lina and I drove to the hotel. We walked into the lobby and Lina asked the receptionist to let Jose Luis know that she was here.

He answered his phone and told the receptionist to send Lina on up to his room.

We took the elevator to his floor, found his room and knocked.

When he opened the door and saw us standing there Jose Luis exclaimed, "Hola Nenas!" ("Hi girls!")

Lina hugged and kissed him on the cheek, then introduced me. "This is my other sister, Shirley."

"Hola, Puma! Mucho gusto," ("Hi, Puma! It's a pleasure,") I said embracing and kissing him on his cheek.

Lina and I were nervous. We couldn't believe we were sitting with this gorgeous sexy man in his hotel room. We exchanged a few words but I could tell he was aware that we were uncomfortable.

"Are you twins?" he asked.

"Yes we are," we said at the same time. We were frequently asked this same question and didn't think it was a big deal. We did it for fun.

We were in his room for no longer than fifteen minutes. He immediately got the message that we were not the kind of girls who wanted to jump his bones and screw him. This gorgeous man was incredible; he was never disrespectful or tried anything weird toward us. He was classy, sweet, and we could tell that he had a beautiful and kind heart. A welcome relief after our experience with piano teeth, Iglesias.

He picked up his phone, called someone, then said, "Nenas, let's walk to the lobby."

Oh shit! I thought he was going to tell us, "Go home to your casitas," but to our surprise we were met by a Hispanic gentleman in his early forties, thin, with black wavy hair. Lina already knew he was El Puma's manager. She had met him at the record store and at the concert the night before.

El Puma introduced me. I believe he was from Argentina.

"Do you ladies know of a good place to go for lunch?" El Puma asked.

"Yes!" I volunteered. "How about Gladstone's in Malibu?"

"Sounds like a plan. We'll follow you in our car," El Puma nodded.

When we got to the restaurant on the beach, we valet parked and walked together to Gladstone's. As we entered the restaurant, the actor Andy Garcia was just leaving. El Puma extended his hand and said, "Hola Andy." He then introduced Lina and me to Mr. Garcia. Andy was very pleasant.

We were waiting to be seated, and Lina decided to talk to the hostess. She requested a private table since a lot of Hispanic people recognized El Puma and were all over him asking for autographs.

The hostess put us in a secluded corner, we ate lunch, enjoyed a few cocktails, and after a few hours, it was time to go home. We took pictures with El Puma and his manager outside of the restaurant while waiting for our cars to arrive; then said goodbye and thanked him for letting us hang out with him.

"Nenas, Muchisimas gracias por traernos a Gladstones, tuvimos un tiempo maravilloso." ("Girls, I had a great time and thank you both for bringing us to Gladstone's.")

That was our beautiful day with the handsome gentleman El Puma.

A sidebar: Genesis Rodriguez is the daughter of El Puma. Genesis is an actress. She's in the movie, *La Casa De Mi Padre*, starring Will Farrell. She's also featured in the movie, *What to Expect When You're Expecting*, among others.

Chapter 21

The Crazy Cop - 1980s-2008

One summer evening, Lina and her friend Karen went out dancing in the Valley. Upon leaving the bar about two in the morning, laughing and swaying from side to side, they didn't notice the two police officers, Rod and his partner Matt, who were parked outside the club. Rod saw the two girls leaving the club and practically falling into their car, and he didn't waste any time starting his cruiser.

The two cops followed them and two blocks down the street, they hit the flashing lights.

Karen pulled to the side of the road and stopped. "OMG! We're fucking going to jail!" Lina and Karen had been drinking a little too much and knew they were in trouble.

Matt went to the driver's side to ask Karen a few questions while Rod walked over to the passenger side where Lina was sitting nervously. Karen and Lina thought for sure they were going to be arrested; but it turned out that Rod just wanted to talk to Lina. Instead of asking for her driver's license and registration, he asked for her phone number.

Lina liked Rod the minute she saw him so she went ahead and gave him her telephone number.

In fact, it was a no-brainer: Rod was in his 30s, very good looking with a great body and a charming personality. He called Lina the next day and after talking and laughing for about an hour, he asked her out.

Lina was very excited about her date with him; she said, "Rod is a real funny guy. His laugh is like no other."

Rod loved Latin women; he was married but separated from a Colombian girl he had known since high school.

Lina was soon seeing a lot of Rod and having a great time with him.

Rod made Lina laugh all of the time. He had the kind of laugh that if you heard him even without knowing what he was laughing about you ended up laughing too.

Lina dated him for a few months and all of a sudden, he just disappeared, he didn't call her anymore. She was very disappointed because she thought

Rod liked her too. Lina decided to move on and forget about him, thinking maybe he'd gone back to his wife.

A few months later, Rod called Lina and asked her out again.

Lina was upset and barked at him, "You're an asshole for not calling me! How dare you come back and ask me out like nothing happened."

Rod of course laughed and said, "I went back to my wife to try to save our marriage, but it didn't work out."

Lina gave him another chance and this time he surprised her by filing for a divorce.

Lina wanted me to meet Rod and see what I thought of him, so we joined him one evening at a sushi bar in The Valley. We ordered sake and sushi and ended up laughing our asses off.

Rod was as crazy as Lina and I were. We were all very loud; every time we said something, Rod laughed hysterically; he thought our accents were hilarious. He was a very likeable man, but he had a wandering eye. Even if he was out with the most beautiful girl ever, he'd always be checking out other women. He was a lot of fun but there was no doubt he was a ladies man.

Lina knew the relationship wasn't going to work, but she also liked all the fun she was having with him. She decided to continue seeing Rod but not to get serious with him.

Rod had a security job on the weekends. He'd frequently call Lina and invite us all to huge private parties. He also owned a tanning salon on Ventura Blvd. in the Valley. He became a client of Torreey's and later opened a nightclub in Hollywood.

After a while, Lina and Rod reached an agreement not to date but to remain friends forever. They realized that they loved each other more as friends than as lovers.

Chapter 22

Kim West / Steve Garvey & Steve Sax - 1980s-2006

Lina met Kim West at a bar in The Valley one evening when she was out with a girlfriend having cocktails at The Bicycle Club in Thousand Oaks.

When she got home, Lina said, "I met this guy named Kim."

I laughed and said, "That's a girl's name." So I changed his name to Kimmi Coco. He was an attorney at a firm in Downtown Los Angeles.

Kimmi and Lina started dating. She liked him, but not enough. "He's a nice man, but he's too boring and too old for me. Plus, he has a bad leg – he limps when he walks, "she complained. It was from an illness in his youth (maybe polio). She wanted to go out with someone who could dance with her. She later told me that his uncle was Jerry West – the Lakers coach.

But Lina and I didn't care about who was who. She never made a big deal about any of her boyfriends.

Lina and Kimmi went out many times. Kimmi took her to a Lakers' game and they sat in the floor seats of the Lakers' arena. He introduced her to his uncle, Jerry West. After all that, she maintained, "I'm still not too excited about dating him, he's just too dull."

He liked going to the beach with her; sat and read a book while Lina sunbathed and body surfed. Sometimes when she watched my kids while I was out with Torreey, she'd take them with her so she wouldn't be so bored. Lina and Kimmi dated on and off for a couple of years. She'd disappear from Kimmi for a while, but then called to see him again.

She said, "He goes out on business trips and when he returns he brings me something special, a beautiful dress, lingerie, or jewelry. He's a kind man, I care for him, but I'm never going to fall in love with him."

She stopped seeing him again, then one day; Rick Dees announced on his show that Steve Garvey and Steve Sax of the L.A. Dodgers were going to be his guests that morning. I believe the Dodgers were the number one team that year.

Lina and I were at work when we heard this. "Shit, let's go to the KISS floor and ask the receptionist if they'd let us meet Garvey and Sax," I said without even thinking.

"Are you sure?" Lina gasped. "What if they say no?"

"Well, then fuck it! At least we'd tried," I shrugged.

When we showed up at the front desk of KISS-FM, the receptionist by now knew who we were. I said politely. "Is there any way we can meet Garvey and Sax? Pleeeeeese!"

She stared at the two of us, and then said, "Wait a second." She then called someone inside and a moment later a P.R. woman came out and said, "Ladies, follow me."

"OMG, I can't believe it!" Lina said nervously.

We entered the studio making a lot of noise while Rick Dees was interviewing Garvey and Sax. We both ran over and gave Steve and Steve a hug.

I grabbed Garvey, kissed him on his cheek and stood next to him as he held me around the waist while Rick Dees continued to interview him.

Lina threw her arms around Sax's neck and kissed him on the cheek, Sax hugged her tight.

Rick Dees had on a happy face. He clearly remembered us, but said for his listening audience, "Hi girls! What are your names? And who do you girls work for?"

We both talked over each other, saying, "I'm Shirley – I'm Lina –I work at John's & John's Advertising – in the same building – on the ninth floor."

That morning, Kim West was on his way to work, had his radio on KISS-FM, and heard the interview with Garvey, Sax, Lina and me. That afternoon he called Lina and the affair started up again.

Later, in the late 80s, Lina came to live with Torreey and me in Redondo Beach. Kimmi was then living nearby in Manhattan Beach on a hill overlooking the ocean. He invited Lina over and we ended up at his place having cocktails and watching the beautiful sunset from his balcony. And for the third time, Lina took up with Kimmi. Alas, the relationship was yet another "swing and a miss" and this time it was over for good. As Garvey and Sax will tell you, "Three strikes and you're out."

Chapter 23

Date With El Debarge - 1985

In 1985, Lina met El Debarge at the First Interstate Bank Building where we worked. El happened to see Lina walking into the building while standing at the front desk. He immediately stopped Lina and struck up a conversation with her. A few minutes later he asked for her phone number. He called her that same day and invited her out to dinner.

El DeBarge was with Motown Records; he had a number one hit record with the song *Rhythm of the Night*. El's brother James was married to Janet Jackson.

El picked up Lina at our ghetto house in North Hollywood and took her to Spago's in Beverly Hills for dinner. This time I didn't go with her.

Lina and El couldn't agree on anything. They were like oil and water together. Besides, DeBarge was about twenty-one years old, very well known, and definitely still playing the field.

Lina shrugged and said, "El is cute but very immature and in love with himself." She went out with him twice and that was the end of her fling with Master DeBarge.

Chapter 24

Famous Motown Lover - 1980s

Lina and I ran into Barry Gordy Jr., son of Motown Barry Gordy Sr., in the lobby of our building.

Barry was very friendly and always had a smile on his face. He looked just like his dad.

We were talking with him and I could tell he liked Lina. Lina and I were always very friendly with people. We'd smile and say hello to everyone who said hi to us...and even some who didn't.

But Barry didn't tell us he was "THE Barry Gordy Jr.," the son of Motown's Barry Gordy Sr. He said, "Why don't you girls come and see me on the fourteenth floor where I work?"

"Okay, we'll be up on our break," Lina replied.

Upon entering the reception area, Lina told the receptionist, "We're here to see Barry." The young woman immediately called him and within seconds he was standing next to us. He then took us to a room where they had a pool table and asked, "Do you girls know how to play?"

"No, we don't," we both, said.

"I'll teach you how!" He grabbed the cue stick and began showing us how to shoot pool.

Lina and I were goofing around, laughing, and saying in Spanish, "Hay caramba. Esto es muy duro." ("This is too hard.")

"You girls are silly," Barry said laughing along with us.

I thought. He has a great personality, and the cutest dimples, too.

Ten minutes later we had to go back to our office before our boss started asking for us. But before leaving, Barry said, "Lina, can I get your phone number?"

"Sure?" Lina responded and wrote it on a piece of paper.

Barry called Lina the next day and invited her out dancing.

"Is it okay if I bring my sister, Shirley along?"

"Yeah, of course you can," he replied.

That evening we drove to Beverly Hills and met him at a nightclub. Had a few cocktails and we both ended up dancing with him.

A couple hours later, we got in his car and he took us to his father's mansion in Holmby Hills where he lived with his dad. On our way into the manor, there was a big gate with a security guard who had to open it for us. When we entered the front door there was a huge glass wall tank with real sharks swimming in it. The sharks had blue eyes and stripes, which we'd never seen the likes of before.

Lina and I looked at each other; we couldn't believe what we were seeing. I said to no one in particular, "Do people actually live like this?" It was unreal! We then went into the living room and sat down for a while. A few minutes later, Barry's dad, Mr. Gordy Sr., and his girlfriend, Grace, came in. She was a very exotic looking Asian girl about half his age. Grace had the longest black hair, all the way past her butt. She was wearing a white bathrobe and part of her hair was inside the front pocket.

"Hi Dad and Grace," Jr. said, "This is Lina and Shirley."

"Good evening ladies!" Mr. Gordy said with a broad smile and the same dimples as his son. He was also wearing a white robe like his girlfriend.

Lina and I both said hello to Mr. Gordy and Grace.

We exchanged a few words, then he and his girlfriend said, "Good night," and left the room quietly.

Barry Jr. beckoned us to follow him into the kitchen where a chef stood waiting. "Please cook us some steaks," Barry said.

After finishing our delicious steak it was time to go home. Barry drove us back to the nightclub where I had left my car. We drove home talking incessantly about the incredible mansion.

Lina started going out with Barry, but was upset that she was never invited to spend weekends with him. She became suspicious, and asked, "Do you have a girlfriend?"

"I don't, but I have a little girl from a previous relationship," he explained.

"Oh, I see." Lina raised a suspicious eyebrow. It seemed that Barry didn't want to give her any more information about himself.

So after a while, Lina became tired of just going to his dad's mansion, sitting in the Jacuzzi, talking, and having sex. She felt that Barry didn't want to be seen in public with anyone.

One evening she came home pissed off and said, "That's it! I'm done with Barry. I think he's full of shit! I bet he has a stable of women."

Chapter 25

In Love With A Mobster - 1980s

One afternoon while Lina and I were on a break, playing Pacman in the lobby's cafeteria, Joe Isgro came in to grab something to eat.

I immediately elbowed Lina and said, "Hey, check him out! He's the cool dude with the Rolls Royce."

"OMG, he's so fucking sexy!" Lina whispered.

And yes indeed, Joe was a very handsome Italian, about 5'10, tan, well groomed and had the sexiest eyes we'd ever seen. And did I mention he drove a Rolls Royce?

"Lina," I continued with our conversation, "every time I see him, he says hi and flirts with me." I really wasn't interested in Joe; I was dating Torreey and as I've said, I never liked dating more than one man at a time. "Lina, I think Joe would be good for you. Why don't you flirt with him and see what happens?"

A couple weeks later, Lina and I were in the elevator going to the café. The door opened and there was Joe standing in front of us. He stepped into the elevator and said, "Hi girls," and started a conversation with us.

He asked us for our names and where we worked; then: "Would you girls like to go to lunch with me sometime?" and asked for our phone number.

Lina gave Joe the telephone number of the office.

Joe called the next day and took us to lunch across the street. We had a great time with him. He was not only handsome but also mysterious and somewhat funny too. Lina and I thought Joe resembled the action film star, Steven Seagal. Every time Lina said something to me Joe would imitate her and we ended up laughing constantly. He was fun and made us feel comfortable with him.

Lina began seeing a lot of Joe. When he was out of town, and it was most of the time, he'd call her from Rome, New York, London, Miami, Amsterdam, etc.

Lina confided to me, "Every time I stare at him I get goose bumps all over my body. I think I'm falling in love with him."

One day he invited us to his yacht in Marina del Rey.

Lina and I drove to his gated home in Encino Valley; we were so excited we couldn't believe we were on our way to his mansion. Once inside, we sat in his spacious living room, decorated with expensive modern Italian furniture, while Joe was on the phone. A few minutes later, we all walked to the garage where he kept his beautiful yellow/gold convertible Rolls Royce. We got in the car on a gorgeous sunny day. He took the top down; then drove to the Marina where his yacht was waiting for us. We went on board and took off for a couple of hours, but we came back sooner than planned because I was nauseated.

Another day, Joe and his gigantic, British bodyguard walked Lina and I to the lot where I'd parked my new light blue Honda Civic, a gift from Torreey.

Lina and I got in the car and as we were saying bye to Joe and his bodyguard, Joe tossed two stacks of bills wrapped with rubber bands inside my car. One stack landed on Lina's lap and the other on mine. We both looked at each other and started sobbing, "OMG! OMG!"

"Come on girls, go buy yourselves something nice," Joe announced with a big smile.

We immediately got out of the car, Lina grabbed Joe and kissed him on his lips and I kissed him on his cheek. "Thank you, Joe!" we both said.

Lina continued going out with Joe and by now was crazy in love with him.

One day he said, "Girls, bring your mom and your other sisters to my seafood/steakhouse restaurant and nightclub Stefanino's on Sunset Boulevard in Beverly Hills.

When we got there he kindly instructed us: "Order anything you want."

We ended up with crab legs, lobster, oysters, steamed clams, and shrimp. It was the biggest seafood platter we'd ever seen!

Lina and I went to Joe's nightclub sometimes on Saturdays where he'd hang out with us. Occasionally he'd have business meetings at the club. Lina and I stayed and danced for a while until it was time to go home.

Joe never danced, instead he liked to sit and watch other people dance. He was a very mysterious man. He was in the entertainment business, a record producer, and he executive produced the movie *Hoffa*. What Lina and I didn't know and according to the press was that he was also involved with the mafia. In addition to that, Joe was a Vietnam soldier with a Purple Heart award. He also worked very hard all of his life.

One evening when Lina and I were at his nightclub, Dennis Cole came in. Dennis was an actor, recently divorced from Jaclyn Smith, one of the stars of *Charlie's Angels*. He was very tall, tan, blond and gorgeous. He came to the table where Lina and I were sitting. Dennis started a conversation with me and after a few minutes he asked me for my phone number.

"I have a boyfriend and I don't go out with other men," I said, looking him square in the eyes.

"How come he's not here with you?" he said, sounding like a jerk.

I simply ignored him and got up to go to the ladies room. Before I reached the door, one of Joe's bodyguards stopped me and said, "Stay away from Dennis Cole, he's probably up to no good."

I smiled and said, "Don't worry, I can handle Dennis." I returned to the table and ignored Dennis until he finally took the hint and went looking for other game.

Another time, Joe arrived at the ghetto house we rented in North Hollywood to pick up Lina in a limousine.

After their date, Lina told me, "I feel like Julia Roberts in the movie 'Pretty Woman.'"

The Lina and Joe affair continued, until Lina got tired of just being a sex toy.

Joe had a special love for Lina, but after a while, Lina got the message that he wasn't a one-woman type of man. He was about thirteen years older than Lina. She was twenty-three and Joe was thirty-seven. Joe would call Lina and ask her to drive to his house for dinner. Sometimes she spent the night and other times not.

She always told me about her dates. "He'll have a box sitting on the bed and he'll say, 'Open it!' Inside is always beautiful, expensive lingerie. I'll go in the bathroom, put it on, then, model it for him. He loves for me to pose for him.

"He has a huge king size bed, and when he's asleep he snores like a lion," she said, giggling.

Lina wanted a relationship and knew she wasn't going to have one with Joe. He was slowly breaking her heart. Lina and I both knew that Joe had many women all over town.

She was heartbroken for quite a while and thought there was something wrong with her. She lamented, "Why can't I find the right man like you did?"

A year later, we heard on the news that Joe was arrested for tax evasion and money laundering. He was eventually acquitted.

Lina got a hold of him and he invited us to lunch on Rodeo Drive where he owned a hair salon next to the restaurant. He took us into the salon and said, "Girls, get your hair done." Lina stayed in touch with him for a while until she met someone who didn't have a problem with commitment.

Chapter 26

Playboy Magazine Shoot - 1986-1987

One evening, Lina came home after a Playboy shoot and informed me, "Playboy is doing a sisters edition, and I suggested to them that we'd be the perfect siblings for the job."

Playboy called and scheduled an appointment to meet us at the Playboy Building on Sunset Boulevard. We each had a different appointment to take a Polaroid picture and see if Playboy would want to use us in the magazine.

My appointment was on a Monday at 10 a.m. I walked into the Playboy building; the top of the building at that time had the Playboy bunny symbol, so you couldn't miss it. I was very nervous, but made it to the right floor and entered the reception area. I walked in and saw all the beautiful pictures of previous Playboy bunny playmates. I was excited and couldn't believe I was actually there.

I gave the receptionist my name and said, "I'm here to test for the sisters edition." I sat down, grabbed a magazine, *Playboy* of course, and waited for someone to call me. There were several other pretty girls waiting in the room with me. When a cute staffer called my name, I got up and was anxious but did my best not to show it. She took me to a room in the back. As I walked down the hall, I marveled at the dozens of portraits of nude playmates that lined the walls.

The girl nonchalantly said, "Remove all of your clothing and put on the robe. A photographer will be in to take a test photo of you."

Minutes later a male photographer came in and, of course, I became more nervous; I had never done anything like this before. For every picture of me in the past I was wearing clothes. So I pretended I was at the doctor's office getting a physical exam.

The photographer was a nice man, he was very professional and I knew he was used to seeing naked bodies all day long.

He said, "Hi, my name is Jim, I'm going to take a few shots of your body and face and will be done in a few minutes. Don't be nervous just relax and remove your robe." The shots indeed took only a few minutes and I was done.

My other two sisters had to do the same. We waited but didn't hear anything from *Playboy* for a couple of weeks; we thought we didn't pass the nude photo test.

Lina and I were at work when she got the call from Playboy letting her know that we passed the test and they were ready to shoot us all together for the sister's edition.

Lina rushed her little ass to the back of the office where I was typing away, and squealed, "Shirley! Shirley! Playboy just called me. We're in!"

"Oh shit! Really?" I replied hugging Lina, jumping up and down with her like two little girls. She then called Tanya and Marisa to let them know.

The first thing we did when we saw each other on the day of the shoot was to high five and giggle while I said, "Hey bitches, are you ready for some crazy fun?" We waited in the lobby until a young woman appeared and took us all into a room in the back of the office.

A second girl came in and brought a box of lingerie for us to look at, and said, "What are your shoe sizes?" She then brought some beautiful high-heeled shoes for us to try on.

The third girl came in and said, "Ladies follow me to the makeup and hair room." Two hours later we were all made up and looking like mannequins, and by now we were starving too. Lina asked the assistant. "Can we please get something to eat?"

Twenty minutes later we were eating a salad, half a sandwich and after finishing, a makeup artist came in to do a retouch while the photographer was getting ready.

The gal in charge of the lingerie came in and selected the items that we'd wear for the shoot.

We all put on our beautiful sexy lingerie and now we were ready for the photographer.

"Are you guys nervous, because my ass is shaking?" I asked Marisa and Tanya, puckering my lips.

"I am too!" Tanya and Marisa both replied.

Lina wasn't nervous at all; she was already used to taking off her clothes for the magazine.

While giggling, Lina said, "Relajense y alistense para ensenar las nalgas." ("Relax and get ready to show your bootys.")

In a flash, the photographer came in. "Hi girls! I'm Richard, your photographer," he announced. He was a very nice middle-aged man. Lina already knew him; he'd shot her once before.

He began asking each of us a question about ourselves and then he'd shoot a picture while we were answering him. He was doing a photo test while at the same time trying to make us feel comfortable and relax. "Shirley, you're definitely the clown of all," he said smiling.

"Tanya, you're the intellectual one," Richard added.

"Yeah, but just don't piss her off. She'll go cuckoo on you. I mean cuckoo crazy." I said it without even thinking. Tanya gave me the evil eye.

"And Marisa, you're definitely the shy one." Richard commented.

"Yeah, but just don't get her mad because she can be real moody. Ha! Ha!" I chirped, and we all ended up laughing.

Of course, Richard already knew about Lina.

Lina was my favorite sister, always there to help anyone in need. She's very likeable and lovable, but she cries over anything and everything. She also has a real bad temper; she'd make a scene anywhere she could if you pissed her off.

"Okay, girls! I'm ready. So here we go!" Richard announced. He began shooting us with the lingerie on. Of course, I couldn't keep my mouth shut. I was joking, giggling, and swearing all the time in Spanish. My siblings were laughing hysterically and having a great time until two hours later one of my sisters suddenly became a pain in the ass. She didn't want to be here anymore, and kept turning her head the opposite way.

We ignored her and decided to ask the assistant for a little bit of wine and Latin music to get in the mood.

Richard's assistant brought us the wine, the music was on, and her mood changed to a happy one once again.

Fifteen minutes later, Richard came in and resumed shooting. This time he said, "Girls, I need you to start by dropping slowly a little bit of the lingerie down."

"Got it!" we all agreed.

After drinking more wine we were more relaxed and began removing parts of the undergarments, teasing the photographer while he'd say things like, "Yeah, that's beautiful. Great shot, Lina." (Or Tanya or Marisa or Shirley).

We each grabbed a pillow and began hitting each other, laughing and cursing in Spanish. Minutes later the feathers were coming out of the pillows and were flying slowly all over the room and landing in our hair and also inside our mouths. We began coughing and coughing and couldn't speak.

"Ladies, let's take a break and clear your throats," Richard said with a light cough, too. Ten minutes later, Richard returned. We finished shooting about 9:00 p.m. We came back twice and finished on the third day. We were extremely exhausted but we had a ball.

When the 1986 *Playboy Sisters Edition* came out, it was so fucking exciting to see all of us butt naked. The pictures were classy and beautiful, especially the pillow fight with feathers flying all over the room.

Playboy called us the following year to do another issue for 1987. This time the shoot was in a house located on a hill near Sunset Blvd. The pictures were taken in the winter on a very cold day. The shoot was outside by the pool in bikinis, with us slowly removing parts of our swimsuits. The edition came out and the pictures were again classy and beautiful.

When our advertising agency found out about our *Playboy* pictures, the men went crazy; but most of the women were not happy and, of course, jealous.

Lina and I were having a lot of fun; guys from work were asking us to sign the magazine for them. It was unbelievable how much attention we were getting all over the building. Most of the men started calling Lina and I "The Bamba Sisters."

Everyone knew the two sisters who were in *Playboy*, from the janitor to Joe Jackson. Yes, *the* Joe Jackson (Michael Jackson's father) whose production office was on the sixth floor.

Lina and I had become friends with Joe Jackson's assistant, John Wilson, a very soft-spoken black guy with freckles on his face. He was sweet, nice, and completely in love with Lina. He found out about the *Playboy Sisters Edition* and showed it to Joe Jackson. Joe was interested in us, and had John arrange a business meeting.

Lina, Tanya, Marisa and I met with Joe Jackson at his office. Lina and I had seen Joe many times in the building, so we weren't as nervous as Tanya and Marisa were. We all sat in his office with John. Joe was a scary man to look at; he'd stare at us with those evil eyes and spooky eyebrows. "I like the Playboy Sister's issue and would like to form a singing group with the four of you. John will be in charge of helping you with your vocals. This is going to be a lot of work and I want you all to commit. If one of you quits then the deal is over. You all need to start right away with John."

We all agreed, finished the meeting, and walked into John's office where he gave us a schedule of days to rehearse with him at his place.

The first evening we all met at 6:00 p.m. at John's. Tanya got there late like always and said, "Oh God, I have so many things to do!" She always had an excuse.

Marisa arrived on time, but like always, never said a thing.

Lina and I went straight from work and were bubbling with excitement.

John started with one of us at a time; he wanted to see who could hit low or high notes. He played the piano and asked each one of us to sing the scale.

John had a lot of patience. Lina and Tanya had none. We laughed a lot at each other while practicing our vocals until 11:00 p.m.; and of course my sisters were already complaining.

"I'm tired," Lina pouted.

"I have to get up early for work," Tanya complained.

Halloween was just around the corner, and we all got an invitation from Joe Jackson to join him, John and others at a party.

We drove our car and met them at the location. The four of us girls dressed up like alien women. Our mom helped us sew the costumes. We wore tight silver glittered leotards, stockings and boots, and short white hair wigs with bangs.

Joe Jackson wore a black cape and looked like the devil himself. We all sat at a table with Joe Jackson, John Wilson, and a few others in Joe's entourage. Joe had a bottle of liquor underneath the table and kept on pouring some into his glass.

In the meantime, we continued working on our vocals at John's place, but after two weeks, Lina had enough and said, "I don't have time for this. Playboy is calling me to go to Mexico."

"I have too many things to do," Tanya whined.

Marisa shook her head; and said, "whatever you guys wanna do is okay with me."

I was the only one who wanted to commit, but as Joe Jackson said, "One quits and it's over." That was the end of my dream of being a professional singer; we had the opportunity but my sisters didn't take advantage of it.

As we got older, Lina told me several times. "Damn! I regret not trying hard enough in practicing our vocals and blowing the once in a lifetime chance. Hay que estupida." ("Damn, stupid girl.")

At Joe Jackson and John Wilson's Halloween party in 1986. Marisa, Me, Lina and Tanya dressed as alien women.

Chapter 27

A Night at the Playboy Mansion - 1989

Lina and I were invited to the Playboy Playmate of the Year party at the Playboy Mansion. Kimberly Conrad was the Playmate of the Year 1989; she was also Hugh Hefner's girlfriend.

We got ready and drove my car to a parking structure near Sunset Boulevard where a shuttle bus was waiting for us and other guests to take us to the Playboy Mansion. Lina and I were excited and couldn't wait to get there. We'd both dressed to kill with our beautiful classy black mini dresses. We were hoping to take lots of pictures but were disappointed when we were told there were "no cameras allowed without a special pass."

Upon arrival we were escorted to a table with other guests. Across from our table was Tony Curtis; at another table, Shannon Tweed and other VIPs we didn't recognize.

Larry Carroll, the news reporter from *Channel* 2, was also there. He came to our table and said, "Would you ladies like to dance?"

With a smile on our faces, we both said, "Yes!" got up and had a blast dancing with him; he was handsome and fun.

John Beck, another newsman with *Chanel 7 News*, was also there. Professional photographers were all over the Playboy Mansion party. A picture of Lina and I came out in a magazine called *The Book* with the title, "Double Vision at the Playboy Mansion." We were having so much fun we didn't want the evening to end. This was by far the best party we'd ever attended.

Weeks later, one afternoon while Lina and I were at work, a woman from Playboy called and said, "A gentleman named Jack saw your picture in 'Playboy' and would like to meet you." Playboy didn't release any phone numbers. "Here's Jack's number in case you're interested in calling him."

Lina walked to the back of the office where I was busy with work. "What's up?" I said, typing away.

Lina gave me the news about Jack and said, "What should I do?"

"Just fucking call him and I'll go with you. Okay?"

"Alright," she replied and returned to her workstation. Ten minutes later she was back at my desk. "Jack is staying at a hotel in Beverly Hills. He said for us to meet him at the hotel's lounge around 6:00 p.m."

"Okay," I reluctantly agreed. "Now you got to go so I can finish my work."

Lina and I left the office around 5:30 p.m. and arrived at the hotel within half an hour. We entered the lounge and stood there waiting to see if we could guess who was Jack.

Jack of course knew what Lina and I looked like from the magazine. Suddenly, we saw this little man not quite our height walking toward us. He had gray hair, glasses, and looked like he was in his sixties. He approached us with a smile and said, "Hi, I'm Jack. You're both beautiful, just like the pictures in 'Playboy', except that you have your clothes on."

"Oh, you're funny. Aren't you?" I laughed, thinking, *He's quite a character.*

Lina, winked at me giving me a sign that it was okay to hang out with him for a while.

Jack grabbed our hands and said, "Girls, I'm at the bar with two friends. Let's go join them." We walked to his table and Jack introduced us to Joe Weider and his wife. We couldn't believe our eyes; we had seen Joe Weider many times on TV and in body building magazines. His wife was very pretty with the tiniest waist ever; she was all made up like a doll.

We sat down, ordered cocktails, and a few minutes later, Joe Weider and his wife had to leave.

Jack ordered hors d'oeuvres and vodka shooters. And minutes later we were laughing nonstop. He was hilarious! He was not at all stuffy like we thought he'd be when we first saw him. After a couple of vodka shots I knew I had to stop. I was driving, so I ordered water while Jack kept insisting and saying, "C'mon, Shirley, live a little, have some more shots."

When Jack took a break to go to the bathroom Lina and I had a little talk.

Lina rolled her eyes and in Spanish said, "Hueputa viejo loco seguro piensa que nos vamos a cogerlo las dos," ("This son-of-a-bitch of a little man thinks we're both going to screw him.")

"Oh shit!" I said, taking a sip of water. "I have an idea. Let's pour the vodka shooters under the bar stool before he gets back. This way he'll think we're also drinking as much as he is."

When Jack returned he ordered another round of vodka shots. But every time he turned his head the opposite way I'd take one of the shooters and dump it underneath the bar. Ha! Ha! The little man was pretty wasted and had no idea what Lina and I were doing.

An hour later, Jack said nonchalantly, "Let's go upstairs and go skinny-dipping in the pool."

Lina raised her eyebrows.

I pretended I didn't hear "skinny-dipping" and said, "We didn't bring bathing suits with us."

"C'mon girls, you don't need a bathing suit," he said a little too loud, "I've already seen you both naked in the magazine."

This was when Lina and I noticed that the little man was getting very pushy, or maybe he'd had too much to drink. We could tell Jack was used to getting what he wanted; he was probably a very wealthy man, but we didn't care how much money he had. Lina and I shot each other a look that said, *Let's play along, this could be funny*, and we took the elevator to his suite. Jack then gave us each a white robe and said, "Put these on and we'll walk to the hotel roof where the pool is."

We went into the bathroom, donned our robes, but left our underwear on. By now it was past midnight and there was no one at the pool. Jack removed his robe and jumped in butt naked.

Lina and I looked at each other and made ugly faces. Jack had no ass and a pudgy belly. *Ewwwww!* By then, Lina and I were in tears while Jack merrily swam laps.

Lina and I sat by the side of the pool with our robes on while Jack kept insisting, "Jump in, girls!"

Lina was pissed off and said, "Hueputa viejo loco," ("Son-of-a-bitch crazy old man.") I was laughing like always.

"Hueputa tirese en la piscina para que deje de hodernos." ("Jump in the fucking pool so he can stop harassing us,") I said.

But Lina was still cursing, "Hueputa viejo porque tengo que hacer lo que el quiere." ("Son-of-a-bitch of an old man, why in the fuck do I have to do what he wants?")

After a few minutes more of my prompting, Lina removed her robe and yelled out, "Okay, I'm coming in!"

"You go girl!" I screamed, and busted out laughing hysterically.

Jack stared at me and said, "C'mon, Shirley, it's your turn."

"No, I don't' know how to swim and prefer to just sit by the pool with my feet in."

Jack finally got the message and stopped harassing me and decided to swim with Lina. Ten minutes later Lina had enough and said, "I'm coming out of the pool," grabbed her robe, put it back on, and told Jack, "We're tired and need to go home." We were surprised to see that Jack didn't try to stop us. We went back inside the hotel suite, changed into our clothes while Lina was still cursing about Jack. I was laughing and said, "He likes you, and he wants a piece of you!" We came back out, hugged and kissed Jack on his cheek and thanked him for the evening.

Before walking away, Jack asked Lina for her phone number and said, "Next time I'm in Los Angeles I'll give you a call."

"Sure," Lina responded. But didn't think he'd follow through.

Two weeks later, Jack came back to Los Angeles, called Lina and invited us to the Playboy Mansion. It was during the Jessica Hahn – Jimmy Baker scandal. Jessica Hahn was staying at the Playboy Mansion recovering from her plastic surgery. She was going to appear in *Playboy* magazine. Jack was a friend of Hugh Hefner and wanted to meet Jessica.

When we got inside the mansion with Jack, we stood by the stairs waiting for Hugh Hefner to come down. Minutes later, Hugh descended the staircase; he was wearing his signature silk robe and pajamas, and was holding his pipe in one hand.

Jack introduced us to Hugh as the Villanueva Sisters and reminded him that we were in the *Playboy Sisters Edition*. Hugh was very pleasant and sweet. A short while later, Jessica Hahn came down the same stairs and we were all introduced.

Jessica was pleasant and shook hands with us. She wasn't skinny, rather voluptuous. She wasn't beautiful either; she was just famous because of her affair with Jimmy Baker.

Minutes later, Jack turned to Hugh and said. "Will it be okay if I give the girls a tour of the grounds?"

"Go right ahead, Jack." Hugh responded, while waving goodbye.

Jack immediately grabbed our hands, smile and whispered. "Let's go have some fun!" We got to the zoo and were surrounded by beautiful flamingos, peacocks, cranes, and a friendly monkey that was in a cage. We then walked to the pool and grotto. "OMG this is amazing!" I said, squeezing Lina's arm. We were mesmerized!!!

After a few more calls, and invitations from Jack, Lina knew she had to put an end to it. She wasn't interested in having a romance with and old coot like him.

"I don't know how some of these young girls can go out with someone like him just for the money," Lina said somewhat disgusted.

Chapter 28

The Chapel of Love - 1990

My kids, Luke and Natalie, sixteen and fifteen were wondering if Torreey and I had any plans to tie the knot. In September of 1989, while having dinner at home, Natalie abruptly chirped, "Mom, are you and Torreey ever going to get married?"

Torreey turned and looked at me, then at Natalie and said, "Yeah! Why not?"

"You wanna get married?" I gasped. I was surprised and didn't expect that at all.

Luke and Natalie both smiled and clapped and cried, "Alright Momma!"

Natalie wasn't finished: "When?"

"I will start looking at dates," I said.

After dinner, I called Lina and gave her the news. "We're thinking about getting married next year, 1990. What do you think?"

Lina was super excited. "OMG, I can't wait to help you with all of the wedding arrangements!" She called our mom and the rest of the family to give them the news.

Over the weekend, Lina came by with a few magazines of wedding dresses for me to look at and said, "I've selected a few that I thought you might like."

Over the next few weekends, Lina and I checked out places for the reception. After looking and looking at magazines and reception sites I was completely exhausted and confused. I realized that I had no interest in getting married with a long wedding gown in front of a minister followed by a big reception. This was more what Lina would want.

When Lina came by that weekend, I said, "I can't see myself having the wedding we are planning. That's not me." I decided to think about it and wait until I was ready to do it my way.

After the Christmas holidays were over, Torreey and I were at the beach playing volleyball when he said, "Momsie, (his nickname for me) don't forget to book our trip to Vegas for my birthday." I always made the reservation for our annual trip a couple of months ahead.

In the meantime, Lina kept asking me about the wedding. I didn't have much to say, except, "I don't want to think about it for now."

Two weeks before our trip, while Torreey and I were in the kitchen I came up with a crazy idea and blurted out, "Do you want to get married in Vegas?"

"It's fine," Torreey shrugged in his casual way, "whatever you want to do its okay with me."

"I think it's the perfect place for us to get married," I beamed.

Every year on Torreey's birthday, I'd arranged a trip to Las Vegas to celebrate, and to get a little break from tax season. We loved going to Vegas a couple times each year. We enjoyed playing craps, blackjack, going to the shows, eating at different restaurants, and of course a lot of dancing and plenty of cocktails too. Sometimes we'd take Mom and Lina with us.

After Torreey left for work I immediately called the Las Vegas Chapel of Love and asked them if they could marry us on Friday, March 16. The date was available! They gave me a price of $300 that included a minister and a photographer. It was perfect; I booked it on the spot. Next I called a limousine service and ordered a white limo. Then I called the Clark County Courthouse to arrange for our marriage license.

The only thing missing was my dress. That weekend I headed to the mall to find the perfect gown. I searched and searched, and suddenly, there it was. A dress made more for dancing the night away than parading down an aisle, but I loved it! It cost me about $50.

I didn't tell Mom or anyone else about our plans to get married in Vegas that weekend. Mom made a few quick alterations and the dress was perfect. It was a white lace strapless mini dress covered with sequins and a few pearls. I was the happiest girl, I had arranged everything by myself just the way I wanted it to be.

Torreey and I left for Vegas on Thursday evening. Mom and Lina were staying with the kids while we were gone. On Friday afternoon the limo driver came to our hotel, The Mirage, to pick us up and drive us to the Clark County courthouse for our marriage certificate. Before getting in the limo I said to Torreey, "Let's stop at one of the hotel bars and do a few shots of tequila."

After our shooters we got back in the limo laughing and super excited about our wedding. We both couldn't believe we were really getting married. We stood in line with others waiting to get hitched at the Clark County Courthouse. I was wearing my mini wedding dress with white shiny stockings and a few white flowers in my hair, while other brides were in their long wedding gowns. Some of them were pregnant; some of them had on what appeared to be Halloween costumes. The courthouse looked more like a circus with a bunch of crazy people waiting at the front door – including us.

When our turn came, we handed the clerk $50 and it took no more than five minutes for the county worker to give us our marriage license. We left the courthouse and the limo drove us to "The Chapel of Love" for our wedding ceremony. I selected a bouquet of red roses and we were ready for our wedding. I chose the disco song by John Paul Young, *Love is in the Air*, to play while Torreey and I walked down the aisle to meet the Elvis impersonator who was marrying us. He was waiting for us at the center of the chapel. I was giggling while we were walking. I couldn't believe this was my wedding, presided over by Elvis and attended by just Torreey and me.

After the ceremony, the limousine took us back to our hotel where we had reservations for dinner at Kokomos Sea and Steak House. We toasted our wedding and Torreey's birthday with a glass of champagne: "To love and happiness forever."

We got back home and I screamed, "Mom, Lina, Luke, Natalie ... we eloped!"

They all looked surprised but were also happy for us, except Natalie.

She stared at me and said, "No you didn't, you're lying."

"Yes, we did!" Torreey confirmed.

Natalie made a pouty face. "Damn Mom, you suck, you didn't even want us there!"

I looked at Natalie, laughed, and said, "You suck too," and we both ended up laughing. The following weekend, Lina arranged a little get-together with our family and the kids to celebrate our wedding.

Me and Torreey at our crazy wedding in Las Vegas Chapel of Love in March 16, 1990.

Back at home celebrating our wedding with my family. Gia, Graciella with baby, Mom, Tanya and cousin Dalia in back row. Lina with sunglasses, Torreey, Shirley.

Chapter 29

Southern Lover - 1980s

AUTHOR DISCLAIMER: In the following chapters, certain habits of various characters come into question. In some cases these habits were reported to me by a friend or relative, and I was not an actual witness. To be fair, in the noun case I will use the generic term ... *habit* in italics. In the verb case I will use the generic term *partaking* in italics. For example, perhaps a character in question had an insatiable sweet tooth. Therefore I will say: My girlfriend X told me about her boyfriend Y's ... *habit*. Or: X told me that Y was *partaking* again.

One evening, Lina and I took off to a concert at the Palace in Hollywood. It was a Dick Clark Production and Cindy Lauper was one of the performers.

Our sister Tanya met Lina and I while we were in line waiting for the doors of the Hollywood Palace to open. Tanya showed up with her date, Charles.

Charles had brought a friend with him, Al Collins. Tanya introduced us to both guys and Al immediately glued his eyes on Lina. We all went inside the Palace for the concert and had a great time.

Al didn't waste any time and asked Lina for her phone number. He was a Southern guy from Lake Cormorant, Mississippi, had moved to Los Angeles, and was going to school at thirty; he was five years older then Lina.

Lina started dating Al and was having a good time with him.

They enjoyed going out dancing, drinking, and to the movies; and both seemed to like each other a lot.

One day while having a conversation with Lina, she gushed, "Al is the sweetest man I've ever dated. He always tells me I'm beautiful, he's very affectionate and lovable too. I've never had this kind of relationship with any of the men I've dated. I think I'm falling in love with him."

Al was tall, thin, with light hair, green eyes and attractive; and he knew how to sweet-talk a girl. He was also falling in love with Lina; you could see it in his eyes.

I knew Lina liked him a lot so I had to ask, "What kind of car does he drive?"

She hesitated, then, said, "A beat-up car, but he's going to real estate school."

"How does he support himself?" I continued the interrogation.

"His parents are paying for the school and his living expenses, and he lives in Hollywood in an old rundown apartment building," she admitted.

I took a deep breath and said, "What the fuck? He's somewhat old for his parents to be giving him money. He's not the right kind of guy for you." I was always watching out for her and she knew I wasn't a big fan of Al.

One evening, Lina called me crying hysterically and said, "PICK ME UP!" She was at Al's apartment.

I drove my ass to Hollywood Blvd.' where Lina was already waiting for me at the corner. When I saw her, I yelled, "What the fuck are you doing standing here like a prostitute in the middle of the night? Are you crazy?"

Lina immediately got in my car, shaking and crying. "I'm sick and tired of his shit – he's got a ... *habit!* While I was there with him in the apartment, he was *partaking*. I was so angry I picked up the phone, called his parents in Mississippi, and told them, 'If you want to see your son alive you need to come and get him out of Hollywood. He's not going to school, and he's hanging out with losers. You seriously need to do something about his ...*habit.*'"

A couple of days later, Al's parents flew to Hollywood, took him back home, and helped him get things in order there.

Lina stayed in touch with Al and after a while, he returned to California and got back together with her.

Lina was still working with me at John & John's Advertising, and was also modeling for Playboy. We were out to lunch when she said, "I'm happy and I want to be in a steady relationship. All I want is for somebody to love me."

She wasn't asking for too much, she was a simple, loving, caring human being. She wanted to be loved and to feel safe. She was tired of dating and most of the time she felt used by these wealthy men.

Al was living in a single apartment in Venice, California. She was spending a lot of time with him at his place, but she hated the neighborhood.

Suffice to say, Lina and Al had a very dysfunctional relationship.

One Sunday morning, Lina came over my house while Al was out fishing and said, "I don't know what to do. I'm frustrated with him. He's very cheap and doesn't like to spend money on trips, restaurants, whatever. I want to hang out with you and Torreey and do the fun things you both do."

Torreey and I often took Lina with us on some of our trips. We'd go to Vegas, dinner, dancing, and Lina came along. We always had so much fun together; it was as if we were really twins. Torreey never said no, he also enjoyed having Lina with us, she was beautiful and a lot of fun, and we always had a blast anywhere we went.

Many times, we ended up on the stage with whatever band was performing at the bar. We dressed super sexy and danced while the band guys sang and played their instruments. Sometimes we'd play the tambourine if the group had one while Torreey watched us from where he was sitting.

Torreey and I continued to invite her. Only it got to the point where we were tired of having to pay for Al all of the time. Al seldom reached for his wallet to pay for anything. But apparently he had enough money for the hunting and fishing trips he took every year with his brother, James and their friends; so Lina was always unhappy. He also took up his ...*habit* again, and that made Lina even angrier.

Lina and Al lived together for a couple of years, on and off. She'd leave him, come and stay with Torreey and me for a while, then go back to him. She could never make the right decision about Al; somehow she just couldn't get away from him.

One day, crying, she said, "Help me find an apartment near your house in Redondo Beach."

We both searched for a place and found a one-bedroom about half a mile from my house. Lina was super excited about their move, although Al just complained about how much rent they had to pay. She wanted to be close to me so we could do things together. She was now working for Daily Advertising Agency as a receptionist in West LA. She was content; it was a good job with great benefits for both of them. Al was working as a truck driver for a friend of his near LAX.

Even though she was happy with the move she still complained about Al.

I always listened to her and many times I said the same thing over and over again: "Leave him, he's not for you, you need a man who can take care of you."

When she was thirty-one years old, Lina felt she needed to get married. I think she just wanted to follow in my footsteps. So one day in March 1991, Lina came over my house and said, "Al and I have decided to get married next month in Las Vegas. Can I borrow your wedding dress?"

"Of course you can," I said without any emotion.

I made an excuse and told her, "Torreey and I can't make it, we're too busy with tax season." I could have gone by myself but I wasn't happy with the idea of Lina marrying Al. I knew this was not going to be a happy-ever-after marriage.

She made the arrangements and in April they took off to Vegas with our mom and our cousin Dalia, and got married at the same place I did, The Chapel of Love. Al's parents met them in Vegas.

Al and Lina always fought about his ...*habit*, his laziness, his selfishness, and most of all about money.

One day Lina came over my house and said, "I'm pregnant."

"Wow, congratulations!" I said and gave her a hug. I was excited about the news but I wasn't sure if this was such a good idea. Having a baby was going to make things harder for them. She and Al were always at each other's throats.

She said, "I want to be a mom. In fact, I wish I had a baby when I was younger, like you did." I was in my thirties with teenage kids.

In November of 1995, Lina gave birth to a beautiful baby girl she named Sunny. Lina was very proud of her little eight-pound bundle of joy. She stayed home for three months to take care of her baby, and then decided not to return to work. She didn't want anyone else taking care of Sunny. The only problem was they couldn't afford to live on Al's salary alone.

Six months later, she decided to baptize Sunny and asked me to be the godmother.

Lina and me dancing on the stage in Las Vegas.

Chapter 30

Bike vs. Car - 1990s

Luke was one year older than Natalie. As a child, Luke was a very hyperactive, funny, and loveable little boy.

I was now working in Downtown LA for an Interior Designing Company. My hours were from 8:00 a.m. to 5:00 p.m., Monday through Friday. Every morning I left the house by 6:45 a.m., to get to work on time. The kids' school didn't start until 8:00 in the morning. So both Luke (twelve) and Natalie (eleven) were on their own to school with some of the kids in the neighborhood. Sometimes they rode their bicycles and other times they'd walk. I was always concerned about it, but there was absolutely nothing I could do. *At least they aren't by themselves*, I thought.

Before I left the house I'd go into their bedrooms and shout, loudly, "Wake up guys! Don't be late. Do your homework and chores too. And most important, call me when you get home from school!"

Sometimes I'd get more than one call a day from them. Especially when they got into an argument. Luke and Natalie never agreed on anything. Natalie always called Luke "Buggs," or BUGGER if she was pissed off at him.

Every day I left work at 5:00 p.m., and got home around 6:00 p.m., or later depending on the traffic. I parked my car in front of our crooked house. That evening I noticed that all of the house lights were off. I became worried and more so when I spotted a policeman sitting on a parked motorcycle waiting for something or someone. I just sat there for a few seconds before realizing something was wrong and didn't want to move from my car. A couple minutes later, I opened the car door and stepped out. I turned around slowly, locked my car, and could hear footsteps coming closer to me. I was now very anxious.

The policeman was suddenly behind me saying, "Ma'am? Ma'am?"

I turned around to look at him and said. "Are you talking to me?"

"Yes, ma'am? Do you live at the yellow house in front?" he asked.

"I do," I said nervously.

"Is your name Shirley Webb, and do you have a son named Luke?"

"Yes!" I responded, getting goose bumps on my arms.

"There's been an accident, and your son is in the hospital," the policeman said.

"What happened?" I practically screamed.

"Your son Luke was riding his bicycle and was struck by a car," he said with a frown. "Witnesses said Luke's body flew a few feet up in the air before landing on the pavement and hitting his head."

I instantly started crying and shaking at the same time.

The policeman kindly said, "Ma'am, would you be okay to drive to the hospital while I escort you?"

"I first need to find my daughter, Natalie," I said, and ran inside the house. I called Natalie's best friend and found out that she was there. Later, I also found out one of my neighbors gave the policeman my name, and told him what time I'd be home.

The officer got on his motorcycle while I followed him, trembling and sobbing, on my way to the hospital.

Trying to get to the hospital was insane for me. It felt like it was so far away when it was only five minutes from my house. When I finally got there, I parked my car at the emergency entrance and ran inside the hospital with the policeman. The officer approached the clerk at the front desk and told her I was Luke's mom. The woman pressed a button and the doors to the ER opened up. I hurried inside looking for Luke.

When I saw him lying on the hospital bed, I hugged and kissed him and held his hand. "Are you okay?" I said through my tears.

"My leg and head hurts," he said weakly.

He had cuts and scratches on his face, arms and legs. One of his legs was badly bruised.

Minutes later the X-ray technician came by and took Luke for X-rays. "Luke, I'll be right here waiting for you. Okay? Love you." I whispered. Then I grabbed my purse, stepped out of the ER and went outside to call Mom and let her know what had happened.

Two hours later, I took Luke home with a brace on his left leg and a set of crutches. He was to stay home for the rest of the week.

Nine months after Luke's accident, I was in the backyard hosing the patio. Luke was outside by the driveway on his skateboard, suddenly he collapsed to the ground. I began screaming like crazy. "Help me, somebody! Please, help me!"

Our next-door neighbor, Mrs. Crabtree, a little old retired lady who always complained about my kids, came out and saw Luke flat on the driveway while I was crying and holding on to him.

A month before this incident, Mrs. Crabtree came over our house and said to me, "You need to come over and look at my front door."

I walked with Mrs. Crabtree to her house and saw that her front door was covered with mustard, ketchup, raw eggs and toilet paper.

"I'm sure your two kids did this to my door," she said, very upset and at the same time in a rude manner.

"Mrs. Crabtree," I said, trying to calm her down. "I'll check with my kids when they get home and let you know. Okay?"

Hours later, Luke and Natalie came home and I confronted them: "Did you guys have anything to do with the mess on Mrs. Crabtree's front door?"

They both looked at me very seriously, and Natalie said, "It wasn't us."

But for some reason I didn't believe them. Meanwhile, Mrs. Crabtree was already cleaning up her vandalized door; I felt bad for her and offered to help her with it, saying, "I'm very sorry about the mess but I assure you that my kids were not involved."

Later that evening I went to throw some trash in the garbage cans that we have on the side of our driveway and, lo and behold, when I took the top off one of the rubbish containers I saw empty bottles of mustard, ketchup, and an egg carton. I ran inside the house as fast as I could and went upstairs to their bedrooms where Luke and Natalie were both innocently reading. I opened both doors and yelled, "I found the empty mustard, ketchup, and egg cartons inside the trashcans. Why did you do this? And why did you lie to me?"

They both looked at me laughing and holding on to their stomachs. Natalie piped up and said, "Because she's a complainer and an asshole, and she yells at us most of the time."

"That's not nice, Natalie. She's an old lady," I said, disappointed, but instead of screaming, I ended up laughing with them too. I guess I was also tired of her coming to our house and complaining about my kids' noise and so on.

"Mom, me and my two friends smeared Mrs. Crabtree's door." Natalie confessed.

"Oh God, Natalie. Please don't do it again." I said, exhaling.

Anyway, when Luke collapsed, Mrs. Crabtree went inside her house and called 911. She came back out, held my hand, and said, "I'm going to pray." By then Luke's eyes were rolling back and he was foaming at the mouth. All I could do was to hold on to him and cry. I thought for sure he was dying.

Two paramedics soon arrived and took over Luke's care. One asked me, "Ma'am, does Luke often fall down, or is he diabetic?"

"No," I said on both counts.

The EMTs injected Luke with something and said, "We're taking him to the hospital." I quickly climbed inside the ambulance with Luke and the paramedics and we took off.

The doctor ran a series of tests and diagnosed Luke with having seizures due to the head trauma he suffered in the auto accident nine months before. The ER doctor said, "I'm referring Luke to a specialist for the treatment of seizures."

Luke was put on medication, which worked well to control his seizures as long as he remembered to take it. Sometimes he forgot the medication even if I reminded him. Luke suffered several seizures over the next six years. One grand mal seizure happened on a weekend while Torreey was working on the house. Luke was in his bedroom sucking on a lollipop; his friend Mark came by to play with Luke and all of a sudden, I heard a scream from Mark: "SHIRLEY, HELP! There's something wrong with Luke!"

Torreey and I ran up the stairs to Luke's room as fast as we could and found him on his bed, eyes rolling back, foaming at the mouth, this time the lollipop was blocking his airway. Torreey yelled, "Call 911, I'll try to dislodge the lollipop from his throat."

By the time the paramedics got to our house, Torreey had already removed the sucker from Luke's throat. They asked me about Luke's health status.

"He's on medication for seizures," I said.

The EMT gave Luke a shot and within seconds he was back to almost normal, except he had no memory of what had happened; it was as if he'd had just woken up from a nap.

Over time, the medication was making him very depressed and he didn't want to go to school anymore. The kids at school were calling him "retard". I took Luke to see a counselor once a week and this helped him a lot.

Natalie often got in trouble in school for defending him. The principal called me several times about Natalie's behavior. Finally, he said, "I'm suspending her for beating up the boys after school."

I had to come up with something to help Luke, and also Natalie. I made the decision to pull Luke out of the public high school and enrolled him in a continuation school. Luke was happy and finished all the courses and got his diploma.

Natalie stopped beating up on the boys and also graduated from high school that same year.

Mrs. Crabtree and I became good friends. And my kids and the little old lady learned to like each other.

By the time Luke was nineteen he outgrew the seizures. The doctor had said, "This will probably happen after puberty." We had Luke tested and were relieved to be assured that he was seizure free.

After finishing high school, Luke didn't want to attend college but didn't know what else he wanted to do.

Torreey came home one evening and said, "Luke, I'll get you a job with one of my clients in construction."

A month later, Luke wasn't happy and said, "I hate my job. I'm quitting."

I was afraid he'd turn out like his real dad and become a deadbeat. After all, it was in his genes.

Once more, Torreey got him another job with a different client; construction once again. Luke still wasn't happy, and quit this one, too.

Ever since Luke was a little boy, he was always fascinated with the movie industry. Torreey's biggest client was the Local 44 Union for the movies in Hollywood. Torreey, through his connections at the Union, got Luke a job and finally, Luke was content. He has been working for the last twenty years in the film industry. He bought his own condominium a few blocks from our house.

Luke and his girlfriend, Darcy, a very special, sweet and caring girl, moved in the condominium together. We all loved and care for Darcy very much. But unfortunately, a year later, their relationship was over, and Darcy moved out and went back home to Seattle, Washington.

In 2012, Luke invited his new girlfriend over to our house for dinner. She's a wonderful girl and we're pleased that he has someone special in his life once again.

Luke and Natalie's high school graduation in 1992.

Chapter 31

My Daughter the Fashion Model - 1992

Natalie was not only a bright and intelligent young girl, but she was also beautiful. She was 5'11, thin, with long black hair. She didn't have to study hard to pass an exam; she loved school and always had good grades. She graduated from Redondo High School at age seventeen, but she was somewhat unsure about what she wanted to do next.

During the summer, she partied hard with her friends and spent the nights at her girlfriends' houses most of the time; that way I wouldn't know what time she got home. She knew she couldn't get away with this every night in our home. We had rules that Natalie didn't like and after a while we put a stop to her carousing, because she wasn't doing anything with her life. I knew she was too young to know better and we needed to be strict with her. She was sleeping late during the day and partying all night.

One weekend after spending the day at the mall with friends, she came home excited and said, "Mommm, someone approached me and handed me a business card. He asked if I was interested in appearing in Lenny Kravitz's new video for his number one hit, 'Are You Gonna Go My Way.' I said, yes! But you have to be there because I'm a minor."

"Oh really? Well I'm going to have to think about this," I replied with a very serious face, but of course I was just kidding.

"You suck, Mom!" Natalie responded, furious, until she saw me laughing.

"I'll take you," but I said, "Lina's coming with me."

"Oh no! "Natalie gasped. "You guys are gonna act crazy. Aren't you?"

On the day of the shoot, Lina, Natalie and I drove to a downtown L.A. wherehouse at 9:00 p.m. We were escorted to a back room where a makeup artist was already working on Lenny's face.

"OMG, its Lenny!" Lina said thrilled, while I giggled nervously. Lenny turned to us, gave a slight smile and said, "Hello ladies!"

We approached him and shook hands. He was wearing a sleeveless red kind of jumpsuit. Something more like a woman would wear than a man, I thought for a moment. But that was Lenny's fashion style. He had long dreadlocks falling on his face. He was gorgeous!

Natalie of course was already giving us the evil eye for being loud and silly.

Moments later, Natalie was escorted to the front stage and Lina and I to a row of bleachers where we sat with about fifty other audience members and watched the filming of the video until 3 a.m.

Natalie and the rest of the cast members were dancing while Lenny and his band performed. She looked amazing and was having a blast.

Lina and I were blown away watching more than a dozen crewmembers filming a three to four minute music video. It took over six hours to film, but it was nonstop fun and excitement!

From time to time, I re-watch my daughter dancing in the music video on YouTube to re-live the experience.

One day, Torreey sat Natalie down and said, "You need to do something with your life besides nonstop partying." He encouraged her to focus on college or some kind of meaningful job.

In January 1993, she came home one day and announced, "Mom, I'm moving to Italy with my friend, Janice, to model in Milan." She was eighteen and I could no longer tell her what to do."

Natalie and Janice took off to Italy and lived there for a year and a half. Two months after her arrival, she called me and said, "Mom, I need money to pay for the electric bills that are overdue."

I wasn't sure if what she was telling me was true. "Well, Natalie, if you're not making money to pay the bills, then you need to come home and go to college."

She snapped, "You suck, Mom. Janice's mom is sending her money, so why can't you do the same?"

"Natalie, listen to me. I don't like the idea of you being so far away from home. You're only eighteen and I'm worried something bad might happen to you," I tried reasoning with her.

I felt Janice and Natalie were too naïve to manage in a foreign country where they didn't even speak the language.

Natalie modeling in Italy 1993.

Chapter 32

A Visitor From Italy - 1993

While living in Italy, Natalie hooked up with Francisco. He was fifteen years older than her.

One evening she called me excited and said, "Mom, I met this charming, tall, elegant Italian guy a month ago. I've been seeing a lot of him. He owns a business and travels quite often. He invited me to France and Germany for a week. He's bought me gifts, and I also met his mother."

"I'm happy for you, Natalie. But please be careful," I said very worried.

After a year of dating him, Natalie called and said, "Mom, Francisco, is travelling to California and would like to meet you."

"Oh, really?" I replied, completely surprised.

Two weeks later, Francisco arrived in LA and was staying at the Beverly Hills Hotel. He called and asked me to meet him for lunch at a restaurant on Rodeo Drive.

The following day I drove to the restaurant, walked inside and stood there like a statue looking for a tall, dark haired, Italian man. I didn't have a picture of him so I was just guessing. Somehow, we found each other, and he actually was elegant, and classy.

"Hi, you Natalie's mom?"

"Yes!" I said and extended my hand to shake his. Instead, he leaned over, kissed my right and then left cheek too. A social custom in Italy and many other countries, too.

He stared at me and with a thick accent said, "You, Natalie's mom, is little."

I smiled back at him. "Yes, she took after her dad."

We sat down, ordered lunch and a glass of wine. Then I asked the question I was dying to know: "How's Natalie doing ... really?"

"She's doing fine. She's modeling a little here and there and having a lot of fun too," he said expressing himself with his hands.

"Francisco," I countered, "I think she needs to come back home and go to college. I'm really not comfortable with the idea of her being so far away."

"Don't worry," he said with a pleasant expression, "I'll keep my eye on her. Okay?"

"Thank you," I responded, "but I'm still worried about her."

He made a serious face, paused, then said, "How can I get your daughter to marry me?"

I was completely shocked! I wasn't expecting this at all. "Wow, I think she's too young for marriage." I replied raising an eyebrow. "And I really can't tell you how to make her marry you, either."

"Okay, I'll work on it," he shrugged.

Francisco was a charming man; I think Natalie was simply in another world at the time. She just wanted to party and have as much fun as possible, and relished her freedom. She loved being on her own without any supervision at all — that's my daughter. She never liked me telling her what to do, even when she was a little girl. She was a tough person with a strong personality and a beautiful heart. She was a sweet girl, but she was also a rebel. During her teenage years (fourteen through seventeen especially) she was hanging out with some girls I didn't approve of. The girls' moms gave their daughters a lot of freedom and Natalie wanted the same from me. She and I had many arguments throughout her teenage years. I knew that Natalie and her girlfriends were doing much more than just smoking cigarettes.

We didn't get along when she was a teenager, like most mothers and daughters. She hated to clean her bedroom. Eventually we started closing her door so that we didn't have to look at it. If you came to our house and opened her bedroom door you'd see most of her clothes all over the floor and bed, if you could even find the bed. Natalie would try one outfit after another until she was satisfied, and then leave all the clothes on the floor for days. When she lost something, she'd say with a real sweet voice, "Mom, can you please find it for me?"

"What? Who do you think I am? Your personal maid?" I said with a firm voice.

She then looked back at me with attitude, and said, "You suck, Mom. My friends' moms are all so nice to them, and you're a jerk."

"I like being a jerk, I'm not like your friends' moms," I said cheerily.

We argued most of the time and couldn't stand each other. She always thought I was dressing too sexy. When she got mad at me she'd say, "You think you're hot, but you're not, you're old."

Natalie's boyfriends from school came by our house and knocked on our front door just to see me open it. The boys had found out that Natalie's mom and sisters were in *Playboy* magazine.

Everywhere Natalie and I went she'd give me a dirty look; that was my daughter. Most of the time I ignored her and pretended like it didn't bother me at all, thinking, *She'll get over it some day.*

Chapter 33

The Engagement is On - 1994

A year an a half after she'd left, Natalie came back home from Italy, and said, "Modeling isn't what I want to do anymore." She'd grown up and changed a lot, and was serious about what she really wanted to do with her life. I was very happy to see the difference in her. She stayed in touch with Francisco throughout the years by phone and e-mails.

A month later, Natalie found a job two blocks from our house in a pre-school, The Sound of Music. She loved working with children, had a lot of patience, and was enjoying her position. On weekends she'd babysit for some of the parents who got to know her at the pre-school. She walked to work every day and a few months later my husband helped her buy a brand new car.

Torreey made a deal with her: "I'll put the down payment on the car, and you can make the monthly payments." This way we made sure she kept her job.

A month or so later, Natalie started dating Dave, who she knew from high school. He's half Chinese and half Irish, good looking, sweet and very caring. Dave was the kind of guy any mother would love for her daughter to be with. He was an exceptional human being. Dave fell in love with Natalie and one day he presented her with an engagement ring.

Chapter 34

Goodbye Dave - 1996

Natalie was about twenty years old when she was introduced to James Collins through my sister Lina, who was married to Al, James's older brother.

Lina never wanted children until she turned thirty-five years old. As I mentioned earlier, she then had a baby girl, Sunny. When Lina baptized Sunny, she asked me to be her godmother and Al's brother James to be the godfather. James flew to California for the baptism and that's when he met Natalie.

Natalie at the time was engaged to Dave. He was the perfect man, good looking, sweet, and kind. He was enlisted in the Army and attended college at the same time.

When James walked into the Catholic Church for Sunny's baptism he fell in love with Natalie the minute he saw her.

Natalie was beautiful, thin, with long black shiny hair, minimal makeup, and a perfect nose.

James was ten years older than Natalie; and he knew how to impress a young girl. He was a lawyer in Lake Cormorant, Mississippi working for his dad's practice as a personal injury attorney. He was building his dream house on Lake Cormorant, Mississippi and of course Natalie was very impressed.

The following day, Natalie and James hung out together with Lina and Al. Two days later, James was on a plane going back home to Mississippi. In the meantime, they were staying in touch with each other.

I was concerned because Natalie was engaged, so I had to ask, "What about Dave?"

"Mom, I don't think I want to marry Dave anymore. I'm going to break off the engagement with him," Natalie said in low spirits.

"OMG, I'm so sad for Dave," I said, thinking. How we all loved and cared for him so much. I knew that Natalie was confused about what she wanted to do.

The following week, Natalie gave Dave the news and handed him the engagement ring back.

Dave couldn't believe it and left the house in tears.

I was so disappointed; I knew how much Dave loved Natalie. I thought she was making a big mistake but I couldn't make her change her mind. It broke my heart to say goodbye to Dave.

Natalie when she met James Collins in 1996.

Chapter 35

The Disappearing Husband - 1996

As had long been the case, Lina and Al were not doing well financially. Al's dad and mom flew from Mississippi to Redondo Beach to visit and to meet their new granddaughter. Lina and Al lived in a one-bedroom apartment in Redondo Beach not too far from my house. Lina had quit her receptionist job to stay home and take care of her baby. Al was working for a friend as a truck driver, but never made enough money to live on.

While his parents were visiting, Al's dad offered them a house in Flicker Ridge, Mississippi. The next day, Lina came over my house and said, "I'm confused. I don't want to move to Mississippi. I want him to buy us a house in Redondo Beach." She looked at me with sadness and asked, "What do you think about us moving to Mississippi?"

"I will miss you and the baby, but it's the right decision," I replied. "You'll have a house with a nice backyard and I will visit you. You can always come back here and stay for a few weeks. Right now you're three people living in a cramped one-bedroom apartment with no room to move around. Seriously, think about it."

After her in-laws were gone, Lina was upset and nervous, but she agreed to move to Mississippi. She said, "I have no choice but to take the offer from Al's dad." She cried and cried and told me, "I'll never be able to raise my daughter in California like I wanted to."

Al, Lina and Sunny moved to Flicker Ridge, Mississippi in July of 1996.

Al's dad had the house ready upon their arrival. It was a new three bedroom with a big living room, a spacious kitchen with all the appliances included, and a good size backyard.

Lina was happy with her house but was not content living in Flicker Ridge, Mississippi. The house was located in the country, and surrounded by cows and horses. She called me and said, "I don't know what the fuck I'm doing here? I'm a city girl and I don't belong with cattle. I'm not comfortable living out in the boonies."

The first time I went to visit Lina was for Sunny's first birthday. Mom, Natalie, my aunt Adriana and I flew to Mississippi and stayed for two weeks. We had a blast; Lina was so happy to see us.

"Lina," I said to assure her, "I'm so glad to see that you have a nice, big, comfortable house and a better life for yourself and Sunny."

Lina shook her head. "I love the house, but I wish I were home in Redondo Beach. I miss all the family and mostly you. I'll never be happy here."

I hugged her and said, "Be patient. You need to make friends and give it more time to get used to it. Believe me, it'll be okay."

We enjoyed cooking meals and just staying home. I made our favorite drink, Cadillac margaritas, and we sat outside in the backyard talking and laughing about all the fun and crazy shit we did together.

After I returned to California, Lina and I called each other every day, sometimes more than once a day. She told me lots of stuff about the Collins. One in particular about how she was always home alone: "I gotta tell you something about Al. When he was eighteen, he was out one evening with his friends, and they got in a brawl with some other guys. At the time, Al was practicing karate and had won several trophies. While Al was fighting, he used a karate kick to this guy's temple that knocked him to the ground. Al and his friends left the scene and the next day they found out that the guy he kicked had died. Al was acquitted on the grounds he was simply defending himself. I don't know why, maybe to protect him against retaliation, but Al's parents moved him to another state, and from then on Al drifted from one state to another."

According to Lina, at the time of the incident, Al's uncle was a highly respected member of the community. She couldn't say whether or not that affected the "not guilty" decision, but she felt the ordeal probably screwed him up pretty bad all the same.

"Al leaves the house and doesn't return until late in the evening. His dad calls me several times a day to find out where he's hiding. I always tell his dad he's at work, which is where I think he is."

Al worked for his dad in construction. In addition to being an attorney, his dad bought houses, remodeled them and sold them for a profit. Al would disappear for hours and no one ever knew where he went.

Lina continued, "When Al gets home he's all withdrawn. We fight about this a lot. I threatened him, saying, 'I'm going to move back to Redondo Beach with the baby.'"

She and Al had a free home to live in. Al's dad, Mr. Collins, paid for everything; utilities, phone, cars, auto insurance, food, and the tab on an American Express credit card. The only thing his dad didn't provide them with was medical insurance. Anytime they got sick his dad had them see a doctor friend of his, and the doctor sent Mr. Collins the bills.

When Lina lived in Redondo Beach, before she got pregnant, she started bleeding from her rectum. It was a weekend and Al didn't want to take her to the hospital because he was going fishing. Instead, Torreey and I took her to the emergency room. After a few hours of tests, the doctor said, "She needs to see a specialist."

We took her home and she made an appointment with the specialist for the following Monday. During her visit the specialist recommended a colonoscopy because of our family history of colon cancer. She had her colonoscopy and the doctor found polyps and removed them.

The doctor said, "You need to follow up with a colonoscopy every five years."

Lina never went back to get a colonoscopy while she lived in Mississippi. She said in frustration, "I don't have time. I have to take care of my baby all day long. Besides, I don't care if I die."

"Don't ever say that again!" I shouted.

"I don't care. I'm fucking tired of my life," she cried, and hung up on me.

Chapter 36

Fun Times in Mississippi - 1996

For Sunny's first birthday, October 30, 1996, Mom, my aunt Adriana, Natalie and I flew to Lake Cormorant to celebrate. We were all staying at Lina's new home.

While we were there, James got to spend more time with Natalie. He was excited; you could see it in his eyes. He took us to see the house he was having built on the lake. From there we headed to New Orleans for the weekend where we had a wonderful time. James was very charming, fun, and I could tell that he was madly in love with Natalie.

Back home in late November, I was cooking in the kitchen when Natalie came in. She was bursting with excitement and said, "James invited me to Mississippi for Christmas."

I hugged her and said, "I'm going to miss you but I know you'll have a great time."

Natalie flew to Mississippi for Christmas and stayed with Lina and Al.

Lina was extremely happy that Natalie was there with her and was spending Christmas and New Year's 1997.

But after the holidays were over, and Natalie was back home in early January, she came into the kitchen were I was and announced, "Mom, I'm moving to Mississippi to live with James, and go to college."

"WHAT?" I said, shocked! Natalie had a job at a nursery school two blocks from our house. She was already going to college and was paying off the new car that Torreey had helped buy for her.

"Natalie, how are you going to make the monthly car payment without a job? We're not going to make the payments for you," I argued.

Natalie responded arrogantly, "James is going to pay off my car and ship it to Mississippi."

She had it all planned; she had an answer for every question I came up with. I couldn't stop her, so I hugged her and said, "I love you and will miss you!"

At the end of January, Natalie flew to Mississippi and was absolutely in heaven. She moved into the brand new house James had built on the lake. She called and said, "Mom, I think I love it here." She sounded thrilled and I was happy for her.

That same year in May, I flew to Lake Cormorant for Mother's Day with my mom. The first time I visited I just loved it. The house was perfect for a couple, very cozy with a beautiful view. It was so peaceful; we'd sit on the porch on a rainy day and watch the fish jump in the air. Thunderstorms were events. The lightning was dazzling, the thunder shocking. I was really enjoying my visit there. We jogged along the lake and watched the alligators swimming. I found it so peaceful and relaxing to be away from all the traffic and noise in California. Going from Natalie's to Lina's house only took about fifteen minutes on the freeway.

Lina lived in the country, with livestock. I teased her a lot and said, "Girl, you need to learn to milk them cows."

"Yeah, all I need is a pair of overalls and a fucking bucket," she replied with a laugh.

We cooked dinner, made margaritas and sat in the backyard to talk and laugh. The nights were very dark; we turned all the lights off in the house and walked through the backyard. It was all lit up with lighting bugs. Sometimes we grabbed a few bugs and placed them inside a glass jar, then, took the container inside the house. With the lights turned out, the bugs would fire and light up the whole place like Christmas, it was beautiful!

Natalie really loved it there, she wanted a change from California and I think she found it in Lake Cormorant. Her aunt Lina was there, and my mom and I'd visit twice a year. Natalie easily made many friends, and was always busy doing something.

We went out to the casino boats on the lake for dinner and a little gambling with Natalie, James, Lina, Al and a few friends of James's.

One evening while we were at the casino, James's friend, Rob Marciano, who at the time was the local weatherman in Lake Cormorant, came to the casino to hang out with us. We met him at the bar. He was handsome, quiet and seemed somewhat shy.

A few minutes later we all left the bar and I yelled, "Let's go play craps." I had learned to play with my husband in Las Vegas and loved the game. I always got pretty loud and crazy while playing, especially after a few cocktails.

Rob Marciano was there for no more than ten minutes.

My sister later informed me, "Guess what? Rob didn't want to hang out because you were too loud and crazy for his conservative reputation. I don't think Rob wanted to end up on the news with this crazy girl. It would've probably ruined his career in Lake Cormorant."

That was about eighteen to twenty years ago that I met Rob. In January 2013, I heard Nancy O'Dell from *Entertainment Tonight* announce her new cohost, "Rob Marciano." I was shocked to see him on ET. He looked better than when I met him many years ago – maybe because he was a lot younger and very cautious then. He was still handsome and did a great job as a cohost. In 2014 he left ET and he's currently the weatherman for *Good Morning America* in New York City.

What a difference between the Lake Cormorant conservative meteorologist and the 2015 fun and goofy (at times) personality. He looks like he's having a blast with the rest of the fun news crew.

Lookin' good, Rob!

Chapter 37

Parasailing in Ensenada - 1997

By August of 1997, it was "summer in the city". Lina flew back to Redondo Beach with Sunny and Natalie from Mississippi. Sunny was about two years old.

Torreey and I had planned a trip on a cruise ship to Ensenada with my sisters Gia, Lina, and my daughter Natalie. It was our sister Tanya's birthday that week, and Tanya's boyfriend John had already booked a cruise to Ensenada to surprise her.

Lina talked to John and said, "Don't mention anything to Tanya that we've also booked a trip the same week, we want to surprise her." Lina left Sunny at my house with our mom and our brother Edgar while we were gone for four days.

We were all super excited to go on this trip. Torreey and I had already been on a couple of cruises before, and I knew right away this was going to be so much fun. It was the girls' first time on a cruise ship.

On the day of the cruise, Lina, Gia, Natalie, Torreey and I drove to San Pedro and boarded the ship. At the gangplank to the vessel, photographers were standing by to take a group picture; we all squeezed in real close to each other for the shot. Then we walked on board and were greeted with a glass of champagne. "Girls, let's have a toast!" I announced, raising my glass up in the air. "Cheers! Let's have some fun!" We were all thrilled and happy to be together on this trip.

Then we hurried up to the deck to see if we could spot Tanya and John coming in. Soon, Lina yelled out. "Here they come! Shit, Tanya is going to freak out when she sees us on the ship!"

When we finally got a hold of John, he gave us the cabin number. We took the elevator down, knocked on the door and waited for Tanya to open it, then yelled, "SURPRISE!"

Tanya looked at us and we could tell she was NOT happy to see us. She was hoping for a romantic getaway with her boyfriend and she knew it wasn't going to happen with us around. We all hugged her while she cried and said to John, "Why didn't you tell me they were coming?" She looked very upset with John, so we changed the conversation. Lina rolled her eyes and said, "we're going to have a ball." We felt bad for poor John. He was a kind man. But he was also funny looking; he has a little face with huge ears and looks like the little mouse, Topo Gigo.

After visiting with Tanya and John I turned to the girls and said, "Let's go to our cabins and get ready for the evening." For dinner we had Italian food with plenty more cocktails and afterwards ended at the casino for some gambling. Three hours later we were exhausted and ready for bed.

The next day we had breakfast and went out to the pool area to sun bathe; had more cocktails, lunch, relaxed, and laughed it up by the pool. After a while, Gia stood up and said, "I'm going down on the water slide."

We watched her scream like a little kid and laughed at her every time she waved at us.

Later on we all went back to our cabins around 5:00 p.m., to shower and get ready for dinner and dancing.

Gia of course had already drank too much and never knew when to stop. She's one of the two craziest and most fun of all of my sisters. She's sweet, lovable and reminds me a lot of my grandmother. The best part of Gia is you can't help but have a good time when she's around.

By about 10:00 p.m., Gia was a fucking mess, crying and talking about how she always wanted to be a stewardess. Every time she got wasted she always brought up the same subject. She was like a broken record.

Around 10:30 p.m., Gia was so fucking drunk we couldn't take her dancing. We were worried she'd slip out of the nightclub and end up overboard, or do something equally stupid. So we took her to the cafeteria and ordered coffee. Contrary to most people, caffeine worked like a sedative on Gia.

"Gia, drink the coffee, it will calm you down," I said.

We just couldn't calm her down. So, I whispered to Tanya, "Do you have any pills to give to Gia?"

Tanya always had a medicine cabinet with her.

"I have sleeping pills, " Tanya offered.

"Go to your cabin and bring a few," I said out of the side of my mouth.

Tanya came back and gave me one pill.

We ordered more coffee and when Gia wasn't looking, I dropped the pill in the cup. She was still crying and complaining about her life.

"Gia, drink up and you will feel better," Natalie encouraged.

We waited half an hour and nothing happened. Natalie then looked at me with a straight face and said, "Shit, she's like a fucking horse! The pill is not going to work!"

We all wanted to go dancing but we couldn't leave or take Gia with us, so I bumped elbows with Tanya and whispered, "Let me have another pill."

Natalie opened her eyes wide, laughed and said, "Damn, Mom! You're gonna kill her!"

"Like you said, she's a fucking horse, one pill cannot take her down!" I groaned, then poured more coffee and dropped one more pill in Gia's mug.

She drank the coffee and began to calm down. She kept talking and talking. We all looked at each other, and I whispered, "FUCK! She's not going down!"

A minute later, Gia looked at us blurry-eyed and was slurring her words. She said something we didn't understand, and suddenly dropped her head on the table. The sound was so loud we thought for sure she'd hurt herself.

Natalie looked at me and screamed, "SHIT, Mom, you killed her!"

We all laughed, but I was momentarily afraid I *had* actually killed her, so I took her pulse. "Hay hueputa! Que miedo." ("Fuck! I'm scared.") Thankfully, she was there, just deeply asleep.

I got up from my chair and told the girls, "Okay, let's take her to her cabin." Natalie grabbed Gia's arm. Tanya grabbed the other one. They began walking Gia with her feet dragging.

I was the "point man" in front of them, and Lina was the "spotter" behind them.

People were staring at us as we explained, "She's very drunk and needs to go lie down."

We took the elevator to the cabin. I opened the door and we put Gia on the bed, covered her up, and left the room laughing so hard we were in tears. She really was tougher than a horse!

We were finally happy to make it to the nightclub and had a great time dancing all night long.

The next day, Gia woke up with a horrible headache and said to us, "Que hijueputa majes, no me acuerdo que diablos hice a noche." ("Son-of-a-bitch, I don't remember what the hell I did last night.")

"Hay maje que bruta, you were on the floor dancing like a chicken without a head," I said. We all busted out laughing like crazy. We didn't tell Gia what we did until we got home.

The ship docked in Ensenada, and we girls took off to go to the beach. Gia was not feeling well but she insisted on coming along. Tanya, John and Torreey stayed on the ship to sunbathe and relax.

When we got to the beach, we ordered some cocktails, and walked down to watch the people parasail.

Gia, like always, never knew when to stop drinking. She was already drunk even though she wasn't feeling well. "I want to try parasailing," she said confidently. Gia was never afraid of trying anything. She was fearless.

We all responded at the same time, "No! No! Don't do it!" But she didn't care. She wanted to do it and no one was going to stop her. So I went ahead and paid the lady for Gia's ride.

Gia was still complaining, "My stomach is upset," but insisted on parasailing anyway. Her turn came and a female assistant hooked Gia to the instructor. We sat on the beach to watch Gia and the instructor take off on their flight.

Natalie was already laughing hysterically. Lina kept repeating, "She's crazy...she's crazy..." and I was just laughing and saying, "OMG, this is hilarious. She's not afraid of anything except driving on the freeway!"

A few minutes later, we all watched as Gia and her instructor prepared for liftoff. She was screaming, laughing, and yelling, "Hey majes voy a volar como un pajaro!" ("Hey you guys, I'm going to fly like a bird!") She sounded like a little kid.

We were laughing and waving as she became airborne and flew like a fucking bird. It was the funniest thing ever, Gia screaming loudly and waving back at us. Ten or fifteen minutes later, Gia and the instructor came down to land. Our eyes were glued to her, and when she hit the ground we noticed that her shorts were covered with something.

The Hispanic instructor was yelling at his assistant to hurry up and unhook them. He was saying to her in Spanish, "Esta vieja se cago en mi!" ("This woman took a shit on me!") We of course understood what he said and immediately began howling with laughter.

The Latin lady was unhooking Gia while we asked her, "What the hell happened to you?" Gia's face was white like a ghost. She couldn't even speak. We all got scared and thought that maybe she had a stroke from so much drinking. When we finally got a word out of her, it was "ME CAGE!" ("I crapped!")

Gia ran to the bathroom, yelling, "Me duele mi estomago. Hay! Hay! Ya no puedo mas!" ("My stomach is hurting, I can't take it anymore!") We all followed her still laughing and screaming.

She got to the bathroom but only had time to pull her shorts down, she bent her knees and all the shit hit the wall. The smell was indescribable; the rest of us ran outside gagging. She took her shorts off, washed them, and put them back on. She was sick with Montezuma's revenge.

We took her back to the ship got her some Imodium and chicken soup, and she spent the rest of the day in bed.

The next day she felt better and said, "Hay majes que horrible es estar volando como un pajaro en el cielo y de repente tener un dolor de stomago tan fuerte. Senti que estava dando a luz." ("It was horrible being up in the sky flying like a bird and all of a sudden coming down with the worst stomachache ever. It felt like I was giving birth. I couldn't control it, all the shit came down my legs while I was flying.")

We all laughed and laughed until we could laugh no more. I kept repeating, over and over again, "Gia was a fucking flying crapping bird." "Y se cago en el Viejo!" ("And she took a shit all over the guy!") Ha! Ha! Ha!"

1997 Ensenada cruise: Natalie, Gia, Lina, me and Torreey.

Ensenada cruise. Drunk and ready to party. Tanya, Gia, Lina, Me, Torreey, Mr. & Mrs. Sabatino and Natalie.

Chapter 38

Off-Key Wedding Bells - 2000

As mentioned, Natalie was tall, thin, with beautiful long black hair. James was shorter than Natalie; he had light skin with brown eyes and brown hair. He wasn't an athletic person. Natalie liked to exercise; and enjoyed jogging, roller-skating and taking aerobics classes.

When James met Natalie, he started exercising, running with her along the lake and going to the gym together. When they came to California, we'd go to the beach and run on the bike path.

They lived together for about five years in the Lake House. She was going to college to get her degree in business. Natalie was very likeable and always had many friends around her. She loved to party and learned to enjoy wine when she lived in Italy.

Natalie and James both enjoyed having friends at their house most of the time. Sometimes when I visited, I was overwhelmed; too many people at the house weren't something I liked unless I was having a party. But this crowd scene took place on a daily basis, a.m. to p.m. I really didn't have a chance to spend much time with Natalie alone; there was always somebody there. I did my best not to show her that I wasn't happy, and went along with it. I'd stay at Lina's house for a few days to get a break from the nonstop activity. It worked out best for the two of us.

After five years of living together, one day Natalie called me and said, "Mom, James gave me an engagement ring."

I wasn't shocked; I congratulated her and said, "When are you planning to get married?"

"I don't know yet, but since James is ten years older than me, it'll probably be soon. He wants to have children and doesn't want to wait any longer."

The following year, James planned the wedding. Natalie wasn't the type that would do it; she always left it to others to make various arrangements.

"Do you want to have the wedding in California?" I offered.

"No, because James has decided to have the wedding ceremony in Lake Cormorant at his mother Trisha's house in the backyard gazebo, with their minister," she replied.

While I was on the phone with Natalie, she said, "Mom, I don't want you to spend money on the wedding. I'd feel bad if you spent a lot and a few years later we're divorced."

I didn't say anything, except, "I'll be there for you, but most of the family can't afford to travel."

I bought her dress in California and brought it with us for the wedding. Mom, Dad, Torreey and I flew together to Lake Cormorant.

My son, Luke, did not attend the wedding. He disliked James; he said, "I don't trust him."

"Why?" I asked, surprised.

"Because he never looks at you when he's talking to you – he always looks sideways."

"Luke," I said, "I think you're wrong. He seems like a nice guy and he loves your sister – plus, he's Al's brother."

"Well, I don't feel the same as you do about him. That's just my honest opinion. I can't help it," he said, and refused to change his tune.

On Saturday morning, Lina came over to Trisha's house to do Natalie's makeup and hair. She then put her dress on and looked beautiful.

By now, Lina and I were also ready, so I said, "Let's do a few shots of tequila." Minutes later I asked Natalie, "Are you sure you want to marry James?" I was still thinking about what she told me a month ago about the marriage maybe not working out. There was something Natalie wasn't telling me and I was concerned.

With a slight grin on her face, she said, "Yes, I'm positive, Mom."

For some reason, deep down inside of me, I was still hoping she'd change her mind.

My husband Torreey and my dad gave Natalie away; they both walked her holding an arm on each side. It was Lina's idea to invite our dad to the wedding and Natalie agreed.

I've never told my kids all of the horrible things our dad did to our mom and us, and it was not the right time to say anything to them. I wasn't happy with the idea but decided to let it go. It was Natalie's big day and I wasn't going to ruin it by bad-mouthing him.

Lina was already crying as Natalie walked by us with both Torreey and our dad. I looked at Natalie and winked at her and thought, *How beautiful she looks, so tall, and elegant, her two little pugs Maya and Maylee with their white lace dresses following behind her.* James was standing near the gazebo next to the minister waiting for Natalie.

James and Natalie were indeed married on December 9, 2000 – as planned – at his mom's house in the backyard gazebo.

Natalie signed a prenuptial agreement that James's attorney friend prepared for them.

At first, James was a wonderful husband and took good care of Natalie. He had a maid come in to clean their house every week and to help Natalie with anything else needed around the house. He spoiled her to death. They were very happy and in love with each other. He treated her like a princess. They both loved to travel and took vacations to Italy, France, Belize and Florida. The Bahamas, Costa Rica, and Las Vegas, with Torreey and I. They also came to California to visit us at least once a year.

My husband and I and the rest of my family loved James and got along well with him – that is, except Luke, who maintained his distance.

My sister Lina and Natalie were not only married to two brothers, but they also had the same middle and last names (Lina Emi Collins and Natalie Emi Collins)

Chapter 39

Misery in Mississippi - 1998

By now, Sunny was three years old and hated leaving her little friends behind every time she and her mom Lina came to California. Sunny had become a very demanding little girl; her parents had spoiled her rotten. She had a bad temper and screamed when she didn't get what she wanted. We were afraid to say anything to Lina about Sunny's behavior because she'd blow up at us. Lina was very frustrated, not only with her husband, but also with her own child. "This kid doesn't act anything like our family," Lina proclaimed.

But we knew Lina didn't want to admit that her little girl had some of her personality too. Sunny could throw a serious temper tantrum. Every time Sunny got upset, she grabbed her ponytails, pulled them as hard as she could, or made a fist and punched herself on the head or in her face.

"OMG, I've never seen anything like this in my life!" I said in exasperation. "Lina, make her stop!"

"She beats herself up so I don't have to do it," Lina snorted.

One year, when Lina was in California visiting, she said to our mom and me, "I went to a gynecologist and the doctor told me I have a mass and need to get a biopsy."

Mom and I got scared and told her to get it done as soon as she got back home.

Lina responded morosely, "I don't have medical insurance and besides, I don't care if I die."

"Lina, you have said this more than once, please don't ever repeat it again. Put it on the American Express Card you have," I demanded.

"No," she shook her head vehemently, "because if I do, Al's dad will be calling me, screaming about the charges."

Al's dad, Mr. Collins had a temper – and sometimes blew up with only slight provocation. He basically had a good heart but from time to time could make life difficult for the people around him.

Our mom, my sisters and I kept calling and begging Lina to go see a doctor but it was impossible, sometimes she hung up the phone on us. Other times she'd yelled. "Stop calling me about it!"

I didn't stop calling her; I just didn't mention anything about her mass anymore. The summer and fall ended, winter came, and Lina never bothered to go see a doctor.

For Natalie's birthday in December 2002, I flew to Mississippi to see her, my grandson Mason, Lina and Sunny. Lina didn't look good; she was limping and had bags under her eyes.

"What's wrong, Lina?" I asked, very concerned.

With a pale and a sad expression on her face, she lifted her skirt and showed me a lump she had on her groin.

"Hay Dios mio! ("OMG!") Have you seen a doctor?" I said, alarmed.

She furrowed her brow and said, "I have, and they are doing a biopsy."

That evening Lina stayed at Natalie and James's house. She slept with me in one of the guest rooms. At about two in the morning, I'd woken up to go to the bathroom when I saw an older, petite woman around eighty-five years old. She had white short curly hair, light skin and was standing at the end of the bed. She looked milky, kind of translucent, and was moving her head up and down as if saying yes to me. "Oh fuck!" I said to myself. I was scared to death and immediately fell back in bed and pulled the covers over my head. I thought I'd seen a ghost. I don't know what it was, but we Latinos have always believed in spirits. I didn't say anything to Lina or Natalie about what happened that night but I was definitely freaked out. Days later I was back home in California and couldn't stop thinking about the fucking ghost.

Lina's appointment for the biopsy was scheduled on January 3, 2003. When she got the results she called me right away. She was hysterical and couldn't get the words out of her mouth. When she finally did, she said, "I have cancer. I don't want to die here, please help me!"

"Oh God, Lina!" I said, feeling like I was paralyzed, but my tears were falling. Moments later I found myself crying with her and telling her, "I love you, Lina. I'm gonna call you later. Okay?" I hung up the phone and immediately called Natalie.

Upon hearing the news Natalie decided to go see Lina to comfort her and offered to take her to the charity hospital. They drove to the clinic and the clerk asked a lot of questions about her financial situation.

Lina wasn't able to answer. She was in a state of shock, so Natalie spoke to the service desk worker and said, "My aunt doesn't have medical insurance and has been diagnosed with cancer." The hospital needed a lot more information to determine if they could provide her with medical care. In the meantime, Lina was desperate and didn't want to sit down and wait. She just wanted to go home.

Hours later, Natalie called me, crying and saying, "Mom, Lina is going to die, and I don't know what else to do! Please help us!"

Chapter 40

Cancer Scare - 2003

I had to think fast and figure out how to bring Lina back home to Redondo Beach. And most important I knew that she needed to be around her family. I always had a solution for everything, I never gave up on anything; I was a fighter and Lina knew she could count on me. I remembered the spirit of the woman I saw at Natalie's house nodding at me. I realized that the woman was telling me to bring Lina home to California.

A day later, I called the County Hospital – Harbor UCLA in Lomita, California about 20 minutes from my house. I asked the woman who answered the phone, "Will you see a cancer patient who lives in another state?"

"Yes, you can bring her in, but it is going to be a long day before a doctor can see her," The receptionist responded.

Upon hearing this I immediately called Lina. "Harbor UCLA will see you if you come to California. You need to get a plane ticket as soon as possible, and I'll pick you up at the airport and take you straight to the hospital. Alright?"

Lina started crying and saying, "I won't leave Sunny behind. I can't do it!"

"Lina, calm down and listen to me," I tried to reason with her, "you have to leave Sunny with Natalie until we get you in the hospital. You need to think of yourself first and then Sunny. She'll be fine with Natalie for a couple of weeks."

Lina was sobbing and repeated, "I can't leave my little girl behind. No! No! I don't like the idea of leaving her with Al, and her grandmother Trisha isn't an option either."

When I finally calmed her down, I said, "Think about it and call me back. We can't waste anymore time."

I then called Natalie and she agreed to keep Sunny until we told her to come home to Redondo Beach with Sunny and Mason.

Lina got a plane ticket and flew to LAX on a Monday in January 2003 about 2:00 p.m. My sisters Gia, Tanya and I drove to the airport to pick her up. We sat and waited for Lina's plane to land; when she came out we all ran to hug and cry with her. We left the airport and went to grab a bite to eat before heading to Harbor UCLA hospital.

While eating, I came up with an idea: "Guys, you need to listen to me. We need to have Lina see a doctor as soon as possible. When we get to the hospital, I'm going to park by the emergency entrance. Tanya, you run inside the hospital screaming for a wheelchair. Lina, you'll be sitting in the back of my car with Gia. You start crying while you struggle to get out, and Gia will hold on to you."

Tanya did just that, except that a large black nurse yelled at her and said, "Control yourself, or I'm going to put you in a straitjacket!"

The nurse came out with Tanya and a wheelchair and said, "This woman must keep her composure or else stay out of the hospital."

Tanya, of course, overdid it with her acting. I looked at Tanya and winked my eye at her while we all helped the nurse get Lina in the wheelchair and rushed her inside the hospital. I then gave Tanya the keys to my car for her to park.

The nurse left us at the registration desk with Lina so they could take all of the information they needed.

I had asked Lina to bring with her from Mississippi copies of all the records from her doctor. After taking Lina's information the clerk told us to wait in the lobby, it was going to be a long time before Lina would be called to see a doctor.

The four of us waited and waited patiently, we all sat on the floor, talked in Spanish and laughed, especially about crazy Tanya and the mean nurse. Every time the nurse walked by us we'd look at each other and giggle.

Gia kept farting as she always did; a couple of Hispanic men were listening to our conversation, and laughing about Gia's farts. We made it fun while we were waiting on the floor of the hospital's waiting room.

Hours later, a nurse called Lina's name and we all got up and walked with Lina. The nurse said, "Only one person can come in with the patient."

"I'll go inside with Lina," I said, and followed the nurse to the room where she took her vital signs, then told us to go back to the waiting room again. We waited and waited; when people walked by us we'd have a comment about that person: either saying they kinda looked like someone famous, or we just had to laugh about a mannerism or a distinguishing facial feature. We laughed hysterically until our bellies ached.

Even Lina, who had cancer and didn't know how bad it was or how long she had to live, laughed and laughed. Lina sometimes lost it and started crying, but the three of us knew we had to stay strong for her. None of us had any idea how bad the cancer was, we were all scared, but we didn't want Lina to see it.

About 1:00 in the morning, a nurse called Lina to see a doctor; at this time Gia was sleeping on the floor like a homeless person. I immediately jumped up and woke up Lina and went inside the room with her.

Doctor Jackson, who looked to be in his twenties, introduced himself. He was holding the records from Mississippi in his hands with the diagnosis of colon cancer; he examined Lina and saw the mass in her groin area.

Lina began balling and pleaded, "Please, Dr. Jackson, help me, I'm going to die, and I have a little girl who needs me."

I was holding on to her and telling her to calm down.

Dr. Jackson was not sure what to do; he tentatively said, "I have to go see the head doctor in charge of admitting and present him with the documents and the diagnosis that's already on them. The doctor in charge will make a decision either to admit you or have you come back to run a series of tests."

At this point, Lina and I were hugging and crying like two little kids.

Dr. Jackson looked at us with so much compassion, pain, and love; I never thought in my life I would see what I saw in this doctor. I think he knew Lina was in a lot of trouble.

Lina and I approached and hugged Dr. Jackson together and begged him, "Please make it happen!" While we were hugging the doctor I could feel him trembling inside, this doctor was like an angel to us.

Dr. Jackson made a grim face and said, "Go back to the waiting room. This is going to take a very long time. I can't guarantee you that Lina will be admitted, but I'm going to do everything possible to make it work."

"Thank you, Doctor!" we both replied and went back and sat with Tanya and Gia in the waiting room. We held hands while Gia said a prayer for Lina.

About 5:00 in the morning, the nurse called Lina's name again; we all got up and looked at each other in panic.

I held on to Lina's arm and walked inside the room where Dr. Jackson was waiting for us. When he saw us he gave us a hopeful smile, saying, "We're going to keep Lina for a whole week and run all the tests we need to do. This way we can determine what type of treatment she'll need – chemotherapy, radiation... whatever."

Lina and I were crying, jumping up and down, and hugging Dr. Jackson and each other with joy. "See, I told you, Lina. All that praying we did helped us."

"Go back to the waiting area again, and a nurse will call you when Lina's room is ready," Dr. Jackson told us.

We hugged and thanked him again for helping us.

Lina's room was ready around 6:30 in the morning. The nurse called her and we all walked with her. We were so exhausted and ready to collapse, but we didn't show it. We left Lina in her room, gave her a kiss on the cheek, and told her we loved her and that everything was going to be okay.

She was quiet for a moment, then looked at us with sad eyes and said, "Love you guys! And thank you for everything."

Upon leaving the hospital a little after 7:00 in the morning and getting inside my car feeling like a fucking zombie, all I wanted to do was to get home and go to bed.

Gia sat in front and Tanya in the back. I was startled when my mobile phone rang. I was so tired I didn't even look to see who was calling. I answered the phone and Al's mother Trisha said, "Shirley, how are you?"

She was calling me from Mississippi. I of course was already trembling thinking that she had to be the first person to call me.

I was so upset and tired, I answered her by saying, "How do you think I am? I'm just leaving the hospital after being here for eighteen hours, all because of problems with having no medical insurance."

Trisha didn't respond to that at all. Her next words were, "I'm so worried about Al."

By then I was so fucking mad, I felt like throwing up.

Lina was at the hospital for seven days. We all went to see her every day. She was exhausted from all the tests and was discharged after a week with strict instructions to come back for more tests.

The doctors had to meet with other oncologists to determine how they were going to treat her. This went on for three months before we got an answer. This is what happens when you don't have medical insurance, you are just a number at the County Hospital.

Every week that Lina had an appointment I went with her. We were both tired, terrified, scared of the unknown and most of all just weary of seeing all of the sick people with cancer. Some of them couldn't walk, some of them couldn't move, some of them with no hair, some of them crying, some of them with no life at all; this was the most depressing time of my life and Lina's.

Lina would sit and cry and I'd hold her tight and say, "Don't you fucking give up on me. You hear me! I will fight with you and you will make it!"

Lina knew I was a fighter, she knew I never gave up on anything in life. We went to the basement of the hospital, a place we both referred to as "hell". That's where most of Lina's appointments were to see the oncologist.

I never told Lina that I truly felt like I had died and gone to hell every fucking time we were there. It was extremely depressing. Sometimes after getting home I was sick and would throw up and cry at the same time while I was in the shower. I didn't want anyone seeing me like this.

When we finally got an answer from Dr. Kwan, the oncologist, it was not a good one. He said, "Lina, has stage three cancer and in order for her to survive, we would have to remove part of her hip."

Lina went into a panic, screaming, crying and trembling. I held her tight and calmed her down, saying, "Lina, take a few deep breaths. I need to ask the doctor some important questions."

Dr. Kwan was very patient; I'm sure it broke his heart to have to say what he did, but he had no other choice.

"If you remove part of her hip, how will she walk?" I asked him.

Dr. Kwan looked at Lina and then at me and said, "She will not be able to walk. She'll have to be in a wheelchair for the rest of her life."

At this point Lina screamed so loud that the doctor had to help me calm her down.

She kept saying, "NO! NO! NO!"

Dr. Kwan immediately called a nurse and told her to bring a sedative.

All I could do was to hold Lina tight, cry with her and think and think. "Shit, what do we do now?"

Dr. Kwan just sat there looking at both of us with the saddest face ever. A few seconds later, I took a deep breath and asked him, "Is there any other way of getting to this cancer?"

"This is one way of making sure all of the cancer is removed, but there are other options," he said, removing his reading glasses.

Lina calmed down after hearing this. I asked him, "Would you please check with the rest of the team?"

"I will, but it's going to take some time." Dr. Kwan gave Lina another appointment to come back to see what kind of plan they had formulated.

Lina and I kept coming back to the appointments week after week. Three months later, the team of doctors made the decision to treat her with chemotherapy first. They couldn't perform surgery and remove part of the colon because the cancer was already in her lymph nodes.

Dr. Kwan gave Lina a prescription for painkillers (Vicodin) and other medications to take before they started with the treatment. Then they kept Lina for a whole week in the hospital and treated her with the chemotherapy.

A week later, after Lina was home, Mom came in the bedroom were I was and said, "Shirley, please make an appointment with the Catholic Church for the priest to have a healing service for Lina."

"I'll do it right away, Mom," I said, grabbing my phone.

Three weeks later after Lina was feeling better, our mom, Lina and I attended the private healing with the priest.

Once at the church, Father Johnson prayed for Lina while we held each others' hands with tears streaming down our faces. After the prayer ended, Father Johnson took one of us at a time to a room behind the altar of the church.

Lina went first while Mom and I waited for our turn. After a few minutes, Lina came back out with tears running down her face.

Mom and I hugged her and we all cried together. It was now our mom's turn to go with Father Johnson and my turn was last.

I was a little nervous following Father Johnson to the back room. When we got there, he said a little prayer, and then asked, "Is there something you want to tell me?"

I wasn't sure what he meant. "What do I need to tell you?"

"Your sins, something that you're not proud of doing," he said quite seriously.

I couldn't think of anything bad that I did or was doing except that I curse too fucking much. So I replied, "I like to swear a lot."

Father Johnson raised his hand and said, "Close your eyes." He then prayed for me for a few seconds. After he was done, I followed him back to where Mom and Lina were. We thanked him and left an envelope with a donation in the box in the church vestibule.

After leaving the church and walking to my car, I asked Lina and Mom, "What do you think about the back room healing with the priest?"

"I felt a strange warm soothing presence and feeling inside of me, I cannot describe it, but it was good," Lina said, sounding pleased.

Our mom said, "Si, me senti muy bien." ("Yes, I felt good.")

Lina and Mom turned their attention to me and asked, "What about you?"

"Honestly," I said, "I don't know. I'm confused about it because he asked me to tell him my sins."

"What did you tell him?" Lina asked with a grin.

"Hmm. I told him I curse too damn much," I responded sincerely.

Lina and Mom couldn't believe what I'd just said. They were laughing so hard tears were streaming out of their eyes.

"Well, shit, it's the truth!" I told them. "I couldn't think of anything else bad that I've done!" We got in the car and laughed all the way back to the house.

Lina was living in my house at the beach along with her daughter Sunny and their little five year old, Pekingese dog, Jazzie. They were occupying one of the guest bedrooms.

Our mom cooked all the meals and I spent my time taking Lina back and forth to the hospital. I was also in charge of Sunny, taking her to school, therapy, etc. My life had completely changed overnight.

My husband, the most patient person I've ever met in my life, never complained about anything, he just worked and worked, and if that's what I wanted to do it was always okay with him. He knew how important some of my family members were to me. He didn't care that we were already taking care of my mom and now we had Lina and Sunny in our home.

This is how we Latin people are; always thinking that we have to care for our family for the rest of our lives, especially if you're the one who has more money than the rest of the family. I was not only in charge of Lina but Sunny and our mom too. Mom also had to be taken to the doctor often for high blood pressure, liver problems, arthritis, and other aches and pain.

The chemo treatments were taking a toll on Lina. Two to three weeks after they began, she started losing her hair. She woke up one morning and a big chunk of her hair was on the pillow.

When I heard her screams I rushed down the stairs to her bedroom and held her tight.

"Lina," I said, "you need to shave your head."

"NO! I won't do it. Sunny is not going to like it," she kept insisting.

When I finally convinced her, I said, "I'll take you to a hair salon."

She made an appointment with her hairdresser, a real funny Hispanic gay man who made you laugh a lot while working on your hair.

I rushed to the mall and bought her a little hat that she took to her appointment to have her head shaved. When I picked her up and saw her, I wanted to cry, but I knew not to do it in front of her. I hugged her and said, "You look beautiful and your hair will grow back soon!"

Lina was concerned about what Sunny would say about her hair. When Sunny came home from school and looked at her mom, she gave her a big smile. We were all so relieved.

Lina kept losing weight and couldn't hold much in her stomach.

Every time I went to the market I brought back the Ensure shakes the doctor recommended. Mom was in charged of cooking all of her delicious Costa Rican meals that Lina loved. We desperately needed to fatten up Lina a bit. She was now down to bones; and it was frightening to look at her.

Sunny was 8 years old and hated the way her mom looked. She never said anything, but we could see it in her face. She looked terrified.

Lina detested that Sunny was always so emotionally distant, especially at this time in her life. She needed her little girl to love her and to hug her too.

"Lina," I advised, "you need to accept the way Sunny is. Don't judge her. She's just a little girl with a very sick mom."

After Lina recovered from the chemo and gained enough weight, Dr. Kwan recommended radiation next: "Six weeks of once a week treatments." Dr. Kwan wanted to make sure the tumors were completely gone.

So here we go again, but only this time the radiation treatments where near my house in a beautiful facility. I took Lina to just about every appointment. After four weeks, she lost the weight she'd gained, she had no energy and the radiation burned her body from the stomach to her crotch. With tears streaming down her face she said, " I can't take it anymore, it's too painful, I can't do it!"

I held her and cried with her and said, "It's okay, baby? Cry all you want, I'm right here with you."

Dr. Kwan postponed the last two treatments and said, "We'll wait until she gains some weight and feels better."

She was being tortured by all of these treatments; it was difficult for Mom and me to see her so weak and fragile; we were sad and scared. All I could do was to hold her and tell her, "You're going to be okay." I was just trying to stay positive for her.

I felt so bad for Sunny; all she wanted was her mom's attention. She was an only child and was not used to sharing her mom with anyone.

Sunny liked coming home to tell her mother about her friends and all the little girl gossip in school. She wanted her mom to just sit there and listen to her. Lina couldn't do that; she was too sick, tired, and scared. She had no energy and Sunny didn't understand that at all. Three weeks later, I took Lina back to radiation to finish her last two treatments.

Months later, Lina was feeling better and said, "I'm going to start taking Sunny to school in the mornings, and therapy in the afternoons, once a week." Lina's appetite was coming back; she was now eating better and gaining weight.

Six months later when we visited the oncologist, he said, "I'm ordering a CAT scan and blood work to see if the tumor has shrunk."

The tests results came back negative, and the mass was gone. We were so happy to hear this we were screaming, crying, and hugging Dr. Kwan while I was saying to Lina, "You're going to make it, and we need to live it up!"

After leaving the hospital we took off to a Mexican restaurant and celebrated with a Cadillac margarita, chips, guacamole and salsa.

Al had stayed in Mississippi all the while Lina and his daughter were in California.

My daughter Natalie and some of her friends told me they saw Al out at night with his friends having a grand ol' time. Meanwhile, Mom and I were busting our asses taking care of Lina and Sunny in California.

After Lina got stronger and was feeling better, I had a talk with her about Al. I told her what I'd heard and she was very upset about it. He was taking it easy in Lake Cormorant while we were fighting to keep Lina alive.

I had taken on a big responsibility when I took Lina and Sunny under my care. I was exhausted and angry with Al.

Lina called Al and chewed him up. "Dammit! Why aren't you calling your daughter every week like a father should?"

After ten months of doctors, chemo, radiation and all the responsibilities I put myself through, I was shot. I ended up in the emergency room several times due to stress. My doctor advised me to step back and let someone else take over. I just couldn't do it. Lina depended on me.

She called Al again and told him, "You need to move to California to help my mom and Shirley with Sunny."

After ten months, maybe his dad tired of taking care of Al and the house he'd provided for them? Whatever the reason, Mr. Collins put the house up for sale and Al didn't have a choice but to move to California.

Chapter 41

Sad Sunny - 2003

Lina was going through chemotherapy one day while Sunny (age eight) and I were on our way to school in the morning. The school was about two blocks from my house. Sunny was in the back of my car crying and screaming at the top of her lungs: "I don't want to go to school! I hate my life!"

While I was driving, I looked into the rearview mirror and saw that Sunny had taken her seat belt off and started to open the car door. I immediately pressed my foot on the brake and Sunny's body flew forward. I put the car in Park, got out, opened her door and yelled, "Sunny put your safety belt back on!" I got back in the car and pressed the Child Lock so Sunny couldn't open the door again. Sunny was shouting like a crazy kid, "I hate you! I hate Mom!" and on and on.

I was in tears, myself; I couldn't believe what had just happened. When I got to the school, I parked my car and went to the backside of the passenger door and open it for Sunny to come out. I took a few deep breaths then grabbed Sunny's arm and walked her to the school's office.

The school receptionist at the front desk asked, "What's wrong?"

While sobbing I responded, "I need to see a counselor or the principal, my niece threatened to jump out of my car while I was driving."

The receptionist immediately called the principal and he asked me to step into his office.

I then turned around and told the receptionist, "Please don't leave Sunny alone."

The receptionist took Sunny in another room with an adult to watch over her.

"What's going on?" The principal Mr. Ellis, inquired.

"Thank you for seeing me, Mr. Ellis," I said, wiping away my tears. "Sunny's mom has terminal cancer, and I'm taking care of her and Sunny along with my mom. Sunny just threatened to jump out of my car while on our way to school, and was saying she hates everyone and everything."

I then recounted for the principal three other incidents at the house with Sunny...

One afternoon, Lina, Sunny and I were in the kitchen when the two of them started arguing. They both had real bad tempers and seldom agreed on anything. Sunny got so angry she ran to the counter where the set of sharp knives are and grabbed the biggest knife and screamed, "I HATE MY LIFE!"

Lina yelled at Sunny, "PUT THE KNIFE DOWN!"

Sunny had the point of the knife toward herself. I immediately shouted at Lina, "Go downstairs to your bedroom and stay there!"

Lina reluctantly left the kitchen while Sunny was standing with the knife; the look in her eyes was a scary one for a little girl. It was a terrifying scene; I looked at Sunny and softly said, "Sunny, please put the knife down."

Sunny kept shouting, "I HATE MY LIFE, I HATE MY LIFE!"

I slowly grabbed the phone and said, "If you don't put the knife down I'm going to call 911 and the police will be here in a few minutes and will take you to the cuckoo house where all of the crazy people are."

No response. Sunny was just standing there like she was somewhere else.

"Please Sunny, put the knife down," I begged.

She just kept staring at me like she wasn't there.

Softly I said, "I'm pressing 9 then 1 and then 1." She knew very well that I wasn't bluffing. I was going to call the police for help.

Sunny finally put the knife on the counter, while crying and saying, "I hate her! I hate her!"

I grabbed her and held her tight while she cried. I said, "Sunny, I love you and your mom does too. Please, don't ever do this again."

On another occasion, my sister Graciella and her three daughters came to visit from Illinois.

Graciella is the second craziest of all my sisters. She is the shortest of all and has a thick body, but she's also very sexy. She's super hyper, mouthy, and makes the funniest face when she's talking. She loses her temper at times, but she's also hilarious and a lot of fun too.

Kim was fifteen, beautiful, blonde with brown eyes olive skin, petite with a cute little figure.

Maggie was eleven, also beautiful with brown hair, big brown eyes, darker skin than Kim's, a cute little nose and of course a little figure too.

Becky was two, cute as can be, and funny as hell (definitely taking after her mom's side of the family). She loved to dance and had a lot of rhythm. For sure I know this child is going to be trouble like some of my siblings and me.

Sunny and Maggie were in the living room playing. Sunny got angry with Maggie and decided to open the door to the balcony and jump off. Our living room and kitchen are on the second floor.

I was in the kitchen cooking when I heard the screams and ran to the living room. Maggie was screaming and grabbing Sunny, trying to pull her back from the ledge of the balcony and saying, "NO SUNNY, PLEASE DON'T DO IT!"

I immediately ran to help Maggie and brought Sunny back inside the living room. I was so angry and frightened; I yelled at Sunny, "Why are you doing this? What's wrong with you?"

Sunny just said, "Maggie made me angry."

I calmed Sunny and told her not to do this again. I don't think Sunny would have ever carried through with any of her threats. I believe they were mostly acting out her need to get the attention she felt was missing in her life.

Another day, I was in the backyard replacing some of the flowers in my garden; Sunny was sitting on the patio watching me. Lina was sleeping; she'd had another round of chemotherapy.

Our old cat was asleep in one of the lounge chairs in the garden. I went to the side of the house to the trashcans and came back and to my surprise Sunny was standing and had our fifteen-year-old cat in her arms. She didn't know I was behind her when I saw her toss our cat like she was bored with it.

I screamed as loud as I could at Sunny, "NO! Why are you doing this to my cat?" She looked at me as if nothing happened and softly said, "I didn't do anything." Then she turned and ran inside the house.

I didn't chase her inside because I knew her mother was asleep and I wasn't going to say anything to upset Lina.

I rushed to find my cat and when I did I held her while I cried and whispered, "I'm so sorry Es. I love you. Please forgive her!"

I told my mom what Sunny did and we agreed not to leave her alone with any of the pets again. I lived in fear of my pets being abused by this little girl who had so much anger inside of her.

In the course of a few months Sunny was forced to leave her friends, start a new school, adjust to living in our house, and do it all without a mother or father who could take care of her. It was a lot for a little girl to take. She was angry with her mother for being sick, her dad for not being with her, and angry with me because I was the one in control of her. She took her anger out on my pets, was getting more and more out of control, and needed help.

The school principal got Sunny to see a counselor once a week. He also referred her to counseling sessions outside of the school.

The following week I began taking Sunny to the sessions. The meetings were for children who had lost a loved one or were going through the process of losing a loved one.

When Lina got strong enough to take over some of Sunny's care, she pulled Sunny out of the therapy sessions. She insisted, "I don't want my daughter in therapy, she doesn't needed it." Even though Lina had witnessed the knife incident she still didn't think therapy was necessary. Lina was in total denial.

Chapter 42

Victoria's Secret - October 2004

My birthday was coming up in October and Lina's cancer was in remission. So I declared, "It's time to go to Vegas and celebrate." I grabbed my phone and called Natalie in Lake Cormorant. "Hey, would you like to meet us in Vegas?"

"Yeah, Mom! Sounds like fun." Natalie was thrilled.

Then I called my sisters Gia and Tanya and when Lina was awake I gave her the news about the trip. When Torreey came home I had already arranged our trip. We were all excited and couldn't wait to be there.

On Friday morning, Lina, Tanya, Gia, Torreey and I took a taxi to LAX to catch our plane for Vegas. We all proceeded to board, and when we got to the entrance door of the plane, I was in front of Lina. All of a sudden, Lina started saying as loud as she could while I was trying to find our seats, "She's a famous Latin soap opera star!"

Gia took her camera out and began taking pictures of me. Everyone in the plane was staring and waving at me, so I just went along with it and smiled back at everyone. This is what we sisters do every time we get together; everything is about laughing and having a good time.

Natalie met us at the Vegas airport and from there we took a cab to the Luxor Hotel where I had booked two rooms. One room with double queen-size beds for my three sisters and my daughter, the other room for Torreey and I.

"Girls!" I said when we got to the hotel, "if you guys don't get along and get into a fight or any kind of trouble - DO NOT FUCKING call me! This is my birthday weekend and you guys are not going to fuck it up for me."

They all looked at me with smiles, and Gia said, "No se preocupe hermanita, yo estoy encargada y prometemos que todo va a ser bueno." ("Don't worry, little sister, I'm in charge and we promise to be good.") They all gathered around me with hugs and kisses, and Gia said, "We love you and thank you for bringing us along."

That Friday evening we all got ready to go to Chippendale's. Torreey didn't want to go with us and said, "I'll meet you gals after the show for dinner." The five of us girls were all dressed up. Lina and I always had to dress to kill. Tanya looked very pretty but not as sexy as Lina and I. Gia looked cute, and Natalie very tall and elegant with her beautiful black silky hair and next to nothing makeup, she looked like a model.

We took the elevator down and stopped at one of the bars to have a few shots of tequila before taking a cab to the Rio Hotel for the Chippendale's show. After our tequila shots we walked laughing and joking like always to the front of the hotel to catch a taxi. While waiting for the cab, Gia kept crossing her legs and was saying in Spanish, "Me duele la panocha," ("My cuchi is hurting.") We all looked at each other and began screaming with laughter.

Natalie was already in tears from hearing Gia repeating the same thing over and over, "Me duele la panocha," ("My cuchi is hurting me.")

Gia was wearing a skirt over new Victoria Secret G-string underwear. She kept saying, "I don't know how you guys like the G-string underwear, they torture your panocha." To everyone's surprise, Gia and Lina moved to a corner of the hotel and Gia lifted her skirt. Lina let out a scream of laughter that caused the rest of us and some of the people who were in line with us to turn around immediately.

Natalie yelled, "What happened? What's so funny?"

By then Lina was approaching us with tears in her eyes. She was trying to tell us what happened but she kept laughing and laughing and couldn't get the words out. "Hay hueputa!" she kept repeating.

Gia came walking toward us also laughing.

Natalie kept asking, "What's so funny?" She was laughing without knowing anything so we all ended up laughing together until Lina finally said in Spanish, "Gia, se puso el G-string al rebez." ("Gia put her G-string on backwards.")

Oh my God! We all busted out laughing and screaming at the same time; tears were running down our faces; my stomach was aching, the whole thing was ridiculous. The people in front of and behind us were also laughing without knowing what was so funny.

We were already a little loose from the tequila shots, and hearing about this just put us over the top. No wonder her panocha was hurting her.

A few minutes later we got to the front of the line and climbed in the next cab. The taxi driver was a Middle Eastern man with a very heavy accent. Four of us were in the back of the cab and one in front. We were still laughing and talking in Spanish.

Gia made a bad choice with a hair treatment before coming to Vegas, and as a result was now nearly bald. She looked like a man with a skirt on.

The taxi driver was laughing with us even though he didn't have a clue what we were talking or laughing about. He asked, "Where you girls want to go?"

"To the Rio Hotel for the Chippendale's show," I yelled out from the back of the cab.

He turned around and said, "You ladies having too much fun!"

We all responded with a big YES!

He then asked for our names.

I opened my mouth and loudly said, "Her name is Victoria," pointing to Gia."

"Ohh, I like it Victoria," the taxi driver nodded approvingly.

"Oh, shit!" Tanya responded, while we exploded with laughter.

Gia protested, "That's not my name!"

Of course, I interrupted her and said to the taxi driver, "Victoria is her name, and she also has a secret."

This time we all screamed even louder.

With a smile, the taxi guy said, "You crazy girls. You got secret, what secret?" This driver was just as funny as Gia.

"You want to know what her secret is, taxi man?" I shouted.

He said, "YES! YES! YES!"

Gia, by this time, was trying to cover my mouth and saying, "Maje, no, no, no le diga lo del calzon, me da verguenza."("Hey, no, no, don't tell him about my G-string, I'm embarrassed.")

We were getting closer to the Rio Hotel, so I said, "Taxi man, Victoria put her G-string underwear in front instead of the back and the G-string is torturing her panocha, that's why Victoria has a fucking secret!"

Natalie, Lina, Tanya and Gia were roaring with laughter and holding on to their bellies, they couldn't believe I said that to the cab driver.

By now the taxi man was also in tears, he dropped us in front of the Rio Hotel but before we got out, he asked, "What 'panocha' mean?"

Instead of saying the word I decided to spell it out: "P---Y."

The taxi man busted out laughing and said, "You girls too crazy!"

"Here, taxi man. I'm giving you a nice tip for being such a good sport and for putting up with five drunken bitches."

"Thank you for showing me good time, and stay out trouble," he shouted, driving away with a smile on his face.

We got inside the Chippendale's nightclub and found a table in the middle of the front section. The show started and the gorgeous men began dancing. The women went crazy, screaming and clapping. In the middle of the show, one of the dancers came down from the stage. Tanya, Lina, Natalie and Gia were pointing at me, trying to get him to sit on my lap. The performer approached our table and instead of sitting on my lap, he sat on Gia's. We couldn't believe it, so here we go again, screaming like crazy. He was dirty dancing on top of

Gia while she kept repeating, "I'm a grandma, I'm a grandma," but the dancer didn't seem to care. After a while he moved on to another girl, leaving Gia helpless with laughter.

When Gia could speak again, she said to me, "Maje, vamos al bano." ("Hey, lets go to the bathroom.") On the way there, she complained, "This fucking G-string is killing me and I need to get it off." Gia went into one of the bathroom stalls and I followed her into the stall next to hers. While Gia was trying to change her G-string, I climbed on the toilet seat with my camera and snapped a picture of her. Gia looked up, saw me with the camera, started laughing and said, "Hueputa, Maje, no me tome fotos en el escusado." ("Hey, don't take pictures of me in the toilet.") I was laughing so hard I almost fell off.

The show ended and Torreey was already waiting for us outside. We all walked to Buzzio's restaurant for dinner and drinks. Two hours later we were dancing at the Luxor Hotel where we got pretty wasted. We were out until 4:00 in the morning; then we decided to give it a rest and go to bed. Gia, Tanya, Lina and Natalie went to their room. Torreey and I went to ours.

The next morning about 10:00, the phone in our room rang. Natalie was calling me and said, "Mom, you need to go with us to find an optometrist for Tanya."

"Natalie," I said, "remember what I told you guys before coming, DO NOT BOTHER ME WITH ANY SHIT! You guys deal with it yourselves. I'm fucking hungover and don't want to hear anything about Tanya's eyes."

So the girls all went together and found an optometrist for Tanya to buy new contact lenses.

After they got back to the hotel, Tanya wanted to stay in the room to rest. Gia, Lina and Natalie put on their bathing suits and came out to the pool where Torreey and I were sunbathing and relaxing.

Torreey got up and went to sit in the pool; Natalie sat next to me and said, "Mom, I got to tell you what happened last night." She was already cracking up.

Gia opened her mouth and said, "Natalie don't ruin your mom's birthday."

Lina was laughing hysterically.

The waitress came by and we ordered cocktails. Natalie looked at me and said, "Okay, this is what happened after we got in the room last night..."

Gia had quickly put on her PJs, Lina and Natalie did the same. Tanya was the last one like always. Tanya kept talking to herself while Gia, Lina and Natalie were cracking up at her. Tanya forgot to bring her container for the contact lenses, so she grabbed a drinking glass, poured the solution and placed her hard contact lenses in the glass. She said, "Make sure NO ONE touches this glass!"

Gia kept farting and farting and, after a while, they all fell asleep. About three hours later, Gia had to pee. She was also very thirsty from drinking so much booze. When Gia got up, she immediately grabbed a drinking glass and drank up the water. Then she peed and went back to bed.

About 9:00 a.m., Tanya woke up and was screaming so loud they all jumped out of bed and asked, "What's wrong?" By this time, Tanya was out of control, her eyes were popping out and she was in psycho mode.

Lina was shaking, and Gia was just sitting there. Her hair was sticking up like always when she woke up in the morning. "She looked like Don King," Natalie characterized her.

Natalie calmly asked Tanya, "Why are you yelling?"

Tanya turned around and said, "I told you guys not to touch this fucking glass, and my contact lenses were in there!" She screamed, "Who the fuck took my lenses? I can't fucking see a thing, you fucking bitches!"

Lina, Gia and Natalie looked at each other and all of a sudden Gia opened her mouth and said, "I tink I drank that and I have soom ting in my troot." Gia started coughing and Tanya jumped on the bed to smack Gia. But Natalie grabbed Tanya and pulled her away from Gia.

Listening to Natalie's description, I was laughing so hard with Lina, and Gia, I could hardly breathe. Natalie could barely tell me the whole story because she kept laughing while she was explaining what happened.

Natalie was able to calm Tanya down, and that's when they called me to go with them to find an optometrist.

We got our rest by the pool but kept laughing and imitating Gia swallowing and gagging on the contact lenses.

Tanya never came to sit by the pool with us. She was still upset. Later, we went back to our room, bathed, and got ready to go out to dinner. We all met downstairs at the bar and had a few cocktails. Natalie sat next to me and said, "Hey Mom, I gotta tell you what happened in the room again." Natalie was laughing once more; I was already cracking up because I knew more shit was going to hit the roof. Anytime you put Lina, Tanya and Gia together in a room for twenty-four hours is a mistake.

"Mom, this is what happened, Natalie continued. "Gia was constipated and full of gas and couldn't take a shit and we all kept laughing at her. Gia sat on the toilet and finally crapped but when she wiped her butt the toilet paper had a little blood. Gia came out of the bathroom and told us what had happened while Lina and I busted out laughing."

Tanya didn't say a word she was still seething.

I turned around and said, "Gia, you know why your booty was bleeding?"

Gia shrugged. "I constipated."

"No, you're not! The hard contact lense came out and ripped your *culo*!" ("butt!") And here we go again! Laughing like crazy.

After a few drinks we all got up and went to meet a couple of Las Vegas friends for dinner at the Mirage Hotel. We ate and had drinks for at least four hours and then our acquaintances had to go home.

Gia, Lina, Tanya, Natalie, Torreey and I went back to our hotel and gambled a little. Torreey was having some luck at the blackjack table and played for a while.

The girls were not really gamblers, so we went to one of the bars and had a few more cocktails. After the bar, we walked around and ended up in a store that had oxygen treatments. Lina asked the guy behind the counter to explain how the treatment worked.

He showed us a piece of a plastic tube and said, "You insert the tubes in your nostrils. The oxygen will make you feel better the next day after too much drinking." The tubes looked just like the ones they use at the hospital when you need oxygen.

"Let's try it," we all shouted. To our surprise, the oxygen came in various flavors. We each selected a different one; melon, lemon, orange, strawberry, pineapple, and began our treatment.

We all sat down with the tubes in our nostrils and we were making a lot of noise; people walking by were staring at us. We waved at them and had them come in and try it too. A bunch of guys walked by and saw us laughing and having fun, so they came inside and joined us. After a while we had enough and left the store; by then it was close to 2:00 a.m., and we were getting tired since we were out late the night before. We found Torreey back at the blackjack table and retired to our rooms.

The next day we all met downstairs with our bags, ready to go to the airport and fly home. Natalie came over and said, "Mom, guess what happened last night?"

"Oh shit, not again!"

"Tanya got into it with Gia and I had to stand in the middle so Tanya wouldn't hit Gia," Natalie whispered. "Lina was sitting on the bed crying and wailing about having cancer. They were screaming so loud that security came to the door. I opened the door and the security guy asked me, 'What's going on in the room?'

" 'I'm a therapist and I'm having a session with them.' I told him, dead serious.

"He goes, 'Okay, ma'am. But you need to keep it down or else I'll be back and I'll have to kick you all out of the room.'

"Yes, sir! 'I'll make sure to keep it quiet,' I promised him. So I went back inside and the girls were already calmed."

Tanya was the one who always started something.

Gia was already in bed and had covered her whole body and head with the blanket; she was afraid of Tanya attacking her.

Lina had taken her anxiety pill and was already relaxing.

Natalie rolled her eyes, laughed, and said, "OMG Mom, this was a fucking crazy trip with all the psycho sisters!"

They say. "What goes on in Vegas, stays in Vegas." But not in our case; it all went back to Los Angeles and Lake Cormorant too.

Chapter 43

Disneyland Disaster - 2005

It was now spring of 2005. Natalie was coming home to Redondo Beach with her son Mason for a week during Spring Break. We had plans to go to Disneyland with Mason and Sunny. I had reserved a room to stay at the Disney Hotel with Natalie and the kids. Lina was going to stay home with Mom and take it easy.

At this point, Sunny was ten years old and very demanding. Lina yelled and screamed at Sunny a lot. The cancer and all of the medication had taken control of Lina. She had gained a lot of weight following the chemo and radiation and, even though she was in remission, she was angry and unhappy most of the time. She was on medication for pain (Vicodin), for sleeping (Ambien), anxiety pills, and an inhaler for asthma.

That morning, Lina came in the kitchen were I was standing, with a grumpy face, and said, "I've decided not to stay with Mom and go with you guys to Disneyland."

My eyes got big. "Really?" I said, worried. Earlier that morning, she and Sunny were in the bathroom arguing. Sunny took a shower and washed her very long hair and Lina, like always, was combing her mane when we heard screams.

Natalie, Mason and I were upstairs; we ran downstairs, opened the bathroom door, and saw Lina hitting Sunny with the brush.

Natalie yelled at Lina, "Stop, don't do that!" and took Sunny away from Lina to the other bedroom.

I tried calming Lina down while she kept repeating, "Fucking kid is driving me crazy."

I could hear Sunny screaming in the other bedroom while Natalie was talking to her.

Lina was trembling, crying, and saying, "She's a brat and I'm fucking tired of her attitude."

"Lina," I said, pulling my hair up in a ponytail, "you need to stay home with Mom. Just let Sunny go with Natalie, Mason and I." Lina needed some time away from Sunny but she didn't agree. "I don't want to stay home with Mom because Mom gets on my nerves too," she said, making a sour face and walking away to get ready.

When Natalie finally calmed Sunny we all got in the car and left for Disneyland. Lina sat in front. Natalie, Mason and Sunny were in the back seat.

Lina wasn't happy at all. She came along with us but all the chemo, radiation, medications and not knowing whether she was going to survive or not was making her angry and scared. She always had a bad temper but her personality these days was frightening. I couldn't blame her; she'd gone through so much pain and suffering to stay alive; she was afraid of the unknown. Was she going to be here next year or not? The future was terrifying.

Lina was also very irritated with her husband Al. He had moved to California and was living in a little apartment about fifteen minutes from us.

She once asked me, "Can Al move in your house with us, too?"

I was surprised and needed to think fast. I didn't want to hurt her feelings, so I said, "I'm sorry, Lina, I just can't have Al living in our house. It's too much for Torreey and I to handle." But I could tell right away that she was already pissed off with my answer.

Sometimes Lina expected too much from me; she was often frustrated and upset. It was as if she hated me for no reason.

I tried to ignore her most of the time; I knew she had gone through a lot. I kept myself busy with aerobics, work, friends, and so on. I encouraged her to find new friends, especially the parents of Sunny's friends. Lina had a different lifestyle than mine. I was used to having parties at the house, and loved going to dinner, movies, and dancing with friends. My life had changed when I brought her and Sunny to live with us. I gave up a lot for Lina and felt unappreciated by her. I gave up the parties my husband and I loved having, the dinners, and the movies, even vacations. Lina acted like she owned me, and didn't like it if I paid too much attention to my daughter and my grandson when they came to visit. Plus, she was infuriated with her husband for putting her in this position.

Lina's attitude was horrible; she didn't care if she hurt anyone. She had become a very different person; she was even mean to our mom.

Mom didn't say anything to me, but one of my sisters called and said, "Mom calls crying, and tells me about how mean Lina is to her." Mom apparently didn't want me to know, and to have one more thing to worry about.

I thought and thought about it and needed to do something, so I went online and got some info. I also asked Lina's doctor about the side effects of chemo and radiation.

Dr. Kwan said, "Everyone's different, but it's evident that Lina's side effects are very ugly and hard to control."

She was very depressed but refused to get any help. She didn't want to accept it and she also didn't care about anyone's feelings. It was more about: "I have cancer and you have to put up with me whether you like it or not." She liked having a cocktail or two and afterwards she used the asthma inhaler that had steroids. The chemo was full of steroids that poisoned her body to kill the cancer cells. As much as I hate to say it, she was like a little monster waiting to explode into something huge.

Dr. Kwan had recommended she see a therapist, but Lina continually declined to get the help she desperately needed.

One time while Lina and I were waiting to see the oncologist, a therapist, Mrs. Heston, appeared in the waiting room. Mrs. Heston introduced herself and told everyone that she was there to help anyone who needed to talk.

Lina and I sat and listened to some of the people talking and crying about their lives, about being scared of death and so on. Lina was not happy about this and said, "I'm going outside for a while. I can't take this shit!"

I thought this was my opportunity to talk to the therapist. So I raised my hand and asked Mrs. Heston, "How can I deal with my sister as her caregiver? She's mistreating my mom and me. We know she's afraid, but we're afraid too. She has a mean temper, lousy attitude, and bad manners most of the time. She's always had a temper, but it's gotten worse. She's making sure our mom and I are miserable, and we don't know how to deal with her crappy attitude anymore. I've been hospitalized several times because of too much stress."

Lina walked in the room while I was still talking and she heard me say how our mom and I were tired of her behavior. She threw me a dark look. I guess she never thought I'd open my mouth and ask for help.

I thought, OMG I'm in a lot of trouble. She's going to kill me!

Mrs. Heston answered, "This is the perfect time to let your loved one know about your feelings. It's not only about the cancer patient but also about the caregivers."

Lina, of course, took it wrong and was very angry with me for doing this. Hmm, I thought for a moment, oh well, it is what it is and there's nothing I can do about it anymore. Except that I felt better by letting it out of my system and Lina had walked in at the perfect time. But I knew for sure she was going to hate me for it. I didn't mean to hurt her. I just needed help.

By the time we got to Disneyland, Lina's attitude had not changed, especially after hearing me talking on the phone with my husband Torreey about a piece of land we'd purchased in Lake Cormorant, Mississippi and had just closed escrow. Lina was infuriated that we bought a piece of land there. She'd said to a close friend of the family, "Shirley should have bought me a house in Redondo Beach instead of a fucking piece of land in Mississippi." She was practically steaming angry by the time we got to the Disney Hotel; she wasn't only annoyed with Sunny but also with Natalie and me.

When we got to our room, we left our luggage and immediately went out to the park to go on the rides. Natalie and I had a great time riding with the kids. Lina pretended to be happy.

Lina didn't want to go on all the rides, and sometimes I'd stay with her while Natalie, Mason and Sunny rode the white knuckler roller coasters. I could tell from her expression that she was still mad, but I pretended not to let it bother me. I just wanted to have a good time with my daughter and the kids.

Around 10:00 p.m., I said, "Let's go back to the hotel and have a slice of pizza and a cocktail." We were going to get up early in the morning, have breakfast with the Disney characters, then go back to the park for more rides.

We stopped by an Italian restaurant and ordered pizza, a margarita for Lina and I, and a martini for Natalie. I drank my margarita slowly and noticed that Lina was already ordering another one. Natalie was also not drinking much since we had to get up early. Lina didn't care and was still on a slow boil.

"Lina," I said, "you need to stop drinking." She ignored me and continued downing her cocktail.

Natalie and the kids were done with their dinner and were already tired. Natalie got up and said, "Mom, I'm taking the kids up to the room so they can bathe and get ready for bed."

"We'll be up soon," I called after her.

When Lina finished her second drink I immediately said, "We need to go up to our room." While walking to the hotel elevator I noticed that Lina was not saying a word. I knew she was still pissed off. The alcohol didn't help her calm down at all. When we got to our room the kids were both bathed and had their pajamas on. Mason was already in bed watching TV with Natalie.

Sunny was sitting on the other bed also watching TV.

"My turn to get in the shower and get cleaned," I said, trying to sound happy. I took a quick shower and put on my pajamas; my bed was in the living room, a pull-out couch. When I came out of the bathroom Lina was sitting on the bed with Sunny. She had opened a bottle of wine that was in the refrigerator and had filled up a glass. She grabbed her inhaler, took a puff, and asked me, "Do you want a glass of wine?"

"No I don't," I said, and reminded her about getting up at 7:00 a.m. to have breakfast with the Disney characters. I also warned her not to mix her inhaler with alcohol, but she pretended not to hear me.

At 11:30 p.m., Mason was sound asleep and Sunny was still awake. Lina continued to drink her wine.

I went into the living room to get my bed ready and heard Natalie say, "Lina, please turn off the lights and go to bed."

But Lina refused to pay attention to her and started saying bad things about her in-laws, cursing each one of them up and down and ending with: "I hate them all!"

By now, Natalie was very upset at Lina for maligning her husband and in-laws. She told Lina with an exasperated sigh. "Stop calling them names – they're also my son's family."

Sunny was sitting on the bed covering her ears and crying.

I could see them from where my bed was so I got up and yelled, "Lina! Stop it!" But she wouldn't.

Lina continued bad-mouthing the Collins, while Natalie defended them and reminded Lina, "Mr. Collins has been helping you with money. He sends you $1,500 a month to live in my mom's house with Sunny. He's not an asshole!"

Mr. Collins sent a monthly check in my name. I'd cash the check, and keep $200 for utilities, and give Lina $1,300 for her to spend on herself and Sunny.

Lina didn't like what Natalie was saying, apparently. I was standing by the door of the bedroom when Lina got up from her bed and jumped on top of Natalie and started punching her.

Sunny was screaming and crying. "STOP! STOP!"

Natalie rose up and pushed Lina off the bed, causing her to fall on the carpet floor.

I yelled, "I'm calling security!" I ran into the living room to grab the phone and all of a sudden found myself face down on the floor. Lina had jumped me from behind. I rolled over and Lina got on top of me, throwing punches and calling me names. I was protecting my face with my hands and couldn't get Lina off me; it was like she weighed three hundred pounds. I couldn't move her; she was incredibly strong.

In the meantime, Sunny kept screaming for her mother to stop, and Natalie was calling security.

I kept yelling, "STOP IT! STOP IT!" But Lina would not listen.

Unexpectedly, Natalie came up behind Lina and grabbed her in a bear hug. I immediately got up while Natalie was holding on to Lina, and yelling. "Open the front door so I can push her out of the room."

I'd hurried and opened the door and Natalie, struggling, finally got Lina outside. Lina was like a monster; like a mad woman on PCP.

Sunny kept screaming and screaming. I immediately grabbed the phone, called security, and said, "Please come, my sister has gone insane!" For some reason, security never came when Natalie first called them.

Sunny was now sitting on my bed, trembling. I went over to her and held her tight while crying with her.

Lina was out in the hallway screaming, kicking the door, and yelling, "Give me my daughter, you assholes!"

Sunny was whimpering, "I don't want to go with my mom, she's crazy."

It was now 1:00 in the morning when I grabbed the phone with my hands shaking and called Al, and told him what had happened. I said, "You need to come right now and get Lina." Thank God, Mason never woke up to see any of this; he was somehow sound asleep throughout the whole ugly scene.

Natalie was looking through the door peephole and said, "Mom, she's near the elevator, charging toward the door, kicking and screaming."

Natalie saw the elevator door open and security grabbed Lina and held her tight. I could hear Lina screaming out of the top of her lungs, telling security, "I have cancer, and they have my daughter in the room."

Security calmed her down and accompanied Lina to the lobby of the hotel to wait for her husband.

A few minutes later, we heard a knock on our door and a gentleman saying, "Ma'am. It's security, please open the door."

Natalie opened and two security guys came in. Sunny was sitting on my bed crying and still shaking.

One of the security guys asked me, "Who are you?"

"I'm her sister," I said.

He asked us if we'd been drinking?

"Natalie and I had one cocktail around 10:00 p.m. Lina had two and she then opened a bottle of wine and drank the entire bottle by herself. She has cancer, had chemo, radiation – and an inhaler that she used after having so much to drink," I explained to security.

The security guys looked at Sunny and one asked, "Do you want to go with your mother?"

"No, please, help my mom. I want to stay with my aunt and cousin," Sunny replied, sobbing.

Security left Sunny with us until Al appeared. They knew that the insane person was Lina, not Natalie or I. They would have taken Sunny from us if they thought that we were intoxicated.

Sunny was a little calmer now, and said, "I want to stay and live with you, Aunt Shirley. My mom is crazy."

"Oh sweetheart, I'm so sorry about your mom," I said while holding on to her.

I'd told security that her father was on his way, so they stayed with us until he arrived.

About 2:00 a.m., Al knocked on the hotel door. He hugged Sunny and said, "You need to go home with your mom and me."

"Al," I said, "if you want to leave Sunny with us to finish her trip at Disneyland, it's okay with us."

"No, I need to take her home with Lina," he insisted.

"Al, I hate to do this and as much as it hurts, I can no longer have Lina staying in my home. Please come by the house tomorrow and pick up all of her belongings," I said with deep sadness.

"Okay, I will," Al, replied.

While Al was driving the three of them home, Lina called our mom, sisters, brothers and Al's family and told them all that Natalie and I beat the shit out of her at Disneyland. I was told by some of my sisters and Mom that Lina called them around 3:00 a.m. Al, of course, believed everything Lina said to him.

I know she didn't mean anything she did to Natalie and me, but it destroyed our relationship for a while. I could no longer trust and keep her in my house. She was no longer the sister I knew.

Chapter 44

Tempestuous Divorce - 2006

James and Natalie were very happy with their lives. After a year of marriage, Natalie got pregnant and had Mason. A year later they moved to their beautiful brand-new two-story house by a golf course and lake. They enjoyed traveling and entertaining. James was a good provider; and in the beginning he took good care of his wife and son.

Natalie was a wonderful mother to Mason, but when it came to house chores she wasn't interested at all. She preferred someone else do the housework. When Mason got a little older, she enrolled him in a preschool and found herself a part-time job working for an immigration attorney. She learned as much as she could and thought she'd open her own business someday. She was not the kind of mother that wanted to stay home and just raise her kid.

After giving birth, Natalie had a very hard time dropping the weight she'd gained. She developed diabetes while she was pregnant and wasn't able to get rid of it. She was frustrated and hated the extra pounds. She tried very hard to exercise and eat healthy but no matter what Natalie did, she couldn't lose the surplus weight.

James was making more money and some of his wealthy buddies were divorced, partying and hanging out with young, pretty, thin women.

One day in 2005, Natalie called me upset and said, "Mom, I kicked James out of the house."

"Why?" I said, aghast.

"I have his mobile phone – listen to the conversation..."

It was a woman's voice leaving a suggestive message that I won't repeat here.

A month later, Natalie took James back, but it was too late, their relationship was damaged beyond repair. Natalie was miserable and doubted James was being totally faithful.

That's when Natalie began telling me stories about her marriage: "One weekend we attended a party that got really out of hand. One of the guys collapsed on the floor and I had to give him CPR. One of his friends was boasting that he never worries about getting arrested because some of the cops are his buddies."

I remember when I first went to visit my sister Lina and we got a ticket from a policeman. After the officer handed her the citation and left, Lina said, "I don't have to pay for this ticket."

"Why not?" I looked at her skeptically.

"All I have to do is give it to my father-in-law, and that's the end of it."

One afternoon, with no warning, someone knocked on the door and served Natalie with divorce papers. That was the beginning of her nightmares.

A month after getting the divorce papers, Natalie called me, sobbing. "Mom, I'm at a gas station and my credit cards were declined while I was trying to fill my tank with gas. I called the credit company and I'm shocked to hear that James had canceled my cards. I have no money for gas or food."

"Natalie, listen to me. I'll send you a check right away for you to get around with Mason, okay?"

In the meantime, she borrowed money from some of her friends.

Natalie and Mason stayed at the house for about a year until one day James presented her with an eviction letter.

Natalie was receiving about $1,500 every two weeks for child support, and $800 a month in spouse alimony. A total of $2,300 a month wasn't enough for her and Mason to live the way they were used to. This amount included paying a divorce attorney to represent her. The alimony was only for a year. That was all she could get from James for now. There were times when James wouldn't deposit the money in Natalie's account and she wasn't able to write any checks for her expenses. This went on for a while until she had her attorney file for James to change the payment to automatic deposits.

When she got the eviction letter from James's attorneys she called me, again sobbing. "Mom, I need to move out and find an apartment." She had full custody of Mason.

"Oh God, Natalie, who did you marry?" I couldn't believe James wouldn't provide a place for his own son to live; apparently, he wanted Natalie out so he could bring his girlfriend in. "Natalie, don't worry. By the way, fax me the eviction letter so I can show it to Torreey."

When I received the eviction document from Natalie, I went into Torreey's office and had him read it. I said, "Natalie is going to look for an apartment to live in with Mason."

Torreey looked at me very upset, and said, "What? Get Natalie on the phone!"

I called and put her on the speaker and sat in Torreey's office listening to the conversation.

"Natalie, don't look for an apartment. Find a house for sale. I will buy a house for you and Mason to live. When you settle the community property with James, you can pay us back. We will rent the house to you for $1,500 a month. Also, have your attorney send the bills to us and we'll pay those until you get your settlement. You can pay us back the rent money and the attorney fees we loaned you, and will change the deed on the house to your name, and you will take over the mortgage payments. Okay?"

That was the verbal agreement that Natalie had with Torreey and me.

Chapter 45

She's Gone - 2003-2008

After the ugly incident at Disneyland, Lina and I didn't speak to each other for about eight months. I was very sad and missed her and Sunny terribly. Her Pekingese dog Jazzie stayed with us. She was used to our home, our other three pets, and the daily walks; besides their apartment complex didn't allow pets.

I had gone overboard to help Lina and by now I was physically and emotionally exhausted. I went on with my life; and of course, my siblings were keeping me informed regarding Lina's cancer.

One evening, Gia called me and said, "I think Lina's cancer is back. She has a lump on the side of her neck and she's getting a biopsy in a week."

Two weeks later I learned that the biopsy was positive for cancer. Gia was crying while talking to me on the phone.

I was silent for a few seconds while my eyes filled with tears. "OMG, What next?"

"She's scheduled for an MRI and a CT scan," Gia replied.

"Okay, please let me know when you hear more details," I pleaded.

I didn't hear anything for a while except that Gia was spending a week at Lina's to help her out and accompany her to the appointments.

Natalie and Mason were visiting from Lake Cormorant when Gia called and said she was on her way to my house. When she appeared at the front door with tears streaming down on her face I knew it was bad news.

"Lina's cancer has spread to her kidneys. She's having surgery and will need a bag for her urine," Gia announced with teary eyes.

Our Mom was already crying while resting on her bed.

Natalie and I looked at each other, shaking our heads. "Oh shit!" I said in low spirits.

Natalie walked over to our mom, her dear grandma, and held her tight.

Seconds later, Natalie got close to me and whispered in my ear, "Mom, we need to go see Lina."

"Lets go!" I said, jumping to my feet.

Natalie and I immediately took off to Lina's apartment, knocked on the door and heard Lina say, "Who's there?"

We didn't respond but knocked again.

Lina, in her PJs, opened the door and was surprised to see us standing there. She threw herself in our arms and we all hugged and cried together. Neither of us said a word about Disneyland. We just held each other until Lina, still sobbing, said, "Oh, I missed you guys so much!"

"We missed you too," I cried.

"Let's go to my mom's house," Natalie said cheerily.

"Okay, let me change clothes," Lina replied.

While Lina was getting dressed I looked around the apartment. I couldn't believe the way they were living.

My beautiful and very ill sister was living in poverty. It was the worst place she'd ever lived in. It made me sick and sad at the same time. This was by far the lowest point in Lina's life.

When we got to my house, our mom and Gia were happy to see that we were family again. We all hugged each other with smiles and tears falling down our faces.

And from then on I started my mission again, going with Lina to her specialists' appointments. I helped her move to a better neighborhood and a bigger apartment with the help of her father-in-law, Mr. Collins. He'd agreed to help them with the rent of $1,700 a month.

Lina was excited about moving to a nicer place, but most of all Sunny was going to have her own bedroom. She'd been sleeping between her parents.

One Friday in April 2008, I rushed Lina to Harbor UCLA Hospital. She was experiencing a lot of pain in her lower back. She now had a urine bag on each side of her body due to kidney failure.

The ER doctor examined her, took a look at her record, and said, "She needs to stay in the hospital for a few days." He then ordered more tests and hours later found out that her colon had ruptured. He said, "Lina needs surgery and a colostomy bag for her stool. I assure you she will not live unless we perform this surgery."

Every member of the family who could be there was present on the day of her surgery.

Lina wasn't happy about having the operation, but felt she had no other choice. She had to do it for her little girl. She was now going to carry three bags for the rest of her life, two for her urine and one for her stool.

A few minutes later, the nurse came in to take Lina to the surgery room. We all gave her a hug, kissed; and while holding on to her hand I said, "We'll be here waiting for you when you wake up. You're going to be okay. Be strong for

Sunny." Despite the doctor's assurance that Lina was in good hands, we were all scared she wasn't going to make it.

Lina told me on several occasions, "I would have never gone through any of this shit if I didn't have a kid, and if my husband Al was a different kind of man. I'm trying to fight for my life and for my kid too."

After the nurse took Lina away we all looked at each other in panic and walked to a room where we sat and waited nervously. A couple of hours later some of us were starting to feel hungry and took off to the cafeteria for a fast bite to eat.

"I'll stay here in case the doctor comes looking for us," Ceci volunteered. Ceci is a long-lost sister who lived far away from the rest of us and seldom called or visited. When Ceci became unhappy with her marriage, she decided a break was needed and moved to California into Tanya's apartment, that's when she came to participate in Lina's care.

While we were in the cafeteria, the doctor showed up in the waiting area and told Ceci, "I'm sorry, there's nothing else we can do for your sister. The tumor has taken over her kidneys, liver and colon. She needs to get her affairs in order."

"How long does she have?" Ceci asked, bracing herself.

"About six months," the surgeon replied.

When we got back to the waiting room and heard the news from Ceci, we all looked at each other in fear; crying, hugging and not believing this was real.

I couldn't take the news and had to walk away to the restroom. I locked the door and stood there trembling, sobbing uncontrollably and throwing up in the sink. "No! No! No! This can't be true. How am I going to face her? What am I going to say to her?" I was numb and couldn't believe this was going to be the end for my dear sister.

Lina was still asleep when I walked in the room. I sat on the chair, held her hand, and stared at her while my tears were falling. I just didn't want to believe it.

When she finally woke up, a doctor came to her room and gave her the horrible news. I was standing outside of her room and could hear her sobbing uncontrollably while our mom held her and cried too.

I peeked and saw some of our family members weeping around her bed. So I waited for my turn. I wanted to be in there by myself with her.

When my turn came I walked slowly into her room with my head down. We both looked at each other without saying a word while I threw myself on her chest and hugged and cried with her.

She wasn't going to make it and there was nothing else I could do or say to save her. I had done so much over the last five years and now it was going to be the end.

With a sad face and a raspy voice, Lina whispered, "I don't want to die. I'm scared."

I was so afraid for her, the look of fear on her face and her repeating the same words to me. "I don't want to die. I'm scared!"

I will never forget it. I held her tight and said, "I don't want you to go. I'm going to miss you." We held each other and cried; that was all we could do.

Lina, Al and Sunny had just moved into their new apartment in Torrance before she had the surgery.

The hospital was releasing Lina in a week so I wanted to surprise her by going shopping for furniture with Sunny. I bought living room and dining room furnishings, a bedspread for Sunny's bed, a few picture frames for the bathrooms, decorations, silk plants, towels, and mats. I had it all delivered before her arrival.

When Lina walked into the apartment and saw all the new things, she broke down in tears. She hugged me tight and said, "Thank you! I love it all!"

"No big deal," I said.

I really didn't know what else to do to make her happy. I couldn't give her life, but at least I knew I could provide the furnishings and housewares to make her and Sunny a little happier.

After all I did to furnish her apartment, Al's mom made a comment that I probably got the money from her ex-husband to pay for everything and pretended that I bought it myself.

When Lina heard this from Al, she immediately called and told me. This of course made me very angry so I picked up the phone and called Trisha in Mississippi to clear this lie. She didn't answer her phone so I left a message: "Trisha, you are so wrong about how I bought the furniture. Please call me."

She never returned my call but she wrote me a letter that I still have, apologizing about her indiscretion. This lady just wanted to make trouble for me. She just couldn't believe that I would do anything for my sister.

In May 2008, it was time for me to go to Mississippi to visit Natalie and Mason for Mother's Day. This time my mom didn't come with me. Mom wanted to stay with Lina; she knew it was going to be her last Mother's Day with her.

I also wanted to stay but I knew it wasn't fair for Natalie and Mason not to see me. It was a tradition to spend every Mother's Day with them in Lake Cormorant, Mississippi.

Before I left, I said, "Lina, here's the telephone number of the funeral home." This was very, very difficult for me to do but I had to do it, I didn't want to arrange for her funeral. Lina and Al needed to do this together.

While I was gone Lina and Al called the funeral home and made the arrangements. She selected cremation and paid the fee of $1,500. This included taking her body to the funeral home, cremation and the ashes to be scattered in the ocean in Redondo Beach near my house.

During the last five months of Lina's life, I tried to be with her as much as possible. I played tennis in the mornings and, for lunch, we'd go out to a restaurant. But if Lina didn't feel like it, I'd cook at my house or at her apartment. Our mom and I did whatever Lina wanted. We went to the movies while Sunny was in school. Lina looked good considering she had only five months to live. She still had energy and the will to live and didn't fully accept the fact that she was dying.

It was okay with me. I didn't want to accept it either. I kept telling myself, "She's not going to die." I cried every day and night, before going to sleep, in the shower, while driving, and when I was playing tennis. No one could see my tears behind my sunglasses.

Lina didn't see me cry but she understood how much I was hurting; she was my favorite sister and she knew it. We always had so much fun together. But we also helped each other. I depended on her to watch over my kids when I met Torreey, thirty-something years ago. Now she depended on me. Only this time, I couldn't help her or give her what she wanted-life.

Sometimes Lina asked me to go to the beach with her. We'd take the beach chairs, pack a cooler with sodas and water, and stop by Chui's, a little Mexican stand a block away from the beach, and buy some carne asada tacos. We sat and watched the ocean, listened to the sound of the waves, and marveled at the dolphins swimming and playing. We sat quietly at times until she let it out and cried. We held hands and cried and hugged each other tight.

"Oh, Lina. I'm going to miss you. I don't want you to go. I don't know what I'm going to do without you," I whispered.

"I'm so afraid of dying, of not knowing where I'm going, and most of all leaving Sunny. OMG, shit, what the fuck did I get myself into?" Lina cried.

I was crying too, and with a shaky voice, I said, "Lina, imagine the most beautiful place on Earth, that's where you're going to."

Lina never once said she felt bad about leaving her husband, Al. She said, "Al lets Sunny do whatever she wants."

Lina knew it was not going to be good for Sunny to have all of the freedom she wanted, but there was nothing she could do about it; she would soon be gone.

Lina was getting weaker as the days went by. She was taking a lot of medication for her pain. She was also seeing a therapist and a chaplain that hospice provided for her.

Max, the therapist, a short Hispanic man with black hair and a very soft voice, saw Lina once a week.

Larry the chaplain, a slim and tall Caucasian man, and a kind and loving person, came once a week too. If Lina needed them more often they'd come. Both men were wonderful; we all cared and loved them for their support and help, not only with Lina but with the entire family too.

July came and it was getting close to Lina's forty-eighth birthday so I organized to have a birthday party with the family and a few friends of Lina's at my house. I ordered a beautiful cake with Lina and Niki's (our dog) pictures and names. It was also Niki's birthday. We had the party in the backyard of my house.

Lina spent most of the day on one of the lounge chairs in the backyard, wrapped in a blanket. We had a beautiful celebration for her; we all knew it would be her last.

By the end of July, hospice brought in a hospital bed to her apartment. "I don't want the hospital bed in my bedroom. I want to be where everybody always is, in the living room next to the kitchen," Lina demanded.

It was a great idea, particularly for our mom. She didn't have to go up and down the stairs to the bedroom. Mom had bad knees so it worked out for everybody.

Hospice also brought an oxygen tank; medicine was delivered to the apartment, and the hospice nurse was coming once a week to monitor Lina.

By August, Lina was already too weak to stand up, walk alone, or bathe. She had lost her voice; the cancer had gone to her throat and was traveling to her eyes next. She cried and cried while writing on a piece of paper what she wanted.

"Don't cry, Lina," I said. "I'm gonna go out and buy you a bell and a board with special pens for you to write down what you want, okay?"

She stared at me with her eyes full of tears and mouthed, "Thank you, I love you!"

A few hours later I came back with the bell and board and told her, "Write down whatever you want for lunch and I'll cook it or get takeout, okay?"

Sometimes she'd request lobster, crab legs, lamb chops, steak, spaghetti, fruits, and desserts – anything that she wanted.

Lina's husband Al was being unreasonable. He refused to buy any expensive food. He said, "We don't have money to spend on that."

On several occasions I argued with him, saying, "You have money for cigarettes, but not for your dying wife."

Al was working as a limousine driver. His dad paid the rent, and Al was receiving a check every month from his dad's business.

My impression of Al was that he was self-centered and he could be stingy when it came to Lina. He always had money to go fishing and hunting but it seemed like he seldom had money for her. He knew I'd buy anything that Lina wanted to eat.

He was also helping himself to Lina's Vicodin. He said, "I have migraine headaches and need the pills."

One evening, Lina's neighbor, Kerrie, witnessed that Al refused to buy a steak and fruit that Lina wanted for dinner. Here's what happened:

Lina couldn't get out of bed; she had the phone by her side of the hospital bed. She didn't have a voice. She'd dialed my number and when I picked up the phone I knew who it was. She was trying to tell me something but couldn't; I could hear her whispering at the other end.

"Lina! Lina!" I said, "I know it's you, okay. I'll be there in a few minutes."

I immediately called Kerrie and pleaded, "Please go next door and see what Lina needs."

Kerrie knocked on the door and Al opened it. Kerrie saw Lina crying and rushed to her side to hug her, and asked, "What's wrong, honey?"

While crying and with her hand shaking, Lina wrote on the board, "*I want a steak and fruit and Al won't buy it for me.*"

Kerrie responded, "Babe, I'm going back to my apartment and will bring you the steak and fruit you want, okay?"

When I got to Lina's apartment, she was still crying. Al immediately went upstairs to his bedroom to watch TV. I'm sure he didn't want to look me in the eyes.

I hugged Lina and told her to calm down. She showed me what she'd written on the board. OMG, *are you kidding me, Al?* I raged inwardly. I wanted to kick his ass if only I was bigger and stronger.

Five minutes later, here comes Kerrie with a beautiful thick and juicy steak and fruit for Lina.

Kerrie and I sat down with Lina while she ate. We were both so fucking mad at the whole situation. Lina was still crying and shaking while eating her steak and fruit. It was so painful to see my sister was dying and still her husband was so oblivious, as if he just didn't get it.

Our mom and our sisters Gia, Graciella, Ceci, Tanya, and our sisters-in-law, Sofia, and Cita came by and helped with Lina's care. Sofia was married to my older brother Edgar. She's Hispanic, about 5'2, very voluptuous, with black curly hair. She's sweet, caring and very helpful, but she will tell it like it is if you get into an argument with her. I've never had a problem with her. We always got along fine.

Cita, my younger brother Evan's girlfriend of many years, is Filipino, short with brown hair, and older than my brother. She's sweet, funny and caring too.

The hospice nurse was coming at least twice a week to bathe Lina.

Lina wasn't getting out of bed anymore. She still had the colostomy bag for her poop, and two nephrostomy bags for her urine, one on each side of her body. The belt that was holding the bags was wrapped around her tiny waist. Cleaning, removing and replacing the stool bag was the most horrible thing anyone can do. The smell was the most awful thing I've ever encountered. Every time the bag was changed, the whole apartment reeked like a sewer.

My sisters and our mom would open all the windows and light up a scented candle so that the stink would go away faster.

I'd go outside and stay until the foul odor dissipated. It was nauseating! I didn't want to hurt Lina's feelings, but she knew I couldn't do the cleaning of her bags, so I gave her foot massages instead.

One Friday evening, Al called me around 7 p.m. and said, "Shirley, you need to take Lina to the hospital. She's in a lot of pain."

According to Lina, his mother Trisha had come to help and be by her son's side when she found out from Al that our family was not too happy with his behavior. His mother came to protect him; she never wanted to accept that her son was a disappointment to Lina and me.

By this time, our family and Al's family were not on good terms. Natalie was going through a nasty divorce with Al's younger brother James.

I was furious because James refused to let Mason, my grandson, come and say goodbye to his dying Aunt Lina.

That evening, my mom and I drove to Lina's apartment, knocked on the door and rushed to Lina's side. She was lying in the hospital bed in the middle of the living room.

I couldn't lift her so I said, "Al, please carry her to my car." I had parked my car in front of their apartment.

Oh, I was so fucking mad, I wanted to kick his and his mother's ass but focused my attention on my sister instead. I just wanted to get the hell out of their way and take Lina to the hospital.

I drove my car as fast as I could, hoping that a police officer didn't stop me. The Harbor UCLA Medical Hospital was about fifteen minutes from Lina's apartment.

While driving, I glanced through my rearview mirror and could see our mom and Lina in the back seat. Mom holding her daughter, crying and telling her in Spanish, "Se va a mejorar, mamita." ("You're going to get better, my little girl.")

My tears were rolling down on my face like a faucet while I was driving; all I kept thinking about was that thoughtless husband of Lina's. *Huh? Huh?* How could someone be so cold to his dying wife? Lina needed him. She didn't deserve this kind of treatment from anyone, especially her husband.

Al wasn't helping with Lina's care. It was painful to see the man she married and had a child with be so indifferent. Lina told me she fell in love with him and married him because he was sweet, kind and loving toward her. What Lina didn't see at first, but informed me of later, was that he had two faces and was only concerned with what he wanted.

I parked my car at the emergency area, got out and said to Mom, "Wait in the car with Lina while I go inside to find a wheelchair."

I ran inside the hospital, grabbed a wheelchair and pushed it to the side of the car where Lina was sitting. Our mom was still holding on to her.

Lina was so weak she couldn't even sit on her own. I tried to move her to get her to sit in the wheelchair but it was impossible. I couldn't lift her; she was dead weight.

Lina kept crying, hugging me and whispering, "I can't do it."

I was sobbing with her and saying, "You can do it. I know you can do it, please Lina! Please help me!"

There was a black man outside smoking a cigarette who saw me crying and struggling with Lina. He rushed over and said, "Here, let me help you." The gentleman lifted Lina and sat her in the wheelchair.

"Thank you, sir, I really appreciate it!" I said, and rushed Lina with our mom by my side into the ER.

When I got to the front desk I spoke to the woman in charge: "My sister Lina is with hospice and she doesn't have much time to live."

The woman ignored me and perfunctorily said, "You'll have to wait like everybody else." She then turned around and disappeared into a back room. Some of the employees at Harbor UCLA Hospital were very rude and cruel, and this lady happened to be just one of them. The ER room was crowded as usual; there were no empty chairs. We waited over thirty minutes until a nurse called Lina's name. I grabbed the wheelchair and went inside the room with Lina and the nurse. She took Lina's vital signs and said, "Wait outside until they call you again."

Around 10 p.m. another nurse called Lina's name. I went inside with Lina where a doctor awaited us. This doctor was very unfriendly and rude; he was tall, bald and, I think, racist. He examined Lina and said, "You have to wait out in the waiting room. We have to see the critical patients first."

Lina was not coherent at this point, she was just sitting there with no life and this asshole doctor was telling me she was low priority. I wanted to scream; I couldn't understand this kind of treatment, especially by an ER doctor.

But I wasn't going to sit idly by while my sister was in desperate need of medical attention. So I left the room in a hurry, pushing the wheelchair with Lina's lifeless body, and went straight to one of the nurses; at this point I was sobbing.

"Please help me! My sister is with hospice, she's dying, the ER doctor was rude and told me to sit and wait again. Please look at her and get her inside to see a doctor who actually cares!" I begged.

Lina was just collapsed in the wheelchair, her eyes were closed and her skin was grey. I couldn't take it anymore. I wanted to scream at the top of my lungs, "Who ARE you people?! Does any one of you have an ounce of compassion?"

The nurse came back out, called Lina's name, and said, "I have a bed for her to lie down, but it might be a while before another doctor can see her."

"Thank you, thank you so much, we'll wait!" I breathed a sigh of relief.

The nurse and I put Lina on the bed in the private room and covered her with a blanket. I sat next to the bed, held her hand, then placed my forehead on the side of the bed with my tears falling in a steady stream. That's when Lina squeezed my hand like she was saying. *Don't worry. It's okay! It's okay! You've done enough.*

A few minutes later I lifted my head and could see the tears running down Lina's face as well. Her eyes were closed and she wasn't making any noise. It broke my heart to see my dying sister with no strength at all. Only teardrops on her face. I just sat there staring and crying with her in that little room.

It was past 2 a.m. when a female doctor finally came in. She examined Lina and saw that my sister was very weak and disoriented; her little body now weighed about sixty pounds. The female doctor looked at me with sad eyes and said, "She doesn't have too much longer to live."

"How much, doctor?" I asked with lips quivering.

"Two weeks, the most. There's nothing we can do at the hospital but to give her an IV and send her home," the doctor said sadly.

I don't think Lina heard any of this, she was already in a semi-comatose state. The doctor left the room and I sat there numb. My poor Lina was dying and there was nothing I could do or say that would change anything. I climbed on her bed and lay next to her. I hugged her tight and squeezed her hand and felt her weak little fragile hand squeeze mine back. I said, "Lina, I'm right here with you." I was happy that she knew I was there with her, holding her tight. I was scared and so was she. She was slowly dying and I didn't want to let her go. By then I was so exhausted I fell asleep with Lina in my arms.

At about 4 a.m., a nurse came in, woke me up, and started Lina's IV. The nurse informed me it was going to be a couple of hours before they sent Lina home.

I got up and went out to the waiting room where my mom was sitting asleep on a chair. I woke her up and said, "Mom, we're going home. Lina has an IV on and it's going to be a while before she can go home."

While walking to the car and holding on to Mom's arm. I called Tanya on my cell and explained what had happened that evening, and how I was totally drained and in need of some sleep.

"Don't worry, Shirley. I'll come by the hospital, pick her up, and take her home," she promised.

Tanya got back to the apartment with Lina after 9 a.m.

That night was the last time I saw Lina's eyes open. The week went by fast, our mom and my sisters Gia and Ceci stayed twenty-four hours a day at Lina's apartment.

Mom slept on one sofa and Gia and Ceci on the other. Lina's bed was in the middle of the living room. There was not a lot of room to walk by. She had stopped eating a week before; she had the morphine pump going into her vein. She could no longer push the button for the morphine so Ceci was in charge of pressing the control if Lina frowned or if we observed that she was not comfortable.

Ceci was the only one who could do the morphine job. She never felt like a sister to me; she never seemed to be on the same wavelength as the rest of us. She wasn't really a family person; she was married but never had or wanted kids. When we were young, she seemed to dislike Lina and me because we were more popular with the boys than she was. She always thought she was special since she went to college. She acted like she was superior to the rest of us. She wasn't a fun-seeker like Lina and me; didn't like to drink or go out dancing. She could be a pain in the ass; it was her way or no way at all. She liked to control the people she hung out with, including her husband. So she was the perfect person to push the morphine button at the end. I couldn't have done it!

Al's mom had been at their apartment for about three weeks. Al's lesbian sister Elise came to stay the last week of Lina's life. Lina didn't want them there but had no choice.

Weeks before Lina went into a comatose state, when her mother-in-law got near her bed to touch her, Lina would open her eyes as wide as possible and make faces at her. Since her voice was gone and she couldn't speak, her eyes were doing the talking.

She did the same when Al got near her bed. She knew she was dying and finally understood she had made a big mistake by marrying him. One afternoon while Mom and I were alone with Lina, she wrote. "Don't leave me alone with them. I don't trust them."

Maybe it was the medication talking? I don't think they actually wanted any harm to come to her. I think they just couldn't deal with the situation.

Three days later, I noticed that her feet were turning inwards so I called the hospice nurse.

The nurse came over, checked her vital signs, and said, "Lina has a few days left."

Lina had been in a coma for already a week, she was no longer with us and didn't look like our Lina anymore. Her face was very puffy because of kidney failure. On her neck was a huge mass surrounded by small ones that had taken over her voice box. Her body was very thin; you couldn't see it because we'd covered her with blankets all the way to her neck. All of her beauty was gone, gone, forever. She was unrecognizable; it was like she had already died months ago.

My siblings were staying at my house when we got the call from Ceci around 6:00 a.m., on Sunday, September 14, 2008. She said, "Get everyone up and get to Lina's place ASAP!"

We arrived at Lina's apartment by 7:00 a.m. We knew this was the end. We were scared and helpless but wanted her to go in peace.

Lina was holding on for as long as she could for her little girl. We all gathered around her staring at her still, grey body with tears in our eyes, waiting for the inevitable moment when her pain would finally cease.

Sunny, who at the time was twelve years old, was so very strong. She didn't know how to show her emotions. She couldn't let it out and cry. She was the opposite of her mom.

I knew she was hurting inside and I didn't know how to help her. I was drained, tired, scared, and angry. Poor little Sunny, we were all too busy concentrating on Lina.

Sunny had become a rebel. She wanted freedom and usually got it. Her dad let her spend many evenings at her girlfriend's house, sometimes she didn't even come home after school. She knew her mother was dying and didn't like coming home to it.

At one point I urged her, "Sunny, please get close to your mom and tell her you love her and that it's okay for her to go."

Poor Sunny, it was the hardest thing for her to do but her mother needed to hear it from her little girl. Lina needed to go.

My tears were rolling down my face hearing my twelve-year-old niece saying, "Please go, Momma, please!"

By then Sunny's tears were streaming down her face also. She'd finally let it out and cried.

I immediately grabbed and hugged her tight and kept her close to me. We were all crying and saying our goodbyes, and telling Lina it was okay to go.

At about 8:20 a.m. I sat by Lina's bed, held her hand and whispered, "Lina, Lina, it's me. Climb up the ladder and don't look back. Go all the way to the top. He'll be waiting for you. You will no longer have any more pain and you will be free. Spread your wings and fly. I can't go with you. Not this time. You have to do it alone. I know you can do it! I love you and I will miss you very much, you will always be in my heart no matter what."

Right after I finished my last sentence Ceci yelled out, "She's gone! She's gone!" Ceci had been monitoring Lina's heart while our sister-in-law Sofia was checking her pulse.

After hearing Ceci's words, the rest of the family gathered around her bed, held her hands, kissed her on the forehead and cried.

Her husband Al was not at the apartment when Lina passed away. He had left earlier with our sister Graciella's husband Johnny to get donuts for everyone.

A few minutes later, Ceci called the hospice nurse and informed her that Lina had passed away.

Larry the chaplain showed up and disposed of all of her medications. He also called the funeral home to pick up Lina's body.

I shook my head in disbelief and moved away from Lina's body. I sat down on the couch staring at her. Even with the oxygen tubes in her nose, she looked so peaceful lying there on that hospital bed. It brought back memories of our time in Vegas laughing with the flavored tubes in our nostrils. One of my sisters pressed on her chin so that her mouth would stay closed.

The funeral home called and said, "It will be about four hours before we can pick up her body."

I turned to Sunny and asked, "Would you like to help me put makeup on your mom?"

She nodded her head up and down and said, "Yes." She walked upstairs to Lina's bedroom and brought back her makeup purse. She pulled out a small brush and gently began to cover her mom's eyelids with eye shadow.

I grabbed a lipstick and the blush brush and completed her makeup. Even with a little bit of makeup, Lina didn't look like herself any longer. It was a totally different face that died in front of us. My sweet, beautiful, caring, and loving sister had left us with so much pain.

"Sunny," I said, "will it be okay with you if we cut some of your mom's hair to keep with us?"

"Yes," she said.

I took a pair of scissors and cut a piece of Lina's hair and placed it in a plastic bag for myself, and did the same for some of my siblings.

The funeral van arrived four hours later and it was time to say our good-byes forever.

We had our mom and Sunny go up the stairs to stay in Sunny's bedroom. We didn't want them seeing Lina's body taken away.

I moved away from Lina's body and sat on the sofa with my knees curled up staring at her peaceful face. As much as I didn't want to think about it, my sister Lina got what she wished for. I kept hearing her words, "I don't care if I die." Next, I experienced a strange shock to my body, as if I had found myself in a movie rather than in my own life.

The two Hispanic men who arrived asked us if we wanted to say our good-byes one more time before they took her body away.

I slowly got up and took a few steps toward Lina's bed, kissed her on her forehead while my tears rolled down my face and fell on hers. She looked like she was crying too.

I sat back on the couch and watched the two men cover her body. They began wrapping a white sheet over Lina's lower body and when they finally got to her face I let out a scream, "NOOO!" I was now sobbing uncontrollably, I couldn't take it anymore.

My sister Graciella jumped up grabbed me and held me tight while we cried. I could hear the rest of the family sobbing; that was the last time I saw my sweet sister's face.

Lina died with a lot of anger, partially at her husband Al for not taking better care of her. She was also angry for leaving Sunny behind. She knew that Sunny needed more discipline than she was getting at home. She was furious with her mother-in-law Trisha for always covering for her son; and at her father-in-law for not providing her with medical insurance, and not buying her a home in California like she'd wanted.

Even though she loved me, she was irritated with me because I had the life she wanted; the good husband, the big house, the new car, the frequent exotic vacations, the lavish parties, and so on.

She was angry with our mother; she always told me that Mom preferred our two younger sisters, especially Ceci, the mean one.

Al's sister arranged a mass at Saint James Catholic Church and from there I had a memorial service at my house that was attended by our family and friends only.

Lina was cremated and her ashes were scattered in the San Pedro harbor by the funeral home. Her wishes were to have her ashes scattered on Knob Hill Avenue in Redondo Beach near my house. We didn't obtain any of her ashes from her husband Al and her request was never granted.

Vita's Hospice did an excellent job in providing everything needed for my sister to be comfortable and leave this world without any pain. From the hospital bed, to the therapist, to the chaplain, to the nurses and all of the medications needed. We couldn't have asked for anything more. We are extremely grateful for all of their support and help. We couldn't have done it without them.

Jazzie, Lina's Pekingese, stayed with us after she passed away. Jazzie had been living with us for the past five years. She was a sweet little dog but she had a bad temper just like her owner, Lina. Jazzie was thirteen years old on October 31, 2012. By then she was incapacitated, I had to carry her up and down the stairs every day. I talked to Jazzie daily and told her, "You will soon be going with your real momma, Lina." Jazzie had a very happy life with us; we loved her just as much as the rest of our dogs.

On Wednesday December 5, 2012 at 7:45 p.m., I rushed Jazzie to the veterinary. The doctor immediately gave her a shot to relax her and gave me enough time to say my goodbyes to Jazzie. I rubbed her little hairy head, gave her a kiss on her forehead and whispered softly. "I love you, Jazzie, and I'm going to miss you, but it's time to go see your real mommie." I broke down crying when the doctor injected her to go to sleep forever.

I had Jazzie cremated and got her ashes a week later. I scattered them with red rose-petals at the beach in Redondo Beach in Lina's memory, just as Lina had wanted done with her ashes. We loved Jazzie dearly and miss her still.

Following Lina's passing, I kept having flashbacks of our crazy life together. I was remembering when we were in our twenties; we rented the movie *Beaches* with Bette Midler. We drank wine and laughed and cried, it was a beautiful movie about two best friends. Lina loved it; it reminded her of the two of us except that we were sisters. The times we spent at the beach together, especially at the end of her life were sad and precious. We held each other and cried knowing that she was leaving this world, leaving her little girl, leaving me, and the rest of her family forever. Just like in the movie we had watched together so long ago.

Wind Beneath My Wings was Lina's song to me. She always told me she admired me for being strong, for not giving up on anything, for always being true to myself, for not changing for anybody, and for always making her laugh.

She said, "You were the wind beneath my wings because you pushed me to do the things I never thought I could do."

Lina was a sweet girl with both a beautiful heart and a bad temper. It was okay with me. I loved her just the way she was, nobody's perfect. She was my favorite sister and my best friend too.

One of our favorite songs was *Girls Just Want To Have Fun*, by Cindi Lauper. Anytime we heard that song at nightclubs we jumped on the dance floor to sing along. It was a beautiful time! When I hear the song on the radio or anywhere else, sometimes I get emotional. Other times I can picture the two of us singing, dancing, laughing and hugging each other. The memories make me smile, and give me the strength to go on.

Every week I take a walk on the beach. Then I sit on a bench for at least a half hour. I can still see myself with Lina, hugging and crying about her dying. I will never forget the look in her eyes, her tears, her fear and mine. The memories at the beach will always be with me. Sometimes it brings me comfort and I feel her presence with me. Sometimes I smile while I'm there remembering the happy times we had together. She knew she was my favorite sister and she will always be, I cannot replace her with any of my other siblings, there's only one Lina. We had a special bond. After all that happened, good and bad, and after not receiving an apology for that horrible night at Disneyland, I still love and miss her with all of my heart.

The plastic bag with Lina's hair I keep in a small wood box. I take it out once in a while and can still smell her scent.

A month after Lina's passing I booked a ten day Mediterranean cruise to Italy for Mom, Torreey and me. We had a mini suite with two bedrooms, two bathrooms, a living and dining room and a balcony. Every evening before going to bed we left the door open so we could listen to the sound of the ocean. It was soothing and relaxing while falling asleep.

One evening at about 4:00 a.m., on our way to the Island of Malta, we heard a loud strange sound that caused us to wake up. Torreey and I jumped out of bed and slowly walked to the living room. "OMG, look at the little bird!" I exclaimed.

This small blue-gray bird was trapped inside our cabin and was trying to find her way out. We tried to help but we weren't successful, so we called the front desk. While waiting for assistance to arrive, I sat in the living room watching our feathered visitor. I remembered what I told Lina a few minutes before she left this world: "Spread your wings and fly." I immediately felt Lina's presence and thought this was a sign from her. I just couldn't believe this was happening to me. It gave me chills and tears but also comfort.

As I previously said, we Latinos believe in spirits and we're also extremely superstitious.

We had a wonderful time even though our hearts were broken into little pieces; but we managed to stay positive and celebrate Lina's life.

Chapter 46

New Love - March 2008

Luis and his Colombian friends were playing soccer one afternoon at a park when Natalie's friends introduced them. They immediately liked each other the minute they met.

Luis was from Colombia. He had olive skin, brown eyes and was the same age as Natalie.

Natalie's friend Dorothy was a sweet, caring and fun person with big brown eyes, brown hair, fair skin, a slender figure, and thirty-two years old. Dorothy was attracted to one of Luis's friends. They'd exchanged numbers and, a day later, the four of them were out on a date together.

Natalie and Luis spoke to each other in Spanish. He was the manager of a sugar cane field that was owned by one of his Colombian friends in Lake Cormorant.

Natalie had opened her own business in Immigration Law Services and they instantly talked about the business. The sugar cane company needed Hispanic laborers to work in the fields. Natalie and Luis thought it was the perfect opportunity to do business together. Natalie would take care of all the paperwork bring the Hispanics from Mexico with working visas for a few months, and place them in Luis' company. They soon were dating each other exclusively.

Natalie called me one evening in March 2008 and told me all about Luis. She said, "Mom I like him a lot and I'm having fun with him."

For Mother's Day, May 2008, I flew to Lake Cormorant to spend a week with Natalie and Mason and got to meet Luis. He was soft-spoken, with good manners, kind, and at the same time shy. The minute I met Luis I could see how much he cared about and loved my daughter. He called Natalie, *Mi Princesa*, (My Princess) and was very attentive toward her. I immediately liked him and was happy that she had someone in her life who adored her.

In late November, my mom and I flew to Lake Cormorant to stay for a week. Torreey flew in on Wednesday evening.

On Thanksgiving Day, Luis came by Natalie's house and met my mom and my husband and we celebrated the holiday together. Mom and Torreey also thought Luis was very nice and were pleased to see that Natalie had met someone new and was happy.

The following day, I walked into Natalie's bathroom while she was blow-drying her hair, and said, "Hey, why don't you marry Luis and get the hell out of Lake Cormorant?"

Natalie looked at me with a smile. "Um, maybe I will." She was getting closer to settling her community property against her ex-husband James.

He owed her close to $400,000 from her divorce settlement that had been dragging on at this point for four years.

A few months later, the company that Luis worked for closed down and he found a job an hour from Lake Cormorant. He rented an apartment and stayed there weekdays for work. Every other weekend, when Mason was with his dad, Luis drove to Lake Cormorant and stayed with Natalie. He couldn't stay with Natalie when she had Mason. This was an order that the divorce judge gave to both James and Natalie. Neither could have a boyfriend/girlfriend spend the evening while Mason was there with them.

Chapter 47

Dirty Tricks - 2009

My youngest sister Graciella came to visit from Illinois with two of her friends in April 2009. It was "spring in the city."

Gia, our oldest sister, came from the Valley to spend the weekend with us. Graciella wanted another tattoo and Venice Beach was the perfect place to go.

The next day we took off to the beach, walked around and saw the freaks on the boardwalk, then stopped for lunch and had cocktails. Gia always drank too much; she got a little wasted and ended up dancing with a Michael Jackson impersonator.

Graciella found a tattoo parlor and I decided to get a tattoo along with her. Graciella went first; she added a third star on her back for one of her kids.

I was second; I got a red rose on my right ankle in memory of Lina. While the guy was doing my tattoo the radio was playing a song with the words, *how does it feel?* We had a couple of cocktails in us so I was feeling brave. The guy started drilling on my skin and I begin singing very loud, "HOW DOES IT FEEL? OUCH, OUCH, MOTHERFUCKER!"

Graciella was laughing hysterically with me and so was the young guy who was doing my tattoo. We had a good fucking time getting our tattoos. It was hilarious. We were playfully harassing Gia to get a tattoo but she kept saying, "No, no, no, I don't like tattoos, I'm a grandma."

On Saturday evening, two of Graciella's girlfriends from grade school came to spend the night at my house. Irene a brunette, half Hispanic, half Caucasian, crazy and fun just like us. And, Fiona, Italian, with dark hair big brown eyes, petite and very sweet. Not crazy like us but she loved laughing at all the insane shit we did. They've been Graciella's friends for over thirty years.

Torreey dropped us at Tony's on the Pier in Redondo Beach for dinner. After our delicious meal I called a taxi and we took off to Hermosa Beach for dancing. We didn't stay in Hermosa for too long and ended back in a cab headed for the Redondo Pier.

The cab driver was a Mediterranean man with an accent. We always seemed to end up with a Middle Eastern taxi guy. There were five of us girls and we sat on top of each other. Our screams and laughter poured out of the cab windows as we sped through the night. At the pier, I was the last one out of the cab and feeling fabulous, so I grabbed my boobs and told the cab driver, "Hey check these out!"

The girls were screaming with laughter, the taxi man's jaw dropped and when he could finally speak, he said, "Thank you, I like it very much!" So I did it one more time. By then Mr. cabbie was speechless.

"Taxi driver," I said, "I'm giving you a good tip and a tit show too!" These were my last words to the driver while we all took off laughing and running to the pier while Graciella was yelling, "You fucking crazy bitch!"

Once at the pier we found a little bar and danced until midnight. I then called Torreey to come pick us up. After we got home we quickly got our PJs on and I yelled out, "Let's play a game!"

Graciella and I had already planned it so we told Gia she was to go first.

"Gia," I said, "Lay down on the bed on your stomach."

Gia kept asking, "What kind of game is this?"

"Be quiet, lay still and I'll be right back," I instructed.

I ran up the stairs as fast as I could, grabbed the plastic bag with the peel and stick black letters that I'd already cut earlier in the day. I then ran back down to the guest bedroom. The girls began rubbing Gia's feet while she laughed and said, "Ay, majes que mirda me van a hacer." ("What kind of shit are you doing to me?")

"Gia, be quiet and stay still," I said.

I immediately stuck my hand inside the plastic bag and grabbed the first letter, and stuck it on the ball of her foot underneath her toes. Then grabbed the second letter, the third letter, and the fourth letter.

We were all laughing so hard my hands were shaking and my tears were coming out. Graciella and her friends were holding their stomachs.

I quickly went to the other foot and grabbed three more letters and stuck them on too. "OMG," I said, "this is too fucking funny," and by then we were on the floor laughing hysterically.

Gia wanted to get up to see what was so funny, but we told her to wait until we took some pictures.

Torreey heard us laughing and making so much noise he decided to open the bedroom door. When he saw Gia on her stomach with the letters on her feet, he said, "Wait, I gotta get my phone to take a picture."

By then our mom was in the bedroom with us laughing and saying in Spanish, "Ay que chiquillas mas malas." ("You bad little girls.")

We couldn't stop from laughing. It was too fucking funny.

Finally we told Gia to get up and when she did, she looked at her feet but couldn't read it, so she sat on the bed raised, her legs up so she could see it in the mirror. With her hair sticking up like Don King's, Gia made a crazy face and said, "Oh shit!!

Again, we all went down to the floor with laughter while holding our stomachs, screaming and cursing.

This is what Gia's feet looked like after we were done:

LEFT FOOT	RIGHT FOOT
F	Y
U	O
C	U
K	

The following day we had a few friends and family over for lunch. I ordered Chinese takeout and brought back a bunch of fortune cookies. After our lunch, Graciella and I took one of the fortune cookies unwrapped it and removed the small piece of paper that was inside the cookie with a tweezers. We replaced it with our own piece of paper on which we'd written our own "fortune". We enfolded the fortune cookie back with the clear wrapping paper and placed a small piece of tape at the edges.

Graciella and I gave everyone a fortune cookie and I made sure Gia got the doctored cookie. I told everyone, "We want to hear your fortune one by one." I then asked the first person to read her fortune while the rest of us clapped and made a comment. I made sure Gia would be the last one to read hers. By then Gia was super excited and couldn't wait to read her fortune! She already had plenty of cocktails and was acting crazy like always. In the meantime, Graciella and I couldn't wait to see Gia's face while she read her "destiny."

Gia's turn came and she excitedly unwrapped her cookie, and then broke it in half. She unfolded the piece of paper while Graciella and I tried not to look at each other, we were already laughing.

Gia read the slip of paper, gasped, then, eyeballed Graciella and me. She loudly said, "Oh shit, 'Fuck You'!"

Everyone was laughing hysterically until his or her bellies couldn't take it any longer.

Graciella and I were staring at each other with tears of laughter dripping down our cheeks. OMG, this was insane!

Gia was calling us, "chiquillas cabronas," ("little assholes") but laughing at the same time.

Poor Gia, we have always pulled something like this at one point or another with her. She never gets upset with us and ends up even laughing at herself.

She then got up from her chair and noisily said, "Hueputas, ("Son-of-a-bitches,") I'm having another fucking drink and fuck you all."

Chapter 48

Skiing at Bear Mountain - 2009

On Christmas Day in 2009, I picked up Natalie and Mason at the airport. They'd been coming home for Christmas Day through January first for the last four years.

Mason loved to see me waiting for them at the airport's baggage claim. I'd always be there when they came down the escalator and as soon as I saw them I'd spread my arms out and yell, "My Papacito." (My little handsome boy.) Every year he was taller, cuter and a lot more fun to be around.

This Christmas we were going skiing at Bear Mountain in Wrightwood, California, about three hours from my home in Redondo Beach. Sunny was also going to join us on this trip.

After getting home from the airport, Natalie said, "Were hungry, let's go out for sushi."

"Sounds good," I agreed.

While eating sushi, I asked Mason, "Papacito, would you like to go to the theater to see 'A Christmas Carol?'"

"Yeah, Bebe!" Mason responded. (Bebe is my nickname for Grandma.)

After getting home from the movies, Natalie and Mason were exhausted and ready for bed.

The following day we left at noon and arrived at the mountain before it got dark. We went to our cabin, unpacked, and Natalie softly said, "Let's go out to a Mexican restaurant, I want a bean burrito."

"Oh, no!" I declared, "we're in trouble now."

Mason looked me in the eye, smiled and said, "Bebe, my mom is going to bomb us later."

"I know that, babe," I said, laughing with everyone and hugging and kissing my Papacito. "I love you, sweet pea," I told him.

From our cabin we walked to the Mexican restaurant. It was a beautiful crispy evening with snow on the ground. On our way, we picked up snow and threw it at each other while giggling. Mason was having so much fun. Every year he looked forward to his California trip with his mom. He knew that Bebe always planned a super special vacation for him.

Two hours later we were back at the cabin taking showers, getting our PJs on, and watching TV.

"Hey, Bebe, I wanna show you a new dance!" Mason said, blinking his eyes rapidly.

"Okay, babe, I'm ready. Show me what you got!"

Mason began dancing like a little nerd while busting out laughing at the same time.

It was too funny. "OMG, Natalie, this kid is crazy," I said, cracking up.

"Yeah, Mom, he's just like you," Natalie replied, shaking her head. Twenty minutes later Mason was in bed cuddling up to his mom.

Natalie and Mason were sleeping in the bedroom.

Sunny and I slept on the sofa bed in the living room.

All of a sudden, Natalie called out, "Hey, be quiet and listen to this…" and blasted the loudest fart ever. By now she was in tears from laughing and holding on to Mason as tight as she could.

Very serious, Mason said, "I told you guys she was going to bomb us." And then with a grin on his face he added, "Mom, um, smells delicious. Ha! Ha!"

My poor little Mason was used to being bombed by his mother all of the time. He never got upset with her and always thought it was funny.

Our night ended with everybody farting except Sunny. She had a great time laughing; but we always wondered how come she never farted like us.

The following day we were up and ready to drive to the mountain. We got to the slope and rented our skis, boots and poles. I purchased a family ski package that included lessons with a ski instructor; this way we didn't have to wait too long in line for the chair lift.

"Bebe, I want to snowboard," Mason announced.

"Are you sure, Papacito?" I asked.

"Yes, I'm sure, Bebe," he replied.

"Okay, I'll get you a snowboard lesson with the other kids."

Sunny, Natalie and I took a lesson with regular skis.

We had the best time skiing; every time we came down the mountain we stopped and yelled out, "Hey, Mason!" and waved and smiled at each other.

We could see him snowboarding with his group of kids and instructor. He was so happy and was having such a wonderful time.

The following day, Mason changed his mind and said, "Bebe, I want to ski with you guys."

"Okay, you got it, Babe. We'll get you regular skis. Whatever Papacito wants, Papacito gets!" I chirped.

We had a family lesson with an instructor for the next two days. And we had the best time laughing at each other whenever one of us fell down.

After three days of skiing we were ready to go back home and rest for a day before going to Disneyland.

That evening, while my son Luke, Sunny, and Mason were in the living room watching a movie, Natalie came in my bedroom where I was relaxing and listening to light classical music.

She had on her red silk pajamas that I had given her for Christmas. Niki, our white Dalmatian/Lab, and Sunami, my pug, were also on the bed with us.

Natalie lay next to me and in a soft voice said, "Oh Mom, I love my business. I'm getting some new accounts and I'm going to be making a lot of money in 2010. I'm so excited and can't wait!"

She continued, "My plan is to build a new house on the lakefront property that you and Torreey purchased. Mom, I have a lot of projects and plans. My life is packed full with raising Mason, playing tennis, and working."

At one point, she glanced at Niki, then turned to me and said, "Why is Niki staring at me like that?"

I looked at Niki and also thought it was a weird stare from her. I said, "I think Niki knows something about you that I don't know. You're hiding something from me. Aren't you?"

Natalie looked at me and laughed loudly. "Ha! Ha! Ha! You're crazy, Mom."

"Ahh, you're up to something and I know it!" I said with a grin on my face.

A few minutes later, she hesitated, and with a solemn face Natalie said, "Mom, I feel like I'm sitting on a time bomb – tick...tick...tick."

She had said this to me a couple of times during the months following her divorce.

Natalie grimaced. "James is not happy about the money he owes me, and he knows it's getting closer to the day he has to pay me."

A strange look came over her face. Very softly, very seriously, and very out of the blue she said, "I don't think I'm going to be around for too long."

I looked at her aghast; my heart was beating fast. Where did that come from? Why are you saying that?

"I don't know, Mom, there's something I feel inside of me," she said ominously. But she couldn't explain the feeling she had.

I looked at her and was very concerned and afraid. She was dead serious. I said, "Natalie, get those thoughts out of your head."

She didn't respond to that; she looked like she was somewhere else. Seconds later, she stood up and said, "I'm tired, I'm going downstairs to bed. Good night, Mom."

I stayed in my bedroom thinking about what she'd just told me. I was scared for her; it gave me chills so I decided not to think about it any longer. I got up and sat on my massage chair for fifteen minutes before going to bed.

On December 30, 2009 my son Luke, Sunny, Mason, Natalie and I took off to Disneyland. We had a blast; we went on the rides, had lots of fun, had dinner at the Captains of the Caribbean restaurant, saw the most beautiful fireworks show ever, and left Disneyland at midnight.

On December 31, 2009 we stayed home and celebrated New Year's Eve.

Sunny went back home to celebrate with her friends.

Natalie invited her best friend, Harvey, to come by and celebrate 2010 with us.

Mom was in Costa Rica so it was Luke, Natalie, Harvey, Mason, Torreey and I.

After dinner, Luke said, "Good night and Happy New Year to all," and went back home to his condo.

The five of us played blackjack. Torreey was the dealer. Natalie, Harvey, Mason and I were the players. Mason sat next to me while I taught him how to play.

Before midnight, I brought out a bottle of champagne and four glasses to celebrate the New Year. We waited for the countdown and watched the ball drop in New York's Time Square on our television. We gave each other a kiss and a hug and went back to playing blackjack before going to bed.

Natalie and Mason were catching a plane back home to Mississippi the following day.

Chapter 49

Water Damage - 2010

One late evening in January 2010, I was on the phone with Natalie for over an hour. She was leaving on a business trip to Florida the next morning with her friend and co-worker Diane. After our long conversation about her business and personal matters we finally said goodnight.

Fifteen minutes later, Natalie called me, scared and frantic. She was screaming on the phone, "MOM! MOM!"

I was alarmed and said, "Natalie, calm down, I don't understand what you're trying to tell me."

She was breathing heavy while saying, "After I hung up the phone with you I was going to sit at my desk to check something on the computer that I needed, but for some reason I changed my mind. When I got up from the sofa I heard a very loud explosion like somebody was shooting at my house."

She took a deep breath and continued, "I immediately dropped to the floor of my living room and layed still, I thought I had been shot at for sure."

Mason wasn't with her that evening, he was at his dad's house.

"I waited on the floor in silence, gradually realizing that I could hear something dripping. I crawled on my stomach to where I was hearing the dripping coming from and saw that my desk, computer and part of the ceiling was all over the floor, water was pouring down from the ceiling and was flooding the house.

"I got up and ran to Lance's house, my neighbor, and called my friend Nancy. Her maintenance guy came over to help me with the mess." Natalie's voice quivered with fear. "The hot water heater upstairs exploded."

"Natalie," I said, "hold on, let me get Torreey on the phone." By now I was in shock and ran to the kitchen to grab a glass of water.

Torreey grabbed the phone and said, "Natalie, listen to me. Call the insurance company immediately and let them know it's an emergency. Call me back after you talk to them."

Within an hour or two, the insurance company sent a cleaning crew to suck up the water that was all over the house. The office, kitchen, dining and living rooms were completely flooded.

Natalie left the next morning on her business trip and came home after three days to deal with the insurance company and the mess of the house.

She then called me. "Mom, what a fucking mess. The tile floors are coming apart. The walls are ruined and so is some of the furniture."

"Don't worry about it, it will be taken care of by the insurance," I assured her.

The house had to be repaired by a contractor that the insurance paid for.

A few days later I was on the phone with Natalie when she said, "Mom you should buy a million dollar insurance policy on me."

"Why?" I gasped.

"I could have been killed. I was going to go sit at my desk but changed my mind. If you had a million dollar policy on me you could have collected from them."

"Oh, c'mon, Natalie," I yelled out, "don't say that. I don't want to think about you dying."

"Damn, seriously Mom, you should think about it," she said without an ounce of jest.

Chapter 50

Cinco de Mayo - 2010

For the past eight years, Mom and I had been celebrating Mother's Day in Lake Cormorant, Mississippi with my daughter Natalie and grandson, Mason.

Natalie made it a point not to schedule any meetings or trips away from home while we were there for a week. We wanted to spend as much time as possible with each other. This year I suggested having Mason see a therapist while I was there, so she scheduled an appointment on Wednesday, May 5, at 10:30 a.m., near her office. I agreed to go with her and Mason.

Mason was having a difficult time dealing with the divorce, and more so with the eviction. He was only four years old when he was forced to move out of his home with his mother. He wanted his mommy and daddy together. Many nights he saw his mother crying. Several times I watched him hugging her, and saying in his sweet and kind voice, "Don't cry. I take care of you, Mommy."

It broke my heart to see my little grandson comforting his mother. Even though Mason was only four years old he already had a large vocabulary. He was used to hearing big words around the house. He overheard his mother on the phone talking to her girlfriends about the eviction letter. He asked with a sad face, "Why Daddy evict us?"

"Because he wants the house back so he can bring his girlfriend here," Natalie explained, holding him close to her chest.

Mason wanted answers to all of his questions. Natalie was always honest with him and explained it as best as she could, but the word "why" was always in the back of his mind.

Natalie and Mason were at the airport when we arrived at 5:30 p.m. I hugged Mason and said, "Hay que Papacito mas lindo, ("What a handsome little boy!") You're so much taller than the last time I saw you at Christmas."

Mom and I kissed and hugged Natalie, then walked to baggage claim to find our luggage.

On our way home we stopped for sushi, then headed for Natalie's house.

As we walked toward the entrance of the house, Natalie very excitedly said, "Mom, Grandma, look at my lovely decorative wheelbarrow that my boyfriend Luis gave to me as a present!"

"Oh, it's beautiful, it smells great and it looks perfect in the entryway!" I said.

"Yeah, Omar planted cilantro and spearmint herbs inside of it." Natalie replied.

I could see how proud she was of the gorgeous wheelbarrow.

Omar and his family were Natalie's friends of eight years. He's about 5'10, medium built, black hair, olive skin with big brown eyes and the longest eyelashes I'd ever seen on a man. When he laughed he sounded like a snorting pig. It was hilarious!

Besides working with Natalie at her Immigration Law Services office, he also helped her around the house with any repairs, or with Mason if needed.

Omar was married with two grown sons and a daughter. He and his family were very religious and attended church every Sunday. Natalie and Mason were like family to them.

Once inside, Natalie and Mason got ready for bed. Mom and I unpacked and an hour later we were prepared for a good night's sleep.

On Friday morning, April 30, Mom and I slept in till 9:00 a.m., Los Angeles time. It was two hours later in Mississippi. We felt rested and were now ready to begin our day.

Natalie left early to drop off Mason at school and from there she went to her office. She was coming home early due to the USTA (United States Tennis Association) tournament she had signed us up for.

That weekend was Mason's turn to spend with his dad, so we wouldn't see him until Monday.

Natalie was super excited and said, "Mom, you gotta meet my tennis partner, Lisa. She's a trip. She's blonde, about five-one, with brown eyes and a stocky frame."

Natalie and Lisa were playing in the women's doubles 3.0 Team.

I was on the 3.5 Team, and was not scheduled to play until Saturday afternoon. The tournament started on Friday, April 30 through Sunday, May 1.

On Friday late afternoon, Natalie and I drove to the club. The weather was perfect for tennis. It was sunny with no humidity or mosquitos for now.

I was there to watch her match and cheer for them. Natalie registered and, before going to the court to warm up with her partner, she turned to me and said, "Mom, don't be too loud, okay?"

"I can't promise you that!" I answered with a laugh.

I walked to the side of the courts, positioned my metal chair on the ground, and sat to watch them play. Natalie, Lisa and their opponents were getting ready to start their match.

At first I sat quietly and just watched them, but then I got bored. Soon I was cheering and clapping loudly every time they made a great shot. "Alright, do that again, Natalie!"

At times Natalie waved at me or made a funny face trying to tell me not to be so loud. She looked so happy; I could see it in her face. She was becoming a better player and was enjoying tennis a lot. I also noticed that she wasn't smoking as much. I think she finally got my message: "Tennis and cigarettes don't go together."

Two hours later, Natalie and Lisa won their first match. I went crazy jumping up and down, clapping and shouting, "Good job girls, you rockkkk!!"

We celebrated their win with a few cocktails, and then we were done for the night.

On Saturday May 1, Natalie and Lisa played their second match while I watched them and yelled out whenever they scored a point. "Damn, good shot! You go girls!" An hour later they won their match.

My partner, Kat, a fifty-three year-old blonde with short hair, blue eyes and an athletic figure, was sweet, and funny too. Natalie had nicknamed her Mr. Miyagi because when she grunted she sounded like the old man from *The Karate Kid* movie.

Kat and I lost our first match. I played like shit, couldn't get my shots to land inbounds. Plus, the weather was as humid as could be; it had completely changed from one day to another. "We'll get them next time," I told Kat.

By 7:00 p.m., we were so exhausted we decided to go home and chill out. An hour later, Natalie came into the kitchen were I was standing, next to the stove, pouring a cup of green tea. "Hey Mom, I want you to be at the club to watch me play my last match tomorrow," Natalie pleaded before going to bed.

"Oh God, I would but I'm so tired. I need to stay home and catch up on my sleep. The humidity kills me, and I'm not use to playing tennis in this kind of weather," I replied, sipping my tea.

Natalie frowned. "Damn Mom, you suck!" She sighed and said as a compromise, "Okay, I'll have your partner, Mr. Miyagi, pick you up on her way to the club before noon."

The next day on Sunday morning, Natalie left the house before 8:30 a.m., for her match. Around 10:45 a.m., Natalie texted me: *Mom, Lisa and I just won our final match. We kicked butt!*

Great, I'm so happy for you! I texted back.

Kat picked me up around noon and we headed to the club. Natalie was already celebrating with a glass of wine. She was all excited, telling her friends about her match.

Joyce, another good friend of Natalie, was also there watching her play. She wasn't a tennis player but she attended most of the events that Natalie was involved with. Joyce was a beautiful black girl, slim with short light brown hair. She reminded me of Grace Jones, the disco singer. She was soft spoken with a caring soul, and she loved Natalie with all of her heart. She was a social worker who dealt with troubled kids. I've always called her "Joy to the world."

"Congratulations!" I told Natalie while hugging her.

She was so happy, laughing and saying, "Mom, Mom, I kept farting on Lisa while we were playing. It was hilarious. I also hit the ball and farted at same time!"

"What did Lisa do?" I asked, laughing.

"She made crazy faces back at me."

"I can't believe she puts up with you," I said, shaking my head.

Natalie had become an accomplished tennis player as evidenced by her wins in both the 3.0 Women's Doubles Division Clay Court Championship at Brayden, and the Courterband Championship at Lake Cormorant Club.

At 1:00 p.m. it was time for Kat and I to play our match.

This time Natalie watched and cheered for us.

I could see her standing on the top of the balcony of the club, drinking her wine and yelling, "Go Mom, go. Momma didn't raise a quitter!" Those were her favorite words, especially when I got on her case about smoking cigarettes. This became Natalie's signature line whenever the going got tough.

A couple of hours later Kat and I finally won our match. I immediately began dancing and clowning around on the court; and of course one of our opponents was very upset. She looked me in the eye and rudely said, "I'm not shaking hands with you. You're crazy!" then stomped off the court.

I just continued with my dance and whispered, "It's okay with me, fucking looser."

We stayed at the tennis club for an hour and celebrated with wine and snacks. A few minutes later, Natalie said, "Lets go home and pick up Grandma and stop somewhere for Chinese food."

"Sounds good to me," I said.

After our meal I suggested, "Manicures, pedicures, and foot massages anyone?"

"Alright Momma!" Natalie cheered.

After our spa treatment, Natalie proposed, "Hey, let's get the movie, 'The Lovely Bones,' a bottle of wine and go home, and relax. I really wanna see this movie with you and Grandma."

"Okay, let's do it!" I agreed.

The movie was very intense and sad; we were at the edges of our seats. It was about death and trying to go to heaven, but first the girl had to finish something on earth. At the end she finally gets into heaven.

Natalie turned to me and very softly said, "Mom, wouldn't that be nice if heaven was anything like that?"

I looked at her and said, "Yeah, if we only knew. If it were anything like that it would be a beautiful place to be." I didn't want to show it, but this movie where the girl is abducted, presumably raped, then murdered, really scared the shit out of me. I found it very depressing.

"Grandma, y tu que piensas?" ("Grandma, what do you think?") Natalie asked.

"Demasiado triste." ("Extremely sad.") Mom responded.

We were all quiet for a few moments, then, I stared at my daughter's face. She had an expression that I'd never seen before and could not explain it. She was wearing the red silk Victoria's Secret pajamas I had given her the prior Christmas and was sitting in her recliner chair in the living room holding her glass of wine and staring at the ceiling as if she was somewhere else. A few minutes later, we finished our wine and went to bed.

On Monday morning, May 3, Natalie dropped Mom and me at the airport and drove to her office. I was picking up the rental car I had reserved so that we could get around while Natalie was at work.

Mom and I went and bought some things we needed at the house, and from there we picked up Mason at school. I was taking him to his tennis lesson after.

While Mason took his lesson, I snapped some pictures of him. An hour later, he was done. We grabbed a bite at the club's cafeteria, got back to the house for Mason to shower, do his homework, and work on his Legos before going to bed.

Natalie called at 6:00 p.m. and asked, "Mom, do you wanna join me and some friends for tennis after I'm done with work?"

"I'm not in the mood for playing right now," I begged off. "I'll stay home with Mason and Mom."

Natalie came home from her friendly match after 9:00 p.m. The minute she walked in she went straight to kiss and hug Mason. "Hey, how you doing, babe?"

With a smile on his face, Mason, looked at his mother and said, "I'm good." He then turned to me and said, "Right, Bebe?"

"Papacito, is always good," I smiled back.

Hey, Mase, did you do your homework?" Natalie asked, using her nickname for him.

"Yes, I did Mom!"

"Okay, I'll check it and then we're going to bed," Natalie said with a yawn.

Mason slept in Natalie's bedroom every night. He had his own bedroom upstairs, but Natalie loved having him next to her to hug.

Anytime I walked into her bedroom in the evenings, she had her arms around him. She gave him a lot of love, taught him to be kind, to love animals, and to always tell the truth.

As I was walking away from her bedroom, Natalie said, "Hey Mom, I almost forgot. I need you to take Mason to school on Wednesday. Diane scheduled a meeting on domestic violence two hours away."

"What about Mason's therapy session?" I asked.

"I had to change it to Friday instead," she replied.

"Mason's therapy is more important. Besides, we agreed, no meetings outside of Lake Cormorant while I'm here," I said, a little upset.

"Well, Diane's driving me crazy with this case she has and wants to get it done right away," Natalie insisted, but she sounded exhausted.

Natalie's friend Diane was working with her in the Immigration Law Services office. She was a lawyer and was renting one of the offices from Natalie. Diane was a brunette with hazel eyes, somewhat slender and a mouth that didn't stop. You'd end up with a pounding headache if you were around her for too long. She was married to an unsociable man, and they had no children. She spent many nights at the office instead of going home. She was unhappy with her marriage, but tolerated it anyway. She always claimed that she felt sorry for him.

She was also representing Natalie on the community property settlement against her ex-husband, James.

Natalie was the co-founder of The Peoples Advocate of Southwest Mississippi, was certified to practice immigration law, and worked closely with the District Attorney's and Sheriff's Offices, and the Police Department to protect immigrants' rights. She volunteered at the Family House of Hope, an organization that helps shelter families and their children, and with A Dogs New Life, a program in which young people at the Juvenile Detention Center train and adopt out homeless dogs.

She also worked with The Women's Shelter, Wishing Project, and the Lake Area Partnership for Animal Welfare.

She was recognized in the media for protecting victims of domestic violence and animal cruelty, and coming to the aid of immigrants and juveniles in need.

My daughter Natalie was a phenomenal civic-minded person. She'd risk her own life to help others. She was the Robin Hood of Lake Cormorant to the Hispanic people. She found them jobs, shelter if needed, and provided them with work visas.

A couple of years back, she called me, super excited, and said, "Mom, I got tell you want happened today! I've been working desperately with the Police Department on finding a four-year-old little boy who was kidnapped by his father after the dad slit his mother's throat and left her to die."

"What the fuck? Are you insane!" I'd shouted nervously.

"Well let me finish," she said.

"Okay, go ahead, but I'm not liking what you're telling me," I backed off.

She went on, "After the guy, Ramon, slit her throat, Maria was brave enough to wrap a cloth around her neck and call me for help. Luckily I was in the area and rushed to her side while calling 911. By the time the paramedics got to her, she had lost a lot of blood. She was taken to the hospital and after a couple of weeks she was slowly recovering but couldn't use her voice. After she was released from the hospital I placed her in the women's shelter. I saw her cry day and night for her child, and it broke my heart. I promised her we were going to find her boy. After desperately working with the police for nine months, someone called me and gave me Ramon's whereabouts. I gave the person my phone number and told him in Spanish to have Ramon call me. A few days later, Ramon called me and after chatting and chatting with him I told him if he returned his boy to the authorities they would reduce his time in jail. I then convinced him to meet me at a restaurant during the day. On my way to the restaurant I started thinking, what if he has a gun and shoots me? But then I thought of the little boy, Daniel, and his mother. So I went ahead with my plan. I parked my car at the restaurant, went inside, and there was Ramon sitting at one of the tables. I recognized him because his wife Maria had given us a photograph of him, and besides we had posted flyers of Ramon and Daniel all over the town."

"OMG, Natalie!" I said anxiously.

"Okay, so then, within seconds of me sitting at the table, all of a sudden the restaurant was surrounded by police cars. Ramon didn't have a chance to escape. The police came in, handcuffed him and we began interrogating him about the location of his son. At first he didn't want to talk, but when I interpreted for him and told him what was going to happen to him if he didn't give us the information about his son, he decided to talk. He gave me the name of the motel where he had left Daniel. I quickly got in the police vehicle with two officers and we took off to rescue the boy."

"Oh, Natalie, that's a heartbreaking story. How was the boy when you found him?" I said, wiping my tears away.

"Well, we got the manager to open the door and there was little Daniel sitting on the bed watching TV. I approached him and in Spanish I said, 'Hola, como te llamas?'" ("Hi, what's your name?")

"In his squeaky voice," he said, 'Daniel.'

"'Daniel, me llamo Natalie y te voy a llevar donde tu mama. Okay?' ("Daniel, my name is Natalie, and I'm going to take you to your mom. Okay?")

"Daniel looked at me with a smile while moving his head up and down and then said, 'Mi mama.' ("My mom.")

"I said, 'Yes,' held his little hand and walked with him to the car that would take him back to his mother forever."

"Ohhhh, how sad, poor little boy and his mother too," I said with a lump in my throat. "Shit, how come you didn't tell me you were involved in this?"

"Because I didn't want to worry you," Natalie responded.

"Yeah, but you put yourself in danger, you know," I objected.

"It's okay, Mom. It's over."

"I am so proud of you, Natalie," I said with chills all over my body.

Natalie always did this to me. She never told me what she was up to until it was over. She knew I'd have a lot of questions and of course, after the fact, she would have all the answers.

On Tuesday morning, May 4, Natalie left the house with Mason at 7:15 a.m., she was dropping him off at school and then heading to her office.

At 10:30 a.m., I called Natalie. "Can we come by your office and have lunch with you?"

"Yes!" she said with enthusiasm.

We got to Natalie's building by noon. Mom and I walked in and immediately gave Diane a kiss and a hug. We then took the few steps to Natalie's office.

Natalie and Diane had a meeting that morning about domestic violence on a young Hispanic girl who didn't speak any English. A retired older policeman in his mid sixties with silver hair and a potbelly was sitting in the front of the office with the young girl. She looked to be about twenty years old.

Natalie exited her office and addressed her partner. "Diane, go ahead and fill out the paper work with the officer while I'm out to lunch with my mom and grandma. I'll be back in an hour and I'll interpret for the girl."

Natalie, Mom and I walked a few doors from her building to Café Mira. We ordered lunch and I noticed that Natalie was upset, so I asked, "What's wrong? You seem uptight?"

With a grin on her face, Natalie responded, "Diane sometimes pisses me off and gets on my nerves. She always tells me what to do and when to get it done. She has a lot of personal problems that she brings to the office. She's upset because she wants me to stay and interview the Latina girl now. She doesn't want me to go to lunch. I need a break and want to spend some time with you both. Plus I found out that the retired officer and the girl are having an affair.

"Ahhh, there's more shit to the story," I said, rolling my eyes. "Natalie, did you know about Diane's bad habits in the beginning?"

"I knew some of it, not all," Natalie replied. "I'm just fucking tired of it all."

"You need to do something about it," I said, agitated.

An hour later, we finished lunch, paid the bill, got up and went to leave when all of a sudden this tall, good-looking, mulato guy grabbed the door handle for us and opened the door. We all stared at him and said "Thank you!" at the same time.

As we were walking, Natalie turned to Grandma with a huge smile and in Spanish said, "Hay Grandma, que guapo!" ("What a handsome man!")

"Yeah, he's hot! Hot!" I concurred.

He was about 6'2 with beautiful medium dark skin, and an incredible physique. You could tell he worked out a lot.

Natalie walked into her building with a big smile. Mom and I drove off to pick up Mason.

At the school, I stood on the sidewalk with my arms wide open to give him a big hug and kiss; he always looked so happy to see me. "Hi, Papacito, how was school today?" I asked.

"It was good, Bebe," he responded.

"Hey, Papacito, we're going to Best Buy to get a computer for your Mom. I'm also buying something for you, too," I said.

Natalie's last computer was ruined when the water heater broke in January 2010 and flooded the house. Mason was now very excited and couldn't wait to get there.

"Bebe, can I get a video?" he pleaded.

"Of course you can, babe."

Half an hour later, I paid for the computer. I took the monitor home but had to leave the PC for them to install the software. I called Natalie to let her know.

"I'll pick up the computer on Wednesday after my meeting," she said.

After we got home, I fed Mason. He did his homework, took a shower, put on his PJs and was ready to play with his new video game.

By 9:00 p.m. I was feeling tired and decided to run up to my room, take a shower, then came back down to watch TV. By then, Mason had already gone to bed and was asleep.

Mom was also getting ready for bed.

At 10:00 p.m. I went to bed in Natalie's room where Mason was and waited for Natalie to come home.

When I heard her arrive, a little after 10:30 p.m., I immediately got up from her bed.

Before I left her room, she asked, "How was Mason?"

"Good as always," I responded with a yawn.

"Mom, don't forget that you're taking Mason to school in the morning at 7:15. I have an important meeting to attend with Diane and two other people an hour away from here. I need to leave the house and pick up Diane by six."

"Don't worry, I'll be up at six," I assured her.

I walked up to my room, jumped into bed, and was asleep within minutes. Around 4:30 in the morning, I woke up with a horrible stomachache, nausea, chills, and my entire body was trembling. I didn't know what the hell was wrong with me. It was a strange feeling like no other. I got up and walked downstairs to the kitchen to find Pepto Bismol, or something similar, for my stomach. I couldn't find anything so I went back to bed shivering and hoping it would go away; but that was a useless wish. I didn't want to wake up Natalie, and stayed in bed hoping that I'd eventually feel better. I kept holding my stomach and had covered myself up with the blanket.

But I couldn't go back to sleep; the stomach cramps were becoming worse. I waited to hear a sound that indicated Natalie was awake, but nothing happened.

At about 5:00 a.m., Wednesday, May 5, I heard Natalie's footsteps. I rushed to get up and went halfway down the stairs. Natalie was walking into the kitchen. She was wearing a long red dress. She saw me standing on the stairs and could tell something was amiss. "Mom, what's wrong?"

"I don't feel well, I'm sorry. I don't think I can take Mason to school," I said with a shaky voice.

Natalie looked at me, disappointed, and said, "Oh no, I have to pick up Diane by six. I cannot take Mason to school."

"I'm sorry, maybe Nancy or Eva can swing by for Mason," I suggested.

Natalie immediately got on the phone. "Eva, nesecito tu ayuda, puedes venir por Mason? Mi Mama esta enferma y no puede llevar a Mason a la escuela. Tambien, traele Pepto Bismol. Okay, gracias." ("Eva, I need your help, can you come by for Mason? My mom is sick and cannot take Mason to school. Also, can you bring Pepto Bismol? Thanks.")

By then it was 5:30 a.m., when Natalie left the house and was on her way to pick up Diane.

Mom took care of Mason until Eva showed up.

I took two doses of medicine, went back to bed, and fell asleep until 10:00 a.m. I got up and felt better with the stomach cramps but still had the shakes. I walked downstairs to the kitchen, had hot tea and crackers, and sat in the living room where Mom and Eva were. At 11:00 a.m., I had a bowl of homemade chicken soup, and after sat on the sofa and fell asleep while my mom snored like a gorilla.

Around 2:00 p.m., the phone rang, and it was Natalie. "Hey, Mom, are you feeling better?"

"Yes, I feel better, but not a hundred percent," I answered while having vanilla ice cream.

"Okay, good. We're done with our meeting and are on our way back home. Do you think you'd feel up for playing tennis around 5:00 p.m.?"

"I'll wait until you get home to see if I'm feeling up to it," I responded.

"Okay, I should be home within an hour," Natalie happily said.

Around 3:00 p.m., I heard a noise in the garage. One of the cats was meowing and making strange noises. I got up from the couch and went to investigate. The cat was scratching the side of one of the cardboard storage boxes. "What are you doing, Jack?" I said to the cat. Jack was one of Natalie's rescued pets, a beautiful and very sweet gray tabby that slept with me while I was visiting.

I leaned down, moved the box to the side and saw a small lizard. "Oh, shit, fuck, I hate lizards!" I ran to the kitchen, put on a glove, went back to the garage, and tried picking up the little creature – but it kept falling off the glove. I tried it a couple of times until I got a good hold of it. I opened the garage door, took the lizard outside, and placed it on some bushes. I went back inside the house and had a cup of tea, sat on the sofa, watched TV and waited for Natalie to come home.

Every Wednesday, Mason spent the night at his dad's house, so Mom and I were home relaxing. After a while I looked at my watch and noticed that it was already 5:30 p.m. I turned to Mom and in Spanish said, "Que raro que no ha llegado Natalie." ("I wonder why Natalie is not home yet.")

"Tal vez hay mucho traffico," ("Maybe there's a lot of traffic.") Mom replied.

"Si, se me olvido que hoy es el Cinco de Mayo." ("Yes, I forgot today is Cinco de Mayo.") I agreed.

I looked at my watch around 6:00 p.m., and had not heard from Natalie yet.

At 6:15 p.m., I was still watching TV in the living room when the doorbell rang. I thought it might be a neighbor as I got up from the sofa and walked slowly to the door. When I opened it, I was shocked to see two police officers standing there.

"Good evening, ma'am. I'm Officer LeGrand, and this is Officer Johnson," he said with no expression. "Is this Natalie Collins's home?"

With a shaky voice, I said, "Y-Yes, it is."

"Who are you, ma'am?" he asked.

"I'm Natalie's mom." My body was wobbly and my voice was weak.

"May we please come in?" Officer LeGrand asked very politely.

I looked at him, very scared, and said, "Yes, of course." I knew right away that something dreadful had happened.

I led them into the dining room. Mom was in the kitchen and Officer LeGrand immediately asked, "Who is she?"

"My mom," I said.

"Ma'am, please sit down." Officer Legrand indicated a chair.

Both officers sat down with Mom and me.

I was already feeling terrified by the serious expressions on the men's faces. I sat quietly not wanting to ask anything. I was just staring at the dining room table. I was afraid of making eye contact with the officers. I knew something horrible had happened for them to be in my house. You see this in movies all the time except that this time was real and in my daughter's home.

Officer Johnson looked at me and spoke for the first time. "Your daughter was involved in an accident."

I stared at him not wanting to ask anything but I had to. My heart was ready to come out of my chest and finally I said, "Is she okay?"

With a very sad face, he said, "No ma'am, she was killed."

I started screaming and pounding my fist on the dining room table. "NOOOO, its not true!" For some reason I couldn't cry. My mom was also shouting but she was crying as well. I turned to Officer LeGrand. "Take me where she is. I need to see her right now. I think you're wrong. Its not her!"

"I'm sorry, ma'am, I can't take you yet, the funeral home is cleaning her up, and they will call me as soon as she's ready," he said in a soft voice.

Both officers kept staring at me, probably wondering why I wasn't asking them any questions. Like if anyone else was killed, the extent of their injuries, who was at fault, and so on. I guess most people would want to know everything about the accident, but I wasn't interested at all. I knew I would find that out later. All I wanted was to see my daughter and the hell with the rest.

I grabbed my mobile phone and called my husband, screaming at the top of my lungs, "Natalie's dead! Natalie's dead!"

Torreey didn't understand me. He asked me to calm down and to tell him again.

I lowered my voice. "She's dead, dead!" but he still didn't understand me.

"Momsie, Momsie, listen to me," Torreey tried again, "I'm in my car and the reception is not very good. What's wrong?"

I took a deep breath and said, "Natalie was killed."

He gasped, "OH NO! How?"

"I don't know all the details, except a car accident. All I want is to go see her now," I cried.

I hung up the phone, and quickly called my son. "Luke, Luke, Natalie was killed in an auto accident," I said while sobbing.

"WHAT? SHIT!" Luke yelled out, and then calmly said, "Mom, I'll make arrangements to fly to Lake Cormorant with Torreey as soon as possible."

I then called my younger sister Graciella in Illinois and gave her the horrible news.

Graciella started crying and screaming.

I said, "Please call the rest of the family and let them know."

I then sat in the dining room with the officers waiting for the call to go see Natalie. By now, I was completely numb.

Officer LeGrand then said something to me that made me look him in the eyes. "Were you, your mom and your daughter at Café Mira for lunch yesterday? I opened the door for you all when you were leaving the restaurant."

"OMG, I can't believe this." I was stunned. This guy was the same person with the beautiful smile, except this time he wasn't smiling, and he was now wearing a uniform. Just yesterday he indeed opened the door for us; and Natalie was so excited telling Mom and me how handsome he was. This good-looking officer was now in my daughter's house telling me she was dead. *How can this be possible?* I thought.

A short while later, Officer Legrand got a call. After hanging up, he turned to me and said, "It's okay for us to go to the funeral home to see Natalie."

By then, Natalie's house was full of friends. I had no idea how many people loved my daughter until that evening.

Natalie's boyfriend Luis came to the house after hearing the news. I can barely remember hugging him and crying with him.

Natalie's friend Kat came by the house. Kat told the officers that she'd take over from here.

We left the house and drove to the funeral home; it seemed like we were in the car forever. I felt like this wasn't true, *this cannot be happening to me, it's only a dream.* When we finally got to the mortuary, I got out of the car and walked toward the front door. It was a very strange feeling. I felt like I was walking on a cloud, almost as if I was floating in the air.

When we got inside the mortuary, someone directed us to the viewing room. I opened the door and there was my Natalie. She was laying on a small gurney. She looked like she was just sleeping. As I walked and got closer to Natalie's body it felt like she was so far away from me; like I was moving in slow motion and couldn't get there any faster. When I finally reached her, I broke down crying, touching her face, her cheeks, her hands and her hair that was wet from the bath they had given her. Her face was still warm and rosy; her fingers were also warm and I could still bend them. I kissed her forehead and my tears were running on her face; it almost looked like she was crying with me. She had no makeup on. She had a small scratch on the right side of her cheek. Her right eye was a little bruised. But her face was not disfigured at all. Her nose was still straight and beautiful.

I realized my mom was by her side, also crying and kissing Natalie.

Eva was sobbing and touching her hair. Eva used to color and style Natalie's hair every time she went out with Luis or girls' night out. Eva was Hispanic and didn't speak much English. She was short, thin, with olive skin; married with two boys. Eva loved Natalie like a sister. Natalie had helped Eva, her husband and kids obtain their green cards to stay in the United States legally. Eva and Natalie were friends for eight years. She cleaned Natalie's house and babysat for Mason. Losing Natalie was very difficult for Eva. Eva depended on Natalie perhaps a little too much.

I don't remember how many hours we were at the funeral home and I don't recall who took us home. I just didn't want to go home without my sweet daughter.

Later that evening Mason asked to see me.

Kat – Mr. Miyagi as Natalie called her – drove me over to James's house where Mason was waiting for me.

I walked in the master bedroom where Mason and his dad were laying down. Mason climbed off the bed and came over to me.

"I love you, babe," I said, hugging him tight.

I turned to James, still holding on to my grandson. "Please don't prevent Mason from seeing me," I begged.

"I won't do that," James said, but not convincingly.

"Are you going to allow Mason to see his mother at the funeral home?" I asked. I was frightened he would say no.

"I'll think about it," he responded, very noncommittal.

On my way out the door, James's mother Trisha followed me. "Trisha, please talk to James about letting Mason see his mother one last time," I pleaded.

James's girlfriend of four years, Rhonda, her mother and Kat were in the kitchen. When Rhonda heard me ask Trisha to talk to James about letting Mason see his mother, she immediately walked over to where Trisha and I were standing and very rudely said, "Mason doesn't need to see her like that!"

I didn't look or answer her back. This woman had the nerve to get in my face and say that to me. For crying out loud, I had just lost my daughter! She was lucky I wasn't Lina or Graciella. They would have kicked the shit out of her. She showed me no respect and now she was going to raise my grandson. *OMG, why is my daughter dead and gone? And now I have to deal with HER!?!* I fretted.

Natalie's friends had informed me that they didn't think too highly of this woman. I won't go into detail, and just leave it that the nickname they came up with was "Ms. Nasty".

I grabbed Trisha's arm and repeated, "This is his mother, and Mason needs to see her." I then turned and left with Kat.

Back at the house, I saw Jean one of Natalie's friends whose husband was a doctor. I said, "Jean, I need something to relax me and help me sleep. Would you ask your husband if he can prescribe something for me?"

"I'll call him right now, Shirley," Jean replied.

An hour later, one of the girls who'd picked up my prescription handed me a pill. Afterward, I was resting on the sofa and started feeling high. I couldn't get up from the couch, move or talk. But I could hear a lot of whispering going on ... "The guy was going over ninety ... They airlifted Diane to a hospital." There were so many people at the house, I really didn't know who was who anymore. I remember one of the girls saying, "Shirley, we went to the wrecking yard where Natalie's car was and brought you back some folders with important information. You need to find out where Natalie's purse is before The Beast gets it."

"Who?" I was so out of it I'd forgotten that was the nickmane they used when they felt Natalie's ex was being unreasonable.

By now it was close to 3:00 a.m., and everyone had gone home. I got ready for bed and said, "Mom? Please sleep with me in Natalie's bedroom. I don't want to be alone."

We finally went to bed around 4:00 a.m.. An hour later, Mom was making weird noises with her mouth, which woke me up. "Mom, Mom what's wrong?" I yelled out.

"No se, no me siento bien," ("I don't know, I don't feel well,") she murmured.

I grabbed the phone and called 911. The paramedics arrived within minutes. The lead EMT asked, "Is she upset about something?"

"My daughter was just killed, " I cried softly. My head was pounding.

The paramedics took Mom's blood pressure and found out that it was extremely high. They needed to get her to a hospital as soon as possible. I jumped in the ambulance, sitting in front with the driver.

An hour later, I found myself on a chair in a hospital room while Mom lay on the bed. I don't remember a lot, I was numb, tired, sad, confused and angry. The nurses had already given Mom a pill to drop the blood pressure to normal. The doctor wanted to keep her there a day or two for observation.

Around 6:00 AM, I called Mina, a Hispanic friend of Natalie's and asked her to pick me up at the hospital.

On Thursday May 6, around 10:00 a.m., my sister Graciella arrived from Illinois. Graciella is my youngest sister. She is a social worker at a school for troubled kids. The kids love her and hate her at the same time. She's super hyper, very mouthy, funny and lovable too.

Graciella was the only sibling who came to be by my side and Mom's. I was so lost, so weak, so shocked I was incapable of doing anything anymore. I let her be in charge of everything. She was brave; she knew she had to be. She needed to stay strong for our mom, and especially for me. I don't know what I would have done without her. All I wanted was to be sedated, to go to sleep and be left alone; thinking that when I woke up everything would be normal again; it was all just a horrible nightmare. My sweet and caring little sister was by my side taking care of me.

While I was napping, Natalie's friends and Graciella got together to discuss the details of the accident. Apparently, they had talked to the police and got the official report.

A couple of hours later, Graciella came into the master bedroom where I was and said, "Shirley, you need to know what happened."

"I already know some of it. I overheard the girls last night," I said, forlorn and agitated.

"Okay, but you need to know what I found out." Graciella insisted. "I'll go and bring you a Xanux so you can relax, okay?"

Twenty minutes after popping the pill, Graciella came back and sat on the bed, looked me in the eye and said, "The guy that killed Natalie was Ronald

Thomas. He's forty-five, and the head football coach at Brighton High. He fell asleep at the wheel and his vehicle crossed the median and struck Natalie's car head-on. His wife, the only other passenger, was also killed."

"Oh God, why did he fall asleep? What the fuck was wrong with him? It was only 3:30 in the afternoon?" I cried, placing my hands on my face.

"There's more, and it's not easy for me to tell you." Graciella came over, sobbing, and held me tight. In a shaky and low voice she said, "Natalie was killed instantly. Her neck was broken and she sustained internal injuries."

"OMG, that son-of-a-bitch! Where is he now?" I demanded, crying uncontrollably.

"I don't know. But I do know the police retrieved blood samples from Ronald, and toxicology tests are pending," Graciella told me, wiping away her tears.

On Thursday afternoon, Graciella and I went to the funeral home to meet with James and his mother Trisha to make arrangements for the funeral service. I had taken a couple of pills to calm me down and didn't feel I was there at all. I just wanted everything to go away and to be left alone.

A female funeral director came in and introduced herself. "Hi, I'm Debra. I need to ask some questions regarding the deceased."

"Hi, I'm Graciella, Natalie's aunt." She put her hand on my arm. "My sister Shirley, Natalie's mother, is not well, so I'll be answering for her if that's okay with you."

I remember listening to some of the words but I just couldn't speak. My mouth was locked and my mind was somewhere else. It was fortunate that I had Graciella to answer questions for me.

"Is your daughter married?" Debra asked.

"She's divorced," Graciella replied.

James jumped in. "She was married."

"What do you mean, James, you guys were never divorced?" Graciella said with bewilderment.

"Natalie was married to Luis," James sneered.

Debra marked an X next to married on the document.

I was in the room but felt like I was floating in the air, until I heard his name, "Luis". I came back down to earth, opened my mouth and said, "I know Luis!" I paused for a moment, then, asked Debra, "Do you have my daughter's purse?"

"Yes, I do," she said this tentatively.

"Please, I would like to have my daughter's purse," I said.

James immediately objected. "The purse belongs to my son."

"The only person that I can give the purse to is her husband, Luis," Debra announced.

I just couldn't believe James was doing this to me. At this point I was very angry, high on pills, but keeping my cool. Something inside me was telling me, *Be strong and don't give up.* I grabbed my phone, called Luis, and in Spanish said, "Luis, soy yo Shirley, necesito un gran favor?" ("Luis, it's me Shirley, I need a big favor?")

"Si, si que necesitas, Shirley." ("Yes, yes, what do you need, Shirley?")

"Este hombre el papa de mi nieto esta reclamando la cartera de mi hija. La senora Debra del funeral dice que a la hunica persona que le puede entregar la cartera es a ti y necesita tu firma. Tambien, es cierto que tu y Natalie estavan casados?" ("This man, the father of my grandson, is claiming my daughter's purse. The funeral woman, Debra, said the only person she can give the purse to is you, the husband. Also, is it true that you and Natalie were married?")

"Shirley, no te preocupes, voy para haya immediatamente. Si, si, es verdad que yo y Natalie estabamos casados. Te lo iva a decir pero pense que no hera el tiempo appropiado. Por favor perdoname" ("Shirley, don't worry I'll be there immediately. Yes, yes, Natalie and I were married. I wanted to tell you but I didn't think it was the appropriate time. Please forgive me.")

The room was pin-drop quiet while I was on the phone with Luis. I could see on James and Trisha's faces that they were not too happy with my Spanish conversation. They didn't understand a word I said.

After I hung up, I said, "Luis will be here in an hour."

James's face turned an angry red after hearing this.

We were still in the room with James, his mom, and Graciella when Luis arrived. He came in and introduced himself to Debra.

"May I see your identification?" Debra asked.

Luis handed her his ID.

Debra looked at the card and nodded. "You can sign here for the purse." After signing, Debra handed Luis Natalie's purse.

Luis immediately said, "Shirley, this belongs to you," and gave me my daughter's purse.

James and his mother looked at each other, visibly upset, got up, and left the room for a while, and didn't come back until after Luis was gone.

James lost this round and he was NOT happy about it. He didn't get my daughter's purse, but I had a feeling he was not finished. Losing was not acceptable to him.

At one point, Debra asked, "Who's paying for the funeral arrangements?"

Before I opened my mouth, I was thinking about my daughter when she told me not to pay for her wedding, it was like she was telling me again, "Don't pay for it, Mom!"

James piped up in a cordial tone of voice, saying, "I will."

Now that I think about it, I wish I could have spoken up and done it myself. I was supposed to arrange the funeral with Natalie's husband Luis, NOT with her ex and his mother. What James and his mother arranged was not something Natalie or I ever would have wanted.

I supposed he'd probably be reimbursed for any funeral expenses by Natalie's estate.

He chose the coffin, something that Natalie never wanted.

His mother Trisha chose a Catholic priest.

Again, Natalie would never have asked for a priest. She was not religious and didn't believe in priests or churches, though she always respected others' beliefs.

The service was set for Saturday, May 8, 2010 at the Thompson Funeral Home.

James brought Mason by Natalie's house on Friday afternoon and said, "Mason wants to see his Mom at the funeral home."

James, Mason, my mom and I drove to the mortuary together to see Natalie.

On our way there, while holding on to Mason, I said, "Babe, you need to know that your mom's body is going to be cold, in case you want to touch her, okay? Don't be afraid of it, sweetheart."

Mason slowly shook his head back and forth. He had no voice anymore. He was in shock like I was, but the difference was that he was only eight years old, a little boy who had just lost the love of his mother forever.

We got to the funeral home and opened the door to where Natalie's body was laying on an aluminum table. Mason stared at his mom without saying a word or dropping a single tear. He was trying to be so brave.

I took Natalie's hand and asked Mason, "Babe, do you want to hold her hand?"

He just shook his head from side to side.

From the corner of my eye I could see James's expression. At times he looked to me like he was sorry for the thoughtless things he said and did to Natalie. But at other times he looked like he couldn't care less. He wouldn't have to deal with her anymore with how to raise Mason, and could forget about the child support payments.

Five minutes later, James turned to Mason and said, "Okay, we need to go now."

On Friday late afternoon, Graciella and I drove to the airport to pick up Torreey and Luke. When I saw them I hugged them both and cried. There were no words to say. We drove to the funeral home for Torreey and Luke to see Natalie. They couldn't believe that it was her laying dead on that table. No one could believe it. It was impossible.

On Saturday morning at 10 a.m., it was time for us to attend the services. I walked in holding my husband's arm. Luke and Graciella were holding on to Mom. We walked all the way to the front where Natalie's body was in repose inside an open casket. I leaned down and gave her a kiss on the forehead. I grasped her hand and didn't want to let it go; this time her whole face and hands were frozen. A video with Natalie's pictures was playing, and her favorite song by Daughtry, *Home*, was drifting from the sound system. Natalie had always wanted to come back home to Redondo Beach. I couldn't stop crying, hearing her song and looking at her pictures broke my heart into a million jagged pieces. Losing my daughter was the worst pain I've ever experienced; and now nothing will ever be the same for me.

Graciella walked to my side and whispered in my ear, "Rhonda is here with James."

"Tell James she needs to leave. She's not welcome here," I said.

"I'll take care of it," Graciella said, walking away.

Graciella approached James and told him what I said.

"She's with me and she's staying," he responded without emotion.

The priest came out and my husband removed my hand from Natalie's to go sit down in the front row. Luis, Natalie's husband sat next to Graciella and Luke.

I remember looking at the priest talking and talking, but I don't recall a single word he said. I also don't recollect when I got up from the front row where we were sitting while the priest was still talking.

My son and my husband later told me that I stood up, walked to Natalie's casket, started kissing her, and telling her, "Get up! Get up! And go with me." That's when Luke came over and brought me back to my seat.

Mason never came to sit by me during the funeral services. James and his girlfriend kept him on their side. I just wanted to hold him, but it felt as if James had other plans. Mason needed me as much as I needed him. I never even saw Mason at the service that day. James, his girlfriend, his mother, and some of his relatives left the funeral home half an hour before it was over.

Nearly three hundred people attended the funeral service. I don't remember ever looking over my shoulder; my husband later told me that the funeral home was literally packed with people. At the end of the service, people came to the front row where we were sitting to pay their respects. I do remember them hugging me and crying. There were so many of them I was overwhelmed and felt like running away, until this young girl came to me and in Spanish said, "Soy Maria y este es mi hijo Daniel, tu hija Natalie nos salvo." ("I'm Maria, and this is my son Daniel. Your daughter Natalie saved us.") I looked at her and the young boy who was about six years old. She hugged me and so did the boy; and crying, she said, "Tu hija fue un angel." ("Your daughter was an angel.") All I could do was to hold them and cry too.

After the funeral ended, Mom, Torreey, and I drove to the Tennis Club for the reception that Natalie's friends had arranged.

I was told that ninety-eight percent of the individuals who were at the funeral came to the reception at the club. But Natalie, the life of the party, was not there. She was loved by so many for her kindness, fun-loving personality, and most of all the way she always kept everyone happy.

Luke, Graciella, and Luis drove together. Graciella and Luke decided to stop by a tattoo parlor before attending the reception. Luke wanted to have a tattoo done of Natalie's name in her memory.

James and his family all went back to his house for food and drinks.

Torreey, Mom, and I stopped at James's house after the reception was over at the Club. I just needed to see Mason one more time before going home the next day.

After leaving James's house, we stopped by the hospital to see Diane.

Mom, Graciella, Torreey and I walked into the room where Diane was resting on the bed and surrounded by friends.

I immediately approached her, threw my arms around her and cried with her. "OMG, I can't believe my Natalie's gone," I said, trembling inside. While holding each other tight Diane whispered in my ear.

I didn't say anything to her. I was confused and thought I heard wrong. A few seconds later I moved away wiping my tears.

Torreey and Luke leaned down, hugged her, and Mom held her and cried.

Graciella got close to her and held her tight.

Twenty minutes later, we left the hospital and were on our way home to drop off Graciella and Mom. I was sitting in the back with them and turned to Graciella and Mom and said in Spanish, "Estoy confundida, O tal vez oi mal. Creo que Diane me dijo que fue la culpa de ella." ("I'm confused, or maybe I heard wrong. Diane whispered in my ear, 'It's my fault, it's my fault.'")

"OH SHIT, she said the same thing to me!" Graciella replied, alarmed.

"I don't know what to think of it. She looked pretty high on the drugs she's taking for her pain," I told Mom and Graciella. I was confused and didn't want to think about it any longer.

That evening, we went back to the funeral home around 8:00 p.m. A gentleman took us back to where her casket was, near a huge oven, outside of the funeral home.

"Sir, please open the casket," Torreey instructed. "My wife wants to see her one more time."

"Natalie, I love you!" My tears were falling on her face. By now her cheeks were very frozen. I held her hand and didn't want to let her go. On her chest was a drawing of a big heart colored in red, captioned with, "You were the best Mom ever!" that Mason sketched for her.

I brought a red rose and placed it on top of her chest. I turned to Luke and said, "Do you know that Natalie was killed on your grandmother Jereldine's birthday, Cinco de Mayo? (Jereldine was my ex-husband's German mother.)

"No, I didn't know. That's weird, " Luke said, surprised.

Luke had brought a pair of scissors and cut off several strands of her beautiful black shiny shoulder length hair. I wanted to keep mementos of her hair just like I did with Lina's.

"How long does it take to cremate her?" Torreey asked the gentleman in charge.

"Many hours," he responded.

The ashes were going to be ready for us to pick up Sunday morning before going to the airport.

I bought a beautiful dolphin urn made of brass from the funeral home for Natalie's ashes.

On a beautiful Sunday morning, Mother's Day 2010, we drove to the funeral home to pick up the urn with a portion of Natalie's ashes inside of it. The rest of her ashes were in a plastic bag inside a metal container. The other half was going to Mason.

We drove to the airport and went through the checkpoint. Luke was carrying one of Natalie's dogs. Milo, the youngest pug, was the only dog we could take home with us on the airplane. Milo weighed ten pounds; the other dogs were well over ten.

I carried my daughter's ashes with me on the airplane on Mother's Day and found myself thinking how much I regretted not going to watch Natalie play her last match like she wanted me to. Who'd believe that this would be her last tennis game on this world? I had medicated myself so that I could handle the flight. All I wanted was to get home and go to bed.

We got on the small airplane in Lake Cormorant to Houston and then on to Los Angeles. We were seated in the back of the plane. I sat next to my husband by the window. I was holding the dolphin urn close to my chest. As the plane took off I started sobbing, I couldn't stop thinking of my Natalie. This wasn't true – it was just a nightmare I couldn't wake up from.

The stewardess announced on the intercom, "Happy Mother's Day!" When I heard this I couldn't take it anymore. "NOOOOO!" I let out a scream so loud it sent the stewardess rushing to the back of the plane, asking, "What's wrong?"

"She lost her daughter," my husband replied.

"So sorry. Is there anything I can get for you?" the stewardess offered.

No, thank you," Torreey answered.

I took another pill right away. I didn't remember or care what time I had taken the last one. All I wanted was to just disappear from this earth, to be gone like my daughter.

As if I hadn't had enough, we got to Houston late, missed our plane to Los Angeles, and had to spend the night and take another flight the next morning.

After being home for a few days I contacted Luis. I really didn't feel like talking about it but I had no other choice. Diane said she could no longer represent Natalie on the community property settlement. In other words, she told us to find another attorney and didn't provide us with any of the documents. Even though we knew she was obligated to do so, I didn't want any problems with her. I already had too much to handle. So we had our new attorney obtain the necessary documents from her.

Torreey contacted an attorney from Mississippi to help us deal with the mess of the community property. Since Luis was married to Natalie we desperately needed his help, and he agreed to do whatever we asked.

"Shirley, first of all, I want you to know that I'm not interested in any money. I don't want a penny from any of this. I loved your daughter and Mason with all my heart," he promised over the phone.

"Luis, muchisimas gracias por quererla tanto. Te lo agradezco con todo mi corazon." ("Luis, thank you for loving my daughter so much. I appreciate it from the bottom of my heart.") I told him.

"Luis, when did you and Natalie get married?" I asked.

"Natalie and I eloped in April 2009. We didn't tell anyone except Natalie's friend Dorothy who married my friend Marcos the same day. Natalie wanted to tell you at the right time, and besides she knew that you'd have pushed her to leave Lake Cormorant and go home to California with Mason."

"Yes, with Mason and you too, Luis," I admitted. "Luis, did you know that she was about two weeks from settling the community property against her ex-husband James? He owed her $400,000 from her divorce settlement that had been dragging on for four years."

"Yes, she had mentioned that to me," he said.

"Luis, please e-mail me copies of the marriage certificate. I'm not sure what else I'll need but I will be in touch with you soon. Oh, also please call me if James threatens you with anything. Muchisimas gracias!" ("Thank you!")

I'd heard talk that James might try to have Luis deported, since at the time he was on a working visa.

"Yes, I will call you, and please don't worry about James. I'm not afraid of him. I can handle it. Asta luego y cuidate mucho." ("Goodbye and take good care of yourself.")

Chapter 51

A Dragon in My Dreams - 2010

On Thursday, May 13, 2010 (eight days after Natalie was killed) I had a dream with her in it. I woke up crying and thinking about it. Natalie and I were together, laughing and floating in a clear blue sky. All of a sudden, this big dragon came toward us and Natalie screamed at me, "GET HIM, MOM, GET HIM!"

The dragon got real close to us and opened his mouth very wide. I was holding a small ball in my hand and Natalie yelled, "Do it now, Mom, DO IT!"

I threw the ball as hard as I could inside his mouth. The dragon exploded in the sky and Natalie and I busted out laughing uncontrollably.

She then turned to me with a big smile and said, "You got him, Mom. You got him!"

I believe Natalie was giving me messages through my dreams. This vision meant *Mom, don't give up. Finish the community property settlement for me and get back the money I owed you.* She wanted me to have what was rightfully mine.

On Wednesday, May 19, 2010, (sixteen days after her death) I had another dream with Natalie. This time we were in a hotel bedroom and we were both tired. She was sitting on one side of the bed yawning; then she turned around and said, "Mom, I'm going to tell you something. I am now in somebody else's body and I'm real tired, so I'm going to sleep." She then covered her face under the blankets and my dream ended.

"NOOOO!" I screamed.

"Momsie, Momsie, (To this day Torreey still uses that nickname for me. He seldom calls me Shirley.) Wake up, wake up!" Torreey said, shaking my shoulder softly.

I woke up crying and couldn't get back to sleep. I got up, drank a glass of water and swallowed an anxiety pill. My whole body was trembling.

On Friday, May 21, Alana called. "Hi, Shirley I'm going to be in Redondo Beach over the weekend to visit my parents. Would love to come see you."

"I'd love to see you too," I gushed.

Harvey and Janice were also coming by to see me.

Alana, Harvey, and Janice were friends with Natalie since junior high. They'd always stayed in touch. Every year when Natalie came home to California they got together to catch up.

Alana was tall, thin, with long black hair and a beautiful light complexion. She was the same age as Natalie. She was married with a two-year-old son. She was sweet and always made funny expressions when she talked.

Harvey was Chinese and very hyper. He loved Natalie like the sister he never had. He was always very caring.

Janice, as I previously described, was also sweet and beautiful. She was taller than all of them (six feet). She and Natalie lived in Italy for a year and a half.

On Saturday, May 22, Alana and Harvey showed up at my house around 10:00 a.m. I was so happy to see them.

Harvey and Alana hugged me tight while we sobbed and they whispered in my ear, "So sorry, Shirley."

A few minutes later I showed them Natalie's pictures and the ashes. Tears were running down our faces.

We sat down and I said, "I had a dream with Natalie a few days ago." I told them how Natalie said she was now in somebody else's body.

Alana eyes welled up with tears. She looked at me and said, "Do you know that I'm pregnant?"

I looked at her with teardrops rolling down my face and said, "Really? You don't look pregnant."

"I'm just a few months along," she confided.

"Do you know what it is?" I asked nervously.

"No, I don't," she answered.

She then placed her hand on her stomach and with a soft tone in her voice said, "Wouldn't it be nice if Natalie was inside of me?"

Harvey, Alana and I stared at each other with eyes full of tears.

"That's so sweet of you, Alana," I told her.

A couple of hours later, Alana and Harvey had to leave.

Janice showed up around noon with a beautiful tropical flower arrangement and some pictures of Natalie, Alana and herself in high school. We hugged, cried and laughed as we glanced through the photographs.

"I'm so sorry for your loss, Shirley. I miss her too!" Janice told me as she held me tight.

Chapter 52

The Vanishing Wheelbarrow - June 2010

A month after Natalie was killed, my son Luke and I flew to Lake Cormorant to clean and pack up Natalie's house. I wanted to get rid of everything – including the house.

"We need to sell the house ASAP!" I told Torreey. I didn't want to keep anything. I thought that by doing this I would feel better. I guess I was trying to make everything disappear. Natalie was gone so I thought I had to let everything of hers go away too.

My sister Graciella and her daughter Maggie were flying in from Illinois to help us. I offered most of Natalie's furniture to Graciella.

Flying back to Lake Cormorant was very difficult for all of us, especially me. In front of the house to the left side of the door was the decorative wheelbarrow that I mentioned earlier; a gift from Natalie's husband Luis.

Natalie's coworker and dear friend Omar had planted some herbs in the beautiful wheelbarrow.

The minute we got to the house, Luke and I were opening drawers in the kitchen and office. I said, "Luke, you go ahead and start by separating the documents into two different piles. One for trash and the other to keep." I really didn't know where to begin but thought the paperwork was more important for now. I needed any documents that had to do with the community property settlement.

Natalie was never an organized person; all of the drawers were packed with paperwork she didn't need. There was no end to it. I took two big plastic bags and cleaned the shelves in the master bathroom. In one bag, I placed most of the containers that were halfway full or completely full. In the other bag the containers that were almost empty. Tears were streaming down my face while I went through container after container. I couldn't believe I was doing this. I was remembering when my husband and I bought the house and I helped her move in; we were both so excited and happy. Now she was gone forever.

Graciella and Maggie arrived on Saturday afternoon, and now there were four of us cleaning up before Johnny, Graciella's husband, arrived the following Friday to load up a U-Haul truck with the furniture.

Graciella immediately came looking for me in the bedroom. She hugged and kissed me and said, "Shirley, do you know that the wheelbarrow is gone?"

I looked at Graciella with a frown and said, "WHAT!?"

I quickly went to the front of the house and stared at the blank space where Natalie's planter used to be. I started crying. "I can't believe someone would do this."

"I'm going over to Natalie's neighbors, Lance and Sara," Graciella said.

Lance and Sara, a wonderful elderly couple where always there for Natalie. They watched the house for us until we came back to clean up.

"Lance, the wheelbarrow that was in front of Natalie's house has disappeared," Graciella informed him.

"What? I can't believe that. No one would do anything like that around here! The wheelbarrow was there a few days ago when I checked the house!" he responded, surprised.

Graciella picked up the phone and called Natalie's best friend. "Nancy, someone stole Natalie's planter from the front of the house."

"No shit? Who would do such a thing?" Nancy answered, alarmed. Nancy was about 5'10, blonde, with big brown eyes. She was married with four children. She lived across the street from James's house.

On Saturday, June 12, I called James in the late afternoon. "I would like to see Mason on Sunday."

"We're going to be gone most of Sunday, but you're welcome to come by around 5:00 p.m. I'm going to barbeque some hamburgers," James said.

"Can I bring my sister and niece along?" I asked. I didn't want to be at his house by myself. I was upset that I had to do what James wanted. I couldn't pick up my grandson and have him with me.

Around midnight I started feeling tired and decided to take a shower and go to bed. Thank God for the pills my doctor prescribed. I was on Xanax for anxiety, and Ambien to help me sleep.

Graciella and Maggie were very helpful and super fast, we got a lot done by Sunday.

On Sunday around 5:00 p.m., Graciella, Maggie and I got ready to go to see Mason.

"Luke, are you coming with us?" I asked.

"No. I can't stand seeing James. Besides, if I lose it, I'll probably end up throwing a punch," he said with a scowl.

"Okay, I think you better stay then," I agreed.

On our way to see Mason I was thinking about Luke's words back in the year 2000 when Natalie married James and why he didn't attend his sister's wedding. "I don't trust James," he'd said. From the very beginning, Luke saw James for who he really was.

I was also thinking about Natalie's words back in July 2009. She wanted to take Mason on a trip to Italy with some of her friends, their kids and me. When James evicted her from their home, he got a hold of Mason's passport and refused to release it to Natalie.

One day while driving, she called James and asked him nicely for the passport again. James verbally agreed while Natalie had him on the speakerphone; a friend was with her in the car while the conversation was going on.

In the end, James retained possession of Mason's passport and didn't give permission to take him on this trip to Italy. James also sent letters to the local tennis clubs where Natalie was a member telling them not to allow Natalie to make any charges. Finally, he also sent a letter to the US Customs and Immigration Service, telling the agency that Natalie had violated a court order. He claimed that she had taken Mason in violation of the joint custody and visitation agreement. He then further stated that he wanted the agency to flag his son's passport to prevent his "unauthorized removal from the country." In case Natalie had somehow obtained a second passport.

For a while Natalie worried about the power James had in their shared circles within the community. She told me and some of her close friends several times that she believed he could make her life miserable if he really wanted to.

James was a charming man when he met and married my daughter. But by the time he divorced her he'd become a different person. Torreey and I didn't see the other side of James until much later.

We arrived at James's house and I knocked on the front door. No one answered so I said, "Graciella, Maggie, let's go through the side gate." I knew about the side gate because I visited this house many times when Natalie and James were together.

As soon as I opened the gate, Graciella, Maggie and I looked at each other in disbelief. "OMG, they fucking took Natalie's wheelbarrow!" Graciella whispered.

I stood there frozen with my mouth open. "Motherfuck!" I growled. I was shocked but kept myself in control. I didn't want to go crazy and say anything because of Mason. Thanks to my meds, all I wanted to do in that moment was get to Mason and hold him. I said, "Graciella, Maggie, please, don't say anything about the wheelbarrow. I can't do it because of Mason."

"Don't worry, we wont," Graciella assured me.

James and Rhonda were in the backyard clubhouse when we approached them.

Mason and her two boys were in the pool.

We pretended as if nothing had happened but I really wanted to rip their heads off.

Mason got out of the pool and came over to kiss and hug me.

"Hi, sweet pea, how are you?" I asked while holding on to him.

"Good," he responded and went back in the pool.

Graciella, Maggie and I each grabbed a hamburger while James and Rhonda sat in the clubhouse and pretended to watch TV.

I loathed being there in what used to be Natalie's house.

Why didn't he meet Rhonda before he met my daughter? I couldn't help thinking. I needed to get over the wheelbarrow with all of the herbs dried from lack of water.

Around 9:00 p.m., I said, "Mason, we have to go, babe."

I kissed him and said, "I love you!" and left.

When we returned to Natalie's house, three of Natalie's friends, Wendy, Leslie and Cassie, were sitting in the dining room waiting for us. They each had a glass of wine and immediately handed Graciella and me one too.

Graciella grinned wickedly and said, "Guess what? We found the wheelbarrow in James's backyard."

"NO SHIT!" Leslie shouted.

By now all of the girls were furious and started calling James and Rhonda all kinds of names. We were all shocked that they had taken it from Natalie's house. A few minutes later, Cassie grabbed her cell phone and called her friend, Charlie. "Come by the house, NOW!"

Fifteen minutes later, Charlie arrived and the girls gave him the news.

"The nerve of those two!" Charlie bristled. He stood there thinking, then said, "We'll be back," and left with Cassie.

An hour later, around midnight, they reappeared in front of us with smiles on their faces, mischief in their eyes, and the wheelbarrow in their arms. "We fucking took it back," Charlie screeched.

Graciella, Maggie, me and the other two gals couldn't believe what we were seeing. Their feet were all muddy and their faces were lit up like Christmas trees. They put the wheelbarrow down and we all started laughing like crazy. Leslie kept repeating, "We got it back! We got it back! Here's to you Natalie, we know you're in heaven laughing."

"Shirley, you need to take it home with you," Wendy insisted.

"No, can't do it," I reluctantly protested. "What if Sunny or Al came by my house? They'd see it and tell James for sure." Wendy turned to my sister. "Graciella, you take it."

"It's too fucking cold in Illinois during the winter, nothing could survive in it," Graciella objected.

In the end, Charlie put it back in his truck and drove away with it. That was the end of the wheelbarrow. Nobody, except us, would know where it went or who took it. We'd wait until Mason was an adult and give it to him.

The following day, Monday, June 14, Monica Collins (James's cousin) called me and said, "James is furious because you guys took the wheelbarrow from his backyard. You were the last ones in his house, and when they woke up in the morning it was gone."

Graciella and I were in the car when she called me. I had her on the speakerphone. "Monica, you can't steal your own property. It was taken from my house, and James or Rhonda did it! That's the truth whether they like it or not." I said, very upset.

Later that afternoon I called James. "First of all, we didn't steal the wheelbarrow, and second, it was taken from my home and you know it!" I declared.

James was silent for a second, then, said, "Mason wanted it, so Rhonda drove by the house with him and got it."

"Why didn't Mason or somebody call me and let me know that he wanted it? I would have given it to him." I said and flipped him the finger over the phone.

"I forgot to mention it to you," James shrugged it off.

Yeah right!

Months later, I asked Mason about the wheelbarrow.

"Bebe, I never wanted the wheelbarrow. All I wanted was my Legos and my mom's pillow." And those I'd made sure he got.

On Monday afternoon, June 14, Graciella, Maggie, and I drove to Natalie's office. I needed to go through Natalie's desk and take any personal documents that I thought were important. I was looking for anything with Luis's name and the community property settlement.

Luis had asked that if I found any records with his name to please give them back to him.

An hour later, Diane walked in and wasn't very happy seeing me there, sitting at Natalie's desk, going through some of the paperwork. She said hello with an unfriendly voice and I could tell by the expression on her face that she was angry.

"Shirley, what are you doing here?" she continued with a rude tone of voice.

I looked at her in the eye and said, "I'm looking for any personal documents."

"You can't do that!" She spoke like she was in a courtroom, addressing a defendant.

Graciella and Natalie's friend Joyce were standing nearby listening to our conversation.

I answered her coldly, "Natalie would still be here if she had listened to me and not you."

"Shirley, if I could change any of what has happened I would, but it's done and there's nothing I can do about it," she said in a firm tone of voice that carried annoyance.

Our conversation ended when my cell phone rang with Luke calling. "Mom, there's two of James's attorneys here at Natalie's saying we are not to touch or take anything in the house because everything – including the house – belongs to Mason."

"Luke," I said anxiously, "call Torreey right away and have him talk to the attorneys."

I shook my head and started crying. "Fuck!" I moaned. I couldn't take any more pain. My daughter was dead and now I had to contend with James.

Torreey informed the lead attorney, "We own the house and most of the furniture. I'll fax copies of the deed to the house and receipts for the furniture. Didn't James tell you that?"

"No, he didn't," Mr. Soress replied.

Apparently James had told his two attorney friends that Natalie owned the house.

The attorneys insisted on checking the house to see what Natalie had while my son Luke followed. They walked upstairs into the guest room and opened the closet door. Inside the closet were men's shirts and pants.

Mr. Soress asked, "Whose clothes are these?"

"Natalie's husband, Luis," Luke replied.

"James didn't tell us she was remarried," Mr. Soress said, clearly upset.

By now both attorneys looked like fools. Before leaving the house they said they'd get back to us soon.

We kept on packing but I was afraid that when Saturday came and we were all ready to leave, James would send the attorneys or the police to prevent us from taking anything.

Graciella called Mr. Soress and got a letter giving us their permission to take whatever we wanted from the home.

A few months later, rumors were that James's mother was saying her son had bought the house for Natalie and Mason to live after they got divorced and Rhonda had plans to move her mother into Natalie's house, thinking that James now owned it.

Chapter 53

Rescued Pets - 2010

When Natalie was killed, she left behind her beloved rescued animals. Two male pugs, Milo and Otis, one male puggle, Rooney, and two male cats, Jack and Sparrow. She was on the rescue team and originally, she only intended to foster them, but ended up keeping them.

On Saturday evening we drove to the pet store and bought three pet carriers so that each dog could travel with us, but when my husband checked with the airport they reminded him that the weight limit for animals was no more than ten pounds to be in the cabin of the plane. And if they were traveling in the cargo bay they needed a health certificate from a veterinary.

"Oh no, we can't leave them behind. What are we going to do?" I cried, hugging the three little innocent dogs. It broke my heart even more to see the sad look in their eyes. "Why? Why is this happening?" I kept asking myself.

"We can only take Milo with us," Torreey announced. Milo was the youngest pug and weighed nine pounds.

"I'll go and talk to Natalie's neighbors, Lance and Sara, and ask if they'll watch and feed the pets for us while were gone," Torreey said, heading over.

"I'll check with some of Natalie's friends and see if someone wants to adopt them," I said, grabbing the phone. I felt horrible about doing this but we had no other choice. Even if I could bring them all with us, I still couldn't have kept them. We already had three dogs and one cat and Milo would make five. It seemed like every year that I came to visit Natalie she had a new adopted pet. "Natalie, you need to stop keeping all these animals. What's going to happen to them if you're not here for them?" I'd said, teasing her.

Well, then you'll have to take them with you," she said with a smirk on her face.

"I don't think I can do that. There's too many of them," I pointed out.

Sunday morning came and we were ready to leave for the airport. Milo was in the carry-on and ready to go.

I grabbed Otis and Rooney, hugged them tight against my chest and cried, "I love you both. I'm so sorry to do this, please forgive me." They both stared at me while licking my arms.

We left the four pets in the house and Natalie's friend Eva had agreed to come and help Lance with the feeding and care of the animals.

Back at home I was a total wreck. I didn't know how to think, breathe, walk and talk. I was torn in pieces and couldn't figure out how to deal with this. I kept thinking of the four animals all alone waiting for Natalie to come through the door; it was horrible and sad. All I could do was cry and cry.

Days later, I called Diane and left her several messages. "Please help me find homes for Natalie's two dogs." I felt confident that she'd assist me since she was on the animal rescue team, and I never thought she'd abandon Natalie's little dogs; but she never responded to my calls. I knew she was a mess, going through rehabilitation for her injures and therapy for her mind, but she was not the only one. I was a total fucking wreck and I desperately needed her help with Natalie's beloved dogs. She was walking, breathing; she was alive. Yes, I was angry with Diane! My daughter would still be here if it wasn't for her insisting on going to that meeting May 5. I still have the therapist card that I found in my daughter's purse with the date and time of Mason's appointment on May 5 at 10:30 a.m. Natalie rescheduled Mason's session to Friday, May 7, just to keep Diane happy.

I was very disappointed and hurt by Diane's refusal to help, but that is what she chose to do. Natalie would have taken all the dogs into her home. I'd thought Diane and I would stay friends forever. I gave life to my daughter and Diane saw her take her last breaths. But I found out Diane was not a true friend.

Back to my grandson, Mason; I called him twice a week and made it a point not to cry when I talked to him. My instructions from James were to go through Rhonda in order to communicate with Mason. Sometimes I'd call more than twice, leave messages on her mobile, and would not hear back from Mason. Several times I'd called Trisha, James's mother and begged her to have Mason call me back. But I was out of luck if Rhonda didn't feel like putting Mason on the phone, and there was nothing I could do about it.

But I didn't give up. I could hear my daughter saying, "Momma didn't raise a quitter, don't stop Mom!" So I continued leaving messages and texting on both James and Rhonda's mobiles to have Mason call me. When I talked to Mason, I stayed strong for him; if I fell apart I knew James would use it in court to prove that I was not a stable person for Mason to be around. James and Rhonda were probably recording my conversations with Mason in case they needed to file anything against me.

When I was allowed to speak to Mason; this was a typical conversation:

"Hi Mason, how are you?"

"I'm good, Bebe."
"Hey Babe, did Rhonda give you my message?"
"No, Bebe."
"Have you had any dreams with your mom?"
"No, no."
"Mason, Milo is doing great with us. He's the king at our house. He misses you, you know?"
"I miss him too, Bebe."
"Sunami is very jealous of Milo." (Sunami is my female pug) Otis, Rooney, Jack and Sparrow need a home. We couldn't bring them with us. I'm worried about them being alone."

One time, Mason called me and said, "Bebe, I want Otis and Rooney with me."

"Oh, that is so sweet of you, babe." I was so happy for Mason but I knew the dogs were going to be miserable. I didn't get the impression that James and Rhonda were animal lovers.

A day later, Mason and Monica Collins drove by the house and picked up the two dogs.

I was thrilled when Natalie's best friend, Nancy, took the cats, Jack and Sparrow.

Mason got to see them every day since he lived across the street from Nancy's house.

During a conversation with my grandson, he told me that the dogs were kept in the backyard all day long. James and Rhonda did not allow them inside the house. I was angry. OMG, *it's the middle of the hot brutal summer!*

Natalie had a doggie door at her house and the dogs spent most of the time indoors. The dogs were probably suffering and Mason had absolutely no say in the matter.

Every time I called him, I asked, "How are Otis and Rooney doing?"

"Okay, but they're not allowed inside," he'd say.

In June, when I was in Lake Cormorant to clean up Natalie's house, I visited Mason. The dogs, of course, were in the backyard. They were so happy to see me. I felt sad to see them in the yard; the humidity and the mosquitos were horrible for them. They were almost out of breath and had bites all over their bodies.

Several times I told Mason, "If you can't take care of them, let me bring them to California and I promise you I'll find them new homes."

One day I called Mason and Rhonda answered. I said, "I can take the dogs with me if it's a problem for you and James."

"It's not a problem for us," she coldly responded, knowing how much those dogs meant to me.

James's backyard fence had a couple of holes that were never repaired so the dogs were going through them every day. I believe the dogs were trying to find their way back home where they belonged, at Natalie's house.

Every week that I called Mason I mentioned, "Don't forget to tell your dad to fix the fence so the dogs wont get out. Okay, babe?"

"I reminded my dad many times, Bebe," he told me.

Months later, Otis was found dead in the neighborhood. Rooney was run over by a car. As far as I could tell in ensuing phone conversations, Mason never learned what happened to the dogs, which I felt was best.

Milo is the only surviving dog. We give him lots of love. He's sweet and sleeps in bed with us along with three of our other dogs and a cat. He has a wonderful life with us in our home even though our bed keeps shrinking and shrinking from so many furry friends. Animals are by far much better behaved than certain human beings I could mention – but I won't. They love you no matter what; when I'm sick or upset they're all by my side. They bring me happiness and joy. They all have different personalities, even our cat, but I love them just the way they are. They're my true companions. I take care of them but they also take care of me with all their love.

Chapter 54

A Bird Brings a Message - 2010

On Tuesday, July 6 at 1:20 p.m., two months after Natalie was killed, I was in the kitchen by myself eating lunch. My four dogs were with me when I heard the cat growling persistently in the living room.

I ran over and saw that Mama Mia, our cat, had a little bird in her mouth. The bird was flapping her wings so I leaned down and squeezed Mia's mouth until she let it go.

The small bird was fine; she was flying all over the living room trying to get out.

I ran down the stairs and opened the front door. The bird came down and kept trying to find her way outside but couldn't do it. I kept on moving my arms trying to direct the bird to go out the front door.

The bird stopped and sat near the side of the window by the stairs, then tried it a few more times and still wasn't able to find her way out the door. By then I was getting very nervous.

The dogs were all sitting at the top of the stairs staring at the little creature.

Mama Mia the cat was trying to get the bird back.

I just wanted the bird to find her way out the door and fly away. The bird waited a little bit and tried it again. I stood by the entrance of the house and watched as the bird crashed into the window and drop in front of me.

"OMG! OMG!" I yelled while covering my mouth with my hands.

The bird had landed on the stone floor next to my feet. By now I was shaking and sobbing at the same time. I leaned down to look at the tiny beautiful bird and saw that it was dying. She took three final breaths and then was gone. "Oh no, why is this happening to me? FUCK, I can't take it anymore!" For sure I thought I was going insane. My dogs were now at my feet sniffing the dead bird.

"What do I do now?" I knew first I had to calm down, so I took a few deep breaths, then ran to the garage, got a little box and a shovel and picked up the bird and placed it inside the box. I took it outside, dug a hole next to one of the palm trees, and buried it.

Since my daughter was killed, I haven't been able to stop wondering if she suffered before she died. Her neck was broken at the time of the car accident; it killed her instantly, so they said. I desperately needed to have some closure.

By this little bird coming inside of my house, breaking her neck, taking three last breaths and dying in front of me, for some reason I found some peace.

My daughter sent me a message through this tiny bird. She needed me to know how she died and didn't suffer, and wanted me to have some peace of mind.

Chapter 55

Mental Healing - 2010

After my daughter was killed I became fearful some of the time with occasional panic attacks and anxiety, especially when the doorbell rang. I was taking Xanax for anxiety, Ambien for insomnia, and Lexapro for depression. I wasn't teaching aerobics or playing tennis. I was walking at the beach every day with our Dalmatian/Labrador mix Niki. The ocean breeze and the sound of the waves helped me tremendously, but it wasn't enough. I was falling deeper and deeper into despair. The Lexapro was not helping me at all; it was making things worse.

I called Dr. Yawata, our family doctor of over twenty years. "The Lexapro is making me weird. I have suicidal thoughts and have become more emotionally unstable. My hands are shaking at times and I think I'm losing my mind. I want life to be over, I'm tired of it. I want to go to sleep and never wake up again. Don't wanna think about anything except to numb the pain in my heart. I can't handle it any more. I don't like feeling this way and I'm not taking any more Lexapro. I need a therapist as soon as possible."

"How about if we try another type of depression pill?" Dr. Yawata suggested.

"No, I don't think so, Doctor," I replied firmly.

"Okay, hold on for a few minutes and I'll get you some therapists' names and numbers," she relented.

I called three of the therapists she gave me and left my name and phone number on their recorders.

After listening to their messages, I called the one I thought had the nicest voice (Roberta).

I set up a consultation with Roberta that week. I really liked her. She was sweet with a very kind voice. I scheduled my next appointments once a week for an hour each session.

Every week that I saw her I cried.

"It's okay to cry, Shirley," she assured me.

She helped me go back to teaching aerobics, playing tennis, spending time with my friends, talking with my grandson; and best of all staying positive. Roberta helped me focus on taking just one step at a time. I'd found myself so lost, so empty, and in so much pain every single day. To make matters worse, one day in July, a friend of Natalie's called and informed me that James and Rhonda had gotten married in Hawaii.

I couldn't believe it. *How could James do this? Mason's mother was killed just two months ago. Why couldn't James have waited until Mason had time to heal a little more?*

I didn't know how to deal with this tragedy. Losing my daughter was not acceptable to me. I kept waiting for her to call me. Sometimes I found myself calling her and waiting for her to answer her phone. Other times I'd break down, go to my bedroom, and cry until it hurt so bad I could no longer cry, no more tears would fall down my face.

I saw Roberta for about nine months, then, decided I needed to be on my own. I wanted to find out if I could indeed handle it by myself, and I did as long as I stayed positive; but of course it was impossible. I stayed away from my family by not answering their calls. I knew they were concerned about me but I couldn't help it, I just wanted to be left alone. I had no desire to be around people and I had no appetite. I lost fifteen pounds, which is a lot for a person barely over five feet. Waking up in the morning was by far when I felt the worst – until one morning I heard my daughter's voice: "Mom, get up, get your ass out of bed. Momma didn't raise a quitter!"

I opened my eyes and cried uncontrollably. "Natalie, Natalie, please help me to be strong," I begged.

Chapter 56

Vehicular Homicide - 2010-2012

It was May 5, 2010 at 3:35 p.m., when Ronald, forty-five, an African American and beloved high school head coach and mentor was driving north on Highway 55. His ill wife Cheryl was sitting beside him in the passenger seat when he fell asleep at the wheel and crashed into my daughter Natalie's southbound vehicle.

Natalie and Diane were always fighting for the less fortunate, and that day they were on their way home from doing just that. Natalie driving her SUV and Diane the passenger when unexpectedly a white Ford truck crossed the median and struck Natalie's car head-on leaving both autos nearly demolished.

My daughter was dead at the scene and Diane was severely injured and airlifted to a local hospital. Ronald's wife Cheryl also died in the accident. Ronald, the driver at fault, suffered only minor injuries.

State Police took blood samples from Ronald and toxicology tests were pending.

Three months after Natalie was killed, I got a call from Joyce, one of my daughter's friends. "Shirley, Ronald has been arrested and charged with vehicular homicide. He was under the influence of illegal narcotics in his system at the time of the crash."

"Oh God, I'm sorry. I have to hang up," I told Joyce, sobbing and feeling nauseated.

After the horrible news I slowly walked to the shelves near the guest bathroom. With my head down and teardrops falling, I grabbed a picture frame of Natalie and me that was taken in 2009 while I was visiting her in Lake Cormorant. I held it close to my chest, sat on the floor, and cried like a baby. Suddenly, all four of my dogs were by my side, looking up at me with the saddest eyes, whimpering and licking the tears off my face. They stayed with me until I got up and ambled to my master bathroom. I opened the medicine cabinet, took an anxiety and a sleeping pill, grabbed the picture back, pressed it to my chest, collapsed on the bed and was again surrounded by all of my dogs. I felt so lucky to have them by my side.

I kissed and hugged them and said, "I love you," to each one, especially Milo, my daughter and grandson's rescued dog (the only male). I'd brought him back from Lake Cormorant. Milo was a part of Natalie and I knew she was happy he was with us in our home. I could feel Natalie with me just by having Milo around. She knew how much Torreey and I loved and cared for animals. I held him close and stroked his soft head until I finally drifted into sleep.

That weekend on late Sunday afternoon, my son Luke came over for dinner. He asked, "Mom, Torreey, did you hear the news about Ronald?"

"I heard some," I said with distress.

"Well, this is what I found out," Luke said and proceeded to read from a piece of paper he'd hastily scribbled notes on. "State Police have confirmed that forty-five-year-old Ronald turned himself in, and is being charge with two counts of vehicular homicide, one count of vehicular negligent injury, and one count driving while intoxicated. He was processed into the jail Thursday morning, August of 2010, and bonded out soon after. His bond was set at $250,000. As for his job with the school, Superintendent Mr. Harris says, 'He's still got a job until he's actually convicted for the crime.'"

"WHAT? I can't fucking believe this!" I said in tears, covering my mouth with my hand. "OMG, Natalie's dead and gone but Ronald continues working as the high school head coach after the accident! It can't be. This is fucking insane! How can the superintendent allow him to do this?

"It's called, 'Union Rules,' you know?" Torreey explained.

"Well, fuck them all! They should be sued. My daughter's dead because of this drug addict coach." I exploded, wiping away my tears.

"There's more," Luke said, anger welling up. "Ronald was given enough time before he goes to prison to get his pension from his job at Brighton High School and leave everything settled for his daughter to go to college."

I knew that it was not his daughter's fault, but it just made me sick that this man, and possibly others are allowed to get away with things like this! "Oh, I feel sick. I'm gonna throw up." I ran to the bathroom sobbing.

Five minutes later I came back into the kitchen and said, "What kind of example is this for the kids at Brighton High and other schools? That it's okay to be under the influence of illegal narcotics, kill someone, and continue to work? What kind of SHIT is this?"

In November 2010, six months after my daughter was killed, I called my attorney in Lake Cormorant and said, "Mr. Feinstein, I have not been contacted in any way by the District Attorney's office regarding my daughter's case. It's like my daughter didn't have a mother, dad, brother or family at all. What is wrong with the system? They've contacted the Collin's and not me. For crying out loud, I'm her mother!"

"Shirley, I am very sorry for this," Mr. Feinstein said, trying to calm me down. "I'll send a letter to the DA's office with your information, and will ask them to put you on the victim's assistance list in this case, and provide you with the courtesy of dates, important hearings, or any other information that might be relevant to the victim of a crime in this situation."

"I appreciate it very much, Mr. Feinstein," I said and ended my call.

A couple of weeks later I received a phone call from the District Attorney's office apologizing and letting me know I was now on their list of contacts and they would keep me posted.

After a year and ten months, Ronald pleaded guilty to vehicular homicide. He spoke briefly to the press before walking into the courthouse, saying, "I know it's a long time for the Collins family; and I hadn't had a chance to address nobody. But I'd like to say to the Collins family, to Ms. Diane, and especially to the son Mason that there's nothing I could say or do that's gonna change what has happened. I've made a mistake and there are consequences for it and justice will be served. I'm going to let justice do it for my part and the same thing for my wife and her family, my kids too, so that's all I got to say."

I cried and cried listening to Ronald's speech on the Internet. He never once addressed my family and me. *Your daughter had a mother just like my daughter did. Not once did you say you were SORRY! You drug addict son-of-a-bitch!*

Ronald was finally convicted and sentenced to ten years in prison with all but seven suspended. The first three years would be at hard labor without chance of parole. His punishment also included a fine of $1,000.

The months I spent waiting for him to be convicted were not easy on me. My daughter will never be back, but at least I knew he wouldn't hurt another innocent person by driving under the influence of illegal narcotics. Ronald will have plenty of time to think of the horrible accident he caused because of his irresponsible behavior.

Chapter 57

Aerobics Fanatic - 1980s-2015

After moving into the crooked house with Torreey and my two kids, he bought me a membership at a health club called Carson Tennis Club. He was already a member there. I began taking aerobics classes four times a week in the evenings after work. I was crazy about aerobics and couldn't get enough of it. The kids swam while I was in class.

I became good friends with Mindy, an instructor. One evening after class, Mindy said, "Shirley, you should become an instructor. I'll help you out if you're interested."

"I'd love too!" I practically shouted.

From then on every time I came to class, Mindy announced, "Shirley will be teaching for a few songs."

Months later, Mindy, talked to the aerobics director and told her about me.

I needed to be certified. Mindy of course gave me all of the info on how to do it.

To obtain my aerobics certificate I had to pass three exams. The practical and the written I took at a health club in North Hollywood. It lasted all day.

Two weeks later I received a confirmation letter that I'd passed and all I needed was the CPR certificate (Cardio Pulmonary Resuscitation.) I contacted a CPR facility in my area and registered for the course. I showed up ready and anxious to take the exam, along with twenty other students. Six hours later, I was mentally exhausted. I was losing my attention and needed to stay focused. When it was time to pump the doll, I carefully watched the instructor, Mr. Hughes. Then my classmates went up to the front of the room one at a time to administer CPR to the doll.

When it was my turn, I thought, *Okay here I go*. I had already memorized everything and I was ready, but at the last minute I got nervous. "Hueputa mierda." ("Shit, son-of-a-bitch.") As I was walking to the front of the room, I was thinking, *Why do I have to pump that little fucking doll when I really feel like punching the shit out of him?*

Once at the front, I smiled and said, "Hi, my name is Shirley." I then leaned down, got close to doll's face, watched his chest, and yelled out, "CALL 911 while I give him CPA!" Everyone, including the instructor, were starring at each other, stunned.

"What did you say?" Instructor Hughes asked.

"Oh, I meant CPR ... I, I need to go to the bathroom," I stammered, and took off running.

Once inside the stall, I slapped my forehead. *"What the hell did I just do?* For sure I was thinking of Torreey's title, CPA (Certified Public Accountant). That's why I messed up.

Oh, shit I gotta go back in there and do it again, motherfucka! I thought, laughing and taking deep breaths. Minutes later I returned, pumped the shit out of the doll, and at the end I got my certificate. Ha! Ha!

When I got home I told Torreey what happened and he laughed hysterically. "You're a piece of work, aren't you, Momsie?" he said, shaking his head.

"I guess soooo," I shrugged with a laugh.

For the next two weeks I had to listen to Torreey: "Hey Momsie, give him CPA."

After being certified I applied at different clubs and was teaching high impact classes four to five times a week in the evenings or on the weekends. I loved music, and dancing was something I couldn't get enough of, so this job was perfect for me. I was not only getting paid for it but I was enjoying myself too. I always experience an incredible high afterward. I work out to feel great, to look good, and I find music to be soothing and healing. Whenever I instructed the class I felt strong and my energy level was insane. My students loved my technique and all of the Latin music I played. "Come on people, let's get loud and crazy too!" I yelled out, sweaty and with enthusiasm.

Back in the 80s aerobics was the greatest exercise ever. There were many health clubs all over Los Angeles and classes were always packed. If you didn't get there early enough you couldn't find a spot to stand.

The club that Torreey and I belonged to, Carson Tennis Club, one day offered me a permanent part-time aerobics class. I was thrilled about the opportunity, and began teaching once a week. From then on I was requested by many students and soon picked up a second class, then a third. My classes were packed most of the time. I also subbed a lot for other instructors when needed. By teaching three classes a week my membership and Torreey's became free. I made a lot of friends that I still have after thirty-two years of teaching at various health clubs.

Nacho became one of my best friends. He was Mexican, about ten years older than me, short, with olive skin, and funny as can be. He loved to curse just like me and we both spoke Spanish. He was my perfect amigo; we were inseparable. I taught the class with my back to the students and of course Nacho was right behind me. After class, he and I and a few other students went to the club's bar, had cocktails, and laughed our asses off. Nacho had so many filthy and crazy jokes to tell. All of the women loved him. The minute they saw him they'd kiss and hug him, and of course he loved it. We called him Nacho the pervert. He reminded us of Rodney Dangerfield in *Back to School*.

The gang:

Blondie, as I previously described, was kind, sweet, beautiful and a gorgeous figure. She had a boyfriend but she hung out with us a lot.

Rockie was Hispanic but didn't speak Spanish. She was single and attractive, conservative, caring, and sexy too.

Michelle was 6' tall with long blonde hair, thin, elegant and conservative. She was married with children. She reminded me of Jerry Hall the model and ex-girlfriend of Mick Jagger. She loved being around us so she could laugh and have a zany time.

Sandra was from El Salvador, married, and about my height; crazy, sexy with beautiful long black hair and olive skin. We both loved to chatter in Spanish, especially when cursing.

My sister Lina also came to my classes when she spent the nights or if she was living at my house part of the time. We all went out dancing, to the movies, horse races, threw parties; we always had over-the-top fun, laughing and being goofy. Lina and I constantly got into some kind of crazy trouble.

We attended many parties together at Barrymoore's Night Club in the south bay. Torreey didn't attend the parties. He'd rather stay home and watch TV or read. He'd pick me up after it was over; and if my friends were too drunk he'd drive them home too. He knew all of my friends, and Nacho of course was in charge of taking care of us girls. But it often looked more like we were taking care of him instead.

Halloween parties were the best. The club was packed from one side to the other. One year, Nacho dressed up as an inflatable giant penis. It was hilarious! Everyone was calling him Dickie. He had a little motor inside the costume that kept him inflated. At one point we were all on the floor dancing and sweating up a storm when suddenly Nacho's costume started slowly deflating.

"Nacho, you're penis is getting fucking limp!" I yelled out, laughing uncontrollably.

"Oh fuck, I need my Viagra!" he shouted and took off running to the bathroom.

A few minutes later he reappeared with a "hard penis," and ready to continue dirty dancing with about ten of us girls around him. At this point we were all doing tequila shots and almost falling on the floor.

I was dressed as Cat Woman and most of the night I yelled out, "Hey Dickie, meow!"

Toward the end of the night they announced the best costume winners: "Cat Woman for the sexiest costume."

I walked up to the stage, did a little sexy cat dance and the announcer presented me with $50.

Next, they called Nacho's name. He went to the stage and everyone was shouting, "Dickie! Dickie!" The announcer presented him with $100 for the most disgusting costume of the night. Everyone applauded like crazy for Nacho. Some of the guys were so drunk they were going behind Nacho's back pretending to hump him. Nacho was so drunk he almost fell off the stage. This was the craziest party and most fun ever!

All of my five friends and I have always been there for one another. That's how strong our friendship was. Good friends are hard to find these days. That's why I cherish them with all my heart.

When I came home from Mississippi after my daughter was killed, my friends came by my house right away. They all got together and showed up in my bedroom, where I was laying on my bed covered with a blanket. They gathered around me, hugging me, crying and saying, "We're so sorry, Shirley. We can't believe our beautiful Natalie is gone." They all knew my kids since they were eight and nine years old.

Natalie worked a part-time job after school at the health club where I taught aerobics. She ran the nursery room, taking care of toddlers while the parents were working out. Sometimes she worked at the aerobics room making sure all of the students were members. Other times she attended my classes and stood at the back of the room since she was taller. After class was over she'd say, "Damn, Mom, you're wild! I can't keep up with you."

"Oh, yes you can Natalie," I'd laugh.

Years later after Natalie moved to Mississippi and came home to visit she continued attending my classes.

By the time I was forty-five I decided to reduce my classes to three times a week. I realized I was getting older and didn't want to hurt myself; plus aerobics wasn't what it used to be. Back in the 80s and 90s classes were full of young energetic students, screaming, sweating, clapping; even singing to what I believe was the best music ever. Everyone wanted to be fit. These days, the music isn't as good. Students aren't as motivated or consistent about attending classes. It was still fun but I had other things I wanted to do, so the choice was perfect.

After Natalie was killed I took a leave of absence from teaching aerobics.

"I've found someone to fill in for you," was the message Harry left on my answering machine.

Harry was the aerobics director. He was a man in his late fifties with brown hair and was somewhat attractive. He was divorced and had three sons. Harry could be very unfriendly and rude at times. I'd seen him treat people like he just didn't care. No wonder he was never able to remarry. Many members at the club didn't like him. For sure I knew he disliked me, especially after I rejected him when he asked me out. He knew I was married. I was always super friendly with everyone and of course got a lot of attention from the guys even though they all knew I was with Torreey and none of them had a chance with me.

In August 2010 I got a call from Harry. He got right to the point. "I need to know when – or if – you're coming back to teach!"

"Harry," I said, "I'd like to give it a try in November. But I only want Wednesdays."

He let out a puff of steam, then, said, "Shirley, Martin is doing Tuesday and Wednesday. The only class I can give you is Monday's. So, wha-da-ya want to do?"

"Are you serious?" I exclaimed. "It's Monday or nothing?"

"There will be no changes," Harry pronounced, then quickly excused himself, claiming he had to take a call on his other line.

On the weekend, I got a call from Susie, one of the other aerobics instructors. "Shirley," she said with concern, "Harry told me you're not coming back. Is that true?"

"Susie, I'm not sure what's going on." I let out a deep sigh. "This is so frustrating. Either Harry misunderstood me, or he has some kind of grudge against me, for some reason. I never once told him I was quitting. I just said I wanted Wednesdays."

"Martin does Wednesday. Do you know who he is?" Susie said ominously.

"No, I don't."

"He's Harry's son." Susie sounded peeved. "You shouldn't let him get away with this. He runs the club any way he wants to and nobody does anything about it. A lot of the members are tired of it. Harry did the same thing to Lori the massage therapist. She got sick and took a leave of absence. Harry replaced her with his son's wife. When Lori wanted to return to work, Harry would only give her part-time. It's called nepotism."

"Now I get it," I said without hiding my contempt. "He never once mentioned to me that Martin was his son. He knew exactly what he was doing. I was vulnerable. He knew I was at my weakest point in life and he took advantage of it. I'm not well, Susie. I'm on extra medication. Oh, that fucking prick! I'm well liked, my classes are always full, and he pulls this crap! Thanks for all the info, Susie. I really appreciate it. I just don't think I can do anything about it. I'm tired, sad, and I'm not strong enough to deal with this bullshit. I'm disgusted with the whole thing. First I have to deal with losing my daughter, and now this."

On Friday, I called the club and demanded a meeting with Harry. I didn't mince words. "I'm here because I want two of my classes back."

Harry shook his head. "The only class available is Monday's. I'm not going to change that. It's not fair to Martin."

"You mean your son," I corrected him sourly.

"His name is Martin," Harry snapped.

This man wanted everyone to pretend he wasn't giving preferential treatment to his son. *Oh come on*, I thought, staring at the latest in his plastic surgery war against the aging process. He'd had a least three lifts according to various other club employees. He was worse than some of the women with his vanity.

"It's not fair to your son? What about me? I've brought many new members to the club. I took time off because my daughter, who I was very proud of, got killed, and this is how I get treated? Are you kidding me?" I said incredulously, shaking and by now crying at the same time.

"His name is Martin," Harry replied in a sharp voice.

This man is a cold-hearted snake. "Why won't you call him your son?"

"I'm not going to change anything. You can have the Monday class – take it or leave it," he said with finality.

"I guess I don't have a choice. Do I?" I said through my sobs, wiping my tears and thinking, *How can people be soooo fucking cruel? No wonder there's so much crime in the world. Someone else would've probably lost it and punched the shit out of this a-hole.*

I got up and left the room knowing he could have given me my classes back if he wanted to. But he didn't because he was an unhappy and miserable person who got some kind of sick joy out of degrading others.

I went home crying and told Torreey about Harry.

He was furious. "You need to quit that fucking place! I'm cancelling my membership right now!"

When my son Luke heard what happened he called the club and immediately cancelled his too.

"I don't know what to do. My friends are calling me to come back. They don't like Martin's style of teaching. They're complaining to management. I want to quit and then I don't because of my close friends and my passion for music and teaching. Fuck, I'm losing my mind. I can't take it anymore. Why is all this shit happening to me? Why are some people so unkind?" I said, crying hysterically.

"Momsie, you need to take a pill right now and get in bed, okay," Torreey said, hugging me tight.

"Ohhh, I miss my Natalie! I'm going insane." I got in bed, covered myself and waited for Torreey to bring me a glass of water, a Xanax and a sleeping pill, so that I could fall asleep and forget about the incident for now.

To make matters worse, while sleeping I heard Natalie's voice: "Mom, go back, this is what you love to do. Momma didn't raise a quitter!"

After all that happened and as much as Torreey and my son wanted me to quit the club, I just couldn't do it because of my dear friends – and don't forget, "Momma didn't raise a quitter." I felt I had no other choice but to teach the Monday class only.

Months later I got a second class at a different health club. Exercise and music helps me deal with my emptiness and pain; it relieves stress, clears my head but most of all it makes me happy. When I'm finished I feel better and stronger. I release some of my anger and tension. Sometimes when I play certain songs that remind me of my daughter Natalie or my sister Lina, I feel happy – though sometimes sad too.

My dear friend, Blondie, helped me out when I lost my daughter. We became even closer. Blondie was here for me most of the time. She never stopped calling me. I have to say she was almost a pest, but a good one, if you know what I mean. She took time for me when I was at my weakest point in life. I needed a friend to talk to. We took long walks together. Sometimes she'd ask me to go dancing with her. She knew how much I loved doing that, but I wasn't ready yet.

Seven months after my daughter was killed, Blondie called my husband one evening, crying. "Torreey, my husband Charles passed away a day ago. I don't know how to tell this to Shirley."

"OMG, what happened?" Torreey asked, shocked.

"Massive heart attack. He was in Cabo San Lucas with friends on a fishing trip. His friend found him in the morning on the floor of his condominium room," she said, in a daze.

After hanging up with Blondie, Torreey walked upstairs into our bedroom and gave me the horrible news.

"OMG, my poor Blondie. I can't believe Charles is gone!" I wanted to call her but I just couldn't bring myself to do it. There was just too much pain inside of me, and I knew I wouldn't be able to say a word to her.

A few days later, as hard as it was, I showed up with Torreey at the funeral services. When Blondie and I saw each other we hugged and cried.

Blondie's husband of nineteen years died shortly after my daughter was killed. So as a good friend, after the funeral, I was there for her when she needed me. We both had so much pain and emptiness inside, and by spending time with each other we made things a little easier to deal with. We took many walks on the beach and talked about the good times. Sometimes we cried, but then we always ended up laughing.

One evening we went out to a bar and had a few cocktails. A friend of Blondie's showed up all pissed off and started telling us about her bad blind date from the previous night.

Neither Blondie nor I were in the mood for listening to any negative stories. I opened my mouth and instead of saying, "Who was he?" What came out was, "Who dat?"

Blondie looked me in the eye and we had the longest laugh attack ever. We kept saying, "Who dat?" "Who dat?" over and over again until our sides hurt so much we could no longer laugh. Her friend was so annoyed with us she stood up and said, "You guys are ridiculous. I'm going home!" and stormed out angrier than when she came in.

Blondie is one of the sweetest, kindest and caring persons I've ever known. I love her dearly and couldn't have asked for a better friend.

Chapter 58

Competitive Tennis - 2002-2015

I've been playing in a women's doubles tennis league in the South Bay for the last twelve years. The association is called Marine League. The rankings are: A, B, C & D. (A being the highest.) There are nine various teams throughout the bay area. We all compete against each club in the spring and fall, and at the end of each season the division with the highest scores becomes the number one team.

I started as a C player. The higher you are ranked as a player the more competitive the games turn out to be. The first five years were by far the best for me. I began loving the game and played as much as I could. I made a lot of friends who I loved dearly, and still keep in touch with. There are a lot of very nice ladies in the league, but also some mean and rude ones who will do anything to win.

I had no idea there were strict rules of behavior. I thought we were just playing for fun.

When the first season started, every time my partner and I scored a point, I did a little dance and clapped after. Later on, my partner, Marcie, said, "Shirley, our opponents aren't too happy with your dancing."

"Really? Those bitches don't know how to have fun!" I said, rolling my eyes.

The second time, we played against two mean bully-type bitches who, were cheating like crazy just to win the match. But in the end, my partner and I beat the shit out of them instead. They were sore losers and one chose not to shake hands, as was customary. She turned her back on us, grabbed her backpack and started to march away with her partner.

For good luck, I had brought with me my stuffed monkey toy. I quickly pulled it out of my backpack, turned the switch on his tummy and tossed him in the center of the court. The monkey began rolling around and laughing hysterically. Both opponents spun around and one of them glared at me and said, "Are you making fun of us?"

"No, I'm not! He's my lucky charm and I take him with me to every match," I said, sounding serious, but I was so tempted to laugh instead.

Marcie put her arm around my shoulder and whispered in my ear, "OMG, Shirley you are a crazy little thing, aren't you?!"

They both stormed out and went straight to our captain to complain about me.

The captain had a talk with me later. I didn't even have to defend myself. She said, "Knowing those two, I'm sure they deserved it."

"Oh God, I thought you were gonna kick me off the team," I said with relief.

Three years later, after losing my daughter, my whole world had changed. Competitive tennis wasn't as important to me as it used to be. As much as I once enjoyed the game, I now found myself hating it. I didn't feel like dealing with so much bullshit anymore; especially the sore losers. My God, it's only a game.

Having not played for five months, I wasn't sure if I was ready to go back. But I wasn't a quitter, and most of all I kept hearing my daughter's voice: "Mom, go play!" So one day in October 2010, I woke up, e-mailed the captain, and told her I was ready to come back and play for the fall season.

I was very anxious the night before. I kept thinking about Natalie and knew I had to be brave. My biggest fear was having a nervous breakdown on the court.

On the day of the match I got up and the first thing I did was to take my Xanax. Then I showered, fed the dogs, and ate a small breakfast. I left the house around 9:20 in the morning. On my way to Manhattan Beach Country Club for my tennis match I started to feel sick. I took a few deep breaths while my tears were falling down my face. *Fuck, I don't know if I can do this. Hueputa mierda.* I thought maybe I should go back home, but then I didn't. I guess I was totally confused.

When I finally arrived at the club, I parked and sat there numb; not wanting to get out of my car. I remembered my therapist's words: "It's okay to cry, let it out and you'll feel better." So a few minutes later I wiped my tears, put on my sunglasses, and got my skinny ass to the courts. Once there I saw some of my teammates already playing, first, second and third positions.

I was now a B player and was going to play fourth.

I said hello to everyone watching the match, then I slowly moved away a few feet from the crowd and began stretching my body, meditating until it was my turn to get on the court with my partner, Casey.

Casey Braker always has a smile on her face. She has short reddish hair and lots of freckles. I always called her by her last name, Braker; and she called me Webster instead of my last name, Webb.

We started with a 10-minute warm-up and then we began to play. I was calm and relaxed and felt the presence of my daughter with me. I kept hearing her voice: "Mom, you can do it!"

We played our first set and won 6-2. *Natalie, please help me, don't let me break down*, I pleaded in my head, looking skyward.

Every time I made a great shot, I'd say to myself, "That one's for you, Natalie. I know you're here with me, just stay with me all the way!" Even though my heart was beating faster, for some reason it was working. I didn't want to stop talking to her.

We played the second set and 45 minutes later we were tied 4-4. We took the next point making it 5-4 us. We then had them 15-love, 30-love, 40-15. All we needed was one more point. I was on serve and I was going to give it all to win.

"Come on Natalie, let's do it!" I whispered.

I tossed the ball high over my head. Watched it reach its apex and start its descent. *This is for you, Natalie* ... and swung my racket up, over and down with all my might. Our opponent couldn't even touch it. I'd hit an ace.

"OMG, we won! We won!" I yelled, jumping up and down, sobbing and grabbing on to Braker. I couldn't let her go. I whispered in her ear, "This game was dedicated to my daughter and she was here with us all the way."

"It's okay, Webster," Braker replied with teary eyes.

"Braker, please do me a favor. I can't shake hands with our opponents right now. I'm too emotional. Please apologize for me," I begged while my body shivered.

"Don't worry, Webster. I'll talk to them," Braker assured me.

I was shaking and crying and filled with joy to have won this game for my daughter. I could imagine the smile on Natalie's face.

I was happy and sad at the same time and felt like running away as fast as I could. But instead of that, I sunk down on the court, crying like a baby. I couldn't control it. OMG, *this is what I was afraid of*, I thought, but it was already too late.

All of a sudden I felt someone hugging me tight. A few seconds later there were more arms embracing and crying with me on the ground. I just couldn't believe the love and support I felt all around me. It was incredible! I felt so lucky to have such wonderful, loving and caring friends.

My daughter wanted me back on the courts and gave me the strength to go on. She wasn't going to let me quit. After all "Momma didn't raise a quitter!" Right?

By March of 2011, it was "spring in the city" and the first tennis match of the year. I arrived at our opponents' tennis club, Jack Kramer in Palos Verdes at 10:00 a.m. I was playing in sixth position with my partner, Braker. Some of our teammates were already on the courts.

I had plenty of time so I decided to try on a new line of tennis outfits that the club was selling. Braker came in the shop, saw me, and said, "Hey Webster, I'll come get you when it's our turn to play."

"Okay," I waved.

Fifteen minutes later I was still trying on the new designs when Braker stuck her head in the door and yelled, "We're on, Webster!"

"Oh shit, I'll change real quick and be there in a flash!" I shouted from the fitting room.

I got back into my uniform grabbed my tennis backpack and ran outside.

I needed to stop and use the restroom before going to the court. I was in a hurry, looking for it, when I saw a gentleman walking by, and asked, "Excuse me sir, where is the women's bathroom?"

"Go up the stairs, make a left and the lavatories are on the right side," he replied, pointing in the general direction.

"Thank you!" I said, and took off running.

I was in such a hurry I didn't stop to read the sign. I blew in the door and was already trying to pull down my skirt when I looked halfway up and was staring at some penis. I immediately placed my hands in front of my mouth and screamed, "Ahhhhhh, shittttt!" I felt like McCaully Calkin in *Home Alone*.

Two guys were standing, completely butt naked with their arms folded, talking to each other in what I then realized was the men's room. They were just as surprised as I was, only I think I scared them more with my scream. Instead of turning around and bolting out, I walked slowly backwards, saying, "I'm so sorry! I'm so sorry!" Then I turned around and ran as fast as I could into the women's restroom that was a few steps from there. I used the bathroom while laughing at myself. "Oh shit, what the fuck just happened to me?" I couldn't believe it.

I then ran to the tennis courts where my partner and our opponents were already warming up and waiting for me. I immediately apologized and said, "You're probably going to hear about a crazy woman walking into the men's bathroom."

The girls were all laughing hysterically. Thank God the opponents were nice.

"OMG, Webster, you're insane! How many were there?" Braker asked with a humongous smile.

"I think there were only two," I replied, crossing my eyes.

After the laughter subsided we began our match.

Forty-five minutes later my partner and I lost our first set.

"Sorry, Braker, my game really sucks," I said with a frown.

Braker approached me and whispered in my ear. "Webster, you need to concentrate and stop thinking about the penis you saw earlier, okay?"

"Okay, I'll try!" I told her with a smile.

Running into dos penis before a match is fucking crazy, I thought, but couldn't stop laughing, or thinking about it.

We played our second and third set and won. By then, for sure, the penises were completely off my mind.

While our teammates congratulated us, my partner said, "Hey Webster, tell the girls why we lost our first set. Ha! Ha! Ha!"

For the next few days, I was the running joke of the team. I kept getting emails and texts from some of my teammates and friends asking, "Hey, Shirley, how many total penis did you see?" and "Wondering if we'd gone in the men's room would we have won our matches too?"

Something crazy always happens around me, but at least I could now laugh instead of cry.

By the end of the season our team was number one for the second year in a row. The first year we were presented with a fluffy gray blanket sporting an embroidered patch with the words: "Division B Champions of the Year 2011." This year we received white jackets.

Soon it will be five years since Natalie was taken from me. I have continued playing tennis and most of the time I truly sense her presence with me on the courts. It's an amazing feeling!

I'm now an A player, but I feel different about competitive tennis. I'm slowly disappearing from playing leagues and tournaments. I thought bullies were only in school but not true when it comes to women's doubles. There's so many of them it's unbelievable. The women are vindictive, mean, rude, jealous and cheaters too, just the opposite of me. Although I have met so many amazing ladies that I'll definitely keep in my life. But, as I get older, I'm finding out that I more enjoy playing friendly matches. I get to laugh all I want while having fun with loving friends.

To me life's about enjoying the people while you have them and not taking yourself too seriously.

Me and my toy monkey.

Chapter 59

Community Property Dispute - 2010-2012

Natalie was about two weeks away from settling the Community Property when she was killed.

James owed her approximately $400,000.

When James found out, shortly after she was killed, that Natalie was remarried, he immediately filed a petition to be appointed the Administrator of the Natalie Collins Estate. He knew exactly what he needed to do. He even had Rhonda move into his house the day after Natalie was killed. As I previously mentioned, at the time of James and Natalie's divorce, the judge ordered a cohabitation agreement. Neither of them could have a date spend the night while Mason was in the house with them.

To this day I'm still wondering why Natalie's friend, Dorothy chose to tell James about Natalie's secret marriage, instead of informing me. Dorothy was not a friend of James.

In June 2010, we received a letter from James's lawyers. AVC Attorneys at Law informed us that James had decided to resign as administrator after coming to the conclusion that this would be a conflict of interest because of the unresolved community property issue. He then petitioned the court a week later to have Mr. LeBlanc replace him as the succession representative. (Mr. LeBlanc was a friend of James)

The attorneys asked if we knew of any bank accounts, savings, brokerage, or any other asset Natalie may have had, to let them know in order that it may be added to the estate.

Torreey and I were handling Natalie's accounting for her business, including her personal taxes. We provided James's attorneys with all of Natalie's bank accounts, credit card statements, income tax returns, and any outstanding bills including a letter with attached documents supporting our claims against the succession of Natalie for monies we loaned to her for legal fees and for unpaid rent for our house in Lake Cormorant.

These payments were loans to Natalie that were to be paid back to us after Natalie received her community property settlement from James Collins. As I previously mentioned, Natalie was going to pay us back the money we loaned her for the divorce attorneys and rent of the house we bought for her and Mason to live; making it a total of approximately $60,000.

We also provided AVC Attorneys with Natalie's husband Luis's telephone number and e-mail address, along with a short letter. "We lost our daughter in a tragic accident on May 5, 2010. Fair resolution of these outstanding obligations of Natalie would be helpful in assisting us to deal with the misfortune we have suffered. We would like to have peace in our lives, not just for us but also for our grandson Mason so that the next nine years of his life can be filled with happiness and good memories. Let us think of Mason also."

Weeks later, James's attorneys froze all of Natalie's bank accounts.

I was torn into a million pieces. I didn't know what the fuck to do except to cry and ask myself, "Why did this happen to me?" Everything seemed unimportant to me anymore.

In June of 2010, Torreey suggested we talk to an attorney about appointing Luis, Natalie's husband, as the administrator of the community property.

"I can't deal with this shit. Sorry, Dudsy, I just can't do it, anymore," I said in a daze.

"Don't worry, Momsie, I'll handle it myself, okay," my husband soothed me.

Torreey contacted a friend of Natalie's in Lake Cormorant and got the name of an attorney, Mr. Pratt. We hired him to represent Natalie's husband Luis as the successor and remove Mr. LeBlanc. We paid him a retainer of $3,500.

By the end of July 2010, we were getting nowhere with Mr. Pratt, except wasting our money away.

Months later, Luis took another job in Atlanta, Georgia and got the hell out of Lake Cormorant, Mississippi. It was a good idea since James was trying hard to deport him. His temporary work visa was expiring. Luis then hired an immigration attorney to help him stay in the United States legally.

I assisted him with writing a letter to the U.S. Immigration Offices regarding the marriage relationship between my daughter and him.

After that I felt like I couldn't deal with anything involving James anymore. I didn't want to hear about the fucking case ever again – even though I knew that my Natalie wasn't going to leave me alone with, "Momma didn't raise a quitter." Meaning, don't stop!

We decided not to pursue the case any further and wrote Mr. Pratt a letter. "It is too hard on my wife at this point and she doesn't want to deal with the situation anymore."

In October 2010, Torreey gave it some more thought and contacted another attorney, Mr. Weiner, in Lake Cormorant to find out how we should handle the situation regarding Natalie's estate. Torreey told him, "I believe

James, his friend Mr. LeBlanc, and the law firm of AVC, have no intention of paying our claim for $60,000. Natalie left no will. She was only thirty-four years old."

In December 2011, our attorney, Mr. Weiner, filed a petition in court to show cause why the claims of Torreey and Shirley Webb should not be recognized as a debt of Natalie Collins Estate.

On February 2012, Mr. Weiner informed us that AVC attorneys had propounded several interrogatories and requests for production of documents.

Torreey responded: "I have several people who knew about Natalie's obligation to pay us back for the attorney's fees and for the rent. Natalie acknowledged these obligations as repayable to us on many occasions.

"All the people listed, except for Diane Landsberg, are willing to testify under oath to this effect. Diane will probably have to be subpoenaed to testify. Diane was Natalie's attorney, friend and coworker. She was in the passenger seat of Natalie's SUV at the time of the accident. As I told you before, she and Shirley are not on speaking terms any longer.

They are:

    Donald Allen – Attorney and friend of Torreey and Shirley

    Luke Parker – Natalie's brother

    Luis Fuentes – Natalie's husband

    Lance Lovey – Natalie's neighbor

    Michelle Paldrew – Shirley's friend

    Graciella Penderton – Shirley's sister

    Joyce Spelder – Natalie's friend."

Two years went by and we were still dealing with the community property issue.

Our attorney called and said, "You're not going to have your claims paid by Natalie's Community Property unless you sue James. As expected, James didn't agree to pay us anything.

"His attorneys paid all of Natalie's debts except ours. Again James wins, no matter what we do. It seems to me that because it's his hometown, he feels he has the advantage.

I let out a heavy sigh and responded, "I lost my daughter and I might as well just forget about recovering any of the money we loaned to Natalie. I don't think James will stop, no matter the cost, until he gets his way."

In November 2012, we got an unexpected call from Mr. Weiner: "We had a hearing and the judge awarded you the attorney fees of $26,000. To recover the rent of $1,500 for twenty-four months, you'll have to take James to court. My advice is to settle for something instead of having to go to trial. All of your eight witnesses would probably have to appear in court to testify and this would cost more than what he owes you."

Torreey suggested we try to settle for one-third of the rent even though we knew James wasn't going to settle for anything. He'd rather spend $100,000 or more on attorney fees than pay us even one dollar.

I'm sure James was angry and probably pounding his fists on his desk after hearing the news. My thoughts were, even if we don't recover the rent that Natalie owed us, it's still better than nothing and better than letting James win. So, *strike out, buddy!*

I knew Natalie was looking down with a big smile and saying, "Momma didn't raise a quitter! Keep going!"

In December 2012, I received a call from Torreey while I was visiting my sister Graciella in Illinois. "Momsie, our attorney in Lake Cormorant called and said he received a check for $32,000 from James's attorneys to settle the community property."

"Really!" I said somewhat surprised.

"Well, what do you wanna do?" Torreey asked.

It had been two long years of battling with James and his attorneys. "Well fuck it, let's just take it," I sighed. "I'm tired of having to deal with this shit. We need to put this awful matter behind us so that I can go on with my life knowing that Natalie is at peace and that we got *some* of the money her estate owed us."

"Okay, we'll do that, then," Torreey said and hung up.

I raised my eyes to the heavens and whispered, "Thank you, my beautiful Natalie, for being by my side and lifting me up when I was down. I love you and miss you with all my heart!"

I later was told that a friend of James had floated a rumor in Lake Cormorant that I was suing James for the $400,000 he owed to Natalie. All that Torreey and I wanted was to recover our money and for the remaining to go into a trust account in Mason's name, a gift from his mother.

As for the $400,000 community property James owed to Natalie, I guess it ended up back in his pocket. He was probably laughing all the way to the bank. For sure we never saw any of it.

Out of it all, Torreey and I learned a big and painful lesson in life: If you ever loan your adult kids money, make sure you have everything in writing, especially if they are married or divorced with children. As a parent you never think of your children dying before you, but it happens – and it happened to me.

We could have avoided all of this hardship if only my husband and I had my daughter sign a simple letter with the words: "I promise to pay you back."

Chapter 60

The One-Year Coincidence - May 5, 2011

On a sunny, windy and crispy spring morning, May 5, 2011, the first anniversary of Natalie's death, I grabbed the plastic bag with some of Natalie's ashes and a red rose I had placed in the fridge the night before. I walked downstairs to the garage, opened the trunk of my car and placed a metal beach chair, a couple of towels, a cooler with ice, a big jacket; and took off to the Japanese restaurant to pick up my order of sushi (Natalie's favorite food).

I then drove to the beach, sat down and stared at the ocean, watched the dolphins swim by, and the pelicans diving for fish. It was a beautiful day; the only thing missing was Natalie.

I started thinking about all of the good times and suddenly found myself sobbing like a baby, my nose was running, my tears were falling like an open faucet, and I was talking to myself. "Natalie, where in the fuck are you? You were not supposed to go yet! Is there anything where you are? Are you okay? I don't believe in God or anything out there anymore. I prayed every night before going to bed for God to protect you, Mason, Luke, Torreey, family, friends, and our beloved pets. If there's a God, why did he take you, Lina, and not some criminal? Please give me a fucking sign or a dream that there's something out there? That you're okay!"

Around 1:00 p.m., Torreey showed up with his beach chair and sat next to me. I had already calmed down after popping a Xanax and was feeling somewhat better.

At 1:35 p.m., I opened the cooler and grabbed the plastic bag where I had Natalie's ashes and the rose and said, "Dudsy," – my nickname for Torreey – "please film me with my iPhone while I scatter Natalie's ashes and the red rose in the ocean."

Minutes later we were sitting back in our chairs. I grabbed my phone from Torreey and sent the video to my grandson, waited a few seconds, then, called him. "Hey Mase, how are you, babe? I just sent you a video. Did you get it?"

"Hi Bebe, I just saw it," he said in a soft voice.

"Okay, Papacito. I love you!"

"Me too, Bebe!"

Days before, I sent Mason a beautiful decorative wreath of lavender flowers in a shape of a heart with a picture of Natalie and Mason in the middle of it.

On Tuesday, May 10, 2011, I received an E-mail from someone announcing that my friend, Missy's mom had passed away on Thursday, May 5, 2011.

Missy and I have been friends for over twenty years. She's blonde with blue eyes, cute with a sweet personality. She's married with two children and her husband is a client of ours.

I called Missy and left her a message. "So sorry about your mom. I love you!"

I couldn't believe that her Mom died the same day as Natalie but a year apart.

A few days later I ran into Missy at the tennis club. We hugged each other tight and cried.

"Missy, did you know that your mom passed away the same day as my daughter?" I said, still holding on to her.

Missy hugged me tighter and said, "OMG!"

"Missy, I hate to ask you this, but I have to. What time did your mom pass?"

"1:33 p.m.," Missy said precisely and without hesitation.

"My daughter was killed at 1:35 p.m.," (California time) I said in amazement. "Missy, I have goose bumps all over my body. I have to tell you what happened at the beach on May 5," then I relayed the story.

"OMG, Shirley!" Missy gasped.

My daughter and Missy's mom died two minutes apart on the same day but in a different year.

At that moment chills went up my spine. I was convinced and realized that this was the sign that I had asked for at the beach. Natalie sent me a message through Missy's mom. She answered all of my questions. She's okay. There's something out there and I believe that I will see her again.

Missy's mom's name was also SHIRLEE, but with an E at the end.

Chapter 61

Fighting For My Grandson - 2010, 2011 & 2012

As I mentioned earlier, Mason is my only grandson. He was just eight years old when he lost his mother.

Also mentioned: Rhonda, his dad's girlfriend, moved into their house shortly after Natalie was killed. From then on everything changed for Mason; and for me too. My home was in California and Mason's in Mississippi.

Mason is a polite and well-mannered child, the way my daughter raised him. His mother always told him not to be afraid to speak up. But Mason had a weakness for doing just that. Natalie was constantly concerned about Mason's inability to say what was on his mind. He was always afraid of hurting anyone's feelings.

I spoke to James on May 5, after Natalie's passing, about not taking away Mason's visitations to California. James verbally agreed Mason could continue with his trips to my home in Redondo Beach. Even though he said that, I felt I still couldn't trust him. I remembered Natalie's words: "He tells you what he knows you want to hear, then he does whatever he wants to do."

Following Natalie's cremation, I made sure I called Mason twice a week, even if it was just to hear his voice and to tell him "I love you!"

I never once cried or said anything against James or Rhonda when I talked to him. But after hanging up I couldn't stop the tears from falling. I had a feeling James and Rhonda were recording my conversations with Mason for whatever reason.

In June 2010, when I was in Lake Cormorant to clean out Natalie's house, I called James and said, "I'd like to come by and see Mason."

"We have plans, but you can come by the house and see him after 5:00 p.m.," James said in a sour voice.

While there, both James and Rhonda carefully watched me. I felt like a criminal, like I'd done something real bad and I shouldn't be left alone with my grandson.

After returning home, I continued with calls to Mason. I was instructed by James to call Rhonda's mobile phone if I wanted to talk with Mason. Numerous times he was "not available" according to her. I later found out from Mason that Rhonda wasn't giving him my messages. She disliked me for no discernable reason, because whenever I spoke to her, I did my best to be cordial.

A few months later I decided I had enough of these two and pursued legal advice from Mr. Feinstein, whose office was in Lake Cormorant, Mississippi, regarding my grandparent visitation rights. I went ahead and signed a contract and returned it to Mr. Feinstein's office along with a retainer check of $3,000 and a letter expressing my intentions to exercise visitations with my grandson.

My daughter had established a bond between Mason and I, which included telephone calls, letters, gifts, photos, school visits, sports events, birthday parties, holidays, and visits to my home in California twice a year. These visits to my home were usually one week in July, and one week in December (Christmas to New Year's). My trips to Mississippi every year to visit Natalie and Mason were usually one week in May and one in October around Mason's birthday. During those weeks, I'd drive Mason to school, pick him up, take him to tennis lessons, help with his homework, cook for him, etc.

My letter stated: "I would like for Mason to continue his visits to California in June or July for a week – or two if possible. I'm willing to work out a schedule with James if he is agreeable. I've planned to visit Mason on December 16, 2010 to celebrate Natalie's birthday with him on December 17. I will be staying at the Gold Strike Resort and would like to be able to pick him up from school and have him with me for two days. I do not want to have to go to James's house, sit there and be watched while I'm visiting with Mason. That's what happened in June 2010, when I asked to see him.

"I also plan on visiting Mason every year in May for the anniversary of Natalie's death and would like to have him with me for those few days.

"I have been in touch with Mason by telephone once or twice a week since my daughter's death and would like to continue to do this.

"I firmly believe it is in the best interests of Mason to continue our established relationship. He is my only grandchild. He knows he's my special boy as I have always told him so. He's the only part of my daughter that's left, and he knows how much I miss and love him.

"Mason has a deep love for me and I know he wouldn't want to lose that connection too. We have a different relationship than he does with his other, eighty-three-year-old grandmother. She's the Southern Belle with good old-fashioned manners. I'm the crazy, young, fun, loud, dancing, joking, and laughing California granny. He's always had a great time visiting with me. We've never had a dull moment.

"I do hope that James doesn't give me a hard time. I really don't need any more pain and suffering. I'm hoping James will put behind him all the anger and resentment he had toward my daughter. He needs to understand how important this is to not only me but to his own son, Mason."

After my legal actions, James and Rhonda had no other choice but to allow me to speak with my grandson. Even though there were times that I still was unable to reach Mason on the phone.

In the beginning of October 2010, during a phone conversation with Mason, I asked, "Hey Papacito, what are you going to dress up as for Halloween?"

"I'm gonna be a gorilla," he said excitedly.

"Wow, that's going to be fun!" I replied, wishing I was with him. "Don't forget to send me a picture, okay Babe?"

On Halloween, late afternoon, a friend of Natalie sent me a photo of Mason with his Halloween costume on. I was shocked and angry when I saw the picture. He had bandages and fake blood on his head, legs, arms and was leaning on some crutches. I couldn't fucking believe this! I was furious with both James and Rhonda.

The following day, I called Mason and pretended I didn't know anything about his costume. "Hi, Babe, how are you doing? How was your Halloween? I didn't get a picture of your gorilla costume."

"Oh, I wasn't a gorilla, Bebe."

"Oh, okay what were you then?"

"I was an auto accident victim," he said in a low tone of voice.

"Who's idea was this?"

"Rhonda's. She put bandages and fake blood on me."

"Well, that's not a nice costume. You know?" At this point I didn't care if she was recording me.

After my conversation with Mason I shook my head and thought to myself, *How can this woman be so insensitive?* Mason had just lost his mother five months ago and for James to let her do this to his own child was unfathomable to me.

In November, I sent the picture of Mason to my attorney, Mr. Feinstein. I was documenting everything in case I would need it later.

In late November 2010, I called James. "I have plans to travel to Lake Cormorant, December sixteenth through December nineteenth. I'd like to pick up Mason from school on Friday and take him to the movies to see 'Tron' and dinner after to celebrate what would have been his mother's thirty-fifth birthday. Also, I'd like for Mason to spend the evening at the hotel with my husband Torreey and me, and keep him through Saturday."

"We already have plans to take him to dinner at the Chicago restaurant. You're welcome to join us, and I'll see about you spending as much time with Mason as possible. I'll talk to Mason about it," James said, not sounding too thrilled about my plan.

I immediately got the message that he didn't want me to have Mason for those two days. He sounded civil on the phone, but I still couldn't trust him.

"It will mean a lot for Mason and I to be together on Natalie's birthday," I said, biting my tongue.

I was remembering the last Christmas in 2009 when Natalie and Mason came to visit me in California. We went to the movies to see A *Christmas Carol* and when they showed the previews of *Tron* coming December 17, 2010, Natalie immediately said, "That's where Mase and I are spending my next birthday." I wanted to do that in Natalie's honor.

On Thursday, December 16, 2010, we arrived at the Gold Strike Resort Hotel, five minutes from Mason's house.

On Friday, December 17, 2010, Natalie's birthday, Torreey and I drove to the Chicago restaurant to pick up Mason. I had no other choice if I wanted to see my grandson but to play it James and Rhonda's way.

I had taken my Xanax before picking him up and I made sure I was calm. I called James and told him we were on our way.

"We're not done with lunch yet. You're welcome to come inside," James replied, sounding like he was in a courtroom. He was always short and cold with his answers.

Before walking into the restaurant I made sure I took a few deep breaths. Doing this always worked for me, keeping me calm. When we approached the table, there was my little Mason.

"Hey, Babe!" I yelled out! I kissed and hugged him tight, while my teardrops fell. "You look so much bigger, sweetheart."

"I'm almost your height, Bebe," Mason replied with watery eyes and a sweet smile.

"You're getting there, Babe," I said, still hugging him.

I then said hello to both James and Rhonda while Torreey pulled out a chair for me to sit down next to Mason.

Torreey said hello as well and of course shook hands with James.

We sat with them for about fifteen minutes; then I reminded Mason, "The movie is going to start at 4:00, so we need to leave pretty soon, okay?"

One of Natalie's good friends, Dorothy, was waiting for us at the theater with her little boy, Nick. We hugged tight and shed some tears. We didn't want Mason to see us but we just couldn't help it.

Dennis, Mason's best friend was also there.

After the movie we headed to the hotel to celebrate Natalie's 35th birthday. Eight of Natalie's good friends showed up, some with their kids.

I had ordered 25 helium balloons and they were already delivered at the hotel. I took a marker and wrote everyone's name on a balloon. "We're gonna go outside by the pool area and release all of the balloons into the sky before 8:00 p.m.," I said.

This hotel was another of Natalie's favorite places to eat dinner and have cocktails with her friends.

Since James wouldn't allow Mason to stay the evening at the hotel with us, I had to return him to his house no later than 9:00 p.m. It felt as if I was considered the monster grandma. It was okay for Mason to spent nights at his friends' houses, and his other grandmother's house, but not with me.

This didn't make sense to me. James knows exactly how Torreey and I conduct ourselves. We exercise every day, don't do drugs, and we're honest. James has known my entire family for over twenty years. My sister was married to his brother for some of those years. He had no reason for keeping my grandson away from me. He had no reason to condemn me. In my opinion it was more because I know too much about them.

At 7:45 p.m., I gathered everyone together. "Okay, it's time to go outside," I said, handing each person a balloon with their name on it.

Earlier I had called Luis, Natalie's husband, who was now living in Atlanta, Georgia and said, "Luis, were releasing balloons for Natalie. I'll write your name on one for you. I'll call and put you on speaker so you can hear us over the phone."

"Muchisimas gracias, Shirley!" he said with great enthusiasm.

I had seven balloons left without names, so I went ahead and wrote my mom's name, my son Luke, and some of my siblings. At exactly 8:00 p.m., I counted, "One, two, and three!" We let go of the balloons, yelling, "Happy Birthday! We love you, Natalie!" as they floated skyward.

By then my tears couldn't stop from falling while holding on to Mason's hand. Mason's eyes were watery. I knew he didn't want his little friends to see him cry, so I smiled at him and wiped away my tears. Half an hour later, Torreey and I drove Mason home.

Back at the hotel, Natalie's friends were all at a dinner table in the restaurant waiting for Torreey and me. After a couple of cocktails, I looked at Dorothy who was sitting across from me. Tears were falling down her face. As much as we all pretended to be happy, it just wasn't possible. Everyone around me was in so much pain, myself included; there were no words to explain the emptiness, the suffering on everyone's faces. *Life is not the same, not without my Natalie.*

The following day, Saturday, December 18, 2010, we picked up Mason.

"He's not feeling well," Rhonda said, and gave me a bottle of medicine for his tummy.

We drove to a restaurant for lunch. Right away, after stepping out of the car, he threw up on the side of the parking lot.

"Mason, are you okay?" I said, handing him a Kleenex.

"My stomach doesn't feel good," he moaned.

"Do you want us to take you back home?" I offered.

"No, I don't want to." He shook his head emphatically.

"Okay, let's go inside the restaurant and use the bathroom, and I'll help you clean up," I said, taking his hand.

While in the restroom, I pulled the medicine bottle out of my purse. I looked at the expiration date and noticed that it was well past. *Damn, what is she trying to do to, Mason?* I thought. I said, "Mase, this medicine is too old. It expired several months ago. Do you think you'll be okay without it?"

He nodded yes.

"If you feel like you'll need it, let me know and I'll stop at a pharmacy."

"Okay, Bebe, I will."

After lunch, on our way to the mall, I said to Mason, "Hey Babe, how was your trip to Hawaii in July?"

"It was good and bad," he responded with a sad face.

"Good and bad? How can that be, sweetheart?" I wanted to hear it all. "Tell me the good part first."

With a slight smile on his face, he said, "The good part was the hiking." Then he was silent, his eyes were glued to the seat of the car.

"Mason, Papacito. Are you okay?"

He looked at me with teary eyes and a sad expression. In a shaky voice he said, "The worse part was the ceremony."

I had been told about the wedding by one of my daughter's friends. I was upset because Mason had just lost his mother two months ago and thought James was selfish not to think of his son's feelings. James should have waited until Mason healed a little more.

"Tell me about the ceremony," I said.

"My dad married Rhonda. That's why we went to Hawaii."

"How did you feel about that?"

"I could only think of Mom," he whispered.

I reached for his hand and held it tight. He didn't want to look me in the eye. I knew he was hurting inside. It broke my heart to hear his words and to see his unhappy little face. "I'm so sorry you had to go through that. You know that Bebe loves you a lot, right?"

"Right," he nodded.

I immediately changed the subject. "Mase, your dad said you don't want to spend the night at the hotel."

He shook his head. "I want to, but my dad and Rhonda won't let me."

"I'm sorry about that, Babe. Let's forget about it and have some fun, okay?"

When we got to the mall, Mason still wasn't feeling well. I was concerned about him so I insisted we go back to his house and I'd stay in his bedroom with him until the evening. I called Rhonda and told her we were on our way back home.

When we got to his place, he immediately ran to the bathroom and threw up again.

A few minutes later, Mason jumped into bed, covered himself with the blanket, while I kissed his forehead and held him next to me. Natalie always cuddled him, especially when he was sick. I knew right away that he was missing the love of his mother.

At 9:00 p.m., Torreey came by to pick me up.

"Hey, Mason, I have to go now, Babe. We have a plane to catch tomorrow morning. I love you!" I kissed him and walked away toward the entrance door where Rhonda was approaching me from the living room area where she was watching TV. "I'll call tomorrow to check up on Mase," I told her.

"Sure," she responded.

While walking to the car I was thinking about Natalie, when she lived here with Mason as a baby. I learned some things about Rhonda from Natalie. Later, several individuals confirmed what she said, but I will not mention any names. Suffice to say, I was told that she'd kept company with an older businessman who was arrested in January 2013 on charges of forgery, three counts possession of stolen property, and altering or removing numbers of a motor vehicle.

Additionally, her ex-husband was the domicile parent (primary custody) at the time of their divorce.

James provided her with a big home, a luxury car and, exotic vacations. She was now the lady of the house and in charge of everything, including my grandson.

After going back and forth for several months with James and my attorney, Mr. Feinstein, regarding my grandson's summer vacation visit in California July 2011, James had to relent and allow Mason to visit me in California for six days. James flew with Mason, and Rhonda arrived a day later. I of course paid for Mason's round trip airline ticket.

My daughter's two friends, Nancy and Gloria, were also visiting with their children, who were friends of Mason.

When we got home from the airport, Torreey, Graciella, and Becky were all happy to see Mason. Graciella and Becky were from Illinois and were staying for two weeks. Becky, as I mentioned earlier, is my sister Graciella's youngest daughter. She was eight years old.

Our dogs, Niki, Sunami, and Jazzy were jumping all over Mason, also happy to see him. Mason had come home to California with his mother every year since he was a baby. Milo, Natalie and Mason's dog, went up to Mason, but I could tell he wasn't sure who Mason was. It took Milo a while to remember him, but after a couple hours he apparently did and began wagging his tail.

Half an hour later, we went to the beach where we scattered a small portion of Natalie's ashes along with red roses that I gave to everyone.

From there we ended up at Joe's Crab Shack for dinner on the waterfront in Redondo Beach.

On Tuesday July 26, 2011, we took off for Legoland and spent the whole day having fun; then drove to a hotel near Disneyland and stayed the evening.

On Wednesday, July 27, 2011, we were at the Disney Park, riding as many rides as possible. The kids were so happy to be with each other. I glanced at Mason with my sunglasses on and my eyes got teary. I tried to stop myself from crying in front of everybody. I was happy to have Mason with me, but things of course were not the same anymore, not without my Natalie. I missed her so much. I missed her laugh, her beautiful smile, her sense of humor, and most of all the way she'd always call me "Mommmmmmmm!" It just broke my heart to see Mason without his mother. I couldn't accept the fact that she was gone forever.

The evening ended watching a terrific fireworks show, which helped take our minds off our loss.

The next morning, after breakfast, we did all the rides on the other side of Disneyland that's called the California Adventure Park until 5:00 p.m.; then it was time to drive back home to Redondo Beach.

On Friday, July 29, 2011, Graciella, Becky, Mason and I spent the day at the beach. Mason and Becky rode their boogie boards on the waves while we watched them screaming and laughing their little butts off. Mason looked so happy and so was I, even though my heart ached. I felt the presence of Natalie and I knew she was smiling down at us.

On Saturday, July 30, 2011, my son Luke came by the house. He hadn't seen Mason yet due to his work schedule.

Luke was super excited to see Mason. He hugged him tight while a few teardrops fell. Guys don't usually show their emotions. I know it was hard for Luke not to cry, but I'm sure it felt good to do so.

"Hi Mason, how you doing?" Luke said with a big smile.

"Good," Mason replied.

"Are you kids ready to go see 'The Muppets Movie'?"

"YEAH!!" Mason and Becky yelled out.

We took off to the movies, came back home, then both kids jumped in the pool for more screaming and laughing. At 6:00 p.m. we all went out to dinner, including Torreey. It was Mason's last evening with us. He was going back home to Mississippi the next morning.

On Sunday, July 31, 2011, I got up at 6:00 a.m. James and Rhonda were coming by to pick up Mason and go to the airport.

I didn't want James and Rhonda coming inside of my house and hanging out as if we were good buddies. That would be too weird and hypocritical. So I got Mason up, fed him breakfast, packed his suitcase, placed it by the front door, and waited for them to arrive. I grabbed Mason, held him tight, and said, "I love you a lot. I'm going to miss you!"

Mason hugged me back. As much as I wanted to control my tears from falling, it was just impossible to do.

Mason was also crying while holding on to me and saying, "I don't want to go, Bebe. I don't want to."

"I know, Babe," I said with my heart beating faster.

I heard a car pull up my driveway and saw Rhonda, through my glass door window, coming out of the passenger side. I immediately opened the door before James rang the doorbell.

James said hello and noticed that Mason had been crying. He hugged his son and said, "I miss you!"

Mason pulled away from his dad, looked at me once again with his sad little face and teary eyes, then went to the car.

"Bye," I said and closed my door. I returned to the guest bedroom were Mason slept, got in the bed and cried until there were no more tears inside of me. I was extremely sad to see Mason go.

The first year of 2011, I wanted to have Mason stay for two weeks that summer. I asked my attorney to get it for me, but the most he could obtain was six days only.

The second summer vacation of 2012, I had no other choice but to agree with James to take the five days he offered and return Mason every evening to the hotel where his dad and Rhonda were staying. I was of course livid.

Before Mason's trip to California I called him even though I was sure they were recording my conversation. "Hi Mase, how you doing? Listen, I'm so excited about your upcoming visit, but I have to be honest with you. It's difficult for me to drive back home at midnight after being at the park all day long. I'm too exhausted. Also, it's so much fun spending the night at the Disney Hotel. Are you okay to do that with Bebe, Graciella and cousin Becky?"

"Yes, but I have to talk to my dad," he said tentatively.

A few days later, Mason called me and said, "Hi, Bebe, I told my dad I want to spend the nights."

"Oh, that's great, Papacito. I'm so excited!" I said, thrilled I'd get to spend five days and four nights with Mason.

In July 2012, around noon, I picked up Mason at the airport. Once again, he'd arrived with James and Rhonda. I took my sister Gia's grandson, Dylan, with me. Dylan was nine years old, and funny as can be. He loved imitating celebrities, for example, dancing like Michael Jackson. In 2009, while we were at Legoland's park with Natalie and Mason, Dylan got his face painted at one of the booths like The Joker from *Batman*. He imitated his crazy laugh all day long, and we ended up calling him *The Mini Joker*. Mason was now ten and loved being around his funny little cousin.

Back at my house my whole family was waiting to see Mason. I was throwing a "Welcome Home" summer party for him.

On Sunday, we took off to the beach for a while, and in the evening we went to see the movie *Spiderman*.

My son Luke was on hiatus from a television show and this time he was coming with us.

On Monday, the four of us, Luke, Dylan, Mason and I took off to Raging Waters in San Dimas. The kids loved this place; the park was loaded with swimming pools and huge water slides.

On Wednesday, we drove to Disneyland, and the fourth day to Universal Studios. We laughed every minute of it, especially with Dylan along. He was hilarious! We all had the best time ever. It was a blast!

I had a few private conversations with Mason. One time I asked, "Hey, Mase, what do you call Rhonda?"

"She told me to call her 'Mama,'" Mase replied, looking down at his fingers with a sad expression.

"How do you feel about that, Babe?"

"I don't know," he whispered.

"Do her kids call your dad, 'Dad'?"

"No, they call him Mr. James."

"Is she mean to you?"

"She yells a lot and she's a control freak."

"She's the opposite of your mom, Babe," I said, curling my upper lip.

On Wednesday evening, we were driving on the freeway from Universal Studios, on our way to drop off Mason at the hotel in Santa Monica where his dad and Rhonda were staying. Mason was sitting in the back seat; all of a sudden he started crying and pleading, "I don't want to go home, Bebe."

"OMG, Babe, I'm so sorry!" All I wanted to do was to hug him, but I couldn't stop my car in the middle of the freeway. I waited until we got to the hotel, parked my car in front, got out and sat in the back where Mason was still sobbing. I hugged him tight and said, "I love you with all my heart, Babe! I know you're only ten years old, but you need to be strong." I gently grabbed him by the shoulders. "Mason, listen to me. You need to see a therapist. It will help you deal with all the pain you have in your heart after losing your mom."

"My dad and Rhonda said I don't need one," Mason replied with lips shivering.

"You do need one, Babe," I told him, rubbing his hair with my hand. "I went to one, and believe me, she helped me out a lot."

I reminded him, "You need to stay strong. You need to speak up and tell your dad what you want. I need your help with your dad, Babe. You understand? I can't do it by myself anymore. Your dad seldom agrees with me. I got that Rhonda is a control freak, and I'm sure she has a lot to say with this situation. But don't be afraid of her, Babe. You have the right to speak up."

After our conversation, I called James and told him we were in front of the hotel.

A few minutes later, James came down to get Mason. When he approached us he saw that Mason and I were hugging, crying, and saying goodbye.

He stood there watching us, and looking like a freakin' zombie.

I got out of the car with Mason, turned to James and said, "You know, it's okay for Mason to cry and show his emotions. Mason misses his mom, and me too."

James said with that familiar cold tone of voice, "It's okay with me."

I knew very well the reason why he and Rhonda didn't want Mason spending the evenings at my house. My attorney, Mr. Feinstein, mentioned that James told him last year, when he picked up Mason at my house to go back to Lake Cormorant, "Mason cried and had a stomachache for eight hours."

It's only natural for Mason to cry. My house is full of memories of his mother. I remind him of her too. If only Mason had the therapy he needed right after he lost his mother, he'd be better able to deal with this situation. The only time Mason cries is when he has to say goodbye to me, whether he's at my house or at his own in Lake Cormorant.

In my opinion, James and Rhonda were not keen on Mason being too emotional. With me, Mason is allowed to show that he misses his mother very much. With me, he knows he can cry for any reason.

After spending over $10,000 on this Lake Cormorant, Mississippi attorney to help me, two years later, Mr. Feinstein called and said, "Shirley, if you want to sue James for your grandparent's rights I can no longer represent you because of some personal issues I have with James and the Collins."

Later on, I was told that Mr. Feinstein was in some kind of trouble himself. Apparently he got caught having an affair with one of his clients and he was possibly going to be disbarred.

By the end of July 2012, I decided not to pursue with my grandparent's rights, and sent Mr. Feinstein a letter of termination. I had accepted the fact that I was only wasting my money. And there wasn't any other attorney in town I felt could get the job done.

On Thursday, October 18, 2012, Mason's eleventh birthday, I called Rhonda's mobile and left a message to have Mason call me back.

An hour later, I sent both James and her the same text: "*Please, have Mason call me.*"

I wanted to wish him a Happy Birthday, but as usual neither of them gave Mason my message.

Around 6:00 p.m., I called James's mother, Trisha. I felt I had no other choice. She answered her phone.

"Hi Trisha, I've been calling and leaving messages on both James and Rhonda's phones, and I haven't been successful in getting in touch with Mason. Are you by any chance going to see Mason?"

"Yes, I am," she responded evenly.

"Will you please have him call me? Thank you very much, I really appreciate it!" I told her kindly.

At 7:00 p.m., Mason called me and I was happy to finally tell him, "Happy Birthday! I love you!"

Chapter 62

Memorial Counseling Center - June 2011

Natalie was a local advocate for the underprivileged and exploited. She made it her life's work to help people who couldn't help themselves. To honor her memory and work, Jack and Nancy Hillmart provided funds for the establishment of the Natalie Collins Counseling Center. The center named in her memory, in Lake Cormorant, Mississippi, provides a safe place for children to express their emotions, to learn that their feelings are natural, and to help them move through their grief.

On June 26, 2011 I travelled to Lake Cormorant, for the unveiling on June 27, 2011 of The Natalie Collins Counseling Center. Graciella met me in Houston and from there we took a small plane to Lake Cormorant.

I was extremely sad and exhausted, but was glad that my sister would be by my side. Just a month earlier I had gone through Natalie's first anniversary on May 5, 2011.

Torreey couldn't make it due to his work schedule.

Before my trip I e-mailed friends, family, and Torreey's clients a letter with details about my trip and asking if they'd like to make any donations to the center. Days later I was surprised by all the love, support, and e-mails I received letting me know that a check was already in the mail to my address.

I presented the center with a donation of $10,000, all of which was given by our family, friends, and clients in California.

I also make donations to the counseling center every month and will continue to do so for as long as I can.

My trip was beautiful but very emotional. I had the pleasure of meeting the Mayor of Lake Cormorant, and got to spend some quality time with my daughter's amazing friends.

My grandson Mason was not present for the event. His dad went out of town that weekend and took Mason with him. As a result, Mason didn't get to participate in the honoring of his mother. As such I didn't get to see Mason at all when I was there.

Chapter 63

Honorary Tennis Tournament 2011-2012

On August 25-28, 2011, I took off to Lake Cormorant for my daughter's tennis tournament memorial and fundraiser all by myself. Torreey had business obligations that kept him in California.

Torreey dropped me off at the airport in the morning. Even though I wasn't feeling well, I knew I had to be there. I'd been sick with a sore throat for a few days and had lost my voice. I got on the plane and had not removed my sunglasses because I had been crying all the way to the airport. I hated to go back to Lake Cormorant, just thinking about my daughter and grandson not being there to greet me at the airport with a smile, a kiss and a tight hug.

I made a reservation to stay at the Gold Strike Resort on the lake. I was also very sad after James said, "Mason will not be staying with you at the hotel."

While I was on the plane I received a text from Nancy: *Who's coming with you?*

Me: *No one. I'm alone, sick and I miss my Natalie terribly.*

Nancy: *Do you want to stay at my guesthouse?*

Me: *I would love to, but don't want to impose on you.*

Nancy: *No, problem at all.*

When I finally arrived at Lake Cormorant's airport around 8:00 p.m., I was tired and very nervous, so I took another Xanax to calm me down before renting a car.

I drove to Nancy's place, a few minutes from Natalie's house. While driving by Natalie's house I started crying and couldn't control my emotions. My phone rang and it was Torreey.

"Momsie, where are you?"

"I'm passing by Natalie's house," I said, sobbing nonstop.

"Momsie, calm down and call me when you get to Nancy's house."

When I arrived at Nancy's, I walked into the backyard, where Nancy and Gloria where sitting and having a glass of wine.

We hugged, kissed, cried, and chatted for a few minutes before I said I needed to get to bed, feeling extremely exhausted.

The next day on Friday August 26, 2011, I woke up a little refreshed but still had no voice; I could barely talk.

I texted James: *I'm staying at Nancy's guesthouse and want to know if I can have Mason stay the weekend with me?*

I also called the school to find out what time Mason went to lunch. Then I drove to the school and surprised him. "Hey Babe, I'm staying at Nancy's house. Would you like to spend the weekend there?"

"Yes, Bebe!" he replied smiling.

"Okay, but don't tell your dad I came by the school."

"I won't."

After leaving the school I grabbed my phone and texted James: *Would it be OK if I pick up Mason from school? Also, can he spend the night at Nancy's?*

James: *You can meet me at the school at 3:15 p.m.*

The second time, when I arrived at the school, of course Rhonda had come along with him to monitor the situation.

Mason finally came out. I hugged him and listened while James asked him, "Do you want to stay with Bebe at Nancy's house?"

Mason looked at his dad, moved his head up and down and said, "Yes!"

Of course neither James nor Rhonda knew that I had stopped by the school earlier and had lunch with Mason. So I got Mason for two full days.

Saturday morning, Mason and I got ready and left for the tennis tournament and memorial. I played a mixed doubles match and lost. I was still sick and didn't feel well, but participated anyway. By now my voice was completely gone and even though I was stressed to the max I pretended to be happy. My heart was full of pain but I didn't want to ruin the event by crying.

It had been over a year since I lost Natalie, and these wonderful caring friends had put in a lot of time and effort to make this happen, and at this very moment I had Mason with me to think of.

Later in the afternoon, Natalie's friends, Mason and I sat down to eat, and all of a sudden, I felt a pain in my right ankle. I removed my tennis shoe and sock. To my surprise, my ankle was swollen like a baseball.

One of the girls got up and brought me a bag with ice to put over it. I didn't remember twisting my ankle while playing – but something caused the swelling? After a couple of cocktails and food with the girls I was ready to call it a night.

Mason and I got ready for bed and within minutes I fell asleep with my arm around him like his mother used to do.

Saturday, August 27, 2011 – Mason and I got ready and took off to the tennis club for lunch. I wasn't playing because of my foot injury. I had an Ace bandage around it and I was limping. But I was going to watch the matches and hang out with Mason and his buddies. The weather was as humid as can be and mosquitos were everywhere. My arms and legs were covered with bites. Some tennis players were having nosebleeds, and one ended up with a heat stroke.

At 5:00 p.m., we headed back to the house, showered, then got ready for the anniversary celebration at the same tennis club, in the banquet room.

When we entered the hall I was amazed. Natalie's friends had beautifully decorated the tables! There were pictures of Natalie with Mason and friends all over the walls. Candles were lit, and a TV screen was playing a slideshow of Natalie's pictures. I wanted to cry but I stopped myself, took a few deep breaths and felt better. I had to keep myself in high spirits, especially for Mason.

After dinner, Mason and I were presented with gifts from the Counseling Center.

I also had contacted Playboy asking for a donation of any items with the Playboy logo to place in the gifts bags for all the players who were participating in the tennis tournament.

Instead, Playboy donated four tickets for a tour of the Playboy Mansion grounds. The tickets were going to be auctioned at the Tennis Tournament with the money donated to the Counseling Center.

At 8:00 p.m., karaoke started playing, and Mason and his friends were all up singing and dancing. Mason looked happy up there; even though his mother was gone forever, he was trying hard to be the happy little boy he'd always been. I'm not sure how he did it, especially since he didn't get any counseling. *He sure knows how to brush aside his pain*, I thought; but it worried me that this might present a problem for him later in life.

The party ended around midnight and I was very exhausted, still sick, and emotionally drained.

On Sunday morning around 11:00 a.m., we got ready and took off to Toy's R Us with Mason, Nancy's two kids and their nanny Marta. There's not much to do in Lake Cormorant except the movies and the mall. I was going back home Monday morning and had to return Mason to his house at 7:00 p.m.

After our trip to the toy store, we met Nancy, Gloria, Joyce and Lisa at the Chicago steakhouse for dinner. From there we headed back to Nancy's house.

"Mase, gather up your backpack and toys so that I can walk you home," I said, but noticed that Mason had a sad expression on his face. His house was conveniently right across the street from Nancy's.

"Bebe, I'm ready," Mason looked me in the eye and said with teardrops falling.

"Oh, Babe. I love you, Mase!" I said, hugging him tight and sobbing too.

"I love you too!" Mason replied.

I opened the front door of Nancy's house and held Mason's hand as we walked to his house, still crying.

I knocked on the door and seconds later there was James.

"What's wrong?" He looked at me with a cold expression.

"Don't you know how much he misses his mother?" I said, unable to hide my annoyance.

I know Mason didn't want his dad to see him crying, so he ran inside the house and went to his bedroom.

"I'd like to see Mason more often, maybe for Christmas," I stated calmly.

"You can come back at Christmas," he said, sounding unhappy.

"There's practically nothing for Mason and I to do here in Lake Cormorant," I said, then walked away. I hated the fact that I had to go through all this shit that wasn't necessary because James just wanted to be in control.

I went back to the guesthouse and waited for Eva, Natalie's friend and Mason's sitter of eight years, to come by and see me before I went home the next day.

On Monday, August 29, 2011, I flew back to California, still sick, with a raspy voice and extremely depressed. I called our family doctor as soon as I got home. That afternoon, Doctor Yawata saw me, gave me a prescription for antibiotics, and referred me to an ear, nose and throat specialist. My ear was hurting like hell; had a lot of pressure and I couldn't hear from it.

Later, at home, I started screaming like a mad woman, holding my ear and head at the same time. OMG, I have never experienced such an awful pain! It felt like someone was ripping my entire head apart.

Torreey was concerned and called the local pharmacy for advice.

The pharmacist suggested I try an over-the-counter antihistamine for the pressure.

The next morning I woke up, and screamed in panic, "SHIT-FUCK! There's bloodstains on my pillow!"

"Blood? From where?" Torreey said, alarmed.

"I don't know," I cried.

I jumped out of bed, looked in the mirror and noticed the side of my face and left ear had dry bloodstains. I still couldn't hear from that ear. "Oh, shit, what the hell?!" I said, terrified.

I grabbed my phone, called a specialist and went to see him that afternoon.

After an examination, the doctor said, "You have a ruptured eardrum." He cleaned my ear, gave me a prescription, and told me to come back and see him in a week.

By the following week I was feeling much better. Saw the specialist and was lucky to not have permanently damaged my eardrum.

The following year, on August 18-19, 2012, I again flew alone to Lake Cormorant for my daughter Natalie's annual tennis tournament memorial and fundraiser.

I arrived in Lake Cormorant at 2:00 p.m.; as we landed, rain came pouring down with thunder and lightning that caused the airport's electricity to go off for a few minutes. I rented a car and waited for the rain to stop before driving to Nancy's guesthouse where I was spending the next two days.

This year, for some reason, James said it was okay for Mason to spend the weekend with me, but I still felt I couldn't trust him. I was surprised he wasn't giving me a hard time.

I called Rhonda from the airport and told her I'd be at Nancy's by 3:00 p.m. and for Mason to come by.

"Okay," Rhonda responded sounding a little nice, which was unusual.

Around 3:30 p.m., she called back and said, "Mason doesn't want to spend the night there."

"*Oh fuck, here we go again,*" I thought. I took a deep breath and needed to think fast about what to say to her. I remembered when my daughter was on the phone with either James or Rhonda; she was always calm and pretended that nothing bothered her. So right away I said, "It's okay with me if he doesn't want to." I made it sound like it was no big deal at all. I knew that by the time I got to Nancy's and saw Mason he'd tell me something different. There was nothing to be gained by disagreeing; besides I'm not an argumentative person even though I like cursing so much. I always tried my best to keep everyone happy. Unlike some people, I never enjoyed getting into fights with anyone.

After getting my rental car I decided to stop by Natalie's house. I wasn't sure it was a good idea, but for some reason I had to do it.

I parked in front and sat there numb, starring at the house while my tears were falling down, thinking of Natalie and how happy she was when she was living there.

I then drove to Nancy's and went straight to the guesthouse where I was staying. An hour later I found out that Mason was already inside the main house playing video games with his friend Dennis.

I approached him and gave him a hug and kiss. "How you doing, Babe? Hey, Mase, how come you don't want to spend the night here?"

Mason shook his head up and down and said, "I do want to."

"You don't have to stay in the guesthouse with me, you know," I told him, thinking, *No eleven-year-old boy or girl wants to sleep in the same bed with a grandparent anyway.*

"Okay," Mason replied, pressing the control buttons of the video game.

Rhonda was probably going nuts after not getting her way. When she found out she called me and said, "Mason's not to stay up late on Saturday because he has just started school and we don't want him getting sick from staying up too late."

"Okay," I responded calmly while thinking, *What a stupid excuse.*

The celebration started on Saturday morning with the tennis players on the fenced-in courts. This year I decided not to participate, rather to be a spectator. The kids were playing outside the courts, chasing each other and screaming as loud as they could.

Lunch was served at noon and from there I drove Mason and a couple of his friends to the roller rink to skate. I sat and watched them go around and around the floor. I kept my eye on Mase; he reminded me so much of his mother when she was that age. His thin body was the same as Natalie's, the long legs and arms, even the way he skated was all her. All of a sudden, Natalie's favorite song by the Black Eyed Peas, *Boom, Boom, Pao,* started playing. My tears were rolling heavy down my cheeks. I was sure glad that the rink was a little dark inside.

After skating for a couple of hours, we returned to the house and were getting ready for the main evening party when my phone rang.

"Shirley, we don't want Mason staying up late. Also, what time is the party going to be over?" James said gruffly.

"I really don't know what time it's going to be over. Why don't you call Nancy and ask her. She would know," I said politely. I knew that James was just trying to give me a hard time, but I wasn't going to let him or Rhonda get to me. I did exactly what Natalie used to do, remained calm and didn't lose my cool.

The evening celebration was again as beautiful as the first one in 2011. We talked and laughed while pictures of Natalie flashed across the TV screen. At times I glanced at the photographs wishing she were here with us. All of these wonderful, caring people who loved my daughter so very much were here to celebrate her life and to raise funds for the Counseling Center in her memory. I felt so blessed and lucky to have had such a beautiful, caring and loving daughter. Even though she's gone, her spirit lives on with all of her friends in Lake Cormorant. Not too many people are remembered in such a way, long after they die. I am so proud of her and wish I could tell her one more time.

Chapter 64

Derby Daze - 2013-2014

In April 2013, James sent me a text message: *Mason would like you to visit him here this summer instead of him going to California. He would like to go there for five days every other summer and for you to visit him here every other summer. If you choose to do so, he may stay with you the entire time you are here. Please notify me as soon as possible of the dates you plan to visit. I will do my best to accommodate your schedule.*

Yeah, right, I thought. Who does he think he's fooling? Mason didn't say any of this; it was all James and Rhonda's idea.

A few days later I replied: *I will be in town May 3, 4, and 5. I will be staying at the Gold Strike Resort. Let me know if Mason will spend a day or two with me to celebrate his mother's memory.*

James responded: *He may stay with you the entire time, or for as long as you would like.*

But of course, the minute I got there, I had nothing but problems with both James and Rhonda. Like my daughter told me, *He says one thing, but he always does another.*

So for the summer of 2013, I didn't get Mason to visit me in California.

On May 3-5, 2013, my husband and I flew to Lake Cormorant to celebrate Natalie's anniversary and to help raise funds for her counseling center; also to spend some time with Mason. I was happy that Torreey came along with me this year. We had just gone through an exceptionally busy tax season, and it was the perfect time for him to take a break from work.

This year, instead of a tennis tournament, the anniversary was celebrated with an event dubbed "Derby Daze" to benefit The Natalie Collins Counseling Center.

The celebration was at the Hillmart's beautiful horse stables not far from the Lake Cormorant airport. The event, hosted by the Friends of Natalie Collins, brought an atmosphere similar to that at the actual Kentucky Derby's at Churchill Downs in Kentucky.

Attendees had the opportunity to place bets on the race, which was broadcast live on large-screen TVs. We were served cocktails and food was catered from more than ten area restaurants with some chefs cooking meals on site.

KWAC News was at the event. The president of the Counseling center, Gustavo Cervantes, asked me to be by his side for the interview.

"OMG, I don't think I'm ready for this. I don't know what to say and I'm afraid I'm gonna break down and cry," I said, fidgeting and taking deep breaths. Although I was extremely nervous and wished I had prepared better for this, I still made the evening news.

The 2013 Derby Daze sold out, raising $68,000 for Natalie's Counseling Center.

In April 2014, I grabbed my phone and wrote James a text message: *I will be in Lake Cormorant May 1 through May 5 to celebrate the anniversary of the death of Mason's mother. Would love to have Mason with me.*

James never responded back.

By now, Mason had his own mobile phone. I was glad I didn't have to call Rhonda's number any longer. The following week when I called Mason, I reminded him about my upcoming trip. I also told him that I hadn't heard from his dad. Of course, Rhonda must have been standing next to Mason and was hearing my conversation. She got on the line and said, "We were going to call you. James has been too busy with work. We don't have any plans for that weekend so it will be okay for Mason to be with you."

"Okay, thanks," I said, but felt she was up to something again – or the dark side of her was on good behavior for now.

By the time Torreey and I got to Lake Cormorant and I spoke to Rhonda on Friday afternoon, plans of course had already changed. I wanted Mason to come by the hotel after school and spend the late afternoon by the pool and dinner afterwards.

"I'll drop him off at the hotel around 4:00 p.m. Mason needs to be home by 6:00 p.m. He has a race at 8:00 a.m., the next morning and has to be in bed early," Rhonda said with a firm voice, meaning she was in charge.

"That's fine with me. Nancy asked me to join her and some friends for a meeting and dinner. Also, what are the plans for Saturday?" I responded, maintaining good spirits. I never once let her know that I was upset because Mason couldn't spend the day with me by the pool. I wasn't about to play her game.

"After the race, Mason has a birthday party to attend," she said in a firm voice.

"Okay. We're celebrating Natalie's anniversary at 4:00 p.m. Will he be ready before then?"

"Yes, you can come by and get him," she answered coldly.

While we were at dinner with my daughter's friends on Friday evening, one of the girls, Lisa, said, "Hey Shirley, I just saw your grandson at Bonnie's house before coming here."

"Really! I guess somebody's lying," I said, not surprised.

"Why?" Lisa asked.

"Rhonda told me Mason had a race at 8:00 a.m., and had to be in bed early," I said, feeling like I just didn't care any longer. I never knew for sure whether or not James and Rhonda were being straight with me.

"Oh, Mason, my son, and a few other boys are all spending the night at Johnny's house," Sofia said, her eyes going wide.

On Saturday when we picked up Mason, I said, "Hey Mase, how was the race?"

"Oh, I really didn't do it because my leg was hurting," he replied in a low voice.

"Did you go to bed early?"

"Yeah."

Right away I knew he was not telling me the truth. It made me sad that my grandson was covering up for Rhonda.

The 2014, Derby Daze ran on May 3, from 4-8:00 p.m. Tickets to this year's event were $150 per person, which included all food and drinks. Upon arrival, we were greeted by a red carpet that lead to a mint julep bar at the center of the stables.

We were asked to dress in our best derby attire. I wore a bright red top with a colorful tropical mid-length skirt and a beautiful red hat that I had borrowed from my friend, Blondie.

A best hat contest was held for women; men competed for Best Derby Duds. Winners in both categories were awarded with a gift basket.

The stables held a forty-five minute jumping show prior to the race. The event highlighted a center that brings group counseling services to the area's children.

Following the jumping show, Torreey and I glanced through the racing form and picked our horses. Torreey selected Dance with Fate and I went with California Chrome to Win - Place - Show. Then we placed our bets on the race.

As soon as the race began I was already yelling for my horse. My colt was in third place for maybe the last few seconds, and of course, by then I was jumping up and down with excitement. And all of a sudden, he pulled in front and won the race. "OMG, I won! I won! I can't believe it, oh shit, my California horse won!" I screamed like a maniac.

After the thrill of the race it was time for the silent auction: Such items as a 6 x 9 Turkish rug, a weekend stay at a casino resort, the use of condominiums in Florida and Puerto Rico Adventures, Mexico, and much more.

The Natalie Counseling Center is a division of Family & Youth. More than eight hundred children have attended the center for counseling since it's opening in 2010.

One of the things that's interesting about this particular nonprofit is that everything about it was born locally. It was local tragedy that amplified a local need, and it was local people who came together because of the tragedy, to meet the need.

The Natalie Collins Counseling Center offers grief counseling to children, families and individuals. My daughter, Natalie, was a local advocate for the underprivileged and exploited. After her death in 2010, the Hillmart's provided funding to establish the center in 2011.

The 2014, *Derby Daze* raised over $120,000.

It was also the first time James's firm donated a $400 check to the center.

I was informed that someone approached James and insisted he should donate something – to do it for his son. He had donated to other charities in the past but not to the charity of his son's mother.

On Sunday, Mason had another birthday party to go to, and the only time I could pick him up was at 6:00 p.m., and he had to be home by 8:00 p.m. I could only have my grandson for two hours.

We picked up Mason and he brought along his best friend, Dennis. On our way to the restaurant we stopped by Sunny's house and brought her along too. By the time we got to the restaurant it was already after 6:30 p.m. We had only an hour and a half to eat and had to rush with dinner to get him home on time.

At the restaurant, some of Natalie's Hispanic friends were waiting for us. We ate Mexican food, and had tons of fun catching up. It was the only time they got to see Mason – once a year when I was in Lake Cormorant visiting.

Close to 8:00 p.m., I looked over at Mason and noticed that he was crying. He was sitting across from me so I hurried up and went to his side and held him tight. "Oh, Mase, what's wrong, Babe? Do you miss your Mom?"

Mason moved his head up and down, still crying. He couldn't even say a word.

"I'm so sorry, Babe. I miss her too!" I said, hugging him and watching everyone's face turning from happy to sad.

All of sudden his phone rang. Mason looked at the screen and pressed the End button right away.

"Who's calling you, Babe?" I asked casually.

"It's my dad," Mason replied, wiping his tears.

The phone rang again and Mason pressed End. The third time it rang, Mason answered and the speaker was on. James's voice came on. "Hey, what's going on?"

"Nothing, we're eating," Mason replied, sniffling.

It was a few minutes after 8:00 p.m., so I figured Rhonda was going insane by now, because I didn't get him home on time.

On the way to Mason's house, he asked me to go inside and talk to his dad about his California trip planned for this summer.

"Mase, I really don't want to go inside your house," I said with a frown.

"Well, I need them to know that I want to go to California for more than a week," Mason said, sounding a little tougher.

"Okay, I'll do it for you," I conceded.

When we arrived at the house, Mason said bye to Torreey, then turned to me and said, "Come on, Bebe."

I got out of the car, followed him, knocked and waited for the door to open. When it did, James was standing there with no shirt on displaying his nasty beer belly.

Mason ran into his bedroom and I followed him while saying to James, "Mason wants me to talk to you and, oh, Mason threw up at the restaurant."

Rhonda was in the living room and yelled out, "One of my son's is also sick. They got some kind of virus."

Once inside Mason's bedroom I closed the door. James sat on Mason's bed.

I turned and looked James in the eye and said, "We are two adults and we both need to hear what Mason has to say about his California trip this summer." Right when I was saying "California trip," Rhonda came and pushed the door open. She gave Mason a glass with something in it, and said very rude and loud, "Here, drink this. And brush your teeth, NOW!"

Mason took the glass, drank it, went into the bathroom adjoining his bedroom, grabbed his toothbrush and began brushing.

OMG, *she treats him like he's a puppet on a string*, I thought. *No wonder Mason's afraid of her.* I found it unbelievable that his dad just sat there without doing or saying anything to her. I felt awful for Mason. He didn't deserve this. *What the FUCK is wrong with James? He looks like he's tuned out.*

Rhonda then turned to me, and loudly announced, "We're not making any decisions right now!"

"I'm not asking you to make a decision right now," I replied in a firm voice.

Rhonda seemed to lose it. She began yelling at me, "WHO THE HELL DO YOU THINK YOU ARE? YOU COME HERE AND DON'T EVEN SPEND TIME WITH YOUR GRANDSON BECAUSE YOU RATHER GO OUT WITH NANCY!"

"You wait a minute," I raised my voice to meet hers. "Didn't you tell me on Friday that Mason had to be home early because he had a race at 8:00 AM, the next day?"

She got even more pissed off because she knew I'd caught her in a lie and she didn't know how to get out of it.

She came charging at my face, pointed her finger, and went ballistic on me, screaming at the top of her lungs, "GET THE HELL OUT OF MY HOUSE! GET THE HELL OUT OF MY HOUSE!"

"Don't you talk to me in that tone of voice! What are you gonna do about it? come on hit me, why don't you Just try it?" I yelled back, waiting for her to slap me so that I could call the police on her. At that moment, James finally grew some balls and stepped in between us, but she kept on yelling at me.

"GET OUT! GET the hell OUT OF MY HOUSE!" She looked like a maniac who belonged more in a psychiatric ward with a straitjacket.

I slowly made my exit while pathetic James hurried in front of me and opened the front door. I didn't turn back to look at Mason. I just couldn't do it. But I am sure he was crying and felt bad about the way I was treated.

On my way out the door, I whispered. "You're married to that thing? You gotta be sick!" I didn't rotate to look at James's face nor did I hear a word out of his mouth. While walking to the car I was thinking, *What kind of a role model is she to raise my grandson?*

From there we dropped off Mason's friend Dennis and I had a chance to tell Nancy (my daughter's best friend) what happen at Mason's house with Rhonda.

The following day, on Sunday, before going to the airport, I called James's mom, Trisha, and told her about the whole thing, even though I couldn't trust her either. She always protected her sons no matter what. She was that kind of a mother. I did it for Mason and told her Mason needed someone to hug him.

After hanging up, I texted, Mason: *I love you!* Then Torreey and I drove to the airport to catch our plane.

When I got home in the evening I looked at my phone and there was a text from Mason: *U2. See you this summer.*

I was extremely happy after reading Mason's text. He was coming to visit this year! For a moment I thought, *Maybe James isn't pleased either with the* way things turned out, all because of his wife's temperament? This time he's gonna stand up for his son.

But after calling and leaving messages and texts for over three weeks, I did not hear from Mason at all. I became worried and thought for a minute. *I bet Rhonda took away his phone, or blocked my number.*

I decided to send a text to my niece, Sunny. As I mentioned earlier, she's my sister Lina's daughter. Her dad, Al, is James's older brother.

Hey Sunny, have you seen Mase? I briefly mentioned the incident with Rhonda. *If you see him, please tell him to call me. I think Rhonda blocked my number. Love and miss you!*

She texted back: *No, I haven't seen him. I'm not allowed to visit their home. The bitch is afraid I'm gonna tell Mason everything I know about her. That's so sick. Ugh. That just bothers me so much. They're mean people. That's just so wrong if they did that. You are his Bebe, his mama's mother. He has every right to talk to you and even come see you. Love you too!*

I texted: *I know. I'm very sad, but there's nothing I can do. I'm hoping he calls me when he's not at home. But I'm sure she checks his phone everyday.*

On Thursday, May 22, 2014, I called Mason, left him a message and a text.

Later that evening, Mason called me but he sounded so different. It was like he'd been brainwashed over the last three weeks.

"Hi Mase, did you get my messages?"

"No," he said, sounding a bit cold.

"What happened after I left?"

"Nothing," he said hesitantly.

"Really?" I said. "What's the latest with the California vacation?"

"Well, my dad is not totally sure I should go."

"Why?" I said, thinking, *Now what's James up to?*

"My dad said your house is not a safe place for me to be," Mason replied, sounding unhappy. As much as I hated to say it, I thought he was emulating his dad.

"Really? How dare your father tell you that?" I said upset, thinking to myself. *My house is no less safe than theirs, and James knows that.*

"So I guess this means that you will not be coming this year either, right?"

"Well, you need to talk to my dad. I'm just a kid and I'm tired of being in the middle of all this. You and my dad need to make up," Mason replied with a shaky voice. Right away I knew these weren't Mason's words but his Nana Trisha's.

"Mason, I'm not gonna do that. For the last four years since your mom died, I have tried my best, and I cannot do it anymore. You're the only one that can make it happen. Not me. Your dad and Rhonda have made my life a living hell for no good reason. I know you're only twelve, but you need to be brave and speak up. You need a therapist to help you with that. I know very well that's not going to happen, though. So we'll just have to leave it at that." Then the phone got cut off and I surmised that someone was in the room with him – or maybe Mason pressed the End button himself?

I sighed to myself. *Things have gone from bad to worse. Obviously they both want me out of Mason's life for good. I guess everything's working out in their favor. The little boy that my daughter raised to be kind, loving and to always tell the truth is slowly disappearing.*

I also found out that Rhonda posted a picture on Facebook the day after Mother's Day of herself with James, his mother Trisha, and Mason outside of the courthouse, making it official that she had just adopted Mason as her son, and she was now his legal guardian.

I was concerned this might further distance Mason from the memories of his mother, and possibly from me.

Mason needs me. I'm the closest thing to his mother for teaching him the positive values she held dear. He needs as much love as possible from all of his family.

It's hard for me to understand why James was disputatious. As I mentioned earlier, maybe because I know too much about them. Or, maybe I remind him too much of my daughter? I know he was unhappy when I got my daughter's purse after she was killed. Then he wanted the house that Torreey and I bought for Natalie and Mason to live in after he evicted them, thinking that the house was in Natalie's name. But he lost that round too. I filed a lawsuit against Natalie's estate simply to recover our loans. I felt I had no other choice but to file a protest to closing the estate.

James could have done this the easy way. He could have paid us back what Natalie's estate owed us. His attorneys paid all of Natalie's bills, but they refused to pay the estate debt to us.

A week later, when my son Luke came over for dinner on Sunday, he asked about my trip and if Mason was coming to visit this year.

"No, I don't think he'll be coming," I said, explaining what had happened.

Luke was furious. "That's why I won't go there. I'd definitely give those two a piece of my mind!"

Over the following weeks I decided to continue leaving messages for Mason, hoping that one of these days he'll call me back. And if not, someday when I'm ready I'll send him the following message: "My dear Mason, I will always love you, no matter what. In my heart is where I'll keep you safe, my sweet and loving Papacito. If I'm still around when and if in life you decide to call or pay me a visit, I will be here for you. Even though it breaks my heart to not even hear your voice, I think for now it's best for me to step aside and let you do it on your own. Your mother would want you to be a strong and brave young man, just like she was a true fighter. I feel that I'm not helping you do just that. Even though you hide your pain well from others, you can't hide it from me. Part of my decision to let you go for now is only because I love you too much and I want for you to live a happier life. You deserve that and much more. This way you don't have to be in the middle and try to make everyone happy. You're still a boy and shouldn't have to be put in that unfortunate spot. Just remember that Bebe will always love you, and your mom too."

I have realized that constantly putting Mason in the middle of this feud is not fair. For that reason, I have let go of him. But there is another reason that I will discuss later.

As an afterthought to my message: "Mason, I hope it will not be too late, as we all know, we live in borrowed time and before we know it, it's gone!"

Natalie, please forgive me. I know you wouldn't want me to stop even if the words "Momma didn't raise a quitter," haunt me for the rest of my life.

Me at the Derby Daze event, May 2013.

Chapter 65

Awesome Friends in Mississippi - 2010-2015

Nancy was Natalie's special friend. She lived across the street from James's house. She had four children and one of the boys, Dennis, was Mason's best friend. They did a lot of things together with each other and their kids. They took trips like skiing in Colorado with the children; or Italy with some of their female friends. Nancy was like the sister Natalie never had.

After Natalie was killed, Nancy and her husband Jack opened The Natalie Collins Counseling Center in Natalie's memory and committed to donate $100,000 a year for the next five years to the Center.

Nancy is a woman with a heart of gold. She's loyal and will do anything for the people she loves. She's funny but also kind of shy too. Natalie always told me how much she loved the expressions Nancy made with her eyes and lips when they were having a conversation. Natalie adored being around Nancy and her family. They were all very dear to her.

Nancy remains an exceptional and special person in my life and Mason's also. I don't know what I would have done without her and her family.

In June 2010, Nancy emailed me a lovely letter:

> Thank you for being a constant reminder of my beautiful friend Natalie!!! Losing her has been one of the most difficult losses of my life but through that loss I have so many wonderful new friends and family. My mother died prematurely, as did Natalie so, although I can't imagine your pain, I understand it. I will always be here for you and Mason, always!!! Love, Nancy.

Natalie's other good pal is Gloria. Natalie was always there when Gloria needed a friend to talk to. Gloria is as sweet as pie and loved Natalie very much.

Joyce is a beautiful black girl who I have always called "Joy to the World". She's soft spoken and a true loving person, like Natalie's other acquaintances. Joyce is a very caring soul who loved Natalie with all her heart.

Lisa was Natalie's tennis partner and new friend. She's been in charge of arranging the Tennis Tournament/Derby Daze events in Natalie's memory every year. She stopped playing tennis after Natalie died. She said, "Shirley, I'll never find another partner like her."

Kat was another great individual in Natalie's life. When Natalie registered me for the Tennis Tournament, she said, "Mom, I've found the perfect partner for you. She's pretty and real sexy too. She's about your age and loves to work out just like you. I know you and Mr. Miyagi will be good together." In case you don't remember, Natalie dubbed her "Mr. Miyagi" (from *The Karate Kid*) because when Kat hit the tennis ball, her grunt sounded just like him.

Natalie was right, the minute I met Kat I liked her right away. She was kind, classy and reserved, but after a few cocktails she became crazy fun.

Eva was Natalie's Latina *amiga*, (friend) from Mexico. She didn't speak much English, and was Mason's nanny since he was a baby. Natalie loved Eva, her husband Jesus, and their two boys very much. She helped the entire family obtain their green cards. She also found jobs for Eva cleaning some of her girlfriends' big homes, and work for Jesus in construction.

Omar and his family were from Mexico too. Natalie had a special love for all of them. They were her Latino *familia*, (family) in Lake Cormorant. She got them work visas for ten years to work legally in Lake Cormorant and found them all jobs with most of her wealthy buddies.

Omar and his family loved Natalie and Mason like their own.

Diane, my daughter's friend and business partner, who survived the auto accident that killed Natalie, decided not to have any communication with me. I was very disappointed and hurt by her actions, but I now accept that is what she chose to do.

Natalie loved every one of her friends in a different way, but with all of her heart.

Dorothy was also a great person to Natalie. She had a little boy named Nick. Natalie and Dorothy hung out together a lot. They both played tennis and had many play dates with their kids. After Natalie was killed, Dorothy also emailed me a beautiful letter.

> "Shirley, I love Natalie like I love my sisters. I still can't wrap my head around this. I feel like I've lost a piece of my heart. She was the most amazing person I have ever met, truly.
>
> Natalie Webb (she always wanted her stepfather Torreey Webb to adopt her) has been an instigator all of her life. She loved to stir up 'trouble'…whether it was to help someone in need, draw attention to a cause, or just for her own enjoyment. Every time my caller ID would show her name, I immediately thought, 'Here we go again, what next!?' She taught me how to see different sides of every story. She taught me how to love every creature…. even the ugliest dog I

had ever seen. She would take all of her friends (people of every race, creed, ethnicity and socioeconomic background) and have them over for dinner or invite them to events to intermingle and get to know one another. She had several 'cliques' of friends, but we all seemed to end up together.

Natalie would always be singing something.... usually, the latest song on the radio, but she would always change the words and make it her own...she was hilarious. She was always smiling and making eye contact ... even though she was brash and forceful, she could disarm even the most hardened heart and look deep into their soul. She never gave up ... she was the most resilient person I know. She was always fighting and entertaining ... whether it was on the tennis court, for humanity, or for her son. She never took herself too seriously ... no matter how down I felt, she could make me laugh in seconds by singing a goofy song, talking about some interesting guy she just met, or just doing something off the wall. We were always planning to go off somewhere. My best trips have been with Natalie and our sons. We never had a dull moment. We lived to the fullest ... I have learned so much from our ten years together. The most important lesson being to take care of each other ... she was a super mommy to Mase but also a 'mother' to so many others."

The first two years after Natalie was killed, her friends and I stayed in touch with each other frequently. But four years later everything seemed to change. I see them once a year for Natalie's anniversary and fundraiser and a text message for Christmas and New Year's, too. I know deep down that my daughter is always in their hearts.

I love them all so dearly.

Chapter 66

Pinata Vengeance - 1994-2014

Mom worked as a seamstress at a company named Costume Characters in Burbank, California for over ten years. She made a career out of sewing Disneyland characters such as Snow White and the Dwarfs, Mickey and Minnie Mouse, and many, many others. She enjoyed her work and had a great time with the people she worked with. She was sharing an apartment in Burbank with my oldest brother Edgar who at the time was divorced. In 1994 she became ill with nausea and dizzy spells.

Edgar was overwhelmed with Mom's doctor appointments and couldn't take care of her on his own.

Our sisters, Gia, Lina and Tanya, lived in the neighborhood and were glad to help Edgar with Mom.

After months of tests and specialists appointments, my siblings couldn't handle it anymore. They had used up all of their sick leave and vacation time at work.

That's when I stepped in, even though I lived farther away than any of them. I was working in West LA for my husband's CPA practice. I was now the only one who could take time off and attend to our mother's needs. Even though I was super busy I still made time for Mom. I worked weekends or late nights if I had to catch up with work.

After months of examinations we finally got a diagnosis of liver disease. By then, Mom was worn out and too weak to continue working at the costume factory. She was prescribed medication and was told to stay home, rest, and if not she'd be risking her life.

After giving Torreey the news and talking with my siblings, we all agreed it would be a good idea for Mom to move in with Torreey and me. We had an extra bedroom and I was the only one who could take care of her.

Mom was sad to leave her job and friends, but she knew she had to.

After moving in with us, I followed up with all of her appointments and eight months later she bounced back to her normal self. She missed work and all of her friends, but she stayed in touch with them. Her acquaintances came by to visit and Mom became accustomed to her new life with us. She enjoyed having her own room with a television. During the day, after I left for work, she stayed home with our Golden Labrador, Tammy, our Pug, Puggie, and a cat we called Es. She did most of the chores, and of course watched her Spanish soap operas, cooked, and was always on the phone with one of her kids or friends. She never stayed still until she went to bed. I guess that's who I got it from. I'm so much like her.

On some weekends, Mom, my sister Lina and I went out to lunch, movies, walks at the beach; or we stayed home cooking, chatting, or watching TV. In all events, we always ended up laughing. That was a necessity in our life. Laughter is indeed the best medicine, as they say.

In 1994, Lina had just moved to Redondo Beach with her husband Al and was pregnant with Sunny.

My daughter Natalie was back from Italy and my son Luke was working and still living at home with us. We had a full house but it was fun. My siblings came to visit often and we had many, many crazy, fun family parties at our crooked yellow house in Redondo Beach.

Torreey and I also took Mom on our trips to Vegas a couple of times a year. Mom's life changed for the better. She didn't have to worry about paying rent, utilities, or buying food. She retired early and got her social security check that she spent on herself, or gave money to some of my siblings behind my back.

When Lina and Natalie moved to Lake Cormorant, Mom and I went to visit them twice a year.

On her 70th birthday in 2001, we had a party for her at our new Mediterranean house in Redondo Beach. We had moved in December 1998.

My Mom's sisters Nari, Adriana and her husband Carlos, and their daughter Rita came from Costa Rica to celebrate Mom's special day. My aunt Adriana brought a piñata on the plane. It was Bam, Bam a character on *The Flintstones* cartoons.

We had about fifty guests, including family and friends. We had a few surprises in store for Mom.

Before hanging the piñata on a rope from the balcony outside on the patio, I glued a blown up picture of our dad's face over the piñata's face. OMG it was hilarious! We couldn't stop from laughing.

As I previously mentioned, Dad was not a model father or husband. Whenever he got mad at Mom, he behaved horribly toward her – and to us kids, also. So the piñata with his face on it was the perfect joke, and gave Mom an opportunity to get the residual anger out of her system for good.

Mom had no idea what we had planned for her. We blindfolded her while my husband Torreey handed her a bat and began turning her in circles a couple of times.

One person was at the top of the balcony holding on to the rope. Mom began hitting the piñata while everyone laughed. Some of the women were yelling in Spanish, "Hueputa dale mas duro!" ("Son-of-a-bitch, hit him harder!")

After beating the piñata to no avail for a few minutes, Mom decided she'd had enough and removed the handkerchief from her eyes. When she saw Dad's face on it, she snatched the bat from Torreey's hand and shouted, "Huepueta viejo ahora si lo mato!" ("This time I'll kill this old son-of-a-bitch!") She began smacking him as hard as she could until some of the candy came flying out. She still didn't hit him hard enough because she couldn't stop from laughing.

Torreey stepped in and said, "Let me have the bat and I'll show you how to do it." He took a big swing; the candy exploded out, and the piñata's body landed on the ground leaving the head hanging on the rope. Everyone was out of control in tears, laughing so hard. It was absolutely insane!

Hours later, after drinking, eating, dancing and laughing some more, it was time to "pin the tail on the donkey."

"Mom, you're the birthday girl, so you go first," I said with a grin on my face.

Aunt Adriana blindfolded Mom while I taped the donkey without a tail to the wall. I had blown up a second picture of our dad's face and glued it on the donkey's ass.

"Hay Dios mio, que brutos!" ("OMG, how brutal!") My aunt Nari said, laughing out loud.

Everyone including Mom (who was wearing a blindfold) was laughing even though Mom didn't know what we had done – but she knew we were up to no good again.

"Mom," I said, "hold on to the donkey's tail and walk slowly straight ahead." She followed my instructions. "Now, move to the left ... A little to the right ... Stop! Now, press the tail ... Let go and stay still." By now we were all in tears and almost choking from laughing so hard.

Torreey then walked over to Mom, removed the handkerchief and as soon as Mom saw the donkey's ass with Dad's face on it, she let out a huge scream, laughing and swearing in Spanish. "Hueputa viejo, burro!" ("Son-of-a-bitch, you old donkey!")

OMG, we were all holding our stomachs and wiping away our tears of joy!

This birthday was by far the best Mom's ever had. She got to beat the shit out of our dad and then pin the tail on his *cara de culo*, (butt face.) "Que hijueputa, que locura. Pura Vida!" ("Son-of-a-bitch, how crazy was this. Pure Life!") Aunt Nari summed up what we were all thinking.

From 2003 through 2010, our family, but mostly Mom and I, went through a lot. As I previously mentioned, first with Lina's five-year struggle with cancer and passing; then followed by Natalie's sudden death.

After Natalie was killed in May 2010, I was lost and couldn't cope with life. Two weeks later, on a Friday evening, I walked into Mom's bedroom and said, "Mom, por favor no quiero que nadie venga a visitar este fin de semana, okay?" ("Mom, I don't want anyone coming by this weekend, okay?")

Either Mom forgot, or ignored my request, and Saturday morning my self-centered sister Ceci showed up at my house at 8:00 a.m. This was the last person I wanted to see! Even though Ceci knew the timing was bad, she still came by to take Mom to the mall to go shopping for shoes. Ceci never seemed to be happy, and stirred up trouble anywhere she went.

Torreey had gone to the health club at 6:00 a.m., and when he returned home and opened the door to the garage, he was surprised by what he saw.

I was standing in front of the door across from Mom's bedroom. "Mom, did you forget what I told you last night?" I said, crying, shaking, and by now yelling at the same time. I was so fucking upset and couldn't believe Mom didn't listen to me.

"I didn't know she was coming!" Mom responded, shouting.

Ceci stood there frozen and didn't say a word.

"You disrespected my feelings and my house," I said with tears streaming.

Mom felt insulted by what I said.

Ceci quickly grabbed her purse and said, "Mom, vengase conmigo, ya!" (Mom, come with me, now!")

Torreey was still standing by the door, moving his head from one side to the other and not understanding a word we were speaking in Spanish. "What's going on?" Torreey finally said, alarmed.

While still crying and shaking I turned to Torreey and told him what had happened.

"Mom, apurese, vamonos!" ("Mom, hurry up, let's go!") Ceci, yelled out.

Mom ran into her bedroom, grabbed her purse, then followed Ceci out the door, yelling in Spanish, "Me voy a ir al Diablo y me busco otra casa para vivir!" ("I'm getting the hell out of this house and finding me another place to live!") She then slammed the door on her way out.

"What did your mom say?" Torreey asked, stunned.

Still sobbing and shaking I told Torreey exactly what she'd said.

Torreey threw up his hands in resignation. "Maybe we didn't take good care of your mom, and perhaps your sister Ceci can do a better job."

"I'm so sick and tired of so much shit!" I said, feeling like I was ready to pass out.

"Momsie, calm down. You didn't do anything wrong. If your mom doesn't want to live here any longer, then one of your siblings needs to take over. You can't do it anymore. We've done sixteen years. That's enough!"

"I know! I know!" I said, trembling and rushing upstairs to the kitchen to grab a glass of water.

Later that evening, I called my sister Tanya and asked, "Did you know that Ceci was coming by my house this morning?"

"Yes, I did, 'cause I overheard her talking with Mom. I even told her not to go, but you know how Ceci is."

I knew that none of my siblings would give her the quality of life she had with my husband and me, especially now that she was older. But I had just lost my daughter two weeks ago. I was heartbroken, extremely depressed, and I couldn't deal with taking care of Mom anymore.

Ceci had no place to go but Gia's house and later she moved into Tanja's. She was not on speaking terms with another one of our sisters, and now I made the enemy list too. Ceci was a selfish and very jealous woman who never seemed to know what she wanted out of life. A month later, Ceci decided to go back to Virginia to her husband who she'd left a year ago because she suddenly didn't want to be married to him any longer.

That spring, Mom moved out of my house and into one of her adult granddaughter's, Cima, in North Hollywood for a while.

In August of 2011, Mom was diagnosed with breast cancer; she needed a mastectomy as soon as possible.

A month later, on September 11, 2011, Mom turned eighty years old. We celebrated her birthday and hoped that the coming surgery would be all right. We were all scared and concerned due to her age, high blood pressure, liver issues, and all of the medications she was taking.

After moving out of my house, Mom's life was quite different. She was no longer receiving all the luxuries that she was used to with us. But I couldn't take care of her any longer, even if I wanted too. As I said, I was lost and couldn't cope with my mother's problems – not only her health issues but also our family.

I had to seek help from a therapist to be able to manage the pain of losing my daughter. I now needed my siblings to take their turn and help with our mom. I always thought Mom would be with me for the rest of her life, but things changed in an instant. I couldn't take the responsibility anymore. I needed to take care of myself first; and at this moment I wasn't able to do it. I had done way more than my share and didn't need to feel guilty about it. Torreey and I had provided sixteen beautiful years to Mom.

In our house, she had her own bedroom with a bathroom. We had a maid clean our house twice a month. Mom didn't have a lot to do, except to feed our pets, and walk the smallest dog, Jazzie, every day. Water the plants, flowers, and wash our gym and sports clothes in the washing machine. Mom was content living in our house. She had a wonderful life with us. We had a very peaceful loving home. Torreey and I had gotten along well with her.

Mom's surgery was scheduled for September 27, 2011. Three of my sisters and I, my brother, and sister-in-law were with her at the hospital the day of her operation.

After waiting for a couple of hours, the doctor appeared and gave us the news. "Your mom's in the recovery room. She's doing well and will be going home in a few days."

Days later, Mom was resting at my niece Cima's condominium.

After recovering from surgery, Mom had plans to leave California and move to Costa Rica where her younger sister Adriana and her husband Carlos lived. She bought a plane ticket to go in December 2011, just three months away.

We all agreed and thought it would be the best for her for now. She visited her family every year until Lina got sick with cancer. She always said, "I wanna live in Costa Rica when I get older." She was really looking forward to her upcoming trip and thought it would do her good to spend some time with her sisters back at the peaceful farm, with the sights and sounds of nature for some healing time.

Chapter 67

My Loco Elvis-Loving Brother - 2011-2012

My brother Evan was eleven months younger than me. His birthday was September 9, and mine October 9. He was a big Elvis Presley fanatic, and I was a Priscilla admirer. I loved her clothes, eye makeup, and the puffy hairdo she wore back in the 60s. Every year when I called to wish him Happy Birthday, he'd say, "Hey sister, we're twins again for a month!"

Evan was 5'5, with olive skin, skinny as a rail, funny as hell and full of life too. Always clowning around, laughing about everything, including himself. He always had something hilarious to say. Like when I teased him about smoking so much. "Damn, dude, you better quit that shit!"

"Nope, I'll never do that! This shit's good. It's like vitamins to me!" he said seriously, but at the end laughing.

"Well, you stink, man!" I said, giggling while placing a hand over my mouth and nose.

He also had a crazy song he made up by the name of *Si con diah*. Not even he knew what it meant. Every time he sang it he started dancing in slow motion until he got to the end where he was crawling all over the floor while we laughed our assess off. OMG it was crazy fun!

Evan was also a heavy beer drinker. His favorite things were Budweiser Light, Winston cigarettes, carne asada tacos, Tapa Tio hot sauce, and of course, music and dancing. He was obsessed with Elvis Presley. Whenever he got wasted on beer he'd put on a show and did a great job imitating Elvis. Some weekends when he came by my house to visit Mom, he brought along his live-in girlfriend, Cita.

Cita's Filipino, and is ten years older than him. She's shy, sweet, funny; and a caring woman who loved my brother very much. We always ended up laughing like crazy not only about my brother but also about Cita. She has a heavy accent and sometimes when she talks, she says the wrong words.

On Friday, November 25, 2011, the day after Thanksgiving, Evan was diagnosed with terminal pancreatic cancer that had already spread to his liver.

A few months before being diagnosed, Evan had lost his job and was collecting unemployment benefits.

The doctor offered Evan chemo and radiation with the understanding that he'd live approximately eleven months if he took the treatments.

"I don't want any of that shit! I'm not doing what Lina did. I'm fucking finished!" Evan told the doctor and refused the therapy.

Our brother required twenty-four hour care, and Cita couldn't provide that for him. She had a full-time job caring for an elderly woman.

Even though I had the big house and enough room for my brother to stay with me until the end, I just couldn't offer him my help. I was still destroyed over losing my daughter, and honestly I just couldn't take care of another ill sibling in my house.

We were having a family meeting when Gia hugged Evan and offered: "I'll take care of you with Mom here at my house. I love you, and I'm your oldest sister. Don't worry about anything, okay, Papito? Manuel said you can stay with us until the end."

"Thank you for taking care of Evan. I love you!" I told Gia and her long-time boyfriend, Manuel, with sadness.

Our mom immediately postponed her trip to Costa Rica to care for her son. She moved into Gia and Manuel's home, five minutes away from Cima.

Evan was broke and of course was worried that he didn't even have money to arrange for his own funeral.

When Gia found out she took donations from the family, even though not everyone could afford it. At the end, she ended up with a little over $800.

In the middle of January 2012, hospice came in and brought Evan a hospital bed, wheelchair, walker, oxygen tank, liquid morphine, and pills for sleeping, anxiety and nausea.

Evan had no appetite and was skin and bones. He was wasting away very fast and slept most of the time.

Every Sunday morning I drove to Gia's home in North Hollywood and stayed until evening. Sometimes I'd bring food and cook for everyone who was visiting him; other days I'd order takeout. We all cried and laughed with him in his bedroom. Some of us couldn't take it and had to walk outside to cry on our own. It was painful to see my brother going through this, although he was still making us laugh.

He had posters, books, videos and CDs of Elvis. While he was in bed he put on his earphones and listened to the music. At times he looked so peaceful to me.

One afternoon, during a conversation with Gia, I said, "Have you contacted Papa Pablo (our dad) about Evan? Gia and our sister Tanya were the only siblings who stayed in touch with him.

"Yeah, I did," Gia responded.

"Is he coming by to see Evan?"

"He didn't say," Gia whispered and changed the subject.

One Sunday evening, at the end of January 2012, I was coming home, very exhausted and depressed. I had taken a Xanax pill before leaving Gia's house. As I was getting near my house by the beach, I noticed that the fog was so thick I couldn't even see the elementary school or the houses in the neighborhood. I was driving very slow and was glad to get home, take a shower, lay on my bed, and watch TV. I was so exhausted I could barely move.

Around 8:00 p.m., Torreey came up the stairs and said, "I'm taking the dogs out for a walk." He usually walks them before it gets dark, but this evening he got too busy with work.

"Why don't you skip tonight? It's too foggy outside," I said, yawning.

"No, I need to take them out," he insisted. "Besides I need a break from work, too. I'll take the flashlight with me just in case."

Torreey left with the three dogs; Niki the mix Lab-Dalmatian, Milo and Sunami, the Pugs.

I was in bed watching the movie, *The Girl With the Dragon Tattoo*, when my mobile rang. I had it on my nightstand next to our bed. I looked at the phone's screen and saw Torreey's photo. He had been gone no more than fifteen minutes. "What's up?" I said.

"I lost Sunami!" he said in a panic-stricken voice. "I guess she came off the leash while we were walking and I didn't notice until I was about a block away."

"OMG, how could you do that? OH, NO!" I immediately jumped out of bed, shaking; grabbed my big jacket, placed my mobile phone and keys to the house in one of the pockets, and ran out the door as fast as I could, still wearing my pajamas. I didn't care; all I wanted was to find my little Sunami.

I ran down the sidewalk, crying, trembling, and yelling out, "SUNAMI! SUNAMI! SUNAMI!" as loud as I could.

When I got to the corner of our block, still yelling, "SUNAMI! SUNAMI! Help! Help me!" I found myself in the middle of the street. I could barely see Torreey's flashlight shining from far away.

Out of the blue, an older woman came up to me and said, "Honey, are you okay?"

"NO! NO! Sunami, Sunami! I need help!" I said repeatedly.

"Honey, there's no Tsunami coming," she said as if talking to a child. "I didn't hear that on the news."

Another neighbor came out of the house, and started talking to the woman, and I assumed they walked away.

I had no time to talk to them; all I wanted was my little dog to come back to me, right now! I stood in the middle of the street, still calling her name. I could see that Torreey was getting closer to me because of the flashlight.

Suddenly I thought I felt something brush against my leg. I looked down at my feet and Sunami was right there at my toes, scratching my slippers. I grabbed her, still shaking and crying, kissed her forehead and held her close to me. By then Torreey and the other two dogs were standing beside me.

"Where did you find her?" Torreey asked, relieved.

I was so angry with him that I yelled out, "Don't you talk to me anymore! You almost lost my little baby. Ahhh!"

I took off running back to the house, while holding Sunami in my arms. When I got home I put her on our bed, then went into the bathroom and got a Xanax to calm my nerves down. I was a complete fucking mess. Going to see my dying brother every Sunday for the past two months; then to get home and for my husband to lose my little dog was enough to need more than one Xanax. Or maybe by now I needed some fucking morphine to knock me out? OMG! I thought for sure I was loosing my mind. I got in bed and kept my little Sunami next to my side; she was still trembling.

A couple of days after the Sunami event, I was walking the three dogs during the late afternoon. It was a beautiful day and I always made a point of waving and saying hello to our neighbors, even if some of them didn't respond. One of my neighbors saw me round the corner and approached.

"Shirley, what happened to you the other evening?" Sarah said with a note of concern. "Some of the neighbors were worried. They told me you where in the middle of the street crying and yelling 'Tsunami! Tsunami!'"

When I told her what had happened, she busted out laughing so hard I thought she might hurt herself. Sarah finally calmed down and said, "Oh dear, some of the neighbors were saying you must have been on some kind of drug. That you looked like a crazy woman out there. Oh Shirley, I'm gonna make sure I tell them the whole story about your little one, okay?"

What? None of these people know that my little pug's name is Sunami? Oh fuck, shit, whatever! I thought. I hadn't realized I'd created such a bad reputation for myself around our neighborhood. Oh well, what could I do besides laugh? I should be used to it by now, something crazy-foolish always happens to me.

On Sunday, February 12, 2012 I walked into Evan's bedroom at Gia's house. He was breathing heavy and moaning as if he was in pain. Angie, the nurse, was giving him morphine every two hours.

"Angie, can you please give him extra medicine so he's not suffering? I can't take this anymore," I begged. At this point, Evan was coughing up blood and the urinary catheter was filling up with blood, too.

At 10:30 p.m., I was getting ready to drive home when Gia approached me and said, "Can you spend the night?"

"I'm sorry, Gia, I can't do it. I don't wanna see it. You know what I mean. Call me at any time, okay?" I said and walked away crying to my car. I knew this was the end for my brother.

When I got home at 11:15 p.m., I downed an anxiety pill, took a shower and went to bed. I was depressed, exhausted, and my mind and body were completely drained and destroyed.

At 3:45 a.m., on Monday, February 13, 2012, the phone rang and I knew right away it was Gia. "Evan's gone," she said, crying.

"Okay," I said in a daze with tears flowing down my face.

Days later I found out that when the hospice nurse arrived at Gia's house to clean up Evan before the van took him to the mortuary, apparently Mom had given Gia a muscle relaxer and an anxiety pill to calm her down a bit. After taking the pills, Gia was so out of it, that when the nurse asked her for some fresh clothes for Evan, Gia handed the nurse Evan's pajamas and said, "Please put these on him. I want him to stay warm."

OMG, *poor Gia!* I thought, and couldn't stop from laughing and crying at the same time.

My brother Edgar arrived at Gia's house along with my two nephews, Andrew and Ruben. They wanted to see Evan one more time. They helped carry his lifeless body to the van that was waiting out in front to take him to the funeral home.

Gia and Edgar couldn't agree with each other during the whole time that Evan stayed at Gia's house.

Edgar had some issues regarding the power of attorney that Evan apparently changed from Edgar to Gia, since he was staying at her house.

Last thing I wanted was to be in the middle of another family squabble, so I stayed out of it.

Gia somehow arranged for Evan's cremation with the $800 that she'd collected from some of us. It was the cheapest cremation she'd been able to find.

Ten days later, Edgar called me complaining about Gia, and how she handled things, saying, "Gia didn't have a clue what she was doing!"

Fuck, here we go again, I thought. *This is what happens when you have such a big freakin' family.*

I listened to Edgar, but I really didn't want to get mixed up in it. Going through my brother's death reopened the barely healed wounds of not only my daughter but my sister's, too. I had plenty of pain in my heart and I just couldn't cope with anything more.

"Do you know where Evan's body is?" Edgar fumed.

"WHAT? What are you talking about?" I responded, confused. "I assumed the body is at the North Hollywood funeral home."

"His body's is at a Downtown LA mortuary, because Gia made a mistake with the paperwork. I called and that's what I was told. He's been there on ice for two weeks."

I let out a sigh of exasperation. "Well, I don't know what to tell you Edgar, except that we all make mistakes. And if she did, I assure you it wasn't intentional. Gia and Mom did a wonderful job in taking care of Evan until the end. They were by his side day and night." I finished my conversation with Edgar, sat in my chair in the kitchen stunned, and couldn't fucking believe this shit! Instead of crying I started laughing so hard, and thinking, *"What da fuck! My brother Evan is dead and gone. Edgar can't find his frozen body and is blaming Gia for everything.* So I decided to say a few words to Evan: "Hey, you up there! Evan, I know you're laughing your ass off, too. Stop smoking, drinking and dancing and come down and help Gia with this mess! I know Gia's done many crazy things but this is by far the most fucking insane thing she's ever done! *Hay caramba. Dios mio!"* ("Dear God!")

Shit, I gotta call Graciella. I picked up my mobile, laughing while telling her about Evan's frozen body and pajamas. I could barely spit out the words.

"Oh my God, this is just like *Weekend at Bernie's!*" Graciella was laughing uncontrollably.

"You're so fucking right!" I said, giggling.

I didn't want to call Gia or Mom because I knew they were exhausted, sad, and depressed. So I waited until the end of the week to ask Gia about Evan's body.

On Saturday, late morning, I sat at the counter table in my kitchen sipping a glass of water. I grabbed my phone and called Gia. "When are we supposed to get Evan's ashes? It's been over two weeks now. And by the way where is his body? I was told he's not at the North Hollywood mortuary."

"WHAT?" Gia gasped. "I don't know nothing about that, but I'll find out! I'll let you know later."

That evening, Gia called me. "Evan's body was brought back and they'll be cremating him in a week. I told the guy, Fernando, to please call me before he's cremated. I want his pajamas removed and changed into a nice shirt and pants that I'll take with me."

"Hay, mujer que loca! ("Girl, you're crazy!") Leave him with his PJs. He'll keep warm," I said teasingly and thought, *I have no more tears left to cry so I might as well laugh about it now.*

"No! No! I want him to look nice," Gia said, dead serious.

What the hell? My sister Gia does crazy shit without even thinking about it. Just like her backwards G-string underwear in Vegas among many other things. She doesn't mean it; it's just the way it turns out. Ha! Ha! Ha!

My son Luke wanted to be there with Gia to cut a lock of Evan's hair as he did with Natalie. He planned to take Evan's hair to the Burning Man festival and do a ritual.

Like I've said before, we're a crazy Latino family and good or bad shit always happens. I cried and laughed at the same time just thinking about all that's happened with my brother. I'm sure Evan, Lina and Natalie are all looking down and laughing their assess off, too.

A week later, Gia called me, agitated. "I got Evan's ashes."

"Well it's about time! *Que hijueputa, Maje! Que barbaros! Ya han pasado tres semanas y asta por fin lo van a hacer cenizas. Con razon era tan barato,*" ("Son-of-a-bitch! Three weeks later and finally he's become ashes. No wonder it was so cheap.") I said, joking. "I'll arrange a reception to celebrate Evan's life at my house, okay?"

"Norma, the receptionist at the mortuary, told me the reason why it took so long to cremate him was because they cremate more than one body at a time," Gia said sounding convinced.

"WHAT! Never heard of that before. Oh shit! So how do we know if we're getting his ashes and not someone else's?" I replied, confused. I wasn't sure if Gia understood the woman or if she was really telling me the truth. So I left it at that. Didn't wanna question Gia anymore. She had done enough and there wasn't anything we could do about it. I kept telling myself only a few more steps and we'll be done with this.

A few days later, everything was set and ready for the Saturday, March 3, 2012 memorial.

We had a beautiful but emotional celebration of my brother's life in the backyard of my house surrounded by family and many of Evan's friends.

Our cousin Rico put together a beautiful video of Evan's life.

I had Tacos Chihuahua Catering Services at our patio and they served everyone delicious Mexican food in my brother's memory.

I also ordered a big cake with Evan's picture in the center. I decorated the cake with a can of Bud Light beer, a cigarette and a bottle of Tapa Tio hot sauce; all of Evan's favorite things.

Weeks later we scattered Evan's ashes in the ocean at Redondo Beach, the same place where we'd scattered Natalie's.

Manuel, Gia's boyfriend of thirty-four years, was very supportive and helpful with our brother Evan's death. He allowed our brother to stay in his house until the end. Over the years Manuel did many selfless acts of kindness for our family.

Our poor mom had to go through another ugly death. In 2008, our sister of colon cancer that lasted five years.

In 2010, my daughter Natalie was killed in a fatal car accident.

And in 2012, our brother Evan, of a brief struggle with pancreatic cancer, that metastasized over a three-month period.

Life can be so beautiful and yet so painful, especially when parents have to bury their own children. The death of a son or daughter is by far more painful than any other death you'll experience in a lifetime. I can say that for me, with my daughter Natalie, her death felt like a piece of my soul had been ripped away.

We all prayed and went to church when Lina was diagnosed with cancer. But after Natalie was killed, that's when I lost faith in praying.

As far as our dad, he never showed up at Gia's to see his dying son. But he did stop by Lina's to see her before she was gone, four years ago. I honestly believe it was easier for him to see a daughter than a son. Dad has too much pride and can't, or never will, say the words, "I'm sorry." It's just not in him.

Five months after my brother's death, our mom took off to Costa Rica and stayed for almost two years. She's now back in the United States and living with Gia and Manuel in Simi Valley. In May of 2015, Torreey and I brought mom back to live with us in our home in Redondo Beach.

Celebrating my brother Evan's life in the backyard of our house, March 2012.

Chapter 68

In a Search of a Father - 2010-2012

After Natalie was killed, my son Luke got a tattoo of her name on the inner side of his left arm. This was his first tattoo. Months later he walked into our kitchen and said, "Mom, I think I made a mistake about this tattoo."

"Why?"

"Well, because every day at work or anywhere I am, I'm reminded of her and how she was killed. It makes me sad and very depressed."

"Why don't you go to a tattoo parlor and have them redo it with something pretty, like flowers," I said with sadness.

"I don't know, maybe." Luke shrugged.

One Sunday afternoon in 2012 while Luke and I were in the kitchen chatting, and, he said, "Mom, remember the last time at Christmas in 2009 when Natalie and Mason were here visiting? Natalie asked why I never go and visit her in Lake Cormorant? I told her, 'Because I don't like it there.'"

I looked at Luke and saw that his eyes were getting teary and his voice was shaky.

He continued, "'would you go if I die?' Natalie asked me."

"OMG! Luke." I said, choking back the tears. "What did you tell her?

"Yes, I would go if you die," Luke responded sobbing.

I walked over and hugged him with teardrops falling. There were no words for me to say. I was speechless.

"Mom, I'm really trying to go on with my life, but it's so hard. I can't stop thinking about Natalie. And I'm real depressed, too..." Luke hesitated, unable to speak.

"I know, Luke. I know the feeling. I try too, but I miss her so much. You know, when I'm playing tennis tournaments and some of the women start talking about their kids? Sometimes I pretend I don't hear them and I walk away to stretch, or I start bouncing the tennis ball with my racket so that I'm not in the conversation, otherwise I am caught in the middle of it. Sometimes I'm asked if I have any kids. Most of the time I can't respond. I get all choked up and either walk away or I softly say, 'I have a son and a daughter, but she was killed.' The women feel bad and they either tell me they're sorry for asking or they just hug me. I can't get away from this, and I know I never will. From time to time I feel like quitting tennis, but then I don't because I feel her presence with me, and besides she wouldn't want me to give up what I love doing. We just need more time to heal."

I then said with concern, "Luke, why don't you go see the doctor about your depression?"

"No, because the doctor is going to prescribe pills and I'm not gonna take them," Luke stated emphatically.

"Well, you can always see a therapist."

"No, I don't think so," he said, shaking his head.

Weeks later, after having dinner in our kitchen, Torreey walked away downstairs to his office to finish a report for a meeting he had the following day. Luke and I started a conversation about his biological dad, Roger. As I mentioned earlier, Roger vanished after we separated. The kids didn't miss their father at all. They were too young to understand the disappearance of their dad. The few times when they asked about him, I always told them the truth. "He's living with his parents in Virginia."

Natalie always asked, "Why?"

At that moment I was reminded of Natalie's conversation about her father when she was in her mid-twenties. I turned to Luke and said, "Remember when Natalie started searching for your dad on the Internet?"

I had a flashback to the day Natalie called me out of the blue, gushing, "Mom! I found him! I found him!"

"Found who?" I asked.

"My deadbeat dad! You know, your ex?" she said laughing out loud. "He's living in Florida. He's married to a Colombian woman, and on top of that, he had a baby girl with her! I got his address and he's running a small carpentry business. Mom, you need to get him for all the child support he owes you. Also, I should pay him a visit the next time I'm in Florida. He doesn't know what I look like so I can pretend I'm there to buy something." She sounded serious but then she laughed hysterically and said, "Damn loser! Can you fucking believe it?"

"Oh, yes I can!" I replied.

"Mom, I'm concerned because Mason was born the same year as I guess would be my half-sister. What about if some day Mason and the girl meet and fall in love with each other? OMG that would be fucking freaky!"

"Oh please, don't think about that, Natalie!" I pleaded, but I was thinking the same thing she was.

Roger also had another daughter before he met me. This daughter would now be about three years older than Luke.

"Mom..." Luke said tentatively, breaking me out of my reverie, "should I try to find my dad and let him know about Natalie's death?"

"I don't think he deserves to know anything. He abandoned you both. Plus, it's two years now that Natalie was killed," I said, uptight and surprised, not expecting this at all.

"Well, Mom, I owe this to Natalie. She was always looking for him. I need to do this for her," Luke said with a sad expression.

"Okay, if that's what you wanna do." I got up, grabbed my Rolodex and handed him the telephone number of Roger's longtime friend, Eric. I still had Eric's number in my Rolodex because he was formerly married to my sister Gia about forty years ago and he'd stayed in touch with her several times in the past eight years.

Luke contacted Eric and had a nice long conversation. Eric was very sad to hear about our loss. He told Luke he'd tried to get Roger to talk to them, but he wasn't successful at it.

A day later, Luke e-mailed his dad: "Hi Dad, this is your son, Luke. I need to talk to you."

Four days later Roger answered: "Luke, if you and Natalie have a problem or are in some kind of trouble I cannot help you. I'm married to a woman from Panama and helping her raise her kids. You both need to talk to your parents, you're both adults and need to solve any problem yourselves."

Luke came by the house and told me about Roger's e-mail. He was beyond furious.

"Fucking jerk! Are you gonna answer him back?" I said, trying to stay calm.

"I am," Luke spat. "I just need to cool off a bit."

A few days later Luke wrote: "Roger, I'm not asking you for anything. I don't need any money from you. I work and pay my way. And I'm not trying to establish a relationship with you either. The reason I want to talk to you is to let you know that Natalie was killed, and if you want to talk, you can call me." Then Luke left his number.

A day later Luke's phone rang.

"Luke, this is your dad, Roger."

"Yeah?" Luke said nonchalantly, but was surprised that he called.

"Is this some kind of joke about Natalie?"

"No, it isn't. It's all true." Luke replied, but didn't hear a word out of Roger's mouth. "Hello, are you still there?"

Roger was quiet for a moment, then he began sobbing. "OMG, I'm so sorry! I'm sorry for what I did."

"Roger, it's too late for Natalie, but it's not too late for you to find the other kids you have and talk to them. Sometimes life's too short, know what I mean?"

"Luke, your mother and I were too young, and our marriage just couldn't work," Roger said, sounding apologetic.

"I understand that – but not the reason why you disappeared on us. Also, you have a grandson named Mason. He's ten years old."

"Would you please send me a picture of him?" Roger implored.

The conversation continued for a while, and Roger told Luke that both he and his sister Pattie suffered from depression all of their lives. He concluded by saying, "Your mom was a good woman. Please say hello to her, grandma, and the rest of family."

Roger continued e-mailing Luke, but Luke meant what he said, and really wasn't interested in having a relationship with him. He did what he needed to do for his sister, and found some closure himself.

Chapter 69

Rebel Niece - 2008-2012

Sunny, as I previously mentioned, is my sister Lina's daughter. She and her mother moved from Lake Cormorant, Mississippi to my house in Redondo Beach, California when Lina was diagnosed with colon cancer in 2003. I offered to take care of Lina and Sunny with the help of our mother. After three years of living at my house, they moved out and went to live with her husband Al at an apartment ten minutes from me. Two years later, Lina lost her battle with cancer.

Sunny was a beautiful petite girl with long black hair and brown eyes. She was just twelve when her mother passed away. She became a rebel; changed her hair color just about every month from blonde to jet black to red, and so on. One day she chopped off her beautiful long shiny hair, and later was wearing extensions, a lot of eye makeup, false eyelashes, and had shaved off her eyebrows.

My observation was that the poor kid was obviously suffering inside. Her dad never accepted the fact that she needed both therapy, and more discipline. Instead, he gave her all the freedom she wanted and more. He didn't set down any rules, and Sunny took advantage of it.

From what I'd seen of Al, he was pretty much preoccupied with his own wants and needs.

Sunny was partying and hanging out with bad friends. She abandoned the good kids she hung with when her mother was around.

I tried staying in touch with her by texting: *Hey Sunny, why don't you come by my house and spend a night or two?*

Yeah, I will. She responded, but she never did.

The only time Mom and I saw her was on her birthday and at Christmastime when we took her shopping.

On her thirteenth birthday in October 2008, one month after Lina's passing, I sent a text: *Happy birthday! I love you! Would you like to go shopping with me?*

Yes! She texted back.

Me: *Great, I'll come by and get you and we'll go to lunch at your mom's favorite sushi bar in Torrance.*

We did just that and had a great time and never brought up Lina's sad end.

Four years later, when Sunny turned seventeen, the mother of one of Sunny's friends informed me that she was not attending Redondo High School for reasons that she didn't know. Sunny was now going to a continuation school in a bad neighborhood for troubled kids.

A year earlier, I was looking at one of those free magazines that's delivered to South Bay residents, and I came across a picture of a young girl who looked exactly like Sunny. The picture was very provocative. She had a big red silk kind of scarf wrapped around her naked body. *Hey Sunny is this you?* I texted along with a phone photo of the ad.

Half an hour later I got an answer: *No, it's not me!*

Well then she must be your twin! I texted with a smiley face emoticon.

Sunny texted back with: ""

Whatever that means? I thought.

I texted the photo to my sister Graciella who is a social worker in Illinois: *Hey, need help with this shit!*

Graciella called me and said, "You can call Al, but as we all know, he isn't gonna do a damn thing. If you go to the police, they'll tell you that the legal guardian has to report it."

"I'm fucking tired of all the bullshit I've been through, and at the same time having to worry about Sunny," I exploded. "I just can't help her. Anything I say will go through one ear and come out the other."

Six months later, my sister Tanya emailed me a website with Sunny's pictures and profile where Sunny proclaimed she wants to be a model like her mother. Sunny's pictures were too sexy for a sixteen-year-old girl. My first thought was: *I'm sure the photographer didn't know she was a minor.* But after a moment's reflection: *On the other hand, maybe he's a pervert who's telling her he's gonna make her famous?*

My sister Lina would have gone through the roof if she knew what Sunny was up to.

I got the impression from Sunny that her dad seldom kept track of what she was doing – or maybe he just didn't know how to deal with it.

On Lina's four-year death anniversary, I texted: *Hey Sunny, wanna go and get your nails done with me?*

Yeah! Sunny immediately responded.

I was happy when I read her message. I wanted to be with her even if it was only for an hour or two. Sunny needed me just like I needed her. She lost the most important person in her life, her mother, and by that point I'd lost my only daughter, too.

I picked her up at the same apartment where Lina passed away four years ago. I still couldn't believe her dad hadn't moved them out of that place. So many sad memories of Lina were dredged up that I'd like to forget, but they all came rushing back after stopping by to get Sunny.

We arrived at the nail salon and were there for over an hour. I never once mentioned anything about her mom's passing. I just couldn't bring it up and I didn't think I needed to. I was happy she was with me and I knew Lina was too.

When our nails were done, we walked a few doors down, ordered some yogurt with toppings and sat outside to eat.

After the last bite, I proposed, "Give me a call when you're free for sushi, and to see a movie, and do some shopping, okay?"

"I will," she replied with a tentative smile.

I drove her back to her apartment, gave her a hug, a kiss and said, "I love you!"

"Love you too!" she said with a sorrowful expression on her face.

While driving away my eyes filled with tears. I felt this emptiness and sadness inside of me for Sunny not having her mother around. The memories of Lina's last days in the apartment broke my heart again. I could still see the funeral van taking Lina's lifeless body away.

I had a bad feeling that Sunny was slipping away from all of us.

At the end of October 2012, Al's mother Trisha called from Mississippi and said, "Shirley, I'm really concerned about Sunny. She has some kind of viral infection."

"Oh no, poor Sunny!" I exclaimed. "I'll call her and go see her and let you know how she's doing."

"Okay, but please don't tell her I called you," Trisha begged.

"Alright, I won't."

I hung up with Trisha and speed-dialed Sunny.

"Hey Sunny, how you doing?" I asked, pretending not to know she was ill.

"I'm sick with a virus," she said in a hoarse voice.

"Yeah, you don't sound too good," I commiserated. "Would you like me to bring over some chicken soup?"

"Okay. Thank you!"

An hour later I knocked on the door. Al opened, said hello then stepped aside.

From the door I could see Sunny laying on the couch in the living room. "Hi, Sunny, you don't look too good," I said and handed Al the soup. "I better not come inside in case whatever you have is contagious. Eat the soup and I'll check up on you later on, okay? Love you!"

"Thank you, love you too!' she called out.

Back at home I called Trisha. "Sunny's very sick, looks pale and sad, too. Trisha, I don't want you to think that I'm trying to create a problem, but I'm very concerned about Sunny. She's not attending the regular high school in my neighborhood. She goes to a behavior school in a very bad area of LA. On Sunny's Facebook profile, she's posted some very provocative pictures of herself, and talks about how she wants to pursue a modeling career. My family and I are all concerned and afraid for Sunny, and we don't know what to do. If something bad happens to Sunny I wouldn't forgive myself for not letting someone in your family know. Sunny seriously needs help.

"Also, your son Al doesn't look good at all. He's aged a lot. He's depressed and lonely. I also know that he's not working. He needs you, his family, and he needs therapy, too. I know that your family and ours, especially me, had a lot of issues while Lina was sick and dying, but I need for you to understand that I mean every word I've said in a good way. We need to put the past behind and think of a way to help Sunny."

I said all this because I knew Al wasn't going to call his mother or siblings to ask for help. I remembered Lina telling me that Al would never ask his parents for anything. I placed the call knowing my sister would want me to help save her daughter.

I concluded with: "Trisha, I'd appreciate it if you didn't let Sunny or Al know that I said anything to you."

"Thank you, Shirley. I appreciate what you're doing. I'm going to try to go to California, or I'll have one of my daughters pay a visit to Al," Trisha said, sounding sad.

On Monday, November 5, 2012, I received a text message from Sunny: *Hey, just letting you know that my dad and I are moving back to Lake Cormorant at the end of November. Love and miss you and want to see you before leaving. Also I want to come back to California and go to college after graduating from high school.*

Teardrops were running down my face while I read her message. I felt bad she wouldn't be close by, but I knew it was the best thing for her. Sunny was going to be safe. I was alternately sad and happy, but I could see a smile on my sister's face. I texted Sunny: *Do you wanna get together this coming Friday?*

Her: *Okay!*

On November 9, 2012, when I picked up Sunny at her apartment at 1:00 p.m., I couldn't help but exclaim, "Wow you look beautiful! Your hair has grown a lot and it's so radiant."

"Oh, thanks!" she responded in her soft voice and with a slight smile.

I also noticed she had less eye makeup on, wasn't wearing false eyelashes, and her eyebrows were growing back in nicely. I gave her a kiss and a hug and we drove off to the sushi bar.

We ordered lunch, and I tested the water: "So are you sad you're moving away?"

"No, not really." She shrugged. "I wanna go back to a regular school and get my high school diploma and then go to college."

I was practically beaming with delight. "I'm so happy, Sun. It's time to move away from that apartment and all the bad memories that are still there. It's going to be so much better for you — and your dad, too."

She nodded thoughtfully. "Yeah, I think so too."

I didn't want to say anything accusatory about seeing her Facebook profile and the provocative pictures. Instead, I decided to ease into it from another angle. "You already know this, but I wanna tell you a little bit about your mom, when she was modeling for *Playboy*. She was in her early twenties and she loved all the attention she was getting. She had fun posing for her pictures. The problem was, she wasn't making enough money to pay her bills. The jobs were few and far between, and the competition was tough. The modeling world can be very cruel for many of these young girls trying to make it. It's filled with drugs, and nasty, perverted men who just want to use them. Also, when Natalie was modeling in Italy, she lasted less than two years, and then decided to come back home and go to college. Since your mom wasn't able to work steady as a model, I got her a job as a receptionist at the advertising agency I worked for. The two of us ended up having a blast — and we had the security of a weekly paycheck."

I was really hoping that Sunny would open up to me and tell me anything she wanted me to know.

"Yeah, I kind of know that," she said. "I did a video for a band. The lead singer was in his twenties and afterwards he asked me to meet him somewhere in the evening."

"Did you go?"

"No, I didn't," she said without hesitation. "I also did some modeling jobs, too."

"Did you get paid for it?"

"No," she said, frowning.

"It's all bullshit. You don't need any of that, Sun. Do any of these people know you're a minor?" I said with a puckered brow.

"Well, I have a fake ID," Sunny replied with a grin.

"Okay, I get it," I said, not surprised.

I saw a big change in Sunny that I had never seen before; she was finally opening up to me. I felt my sister sitting by my side telling me to keep on asking more questions. It seemed like Sunny wanted to tell me so much more; it was the perfect time for me to get as much from her as I could. "Have you been in contact with any of your old friends from middle school?"

"No, I haven't."

"Who are you hanging out with?"

"A girl by the name of Tracey," she said, then quickly added, "but I'm not speaking to her anymore."

"Why not?"

"Tracey almost got both of us *fuckin' killed!*"

"My God! What happened?" I put my hand on hers reassuringly. I could tell she was regretting having said that, and I could see the wheels turning in her head: *Should I or should I not go on?* The decision was made. She swallowed hard and continued.

"Well, Tracey has a boyfriend in his early twenties. A month ago, me, Tracey, her boyfriend Jerry, and his friend Mike picked us up and started driving away. They were driving by the airport when I asked Mike, the driver, 'Where are you taking us?'

"Mike yelled at me: 'SHUT UP, BITCH!'

"I had my mobile phone in my hand and tried to call someone, but there was no signal. Mike drove to a motel, parked the car, and the two guys got out. Suddenly, police cars surrounded the motel parking lot. The cops grabbed the two guys, threw them on the ground and handcuffed them. One of the officers opened the back door of the car where Tracey and I were sitting, and saw that we were young girls. He asked us for our names and our parents' phone numbers. Another policeman opened the trunk of the car and found ropes, duct tape, a bag of cocaine, alcohol, and the drug called roofies."

I was on the edge of my seat with goose bumps all over my body, and tears were falling. "OMG!" I grabbed Sunny and held her tight.

Sunny was in tears as well.

"Sun, do you know what those guys were going to do to both of you?"

"Officer Benson told my dad and us that Mike had just gotten out of prison two days before. He said Tracey and I were lucky they had Mike under surveillance. The police felt sure the two men were going to tie, drug, rape us, and possibly kill or sell us for prostitution."

"Oh God!" By now I was slightly nauseated. "Sunny, you're mother and my daughter Natalie were with you all the way. They were protecting you. A month ago I kept having dreams with you, your mom and Natalie. My dreams were telling me something about you, Sunny. I was afraid of something bad happening to you. I was positive that Lina and Natalie were trying to give me a sign about you."

I now believe the dream I had about my sister and my daughter was for me to save Sunny by calling Trisha.

I didn't tell Sunny that I had talked to her grandmother Trisha about her and Al.

Trisha and her daughters had convinced Al to move back home to Lake Cormorant along with Sunny.

After this throbbing story I sure could have used a shot of tequila to calm my nerves down, but I decided not to. Sunny was opening up to me and wanted to tell me about another incident, this one at her apartment.

"I was having a sleepover with two friends, Veronica and Mary. Mary was on her way and when she got to my place, Veronica and I noticed that Mary didn't look right. She was mumbling her words and all of a sudden, she dropped on the floor and was having convulsions or a seizure. I yelled for my dad to help us. Dad ran downstairs, called 911, then Mary's parents. The ambulance got to the apartment and took Mary to the hospital. Apparently, Mary had taken a bunch of drugs before coming over."

"Oh God, Sunny!" I said moving my head from side to side. "What else has happened?"

"One evening, I went to a party with another friend, Frances. While at the party some girl had taken some drugs and drank too much alcohol. She was super wasted and kept saying, 'I want to kill myself.'

"I told her, 'don't say that! You don't wanna do that?'

"She goes, 'You think you know everything about death cuz your mother's dead,' only she was slurring her words.

"I yelled at her, 'Stop it, you crazy bitch!'"

"She screamed back, 'Fuck you ... and your mother, too!'"

"Oh shit! What did you do, Sunny?" I said, frightened.

"I had a plate of nachos in my hand so I threw it at her face," Sunny said, laughing.

"Sunny, you don't need these type of friends. Friends come and go all of the time, but it's only a few that you'll keep forever. Most of them are not your real friends. All they want to do is take you down with them. Family is almost always forever. I will always be here for you. The move is good for you. When I go visit Mason in Lake Cormorant, I can see you, too."

"I want to come back for summer. Maybe Mason can come with me?" Sunny said hopefully.

"Sun, when you get settled in Lake Cormorant try to visit Natalie's counseling center. It would be a good place for you to go and get some free counseling. Natalie, your mom and I, will be so very proud of you."

Her eyes lit up with an idea. "I'll ask my Nana Trisha to bring Mason along with me."

It made me happy to hear that from her, even though I knew Mason would not be attending. His dad and Rhonda weren't going to let that happen.

"Mason needs counseling. I'm thankful I had four years to prepare for my mom's death, and I was twelve years old when she passed away. Mason was only eight. He saw his mom that morning alive and she was gone by the afternoon," Sunny said as if feeling his pain.

Sunny was aware of some of the awful things James did to Natalie and that he continues to take it out on me by not allowing Mason to spend time with me in California.

Sunny has changed for the better and I do hope these experiences at such a young age have helped her understand the danger she can be in when she hangs out with bad friends.

After our long and at times frightening conversation, we did our fun-shopping spree. We "shopped till we dropped"... that was one of Natalie's favorite phrases. Next, we drove to the nail salon and had a manicure/pedicure, plus a foot massage for over an hour. I then drove her back to her apartment, gave her a kiss, and told her. "I love you!" I presented her with a copy of A *Time To Grieve*, by Carol Staudacher, that I'd purchased for her at Barnes and Noble. This book has helped me tremendously over the past two years and I'll definitely keep it forever.

"Here Sunny, I want you to have this book. Please read it when you have time. Sometimes when I'm sad, lonely, or depressed, I open the book and just randomly start reading. It helps me to deal with my loss, emptiness, and pain." I hugged her gently.

The first page of the book was a blank one. On it I wrote:

"To: Sunny, with love

From: Aunt Shirley"

I drew a big red heart in the middle of the page and wrote in the center of it: "I will always B here 4 U no matter what!"

Chapter 70

Graciella's Surprise - December 2012

In November 2012, I received an invitation from my niece Kim announcing her baby Kerrie's one-year-old birthday party on December 21, 2012. Unfortunately, I was feeling extremely depressed, with the holidays and of course Natalie's birthday coming up on December 17.

Kim had named her baby girl, Kerrie Natalie, in my daughter's memory. It was so very sweet of Kim to do that, but at this time it made me very emotional. I left the invitation with the baby's beautiful picture on my desk and a couple of days later I picked it up, stared at it with tears in my eyes. With determination, I grabbed my phone and called Kim. "Hi babe, how are you and baby?... Listen, I received the invitation and want you to know that I wanna be there for the party."

"Oh, I'm so happy, Aunt Shirley!" Kim shouted, super excited.

"Can you believe it? I'm finally gonna come visit you all. It's the perfect opportunity. I'll buy a plane ticket as soon as I'm done talking with you. Oh, by the way, please don't mention anything to your mom. I want to surprise her," I said, picturing the look on Graciella's face when I just happened to "drop in" on her.

After finishing my conversation with Kim I immediately called my sister Gia. "Diah mujer, como estas? Maje, quiere ir a Illinois conmigo en Diciembre para el cumpleanos de Kerrie Natalie?" ("Hey woman, how are you? You wanna go with me to Illinois for Kerrie Natalie's birthday?")

"Claro que si, maje!" ("Of course, I do!") Gia responded, overjoyed.

"Okay, I'm going to make the plane reservations for us right away. I'll let you know all the details later on. And whatever you do, if she calls, don't say a word to Graciella about this."

Gia understood what I was up to.

A month later, on Thursday, December 13, Gia and I took off on our trip. We arrived at the St. Louis Airport where Kim was waiting for us. Then we drove the two hours to Carrollton, Illinois. The drive was pleasant and we got to talk with Kim about the baby and her husband, Dan, until we finally got to Graciella's house.

Kim, Dan, and baby were living with Graciella for now.

Graciella had divorced Johnny a year ago and was planning on moving out in 2013. She had a new man in her life, Tom, and after eight months he'd asked her to move in with him.

Her ex-husband Johnny was already renting a place of his own.

Like I said in an earlier chapter, when my daughter Natalie was killed in 2010, I gave most of Natalie's furniture to Graciella. I was feeling fearful of walking inside her house and falling apart upon seeing the furnishings. So I took a deep breath and followed Kim to the side door of the house with Gia behind me. My heart was beating faster and my hands were sweating. As soon as I entered I saw the dining room table and chairs; the sofas and end tables were in the living room area. I felt sad in one way, but also happy that Graciella was getting good use out of everything.

"Aunt Shirley, this is my husband Dan," Kim said, interrupting my thoughts.

Dan approached me and I kissed and hugged him.

The baby was walking around and stopped to stare at me.

"Hi baby Kerrie. You're so beautiful! Look at those gorgeous blue eyes you have," I whispered, but didn't pick her up because she didn't know me yet and I didn't want her crying. Instead, I grabbed her little chubby cheek and told her how cute she was.

I then walked into Graciella's master bedroom where Natalie's big king size bed was. I stared at it and remembered the last time I slept on her bed. On the side of the wall next to the bed was a wood block hanging rack. On the hooks were Natalie's cowboy hats, tennis visors, and some of her party purses. Natalie loved wearing cowboy hats. I was definitely having strange feelings throughout my entire body, but I knew I had to be strong.

"Gia, lets hide in Graciella's bedroom right before she comes home and shock the hell out of her," I said, giggling like a schoolgirl.

At 5:00 p.m., Graciella walked into her bedroom looking for her mobile phone that she'd forgotten that day. When she turned the lights on, Gia and I yelled as loud as we could, "SURPRISE!"

Graciella was so blown away, she threw her arms around us and began sobbing. "CABRONAS!" ("YOU ASSHOLES!") It was sure a sweet and wonderful moment for her.

Night came and Gia and I were sleeping in Natalie's bed. At first I felt nervous. I kept thinking of her and how she had been killed; the last morning I saw her leave the house; our last conversation on May 5, 2010 at 2:00 p.m. All of these memories kept coming back to haunt me, but for some reason it was a different feeling this time there at Graciella's house. I hadn't seen Natalie's belongings for the last two and a half years. But at this moment, I didn't cry;

my feelings were more of maybe letting her go. I felt happy sleeping in her bed; I felt her presence next to me every night. It was a sensation as if she was assuring me that she was okay and I needed to go on with my life; it's an unexplainable emotion.

We spent the following day shopping and laughing at the mall in St. Louis.

Two days later, I had the girls take a picture of me on Natalie's bed, wearing her favorite cowboy hat.

On Saturday morning, while having breakfast, I said, "Hey Graciella, do you know what happened to Natalie's telephone answering machine that she had in her living room?"

"Remember, you told me to trash it?" Graciella looked at me with a sheepish smile, then her eyeballs popped out. "Well... instead I brought it home with me, and it's in the closet."

"Really, you little bitch!" I responded, shocked. "You didn't listen to me, you little shit!" I kept up the act, pretending to be pissed off. "Can you bring it out? I wanna take it home with me."

"Fuck you bitch! I'm not giving it back, it's mine!" Graciella yelled out and then laughed. "Just kidding."

Graciella went to her closet and brought me back the machine, and I promptly stuck it in my suitcase to make sure I didn't forget it. Later that afternoon, we celebrated the baby's birthday, and in the evening we ended up at the Casino Argosy for a few hours where we ended up losing about $200 each, but had a blast doing it.

Sunday morning, December 16, 2012, Kim's husband Dan drove us to the airport.

After getting home and unpacking I placed Natalie's answering machine next to our telephone on the kitchen counter.

On Monday, December 17, 2012, it would have been Natalie's thirty-seven, birthday. I woke up and the first thing that came to my head was to say. "Happy Birthday, Natalie!" I was very sad and depressed, but I was looking forward to listening to the messages that were still on the answering machine. I fed the dogs, made coffee, and had a banana. I was nervous and frightened about listening to the recordings. After a few sips of coffee, I got up from the chair and walked over to Natalie's answering machine. At this point, I was already shaking, looking at the readout on the phone recorder with 42 messages.

I pushed the button and the first message started to play. I deleted the telemarketers and friends' brief messages until I got to #9. The message was from Natalie herself. She was calling Mom and me from her office. We were waiting for her at her home. She'd left a message saying: "Grandma, abre la puerta, ahi esta Mayte," ("Grandma, open the door, Mayte is there.") Mayte is one of Natalie's Hispanic friends. She was dropping off some homemade Tamales for us.

By now, my tears were raining down and my hands were trembling even worse. I couldn't believe that after two and half years of not hearing her voice I was now listening to it like she was still here. I felt so fortunate to be able to hear her lovely vocal resonance again. I felt I could play it over and over and never get tired of it.

Then I listened to several more messages from various friends until her voice came on again. This message was on May 4, 2010, one day before she was killed: "Mom! Mom! Grandma! Mason! I know you guys are there and listening to me. Pick up, pick up! Aha! Aha! Aha!" she laughed with excitement.

This message was a million times better than the first one. Hearing her calling my name, "Mom! Mom!" was unreal. I thought. *I'll never hear her like that again. Her voice sounds so happy, just the way she was for the last three years of her life!*

I pushed the Play button again, and the next message was on May 5, 2010 at 12:25 p.m., the day she was killed. It was Natalie again, but this message didn't sound like her at all. It was long and her voice was kind of rough and sounded nasal. She said, "Mom, I know you're there. Hello, hello? My cell phone doesn't work here in Fair Mells, so if you get a number from 631 call me back. Wait, actually don't call me back." This message was three hours before the accident. I listened to the rest of the messages one by one. After deleting the ones I didn't need, I decided to play the one with "Mom, Mom," over and over and over again, until I finally couldn't play it anymore.

A couple of hours later, I drove to the market and bought a dozen red roses. Back home I got busy with office work. Lunchtime came, and I took off and picked up a meal for Torreey and me. While eating in the kitchen, I said, "Dudsy, do you want to hear Natalie's voice?"

"Of course!" Torreey replied.

I played my favorite message for him.

"Oh, poor Puff," he said with sadness. That was Torreey's nickname for Natalie, because she liked smoking a cigarette or two a couple of times a day.

I'm so grateful to Graciella for not listening to me back then and tossing the answering machine like I originally wanted her to do. At that time I was so lost; I didn't want anything that would acerbate my pain. I'm glad she agreed to take most of the furniture, too. I got to see it, touch it again, and the feeling was unreal. I think Natalie influenced me to go to Illinois; somehow she made it happen, and it turned out good for me. I believe everything happens for a reason, the good, the bad, and even the evil. It makes us who we are.

Around 3:00 p.m., I drove to the beach and scattered the ashes and lightly threw the roses in the ocean. As I mentioned earlier, I have a portion of Natalie's ashes in a beautiful dolphin urn. And the remaining is in a plastic bag inside a container. Every year on her birthday, Christmas, New Year's and celebration of her life on May 5, I'd promised myself I'll scatter a small portion of her ashes along with a red rose in the ocean for the rest of my life.

Now, going back to my day at the ocean: I sat on the sand and silently relived several beautiful memories of Natalie and me. I watched the small waves break and the red roses dancing from side to side. The sound of the ocean was always so relaxing and calming to me.

"Natalie," I called out to the gentle breeze, " I love and miss you with all my heart. I lost you, but your voice will be with me till we meet in the hereafter." In this moment, I was much more happy than sad on her thirty-seventh, birthday, because I'd gotten to hear her voice again...although I still missed her immensely.

Later that afternoon, I called Mason. Rhonda, of course, answered the phone, then, passed it to him. "Hi, Mase! You know that today would've been your mom's birthday?"

"I thought it was yesterday," he said distractedly.

"C'mon, Mase, you know its today," I said with sadness. "Are you doing anything special?"

"We're roasting marshmallows in the backyard, so I'll celebrate when I finish talking with you," Mason replied.

"Okay. Look up at the sky and tell your mom, Happy Birthday and that you love her, too!"

"Okay, Bebe, I will."

"Hey Mase, guess what? I listened to your mom's voice today," I said without really thinking.

"How, Bebe?" He sounded confused.

"I got her answering machine back," I explained. "Do you think you wanna hear it? It's okay if you don't want to, Babe." I knew I needed to let him to decide on his own. I felt thrilled to have heard her voice and hoped Mason would be too.

"Yeah, I want to!" he said, perking up.

I played him the message that said, "Mom! Mom! Grandma! Mason!" After the message ended, I said, "Did you hear it?"

"Oh, I couldn't hear it that well," he said in a very low voice.

At first I thought he was shocked to hear her. But then I thought. *Maybe it isn't the right time to do this?* But then again, I didn't want him to forget his mother's voice.

After finishing my conversation with Mason, I sat in the kitchen chair thinking how selfish of James and Rhonda. Natalie's birthday had always been so important to Mason. He had so many happy memories of celebrating with her. Why couldn't James and Rhonda celebrate his mother's birthday with Mason and help him remember her with love and respect, like a mother should always be?

Chapter 71

BFF Blondie - 2010-2015

As I previously noted, my dear friend Blondie lost her husband of nineteen years to a heart attack in 2010, just seven months after I lost my daughter. We became even closer to each other after our tragedies.

One weekend, in 2013, Blondie was on a lunch date with her new love interest, Larry. She'd met him through Match.com and had been going out with him semi-seriously for about two months. While at the restaurant, she got up and took off to the ladies restroom, where she met a young girl, Tara, who was in her early twenties. They immediately liked each other and started a conversation.

"Is that your husband you're with?" Tara inquired, having noticed Blondie and Larry earlier.

"No, he's a date. My husband passed away three years ago," Blondie said with a tinge of sadness.

"Oh, so sorry," Tara replied. Their conversation continued with them discussing men in general. Then, out of the blue, Tara blurted out, "I think you should go out with my dad."

I'm sorry, honey, but I don't date two men at once," Blondie said, shaking her head.

"Okay," Tara nodded, "but why don't we exchange numbers, and if it doesn't work out with this guy, call me."

"Okay, maybe I will," Blondie shrugged noncommittally.

Fast forward: a month later Blondie calls me and says, "Shirley, I'm going out to dinner with this guy named Paul. I'd love if you can join us. Need you to check him out for me. I'll come by and pick you up, okay?"

"I'm in," I said eagerly.

Later that evening, Blondie came by to get me.

"What the hell happened with Larry?" was my first question.

"Well, he just wasn't my type," Blondie said, as if in apology.

"Oh good, 'cause you know, I didn't really care for him anyway. Definitely not for you! He looked like he had a stick up his ass, or maybe he was just constipated?" I offered.

"Oh God, you're too funny – and too honest, aren't you?" Blondie said, laughing hysterically. "I knew it was a good idea to ask you along!"

We took off, cackling all the way to Ocean Tava, an Indian restaurant in Redondo Beach, a few minutes from my house.

The minute I met Paul I loved him. He was not only good-humored, but also easygoing, and definitely fit in with our crowd of friends. He was also classy and a gentleman, just like my husband, Torreey. His beautiful sweet, daughter, Tara, accompanied him.

I thought, *Wow, no man ever brings his daughter along on a first date! How much cuter can this be!*

I was very impressed and at the same time a little envious to witness how much love Paul and his daughter had for one another. Something my siblings and I never had, nor will have, with our dad. I turned my attention to Blondie and whispered, "Damn, this guy is a keeper, girlfriend!"

Five months of dating and he asked her to marry him. Paul gave her a huge, beautiful engagement ring. The wedding was set for May 2015.

One evening while Blondie, Paul, and I where having cocktails at HT Grill in Redondo Beach, I said, "Hey Blondie, your birthday's coming up. What are you going to do?"

"Well, I'm thinking of having a party." Blondie said with a gleam in her eye.

"Yeah, sounds good! Where?" I asked, excited about her idea.

"I'd love to have it at … your house." Blondie looked at me with puckered lips.

While maintaining eye contact with her, I took a deep breath, a sip of my cocktail, and cheerfully announced, "Yes, I'll do it for you!"

Blondie threw her arms around me and a few tears fell down our faces.

"Oh, honey, thank you! I love you! But you don't have to if you don't feel like you can, okay?" Blondie said softly.

"I love you too! I think it's the perfect opportunity for me to have a party at my house," I said, delighted, but a little nervous too. I hadn't hosted a party since my daughter's death four years ago.

Paul stared at the two of us with a broad smile and said, "I'll cater the whole party for you."

"Oh, sounds even better!" I replied, overjoyed.

We had a month to prepare for the party. I hired a DJ, a bartender, and we invited over a hundred friends and family to celebrate Blondie's birthday and engagement in the backyard of my home. We had a wonderful time dancing, having cocktails and laughing like always. Especially when my sister Gia drank too much, fell in the pool, and ended up dancing underneath the waterfall. It was hilarious!

A month later, Blondie and Paul decided not to wait, and tied the knot in August of 2014. They were happy and in love with each other, and didn't want to wait a whole year to get hitched.

As for me, I'm over-the-top thrilled for my dear friend Blondie. She went through a lot of pain after losing her husband. She deserves to be happy and so much more. She's sweet, kind, generous, loving, and a great friend forever. Life is beautiful for her once more.

Equally important, this event helped me take another step toward opening my home again, and welcoming friends like we used to do so many years before.

Chapter 72

The Invincibles - 1978-2015

My husband Torreey and I have been together a total of thirty-six years. My kids were three and four years old when Torreey and I met. We lived together for twelve years before getting married – eloping to Las Vegas.

I've always believed in myself, and worked hard for a better life for my children and me. It seems unbelievable, but it took meeting Torreey for my life to change for the absolute better. After all these years we have a strong marriage and a deep love for each other. In my opinion, the key to a good marriage is trust. Marriage is also hard work, and can be even more complicated when your children are from someone else. On top of all that, we run a flourishing business together. And fortunately, we still have a fabulous and crazy-at-times relationship. Crazy because something loony always seems to be happening in my life.

As the years went by, Torreey learned to love my children and became a great mentor for both of them, leading by example. I couldn't ask for a better husband, and stepdad. He was the perfect roll model for my kids, and for myself too.

I learned so much with him that I never thought possible. I became a disciplined individual who enjoyed feeling physically healthy by exercising every day, and living a healthy lifestyle just like Torreey did. He taught me how to play doubles beach volleyball. We played just about every weekend; sunny or not, we were there for eighteen years. He even got me to play beach tournaments with him. One that's etched in my memory took place in Manhattan Beach, against Wilt Chamberlain, the famous basketball player. Even though we lost against the giant, and his partner, Renee, it was the most fun I ever had playing the game.

My kids hung out at the beach while Torreey and I played. In the winter we'd snow ski, mostly at Mammoth Mountain. Sometimes Luke and Natalie joined us.

Torreey provided a wonderful, safe and beautiful life for my kids, my mom and me. He never complained about my crazy family, or all the shit my sister, Lina, friends and I did throughout the years. As long as I was happy, he was too.

When I met Torreey in 1978, I had just started working for a doctor as a medical assistant at Wilshire Medical Group near downtown LA, for about a year.

Next, I took a job at the John & John's & John's, Advertising Agency in Hollywood. I was there for ten long but crazy fun years, in the building where Lina and I met many celebrities.

From there I went to work for Thomas & Associates, interior designers in Downtown LA. A year later I had tired of getting up at 5 a.m., and driving twenty miles to work, but my larger complaint was having to put up with certain moody and asshole co-workers, all completely absent of a sense of humor.

Months later, an aerobics friend, Cynthia, who worked at the Space Technologies, got me hired on as a secretary for the Space Technologies Division in El Segundo, twenty minutes from home. I wasn't crazy about the job and hated being a secretary serving under one person. At my previous jobs I was a word processor for many different bosses at a time. The only good thing about working there was that I gained a beautiful friend, Michelle, for life. Michelle is an incredible person. To me she's like Superman, but a woman. She's a wife, a mother, has a daytime job as a secretary. She exercises and walks her two seventy pound Husky dogs every day. And on top of all that she's also a caregiver to her twenty-eight-year-old quadriplegic son following an accident fifteen years ago. She never complains about anything. She always has a smile on her face and makes time for her friends. She's unstoppable and an inspiration for other women, including myself. If I could give someone a heroine trophy, besides my Mom, it would definitely be Michelle. She's amazing!

A year and half at Space Technologies, then I decided it was time to move on and got into temping. The jobs I chose were in my neighborhood. I worked the days I wanted and was always home by 4 p.m. By now, my kids were sixteen and seventeen, and I needed to keep my eye on my troublemaker daughter, Natalie. Luke was going through medical issues after the head trauma from the bike vs. auto accident. It was the perfect situation for me to work part-time and be close to home.

Around this time, Torreey moved his accounting office from Culver City to a West Los Angeles area between Santa Monica and Olympic Boulevard.

Since I had a good amount of free time, one day I asked Torreey, "Can I help you with anything around the office?"

"Yeah, you can. I got plenty of things you can do," he said, then made a little frown, "but I can't afford to hire you permanent."

"Fair enough," I said and began working at his office once a week – then twice, and sometimes more. I was doing all of the secretarial tasks including making deposits at the bank and running errands. I was taking a lot of busywork off Torreey's shoulders, allowing him to concentrate more on his detailed accounting work than the clerical duties he was also used to doing as well. His specialty was in complicated corporate returns and dealing a lot with the IRS.

Since I had over eighteen years of computer experience, with Torreey's tutoring, I quickly mastered the basic phase of accounting, also known as bookkeeping? A month later, I was processing the payroll for his clients. I loved it and wanted to learn more and more, so I pressed the issue: "Why don't I just work for you full-time?"

"I told you before, can't afford you." He shook his head sadly.

"Well, I have an idea," I beamed.

"Oh no, not again!" Torreey teased with a smile.

"Look, why don't you just raise your rates a little?" I reasoned, "that way you *can* afford me! Besides, your fees are way too cheap."

He considered this, and replied, "Yeah, I could do that. But my clients aren't going to be too happy about it."

"You can't keep doing it all, Dudsy!" I pointed to the stacks of paperwork on his desk. "This is too much work for one person. You really need me here and you know it. Let's just give it a try and see what happens."

Torreey knew I was right, and from then on, I was in the office five days, and seven days during tax season. Sometimes we wouldn't get home until three or four in the morning. Even though we worked our butts off, we were both happy. For one thing, I didn't have to work for mean, rude, egotistical, snooty, or tight-ass bosses. But most of all, I really loved what I was doing.

My mom had moved in with us due to her illness, and after recovering, she was happy with her life – and the grandchildren were there for her, too. It sure made life a lot easier for me. Mom was taking care of the house chores along with my kids.

Despite the higher fees, Torreey was picking up more clients, and everything was working out perfect for the two of us. Later on, we moved our office to Torrance, about five minutes from our home.

Five years later, after buying our brand new house in South Redondo Beach, we moved our offices into our home on the bottom floor.

Now I had everything I could possibly want: A husband who adored me, a beautiful home, relaxing vacations, afternoon and dinner parties, great pets, and lots of beautiful, fun, caring and loving friends. Torreey's one of the most honest and generous person I've ever known. And I'm not just saying that because he's my husband. He truly is that and more. I have everything I never imagined I could have, and I appreciate every little thing he does with all my heart. Life was absolutely beautiful!

Shortly after moving into our new four thousand square foot Mediterranean house on the hills, three blocks from the beach with a partial ocean view and a good size dance floor, we decided to throw a housewarming salsa party. We invited our friends and clients, about two hundred fifty people, to celebrate our new home and New Year's Eve 1998. We had a DJ, a bartender, a lavish buffet of food, and even security. The party lasted till four in the morning; everyone was drinking, dancing, and having a great time. Incredible how much fun we all had. It was a total blast!

Torreey and I were so proud of our beautiful home. We decorated the house with a tropical motif. Every time we traveled to Mexico, the Caribbean Islands, Costa Rica, etc., we brought back wood parrots, oil paintings, and other ornaments. The house looks like a Costa Rican or Hawaiian home. Palm trees, exotic plants, small garden statues of frogs and turtles surround our backyard. During the evenings, when the various outdoor lights come on, the yard becomes even more beautiful to look at.

I enjoy gardening and spending many weekends taking care of my beautiful flowers; it's very therapeutic for me. I love observing each flower head. I find myself thinking, "How can this be so beautiful?" It's as if someone took a brush and painted every bit of each bloom. Sometimes dragonflies and exquisite butterflies are all around me. It's an incredible feeling. I feel so lucky to be surrounded by all these little creatures. Amazing!

In 2001, we hired a contractor to redo our backyard, adding a pool, and a hot tub with waterfalls rockwork, and a pond. I wanted something like the Playboy Mansion's Jacuzzi, but of course a mini version of it. My office overlooks our pool and waterfall area. Torreey's has the garden view.

There's a flowerbed in our backyard where I placed Natalie's memorial plaque. It's made of brass with her picture and the words, "Always in our Hearts. Natalie 12/17/1975 – 5/5/2010." The gorgeous flowers, I sometimes replace every month frame the commemorative sign. Every time I water the plants I look at Natalie's image and her beautiful smile. Sometimes I smile back at her; and other times I cry and ask, "Goddamn! Why did you leave me so soon?"

The last four years of Natalie's life we'd become even closer to each other. She was the happiest I'd ever seen her after her divorce. She was moving forward. Her life, her business, and our relationship were at its best. We were enjoying each other's company more and more as the years went by. We'd had many conversations about her childhood, her dad, and especially her friends. One pal in particular (who shall remain anonymous), Natalie related terrible stories to me about her being sexually abused by her dad when she was a little girl. Natalie and I spoke every day or evening. The last thing we always said to each other before hanging up the phone was, "I love you."

One evening, I had a flashback to 2007...I was visiting Natalie and we were having cocktails; she suddenly arched an eyebrow at me and said, "Mom, I'm so glad you left my dad when Bugger (Luke's nickname) and I were little. We probably would have ended up losers like him too. You know, when you sent us to live in Virginia with our grandparents and then we came back? Buggs and I were always pissed off at you and thought you were a jerk for sending us away. But, now that I'm older, divorced and with a kid of my own, I totally understand you. I probably would've done the same if I were in your shoes. I understand the sacrifices in life that some people choose to do. I've seen a lot of it here in Lake Cormorant, especially working with abused women and children."

"Well, I certainly didn't want to do what my own mom did: Wait until the kids were older, and all the damage was already done. So I did what I felt was right. You know very well, Momma's not a quitter. Thank God everything turned out okay for us," I said, clapping and rolling my eyes.

Natalie continued, "Damn, you did good, Mom! Torreey's a good man, and we love him like he was our real dad. He's so caring and if it weren't for him, I wouldn't even have a place to live. He didn't have to buy me a house. That was James's responsibility to his son. He also helped Bugger buy his condominium, too. When Mason gets older I'm gonna change my last name from Collins to WEBBBBB. Momma didn't raise a quitter! Ha! Ha!"

"Now you're talking, girl!" I said with a wink.

"Mom, remember when I was a teenager?" Natalie said cracking up.

"No, I don't wanna remember," I said, making funny faces at her.

"Oh, I use to lie, and sneak out of the house to go party. Ha! Ha! And how about when I stole your car?" Natalie's said, wiping away her tears of happiness. "Damn, Mom, I was a real fuckin' bad juvenile! I'm sure glad I didn't have a daughter. Ha! Ha!" Natalie just couldn't stop talking and laughing. It was insane.

Many of these recollections of Natalie make me realize how lucky I was to be able to spend the last seven days of Natalie's life together. I was with her constantly. Not everyone gets that chance. She was bubbling over with happiness, and living life to its fullest. Best of all, I got to observe it with my own eyes.

Natalie was a free spirit. She walked slow, spoke softly, rarely raised her voice, and was never in a hurry for anything. She loved to burp and fart like a man, and was never embarrassed about it. All of her friends loved her just the way she was: simple, very humble, caring, fun, loving, adventurous and full of life.

One year, Natalie came to visit for a few days with a couple of her friends. Somehow she got tickets for *The Ellen Degeneres Show*. She loved Ellen just like my sister Lina and I did – especially at the beginning of the show where Ellen dances.

It brought back a memory of when Lina had gone through chemo and was very depressed about having to shave off her hair.

That day I needed to think of something quick to make Lina happy. "Hey, I'm making some Cadillac Margaritas, and we're gonna sit and watch *Ellen Degeneres!*" I yelled out! By the time the show started I had already drank two and was feeling goooood!

Lina was still on her first, and kept saying, "Oh, this is the best margarita I'll ever have!"

We were relaxing on my bed and the minute the show opened I quickly jumped up and started imitating Ellen's dance.

Lina exploded with laughter and said, "Hay, huepueta! Hay huepueta! I'm gonna pee in my pants if you keep that up! OMG, you're so fucking crazy!"

We both ended up howling until our stomachs hurt.

As of this writing, I am 59. My daughter always told me she was going to take care of me when I got old. Natalie called me *The Female Benjamin Button*. I still laugh when I think about it. She'd say, "Damn, Mom, you never age!" But I have, I just don't show it, it's my heart that's old after being shattered into a million pieces when I lost her.

I'm 5'1 and weigh a hundred pounds. I've never dieted in my life. I guess I was born with good genes and exercise has helped me stay thin. I've also taken very good care of my skin since I was in my twenties, particularly my face. Even though back then I didn't have the money to spend on expensive facial creams. Instead I used Vaseline to clean up my entire face, followed with a bit of olive oil. Mom's beautiful skin secrets.

Over the past twenty-five years I've been using costly creams such as Lancôme, Estee Lauder, Dermatologica and many other brands. Although, I still can't stop cleaning my eyelids without Vaseline.

My visits to the spa for facials, I call it a necessity. I enjoy them; they help me feel relaxed, and they treat my face with collagen and mint masks to refresh my skin. A little Botox and Restylane here and there twice a year has helped me even more.

I used to drink a few cocktails per week when I was in my twenties, thirties, and late forties; and particularly if I was out with the girls. Sometimes we downed Kamakasis, Tequila shooters, Jack Daniels and other cocktails. OMG, it was crazy girly fun – until the next morning!

But over the past ten years I've cut down a lot on my drinking. Once or maybe twice a month a glass or two of champagne followed with lots of water after, and a good eight to nine hours of sleep. Can't do the carefree drinking anymore. Now that I'm older my body can't take the abuse; plus I feel like shit for the next couple of days. Not worth the trade-off.

In early 1999, I was diagnosed with heart disease, and was put on medication that took three months to kick in. I then bounced back to my normal self. My energy had returned in full range and I was happy that I wasn't dragging anymore. I was afraid that Dr. Rosin, my cardiologist, was going to tell me to stop teaching aerobics; on the contrary he told me to keep it up. It was the best thing for me. My heart was strong except for an irregular heartbeat, a murmur, and a leaky heart valve. So what the fuck, I'm still here. But the doctor did mention I needed to reduce stress. Something I just can't entirely do, because it's impossible to forget everything I've gone through the last six years of my life. Mainly loosing my daughter; then having to constantly battle her ex for the right to see my grandson, Mason.

I've never let any of my medical conditions stop me from exercising. I hide them from people, particularly at the health and tennis club. My teammates and aerobics students think I'm one of the healthiest persons on the planet because of the way I look.

I have now been on serious medication for fourteen years. During my sister's battle with cancer I ended up in the emergency room several times. My heart specialist told me over and over that I needed to step back and let someone else take over. I was under constant worry. Some of my siblings came to help but I just couldn't walk away from Lina. She knew I was never going to quit on her even though at periods she caused me so much pain as her mood swings were becoming impossible to deal with. I still loved her and kept my promise; I was there till the end.

A year after Lina passed away I was diagnosed with rheumatoid arthritis. I have been under the care of a specialist for the last seven years. I'm on muscle relaxers, pain medication for swollen joints, and a pill to prevent joint deformity. Occasionally, I'll get a shot if I have a real bad month, when my joints are very inflamed and tender.

Mornings are the worst part of the day for me until an hour later after my body is warmed up and the pills have been in my system for that period of time. Body massages are a must for me at least once a week, preferably on Friday evenings. By then I feel like the rusty Tin Man from *The Wizard of Oz*. When the masseuse is done, I'm good as new again. All my body parts have been *oiled* and I feel good and relaxed. I also have a massage chair at home that I use just about every evening before going to bed.

My rheumatologist, Dr. Kim, told me to slow down on my activities. I used to play tennis five days a week. I now play no more than three and teach aerobics twice a week. Occasionally my body aches but I don't complain or tell anyone about it, except my husband.

Some days when I'm feeling depressed, my way of treatment is an hour beach walk with our beautiful Dalmatian-lab mix, Niki. After our walk I sit down on the bench and stare at the beautiful ocean, the waves, the dolphins body surfing, the screeching pelicans. I even talk to my daughter and sister too. I let the tears fall and know that no one can see me cry while my sunglasses are on. I feel so blessed that I live a few blocks from the beach. The ocean is my invigorating escape.

It seems like practically each year that I get older I add another illness to my list. I guess it is true that "Life is short, life is sweet, so make the most of it."

I had two reasons why I had to let go of my beloved grandson, Mason. The first, as I told you earlier, was because I love him too much and want him to live a happier life. Putting Mason in the middle of a feud between his dad, Rhonda and myself wasn't fair to him. And the second, as you've likely figured out by now, is my health. I've done what I needed to do for Mason in the last four years – just let him be. He's now fourteen. Four years from now, he'll be able to make his own decisions. And if he choses to see me, he knows where to find me.

Letting go of Mason was a very difficult and painful decision for me to make, but I knew I had to. I'm still not sure whether the step I took will be helpful in the long run. I might have done the wrong thing, but I had to trust my intuition. Sometimes the only way to solve a problem is to put some distance between you and it for a while.

I've learned a lot from the mistakes of the past, and even though my heart is broken, I have chosen to move on and live the rest of my life with my amazing husband with love, peace, and to always remember my daughter with a smile on my face. Hard to do sometimes, but I'm still trying. Happiness is not a permanent state; you have to live life-capturing moments of contentment as best as possible.

I know deep down in my heart Natalie understands my decisions. Sometimes in life you sacrifice for the ones you love.

I was fifty-three when my daughter left this world. Six holidays later, it feels like it was just yesterday that I lost her. We don't always know what we have until we lose it forever. So much we take for granted, and then one day it's too late. It's gone in a flash before we know it.

I miss my daughter, sister and brother's voices. I miss their laughter, all the fun we had together, and even the arguments and fights we had. At times I glance through my photo albums and see the beautiful and crazy pictures of us together, having a blast, laughing and being goofy at times.

There's some moments that I get very emotional, like when I'm driving and hear a song that reminds me of my daughter, sister, or brother, too. But then I have to laugh because we really had some good fucking times! Humor always helps me ease the pain.

Like I've said before, life can be so beautiful yet so painful and complicated at the same time. No one's ever happy every single day. We just have to make the best of it while we're here. The nice thing about life is that we can change it if we want to, by changing our thoughts and how we view it.

There's not one day that I don't think of my daughter; and I do hope there's something out there after this; and if so, I'll get to be with her again someday.

I can tell you how a mother feels when loosing a son or daughter unexpectedly. It's like ripping out a piece of your heart. It will ache forever and never fully heal. I have accepted that she's gone but my emotions I cannot always control. So one morning I woke up and decided to get a tattoo of a rose on my abdominal area as a daily reminder of my daughter, Natalie.

Now, back to December 17, 2012. Natalie's birthday was gone again, and so as Christmas passed, the last thing I wanted to do was to celebrate New Year's Eve. Torreey and I had not celebrated the holidays since Natalie was killed three holidays ago.

This year we were invited to two parties. One of the invitations was from Harvey, Natalie's longtime and special friend from high school, who I mentioned earlier. Natalie and Harvey took trips together to Italy, Greece, and partied their butts off. They also had plans to visit other countries in the near future.

The other party invitation was from one of my tennis teammates; it was going to be at the beautiful Terranea's Hotel in Palos Verdes overlooking the ocean.

When I received Harvey's text asking us to join him and his family at his house, I got very emotional just thinking how sweet and kind of him to think of us.

I texted back: Hi Harvey. Thank you so much for the invite. I'm afraid we'll not be able to attend your party. Torreey and I stopped celebrating the holidays after Natalie was killed. I don't know if I can do it.

Harvey's reply: Shirley, you need to live and have fun for Natalie. I'm sure that's what she would have wanted. She was always proud of her fun-loving mom.

While reading his text, my eyes filled with tears and I knew Harvey was absolutely right! I need to do it for her.

That afternoon, when Torreey came home, I said, "Dudsy, we're going to both parties. Okay?"

"I was hoping you'd say that," he responded.

Early evening, on December 31, 2012, we headed to Harvey's intimate party and had a wonderful time with his wife, family and a few of his friends. A couple of hours later, it was time go to the big party to celebrate New Year's Eve. My friend Rocky and her boyfriend Jerry joined us.

We drove to Palos Verdes Peninsula's gorgeous hotel near the ocean. I was nervous going there, but the minute we arrived, I ordered a cocktail and felt better. By 10 p.m., the place was crowded as can be with people eating, dancing, laughing and just having a great time.

After my second cocktail I got in the mood for dancing. I finally took off my coat (yes, I was prepared to make a break for the door if need be) hit the floor with Torreey and danced the night away. At times I could feel and hear Natalie by my side, smiling, and yelling, "Go Mom! Go!" It was incredible!

Five minutes to the countdown to New Year's 2013. Torreey pulled me close to him, each of us holding a glass of champagne. The DJ started the counting. When he finally shouted, "Happy New Year!" We kissed and held each other in our arms not wanting to let go. Even though a few tears fell, I wasn't going to ruin New Year's for anyone, and particularly not for Torreey. I raised my glass and whispered, "Here's to you my Natalie! I love and miss you with all heart! Happy New Year wherever you are!" I downed my glass of champagne, placed it back on the table, and slowly walked away, holding hands with my husband, and thinking to myself, "Natalie, I have taken another step. I know you're proud of me."

In May 2013, Torreey and I rushed our eight-year old Dalmatian/Lab Niki to the emergency hospital. All of sudden, one weekend, she developed violent seizures. She was put on medication but the seizures continued. The next step was a brain MRI to find out if she had a tumor or a brain infection. We scheduled the exam and were told we'd have to wait a whole week before we could find out what was really wrong with her. The next day, Niki was moaning and in so much pain we just couldn't let her suffer any longer and rushed her to the emergency hospital once again.

Upon arrival, Torreey carried her out of the car and into one of the rooms. He placed her on the floor, while I lay next to her sobbing uncontrollably and holding on to her head. "Niki, Niki, I love you! OMG! Why? Why?" I cried.

The doctor came in, gave her a sedative, and said, "I'll give you a few moments with her."

Minutes later, he returned and slowly injected our beloved Niki.

My hand was stroking her head and my tears were falling like an open faucet. "Goodbye, my beautiful, sweet Niki. I'm gonna miss you." I held her tight while Torreey patted my back. I could hear him crying too. She left us with so much pain.

Two weeks later, I got Niki's ashes and scattered them in my garden next to Natalie's plaque. I guess by now I have my own little burial tract in my backyard. Not only my daughter's ashes but also my brother Evan's, Jazzie, my sister Lina's dog, and now our Niki. Maybe I'll call it WEBB's Cemetery. And for a moment it occurred to me: "How am I ever gonna be able to move out of this house when I have the ashes of my loved ones and so many beautiful memories of them, including my beloved pets? It would definitely be heartbreaking for me." So I walked away not wanting to think about it anymore.

A month later, I couldn't take it anymore and decided we needed to find another dog like Niki. I searched and searched until we finally drove to San Juan Capistrano where there was a ten-week female white Labrador. We fell in love with her on sight, and named her Nina. She's now two years old and crazy as can be, bringing us so much joy and laughter. She's in the pool every single day. Nina's our beautiful girl, but we will always have a special place in our hearts for our beloved Niki.

In June 2014, while bathing my eight-year old Pug, Sunami, I found a lump on the side of her neck. I rushed her to the doctor; had X-rays taken, and was given a referral to the emergency hospital the following day.

Sunami had surgery to remove two masses, and was kept for observation. Three days later I brought her back home. That same afternoon, the doctor called and said, "Sunami has thyroid cancer. It has spread to the lymph nodes. She will need chemo or radiation."

"FUCK! FUCK!" I cried and cried and held Sunami close to me. It seems like tragedy keeps following me and for some reason doesn't wanna leave me alone.

I was glad Torreey wasn't home yet. I'd already made up my mind about the treatments. I wasn't going to tell Torreey until the following day. I thought, *I'll just keep it to myself for now.*

That night I went to sleep even though I was extremely depressed. But I was peppered with thoughts of my little dog and kept waking up. She was leaning on my shoulder while I stroked her little forehead and told her, "Mommie loves you, Sue."

When I woke up in the morning I gave Torreey the news.

"What are you going to do?" Torreey asked.

"Nothing," I said. "I'm going to leave her alone for now. She's happy and she's eating well."

Two weeks later I decided to see the oncologist. Dr. Villalobos recommended chemo pills twice a day along with some herbal medicine.

"As long as Sunami isn't going to be sick from the chemo," I told the doctor, "I will try it."

Sunami was on medication for over two months. She was doing well, still eating, going for walks, and was in high spirits. Although I knew she'd soon be gone from me, for now I was giving her as much love as I could. She knows she's my special little girl.

Four months later, on October 20, 2014, I rushed Sunami to the vet. She was having trouble breathing and wasn't eating or drinking water any more. I knew it was time to say goodbye to my dear loving precious little Pug.

Doctor Hutson came in, examined her, and said, "Shirley, it's time to let her go." She left the room and within seconds came back with a shot of morphine to calm her down. Dr. Hutson left the room again to give me privacy with my Sunami.

I stroked and kissed her little flat funny face and told her, "Mommie loves you for ever and ever," while my teardrops fell on her face. Minutes later Dr. Hutson walked in and injected my little dog. I held her sobbing uncontrollably. I could feel the doctor's hand patting my back and also crying with me. She had known Sunami for eight years. I had her cremated and scattered some of her ashes in my backyard where my daughter's plaque and Niki's ashes are.

I'm now down to two dogs, Milo, my daughter's Pug, Nina, our Lab, and our only cat, Mama Mia.

Torreey and I haven't traveled to any of the exotic islands or Vegas like we did so many years ago. The important thing is that we still have each other. It's been one step at a time just like my therapist told me five years ago.

Little by little I'm opening my wounded heart back to God. I'm slowly starting to heal by letting Natalie go. Many times I was inconsolable and cried uncontrollably. But I now feel better, stronger, and ready to move on and live the rest of my life with my incredible husband as best as we both can. Torreey deserves to be happy. He's done so much for my kids, Mom, and family; and in particular me. All because he loves me and deeply cares about my happiness. For thirty-seven years he's always thought of me first.

I look at life differently now since all that's happened to me. I've certainly made some mistakes, but I've also learned from them. I have experienced deep pain, but I don't let the pain break my spirit. I have chosen to learn from the painful experiences of the past and grow from them. I understand that you've got only one life, and you need to live every day to the fullest.

These days I'm laughing more than I'm crying. It's a sign that one day I'll do the following: First, I'll find the strength to open and read all of the sympathy cards that I received from family, friends and clients, after Natalie was killed. I keep them in a drawer in my office in a big manila envelope. And second, I'll get there and make that reservation to paradise once more.

In the summer of 2014, we were invited to a fake mustache party where we had a wonderful time dancing to the sounds of the 70s Disco songs. It brought back so many beautiful memories, like when I met Torreey, and all the fun my sister Lina and I had back then.

Even after all I've been through I still maintain the belief that life is beautiful. After all, "Momma didn't raise a quitter!"

Torreey and me in our backyard with our beautiful loving pets. Me holding Lina's dog Jazzie. Torreey with Niki the Dalmatian/Lab. Milo, Natalie's male Pug and Sunami my female Pug.

Natalie in red, me in white.

Me and Natalie dancing at a friends wedding in Las Vegas.

Torreey, Natalie and me in Costa Rica.

Lina, Natalie, and me...tres senoritas locas.

Where Are They Now?

Family / In-Laws:

My grandson, **Mason**, is now 15. I have not heard from him for two years.
Mom (85) is back living in our home with Torreey, me, and our three beloved pets.
Dad, also 85, rents a room in a house in Los Angeles.
My son **Luke** (41) lives a few blocks from our house in Redondo Beach. He enjoys his job of over twenty years in the movie industry. He's still single but dating Molly, a sweet and wonderful girl.
My oldest and craziest sister **Gia** (62) is living in our home and helping me with the care of our mom.
Dylan (13) (funny kid who played Mini Joker and Gia's grandson) eventually gave up imitating celebrities in favor of mastering video games.
Tanya (53) another sister, is enjoying time with her two grandchildren. She lives in San Fernando, CA., with her husband Bobbie.
Graciella (49) my youngest, hyper, and also crazy sibling lives in Illinois with her fiancée, Tom.
Marisa (60) the shy and sometimes quiet sister became a born again Christian.
Ceci (52) lives in Montana with her husband. We have not spoken after the shoe episode with Mom two weeks after Natalie's death, six years ago.
Edgar (61) my oldest brother is happily married. He made up with Gia after Evan's funeral disagreement.
Al Collins (60) my sister Lina's husband is presently living in Lake Cormorant, Mississippi. Sources say he and his siblings inherited a good portion of his dad's wealth. He remains single, and apparently is enjoying life at the ranch.
Sunny (20) is currently living in Lake Cormorant. We remain in contact and on good speaking terms.
Luis (40) Natalie's husband, lives in Florida. I found him on Facebook and we've remained in touch with each other.
Roger (65) my ex-husband, and Luke and Natalie's biological dad lives in Panama, Central America with his third wife. Allegedly, he is helping to raise her kids.
Jereldine (Roger's mom) passed away fifteen years ago.

Celebrities:

Julio Iglesias (73) finally married, and continues performing at concerts all over the world.

John Travolta (62) his latest project will be playing Robert Shapiro in the upcoming miniseries about O.J. Simpson.

Steve Garvey (69) is battling prostate cancer.

Steve Sax (55) is a financial consultant and is also co-writing a book on athletes and finances.

El Debarge (55) Clean and sober and back on tour where he belongs.

Joe Jackson (84) is still a talent manager.

Jose Luis Rodgriguez (El Puma) is 73 and resides in California. For the past ten years he's been suffering from Fibromatosis, a condition that affects the lungs and makes it impossible to breathe on your own without the help of an oxygen device.

Rick Dees (67) LA's famous KISS-FM DJ of the 70s, 80s and 90s, left over a contract dispute. He then hosted Movin 93.9 FM until it changed format to Spanish hits and dismissed its radio personalities. Currently, he has a #1 internationally syndicated radio show, The Rick Dees Weekly Top 40.

Kim West (68) the nephew of the former coach of the L.A. Lakers, Jerry West, is a successful attorney in San Francisco.

Joe Isgro (69) resides in California. He is a recipient of Purple Heart and Vietnam War veteran. He is still in the movie and music business and doing exactly what he loves to do. He was charged back in 2014 with money laundering and gambling. According to the previously unsealed indictment Joe and a member of the Gambino family conspired to open an illegal gambling operation in Costa Rica. Authorities claim he is also a Gambino crime family mobster.

Colorful Characters:

Rod (64) the hilarious cop, is as funny as ever, and remains single.

Nacho (69) my best amigo and zany gym buddy is still crazy, except he's no longer drinking tequila shots.

Casey Braker (53) my upbeat tennis partner: Due to conflicting schedules, we decided it was time to split up the dynamic duo, but we remain good friends.

Blondie (51) my closest friend is still happily married to Richard.

Miscellaneous Natalie Friends:

Francisco Guisti (58) Natalie's Italian ex-boyfriend when she was 19 and living in Italy. They stayed in touch with each other for a short while. I still have not found Francisco to inform him of Natalie's death.
Dave (40) Natalie's first fiancé, is married with children.
Alana (41) Natalie's high school friend, is a therapist, married with 2 children.
Janice (41) Natalie's companion in Italy, is now married.
Harvey (41) Natalie's Chinese high school friend, is married and has a beautiful little girl.
Omar and family, Natalie's amazing Latino familia and beloved friends in Lake Cormorant, keep in touch and always remember Natalie with love.
Eva and family, Natalie's dear Hispanic friends and Mason's nanny in Lake Cormorant, tell me they still miss Natalie.
Jack & Nancy Hillmart, Natalie's amazing and best friends, five years later, continue to provide funds for Natalie's Counseling Center in her memory. Nancy and I stay in touch.
Diane Landsberg (45) Natalie's friend and business partner, who survived the auto accident, divorced her first husband and found herself a new love.

And Finally:

Ronald Thomas (53) the man who killed my daughter Natalie and his own wife Cheryl, was found to be impaired when his truck crossed the highway centerline. According to State Police, toxicology tests indicated Thomas was under the influence of illegal narcotics. He is serving three years of a 10-year sentence after pleading guilty to negligent homicide. He had seven of his ten years suspended. After completing his prison time, he will be on supervised probation for three years.

A portion of the proceeds from the sale of the book will be donated to my daughter's Counseling center, a non-profit organization.

Acknowledgements

To Cliff Carle, my editor and publishing consultant, thank you so much for your skilled advice for helping me take this project from beginning to end. I would have never done it without your help. I'm so deeply appreciative for your patience and for your understanding what I was trying to say. And thanks for your never-ending encouragement to press on and finish this book. You made it so such much easier for me. You were amazing to work with. Muchisimas Gracias!

Thanks to Patience, Grace, Meaghan, Michelle, Connie, Ron, and my husband, Torreey for editing and proofreading and for expressing that I had a great story to tell.

Thanks to the wonderful people at Inkwater Press for believing in me.

To my awesome and crazy family, thank you for your love, laughter and even arguments. And, thank you to my dear Mom for your love and support. Love you to the moon and back.

To my dear friends and second family – Louie, Blondie, Rochelle, Michelle, for the twenty five plus years of an incredible and beautiful friendship. Thank you for putting up with all of my crazy shit! You guys rock!! Love you all!!!

To Marla, McNasty, Jennie, Misty, and many, many others. Thank you for your love, support and all the fun and crazy tennis matches we've had. Love you girls!

To my son Chris, my one and only grandson and my beautiful niece D. – I love you three with all of my heart!

Thank you to my beloved creatures and beautiful pets, Tammie, Puggie, Es, Niki, Sunami, Jazzy, Nina, Milo and Mama Mia – for your unconditional love. Love you with all my heart!

To my daughter's incredible friends in Lake Cormorant – thank you for your love, support and all of the hard work in keeping my daughters legacy alive. You guys are amazing! Love you always!!

Finally, this book would not have been possible without the support and encouragement of the most amazing man I know, my husband. I'm so blessed to have you in my life and I treasure every moment we have for the rest of our lives. Love you forever and ever!

CPSIA information can be obtained
at www.ICGtesting.com
Printed in the USA
FSHW04n0058140318
45438FS